W9-BUD-326

Foxfire 3

·ANCHOR·PRESS·
·DOUBLEDAY·

Foxfire 3

animal care, banjos and dulcimers, hide tanning,
summer and fall wild plant foods, butter churns,
ginseng, and still more affairs of plain living.

edited with an introduction by
ELIOT WIGGINTON

Anchor Books
Anchor Press/Doubleday
Garden City, New York

Eliot Wigginton, faculty adviser to *Foxfire* magazine, teaches journalism at the Rabun Gap-Nacoochee School in Georgia. "Wig," as he is known to his students, is currently working with IDEAS, Inc. to extend the *Foxfire* concept of education and oral history to other communities.

The Anchor Press edition is the first publication of *Foxfire 3* in book form. It is published simultaneously in hard and paper covers.

Title page photo courtesy of Dorothy Hill

Portions of this book first appeared in *Foxfire* magazine
Copyright © 1973, 1974 by The Foxfire Fund, Inc.

This book is dedicated to those adults who love young people and demonstrate that affection every day. Without these men and women, the love already deep within all kids would shrivel, for it would have no pattern to go by.

ACKNOWLEDGMENTS

Foxfire continues to be a fresh, exciting experience for all of us because of the basic generosity and good will that run strong and deep within most people.

The parents in the county and the administration of our school continue to trust us with kids. Recently, for example, I took two students (neither of whom had ever flown before) on a week-long trip that leapfrogged us all over the country—they were students whose parents had never met me but who willingly gave their permission.

Residents of the area still greet us enthusiastically when we come to intrude into their lives with cameras and tape recorders. As we were winding up an interview not long ago, the lady whose husband we had been questioning disappeared into the kitchen and reappeared with four pies she had baked especially for our visit; and she insisted that what the kids couldn't eat there, they had to take home with them.

Members of our Board of Directors and Advisory Boards continue to find ways to give us a hand and urge us on—people like John Viener, for example, who put in scores of hours dealing with unpleasant chores like straightening out all our insurance needs and getting those attended to, trademarking our name, and attending meeting after meeting in our behalf.

Old friends from the beginning (and there are lots of them), like Junius Eddy, lie low for a while and suddenly reappear bearing some new gift or piece of news, and you realize with a rush that they've been out there quietly working behind the scenes to make some fine new thing happen for you or the project.

New friends appear—like A. K. Johnson of the Georgia Bicentennial Commission, who urged his commission to sponsor two of the log buildings in our reconstruction—or Peter Haratonik of the Center for Understanding Media who sent Chuck Anderson down to Rabun Gap for a week to help us get our video project off the ground.

And always there are the kids—new ones every year with new ideas, fresh enthusiasm, and different demands and needs—keeping us, in turn, fresh, flexible, and enthusiastic.

With resources like that behind *Foxfire,* it's hard to be anything but strong.

BEW

CONTENTS

INTRODUCTION

In the spring of 1976, *Foxfire* magazine will be ten years old. By all the normal standards of measurement, we should have plenty to celebrate, for *Foxfire* has not only survived, but is being called one of the most dramatically successful high school projects in sight.

By 1976, our first book will have sold well over a million copies. The second book will be right behind it. The telephone in our office rings constantly, bringing requests from film and TV producers, advertising executives, and free-lance writers and photographers. I receive hundreds of letters a year inviting me to speak before various organizations, serve on various boards, lend my name to various proposals or proposed proposals, or accept various jobs. Scores of visitors come through our tiny office with no more reason than "just wanting to see where it's done," or wanting us to introduce them to some "real mountain people." Not long ago, a stranger came huffing the half mile up the mountain to my log house, where a couple of kids and I were spending a Saturday adding a porch, took a picture of us with his Instamatic, and then struggled back down the mountain.

I accept several invitations a year to speak. Almost invariably in the question-and-answer period that follows the presentation, the same question comes up. It goes something like this: "Did you ever dream when you started the project that all this success would happen?"

I usually laugh and answer, "No, never." And that's true. I sometimes don't see how we made it past our second issue. But at a recent talk, something perverse in my character or my mood made me answer, "Say you're a high school teacher who wants to reach his students in a very special way. You start a project with them, and in the early days, you all do everything together. When you walk across the campus, as often as not a kid will come charging up from behind and tackle you, laughing crazily as you roll, wrestling, scattering books and papers across the grass.

"Your project prospers. Your name is in lots of papers and before lots of folks. You come back on campus after a successful four-day speaking engagement, and a kid stands before you looking down, scuffing his feet at something imaginary in the dirt, and says, 'Gee, you're not around much any more.'

"Are you still successful? Do you have anything to rejoice about except notoriety and a stack of invitations? Is that success?"

I think about that a lot now that we're besieged. And I'm finding out, like lots of others before me (some of whom warned me in advance), that success, interestingly enough, turns out to be a mixed blessing. It's bright with opportunity, but it's also jammed up with problems—a lot like walking around town with a rattlesnake in your front pocket.

It's an old story. I've read about it in various books and magazines. I've seen it at work on other people. I never really expected to have to deal with it personally, but here I am, writing this in Room 219 of the Great Smokies Hilton in Asheville instead of at my cluttered desk, because there are too many distractions at home.

Visibility presents rather fragile organizations like ours with a number of problems. Some examples: When a group that's used to getting 3 letters a day suddenly begins to get 40 a day (something like 14,000 a year), and has to answer them with a staff of high school students that can only work on the project part time, and they have a number of other activities that we'd like them to be involved in besides answering letters anyway, then some adjustments are needed. When we run a workshop for teachers interested in implementing the same sort of project in their own locations, and twenty of those teachers ask permission to bring their classes up for a day to see our operation, we know that if we say yes to all of them it's going to mean that the equivalent of *one month* of school days will have been spent giving guided tours instead of writing articles, and that all the groups are going to go away disappointed anyway because all there is to see is a little cluster of three impossibly cramped ten-foot-by-ten-foot rooms cluttered with typewriters and envelopes and paper (we can't take them to visit contacts—you can't fit a whole class into the tiny living room of a mountain home). Yet we know that if we say no to them, we run the risk of seeming brusque and unco-operative and cold, and here we are again—stuck between a rock and a hard place. You get the idea.

So it's been pretty interesting around here for the last year or two. Margie, Suzy, Pat, and I, as a staff, have learned a lot, and we're slowly beginning to develop some techniques for coping; trying to stay positive and helpful whenever we can, but also trying to keep foremost in our minds that image of a kid, disappointed, scuffing his feet in the dirt.

The problem, of course, becomes to figure out a way to grab that thing called success, shake it up, turn it inside out, and make it work *for* us instead of letting it eat us alive. Here's the system we've devised for the moment. It seems to be working in the biggest areas of concern.

The first area is that I jokingly tag the "I know you're busy, but . . ." department since we hear that line many times a day. If the request asks me to come and speak, I ask a couple of questions in return. Is the group that's inviting me willing, for example, to foot not only my expenses, but also those of two or three of the students? If they aren't, I usually don't go. Is the group asking us for some specific input, or is it looking for entertainment? If it's a group of English teachers from the state of North Carolina that are really looking for some ways to get their kids involved; or a high school in Parkersburg, West Virginia, that wants to start a similar project and wants me to come and help get it off the ground; if we can spare the time away from the office, and if it's not during one of those months we periodically set aside *just* for the kids here and let nothing else interfere, then we might go. On the other hand, if it's a group that is a four-hour drive away, and just wants a little after-luncheon presentation to fill a hole in the program chairman's calendar, which for us means a full day away from the office with a good chance that little will be accomplished, we don't go. If it's a local group within our or an immediately adjacent county, we almost always go because we feel it's vital that people in our area know what we're up to.

Using this system, we can get most of the student editors out on at least one good trip (after they've all been once, we usually turn down everything else until the next school year), and we find that some fine things often happen on those trips that add yet another dimension to our program. On numbers of occasions, for example, the kids we've taken with us have never been on a plane before, have never encountered a hotel elevator, revolving doors, escalators, and have never been entertained at a sit-down dinner. They've just never had the chance. Nor have they previously been put into situations where they're asked for autographs, or where they're asked to address a group that may be as large as several thousand people, or where they're asked by teachers for *their* advice as to how teachers should teach, or what it's really like to be a high school student. I've seen them stunned again and again by the fact that adults are asking *their* opinions on certain issues and are seriously considering, accepting, or challenging their answers in a healthy, friendly exchange of views. We try to pull out all the stops on a trip and give completely of ourselves to the sponsoring group. As a result, many of the students we take are put in situations where they have to think seriously about our project—what it's all about and precisely how it works—because they're going to have to articulate all that to people who have never been here. Suddenly they find themselves not only with a new understanding of who, in part, their audience out there *is,* and a new understanding of the fact that lots of people they've never met before *are* watching their work; but they also find themselves evaluating the work they're doing and the whole *Foxfire* project in a new, more serious, and more objective light. Even if the end result of the visit is that nothing specific is accomplished by being there, the kids, at least, come back having had a solid, sobering experience—and often come back, newly recharged and committed, thinking of ways to alter our operation here at home to better serve the other kids, the audience that's waiting for their next magazine, and the community in which they work.

If the request is from an organization that wants to come here and do some filming or some photography, certain other questions come into play, all of which lead up to the big question: into what position is the request going to put the people who might be filmed or photographed? What's in it for them besides publicity that might bring people trooping to their doors, and do they want to be put in that position? But first, the class as a whole decides whether or not they will be willing at the time designated to work closely with a camera crew (if the crew doesn't want the kids around, but simply wants introductions, we don't even consider it). If the kids have recently been through such an experience, and they don't want to gear up to do it all over again, or if they're involved in so many things that they don't feel they can take the time, the project is vetoed.

If, however, they are interested in looking at the project more closely and perhaps want to do it, they ask for more details. For example, the JFG Coffee Company recently decided that it needed a new set of commercials, and Fitzgerald Advertising, Inc., was hired to make them. The plan was to make six commercials, each featuring a mountain person (the JFG marketing area covers much of the southern Appalachians) demonstrating some skill. At the end of the thirty-second scene, all the person had to say was something to the effect that, "It take a lot of skill and patience to do this." Then the announcer would come in and say, "Just as it takes this person time and patience to make butter, so, too, it takes JFG time and patience to make a fine coffee." Something like that.

Thinking they might be able to save filming time, and save trouble, they approached us and asked if we would be willing to locate the subjects for the commercials and prepare them so that all the film crew had to do was walk in, film the six scenes in four days, and walk out. It sounded unsavory at first, but we told them the kids might be willing to do it. They would simply have to come up and present their case and let the kids decide.

The writer and producer flew up from New Orleans, and I gave them a class period to present their story boards to the kids and answer questions. The kids wanted to know if *Foxfire*'s name would be used (they didn't want it to be), or if the name of the county would be used (they didn't want that either after seeing the number of tourists that came through as a result of the movie *Deliverance*), or if the contact would have to drink some coffee (they didn't want that). They also wanted to know how much each would be paid, how long they would have to work, etc. They grilled the ad agency representatives for an hour, then told them they would talk about it among themselves and let the agency know next week.

For several days, that was all they talked about. Finally they decided that they'd co-operate *if* they could find people in the community who *wanted* to do it. They headed out to locate a butter churner, a beekeeper, a man who would plow with a horse, some quilters, a weaver, and someone who would dig sassafras and make tea with it—all skills the ad agency wanted pictured. In two days they had found them all, and they called the agency and said that they could come in if they paid the people in cash just as soon as the cameras stopped rolling, would give us copies of the finished commercials for our archive, and would pay for a community showing.

The agency agreed, came in, and the kids had it set up so they got all they came for in less than four days. The contacts got paid on the spot, and everyone was happy. One of the contacts, for example, came up to the kids afterward and said, "I just want you all to know that I am grateful to you for thinking of me. That's the most money I ever made at one time in my life. That will pay for my seed and fertilizer this year and put me in the black for the first time in years." The party was held, and over a hundred people came to watch the finished commercials before they were to start airing, and they approved. And later, when one of the subjects was bitten by a copperhead, the ad agency sent up a donation to help with the hospital expenses.

Another recent request was from a production company that wanted to film a two-hour television special here. The film would tell the fictionalized story of a boy who came from a city, got involved in a project like *Foxfire,* and through that involvement came to some new understanding about himself and his heritage. The project went through several months of negotiations, script writers even came from California with a sample script in hand, and in the end was not agreed to because the kids insisted that the film should not be called *Foxfire,* nor could the project shown in the film be called *Foxfire,* since the story itself was fictionalized and had never happened here and since our name would pinpoint the location geographically. The company, having already made a number of concessions, balked at that one, and the contract was never signed. I have friends who think that the kids, in that case, made a mistake. Whether they actually did or not is somewhat beside the point. The fact is that they made a decision that they believed in after weeks of real deliberation, and that decision was adhered to even though I personally thought (and told them I thought) that making the film might be a fine educational experience, might be a chance for us to provide an antidote to *Deliverance,* and might be a fine chance for us to help shape what could be a genuinely exciting television offering. In the end, the experience the students went through in the act of having to come to their decision was probably enough. And it was a weighty experience for me personally to watch them at work, see the intensity of their commitment to our project and our community, and see the seriousness with which they deliberated as to how they felt both the project and the community should be allowed to be used by others.

In another vein, if the request is from a person or group that wants to come and visit and be taken by us to meet some of the people we've written about, we turn it down. From the beginning, our hope was that our project would, in part, encourage others to begin to look in their own back yards for the riches that are there, and for the experiences that can come from that involvement with a community. Every neighborhood has its own Aunt Aries and its own kids that could easily be put in touch with them. When people want, instead, to come here and be given a guided tour, we've failed, in a sense, to accomplish part of what we set out to do. We have no intention of putting our contacts on public display, or running bus tours past their homes. That's not only degrading but dehumanizing.

On the other hand, if the request is from a person or group that wants to come and work with the kids, get (or give) ideas, engage them in some serious discussions, or perhaps try to implement the same sort of project back home, then we read the letter in class. If some kids want to host the group and really set up a first-rate visit, we give those kids the letter, and from that point on, it's their responsibility. One of them writes the group back, tells them to come ahead, works out the dates and details, and hosts the group when it arrives. If there are no kids who want to take it on, we write back with our apologies. The alternative (and we know this from bitter experience) is two or three groups a day coming through, no work done here, and, after a time, zero educational experiences for the students involved. The last thing we want is to see them turned into the equivalent of the bored, faceless guides at places like Mammoth Cave.

To handle the requests for craft items the contacts make, the kids each year set up a team that will take the letters, pick up the items, give the contacts the full purchase price, bring the items back, and wrap and ship them at our expense. It's one of many services we try to provide for our contacts as part of our attempt to thank them for the time they've spent with us. The kids get a good sense, through activities like these, of what it's like to give of themselves and use part of their resources to help others.

If the request is for a job with us, we don't usually consider it unless it comes from a community person, or a kid who used to work with us, has just finished college, and wants to come back home. If the request is for us to consider a manuscript for publication in the magazine, we turn it down, because the kids write all the articles. On the other hand, if someone writes in and wants us to find and take a picture of their grandfather's grave, or wants us to provide additional details about something we wrote, or wants other specific information and we have a kid who wants to track that down, we turn it over to him. If we don't have anyone with the time, we usually write back, tell them we're holding the request, and wait until a kid comes along who wants to tackle it. Theoretically, each student should be held responsible for his article and for any questions from readers that it may stimulate. The problem in our case is that by the time the article comes out in book form and begins to draw questions, the kid has already graduated from our school and is out in the world somewhere.

In some cases, we feel that the request really deserves attention whether or not there is a student to handle it. In those cases, we as a staff take it on ourselves on our own free time. By and large, however, the general rule is that if we can't turn what comes through the office into a true learning experience for some students here, then there's no room for it. The alternative is to be swamped, and to watch the main goals of our work go down the drain.

The second area of success is money, and again the question becomes that of how the income can be taken and used by the kids so they can learn and accomplish something in the process. Everyone wants it. Who's going to get it? And who's it going to be given by?

Some time ago, we set up a non-profit, tax-exempt corporation with our own Board of Directors, Advisory Boards, lawyer, etc. The corporation exists within the school as a separate organization. *All* of the income goes into the corporate account. A portion of it is used to pay the staff members who work with the kids, to pay the salaries of the many kids we hire full time to work with us during the summers, to buy equipment and supplies, pay our printing and postage and telephone bills, give scholarships or loans to our kids who want to go on to college and can't otherwise, pay expenses on extended collecting trips into the mountains, and so on.

Beyond those expenses, the students are encouraged to try to come up with responsible, useful ways in which the balance of the money can be invested to provide income to continue the project long after the book royalties have dried up; be returned to the community in which we work; be donated to worthy groups; or be used to help out our contacts.

Two years ago, for example, the students voted to purchase a fifty-acre piece of property to which they wished to move and then reconstruct about twenty endangered log buildings. A check for $35,000 was written to pay for the land, and a fourteen-year-old kid signed it. Millard Buchanan, a retired logger in the community, was hired as foreman; and with him in charge, a collection of community people and students began, in April of 1974, to move the buildings. By Christmas, they had seven log buildings and two barns up and under new roofs. This year, approximately ten more cabins will be added. Then, for years to come, new groups of community kids will be engaged in doing the required finishing work.

The area is divided into three groups of buildings. One area is set aside for the collection of artifacts (looms, spinning wheels, wagons, tools, etc.) the project has amassed over the years. Here, new groups of kids can actually use the collection themselves, or they can borrow from it to take supplies to a contact they've found who can show them how to make an object, but has long since parted with his tools and materials.

The second area will house, in separate buildings, our collection of audio tapes, photographs, videotape, and film. Each building will, aside from the collection, also contain working/editing studios. In the videotape cabin, for example, will be the editing decks and equipment the students use for producing the shows they film, edit, and broadcast on a weekly basis over the local cable TV network. Using equipment they've purchased themselves with book royalties, the kids produce shows that range from basketball games, to community group discussions of local issues, to *Foxfire* interviews that bring the pages of the magazine to life—all shows that we all hope give our community a new sense of unity and interdependence while teaching the kids some very professional skills.

The third group of buildings will be set aside and furnished so that people who attend workshops, conferences, or board meetings that the kids host will have accommodations; or so additional staff members who want to work with us for short periods of time will be able to settle in right away in rent-free housing.

The remainder of the land—some forty acres—will be used as an environmental laboratory for all the students in the area.

The students have decided—in what will doubtless be greeted as an unpopular decision—that the project will be closed to the general traveling public. There are many historic restorations in the mountains that people can visit, and the kids don't want to use their money to pave large parking lots or hire the maintenance people and guides who would be necessary. It will be open to any local community groups or individuals who wish to work with us or visit, or to a limited number of workshops or special guests. Rather than being a museum which tourists visit, it will instead be a working studio, dedicated to the people of this region, from which will come the books and magazines, films, recordings, and video shows the kids will produce in concert with the community people they will enlist to work with them.

Over the next few years, enough money will probably come in to complete the project, but the kids, in an interesting maneuver, are informally approaching groups outside the mountains who may wish to provide a gift that will sponsor the cost of the reconstruction of a building (approximately $3,700). Whenever such a grant is made, a plaque on the building's wall acknowledges that fact, and money that would have been spent there can be set aside to fund yet another project. Recently, for example, just such a gift from the Georgia Bicentennial Commission enabled us to bring out the first book we have published ourselves, *News from Pigeon Roost*. The book is an edited collection of thirty years of newspaper columns written by Harvey J. Miller of Greenmountain, North Carolina, for the Johnson City (Tennessee) Tri-County *News*. Jammed with the affairs of day-to-day living in a tiny mountain community, the book was, as Harvey called it in the introduction, "A dream come true." Part of the first edition was sent as an issue of *Foxfire* to all our subscribers, and the remainder (1,500 copies) was sent free to Harvey to market himself through his still-active weekly column and through stores in the area. All the proceeds are his to keep.

Through all these projects, whether they be donating the publishing costs of a book to someone like Harvey Miller, buying a new guitar for a local songwriter, helping with the doctor's bills for a contact, or providing employment in the county, the kids add yet another dimension to their activities and their education—one that I feel is going to make them ever more willing to step beyond their own needs and extend themselves to others around them. It's success, used as a tool to make positive things happen.

One final area stimulated by success has to be wrestled with, and it's a rough one. It occurs when a person like myself realizes that an organization has been created that has equipment, land, vehicles, employees, and buildings, and he wakes up asking, "What have I done?" It's then that some of the big questions come: "What happens if a plane I'm on goes down coming into Charlotte?" "What happens if a kid falls off the roof of

one of our buildings and breaks his back?" "What happens if I suddenly
find that more and more of my creative energy is going into the maintenance, care, and feeding of the beast itself than into the projects, or into
insuring the flexibility, responsiveness, and creativity of the group as the
needs of kids change from year to year?"

We've all seen it happen. A great idea (like a public school system) is
somehow transformed into a grotesque, clanking, rust-encrusted machine
the basic maintenance of which saps everyone's time and energy to the
detriment of the original goals. Or someone founds a great organization
only to find himself afraid that not a single other person can run it nearly
as well; when senility strikes years later, the individual has made no plans
for the organization's survival, or for a hand-picked successor to carry on,
and the whole thing collapses with a sigh.

And it's not enough to say, "Let it all take care of itself." It won't. In our
case, who gets our land? Let that take care of itself, and it falls into the
hands of a Florida land developer. Who gets our continuing royalties from
the sale of the books? Let that take care of itself and the IRS snatches it.
Who gets our archives and our collection? Let that take care of itself, and
every antique dealer around has a field day.

It's not the problem of whether or not the stuff will be disposed of. It's
how it will be disposed of if something goes awry. Without some attention to
those details, it could all fall into the hands of the vultures who wait on
the sidelines, cheering, and then move in to get a free ride off our sweat and
toil, make money off what we've done, and leave the kids by the wayside
wondering just what the hell happened.

We've tried to cover all that. Early, talented graduates of our school
have been and are being brought back from college as full-time employees
and board members. Money has been set aside to guarantee salaries. Lia-
bility insurance packages have been set up. Luckily, the kids guarantee our
responsiveness and flexibility just because they are kids, and we care about
them deeply—there's a new group of them every year, fresh and demand-
ing, clamoring to step in and take over.

If all else fails, there are documents that will insure that equipment will
be given to appropriate groups, and the restoration will go to the county
as our way of thanking its residents for being so patient and co-operative
with us. And at the very least, we can all rest secure knowing that a number of kids who worked with us were able to share and help direct a great
experiment that took them, for a time, far beyond their ordinary high
school fare. And that's something. But I'm counting on the belief that we
can do even better than that, and I'm working toward it.

Beyond all this, of course, is the ego-burden success can place on a person's head. Groups approach me, convinced that I am something I know

that I am not. Convinced that I came to the mountains with the whole grand scheme intact like a symphony in my mind. And, most distressingly, convinced that it was so brilliantly executed tactically that they could never duplicate it themselves.

That's all baloney. The whole thing was a series of both fortunate accidents (having a fraternity brother at Doubleday, for example, who set up *The Foxfire Book;* or meeting the IDEAS folks completely by accident one day in Washington), and tiny, day-by-day responses to the needs of a group of kids that gradually gave us the shape and form we now have.

The whole thing is now being duplicated so many times (thanks to the help and persistence of IDEAS, which has used our kids as consultants to help start similar projects in places from Maine to Missouri, from Alaska to Hawaii, and which is now making available a complete printed package that details to any interested group the educational philosophy and the various skills and tips helpful to know in pulling it off) that it is now obvious that all manner of individuals, institutions, and informal groupings of good people can get something similar going in their own locations if they just want to badly enough.

I keep reminding myself of all that.

The ever-present collection of people seeking autographs can change a person's head, but the kids are really helpful there. As folks come up, the kids often nudge me from behind and whisper something like, "Think you're a big deal don't you?" And I keep reminding myself that we, as a staff, are guests in this school, and that we could be asked to leave at any time if things went awry. That, of course, would be our death—we would no longer have access to the students, and there would no longer be any reason to continue. All these facts help keep success in some sort of perspective, and that's vital.

Is it going to work? I think so, I think we're going to be okay. Because yesterday, as I was walking across campus, two kids tackled me and the books and papers I was carrying were suddenly scattered across the grass.

BEW

PLATE 1

SIMMIE FREE

W e had heard of Simmie Free long before we first met him. He was the fiesty, good-humored little man—laughed at by some, but far more often laughed along with—that you'd see once in a while on the streets of town with a little half-full half-pint bottle stuck in the left hip pocket of his overalls. Usually he was making the rounds of those who enjoyed his company—A. W. Adams in the bank, for example, or some of the boys down at the courthouse.

He had a reputation as a retired moonshiner who used to make some of the best liquor in the region. So three of us went to meet him, initially to talk about moonshining. As we bounded across the little wooden bridge on the dirt road to the three-room house he and his wife, Annie, live in, he appeared on the porch, waved hello to us with an expansive, warm salute, and was soon leading us proudly through the woods along a dry creek bed littered with barrel hoops and staves from previous operations to show us the snail-shell furnace hidden up behind his house where he made his last batch of pure corn. "The law came and got my copper pot," he roared, "and they didn't even ask me could they. And they never even brought it back, the damn fools! That's wrong to take a man's stuff and not ask him." Then he sneaked a quick look at us to see whether or not we were catching onto his brand of humor, and, seeing that we were grinning at each other, burst out into delighted, infectious laughter. He had us hooked, and every half-dozen steps he'd pause, gesture at something with his stick, and then hit us with another polished one-liner:

"We had a good sheriff then. He'd put me up free every Saturday night!"

"I can't get around as well as them young boys. Know why? 'Cause I'm older than they are!"

"See those turnips there? Get you some. Won't cost you nothing. My name's Free, and they are too! I don't eat turnips raw. Know why? 'Cause I don't have a tooth in my head! Watch out! I'll tell lots a'jokes on y'."

"Them briars is little, but they're like I am. They can sting y'!"

"Man tried to buy my land but I wouldn't sell. Said I couldn't use the money. He asked me what I was goin' t'do with all that land. Said, 'Hell, I'm goin' t'carry it with me!' "

"Know why that corn's so high? It's them sob's goin' t'th'moon. That corn's just took out after 'em!"

"Me and him's a little kin, but that ain't worth nothin'. I got some kin as mean as ever drawed a breath. They're honest, but they'll claw your eyes out!"

On the third visit, we were paraded into the living room, where seats were waiting for us, and were greeted with, "Today we're not going to talk about moonshining. Today we're going to talk about hunting." And for hours he filled us with hunting tales.

Recently Annie had a heart attack, and the eighty-two-year-old Simmie had one shortly thereafter. "I was hoein' my tomaters and all of a sudden it hit me and there I was with my face stuck in th'ground. I reckon I was tryin' to hoe with my nose!"

The last time we visited, they were both back at home, weakened, but full of fun. "Me and her, we have a big time here together."

We're honored that they allow us to share in that.

Interviews and photos by Ray McBride, Don MacNeil, and Gary Turner.

MOONSHINER

Simmie was born on his grandfather's place in Turnerville, Georgia, on January 14, 1892. ("Pa said at five o'clock, and I couldn't argue. I wouldn't of argued to him anyhow. He would have given me a whippin'. That's the way it goes.") His father never owned a piece of land. He lived, raised his fifteen children, and died (at the age of 109) on rented land.

For many years after he was grown and married, Simmie didn't own land either, and moved from place to place, job to job, trying to keep his family supported. They were constantly on the move. They lived, for example, for a short time on his brother Willie's land near the Macedonia Church. "Two of my children are layin' over there right now. Willie and Catherine, they're restin' and will be all right. We've got their graves fixed up as good as anybody could have it. Anyhow, they're over there. That flu epidemic of 1919 like to killed us all. Come damn near killin' me. I held out that the only thing that kept me alive was just saying, 'I ain't gonna die!' Don't never say you're gonna die. If you do, you're shore as hell gonna die. Just don't give up. They was four people layin' at Macedonia Church and nobody to bury 'em or nothin'. Me in the bed with double pneumonia fever and not able to go nor nothin', or nobody else hardly. I'll tell you them was bad times. That 1919 was the awfullest time I ever see'd in my life."

Six weeks after he was married, he had to serve eight months in the Gainesville jail for making moonshine, and when he was released, he and Annie lived at his father-in-law's apple orchard in Habersham County, where he worked for ten cents an hour. "I kept on working for a good long while before I done anything else. Then I took government training about pruning apple trees. I went to working in the orchard and I went ahead and had an expert pruner teach me how to prune. And I stayed with him for a right smart while. I don't know how long I worked there. It got time in the weather that I didn't have much pruning to do there because we had most of it done on his orchard. And there was a feller named Frank Garrison that was up there on the Habersham Orchard just about a mile and three quarter from there. Habersham Orchard was the name of it. I went up there and I don't know how long I stayed up there; stayed up there a long time with Frank Garrison, a mighty fine guy to work for. And that's when our oldest boy was born, Grover. Then I moved back down to my daddy-in-law's. Stayed there a long time. Then another one of our boys was born, Lewis, our second boy. He was born there, and then we moved from there too."

Several orchards, a sawmill, and a son (Harvey) later found Simmie and his family in North Carolina where they moved from Moses Creek in Jackson County to Franklin, Dillsboro, Sylva, Cullowhee, a Blackwood lumber company sawmill, Chaney Fork, and finally to Rich Mountain, where he found another job getting out acid wood. "The boss got me to takin' over the loading of acid wood cars. I had me two hands but I was the one seein' to it, you know. The wood was a comin' five to six, maybe eight miles by water. And it would come in there in a flume—two planks nailed together. We had to make our flumes and everything—make it curve and go down—make it so water would just fly in it to haul the wood. And you could get on a log and ride. I had some that worked for me did do it. Find a place and they could ride for half a mile nearly. Just get on a big stick of acid wood and just sit on it and the water would just push 'em. Then they'd have to get out and walk back. I seen a feller— one of the Parker boys—he was riding by himself and was holding onto the stick right behind him and the wood had jammed behind him and he didn't know it. He was holding on with his hands and had his fingers down in again' the end of the wood. And the jam had turned loose above there and it came right down in there and hit his two fingers and cut them off just like you had taken a knife and cut them off.

"You could get just as wet as water could be. When you got there, it was just like gettin' down in the creek and staying there. The wood would come and fall right in the [railroad] car. Well, we'd go three cars ever' day. That was a day's work. And them two fellers—one in one end of the car and the other in the other—and me watchin' so if they got a car loaded and wood went to pile up on'em, I'd throw the stop in and put the wood out on the ground. Then let 'em catch up with me and pull the stop out and let the wood go right on in the next car. We'd load three cars a day. I worked there for over a year in the acid wood business. They was a lot of people come up from Georgia to work with me. That water didn't suit everybody—didn't suit me—but I was in it just the same as they was. And in the winter time, they wasn't no need in havin' rubber clothes but we did have. When I'd go to take off my overclothes—rubber clothes you know—they'd be so cold they'd be froze. They'd just stand there. Froze just as hard as they could freeze. I believe that's one thing that's causing me to have arthritis so bad today. Mountain water up in there on them Balsam Mountains *stays* cold. I made thirty-five cents an hour there."

Several moves later, the family settled two miles above the Tuckaseegee, North Carolina, post office. "We lived about two mile from there, on Ben Harris' place. That's where I had to go to buy my groceries and get our mail from. We stayed up there, I reckon a year. One of my boys, my third boy then, took th'pneumonia fever, and I had to walk from Ben Harris' place plumb to Sylva—forty mile. Had to walk ever' step of it to get a doctor. And th'doctor weighed 'bout three hundred pound. Big Doc Nichols. He 'uz big enough!

"And so I went down there and got him. He said, 'Well, Mr. Free, it'll cost ya' a dollar a mile, and it's forty-two mile!' And I said, 'Yeah.' I knowed it was that far.

"I said, 'I ain't a'carin' what it costs. I want you to go up there and see what you can do for him. I believe he's got pneumonia fever. I've had it myself several times, and I believe he's got it.' He just got in his car —had a special car built for him—and I just nearly had to stay half-way on part a'one a'his legs to get in. He drove up there then—back home.

"Well, when I got back home, he doctored my boy, and give medicine enough to do, I don't know, three or four days. And he said, 'Now if he's not better', I believe it was two days, 'use th'medicine you got and do just like I tell you and he'll get alright.' Well, we was doin' ever'thing we could, just like he was tellin'—way over in there forty mile from nowhere—right back in th'mountains, too. Plenty of bear and ever'thing right around where we was living. Well, he kept gettin' better and finally got over it.

"I had dogs, and hunted up there lots then; catching coons, foxes, anything for fur. Fur was good then. So I had 'bout six dogs that I hunted with. The doctor had to leave his car about a mile from where I lived. And my dogs followed me back over there [to where the car was parked] and as we went by, we had to pass some old apple trees. Before we got there my dogs had got a animal treed. Up there in them apple trees, the possums had been eatin' apples. They was settin' there treed, and Big Doc Nichols said, 'Boy, I wish I could get a good possum.'

"And I said, 'We'll get one now.' We got there to where they was two up in a apple tree. I went up and got one of'em down, and I said, 'Have you got a box or anything we can put this one in?'

"He said, 'I may have.' He looked, and he found a sack of some kind. He says, 'I've got a sack.'

"I said, 'That's better'n a box.' I said, 'Let's get this one.' And it was a great big, pretty, fat possum. And put it in a sack, and he held the sack, and I went back up in the apple tree and caught that'un and bringed it down. Put it in th'sack for'im, and he said, 'Don't you want to keep one?'

"I said, 'No. I have more coons and possums to eat than I've got any use for. I got plenty a'hogs out around my pasture.' I had a place rented, rail fence around it, and I had about forty head a'hogs just a'runnin' out in the woods. I could kill one anytime I got ready, 'cause they was plenty of acorns an'things for'em to stay fat on. They wasn't like the hogs we got here now. They was raised out in the mountains, and they knowed how to make a livin'. They'd just get fat enough. It was good eatin', too. It wasn't a wild hog, but I mean they was out in the woods. They wasn't scared of me. I could call'em and they'd come to me and I'd feed'em when snow was on th'ground.

"I told my wife Annie there, 'Just as quick as Harvey gets able, no more North Carolina for us—we're leavin'.' And sure enough, just as quick as he got to where he could make it and we could get back home alright, we come back. Moved back down here on Windy Hill, right here at Tiger. Just two miles from right here where I'm a'settin'. I went to work for th'Ordinary up here in th'county—Will Smith—he's dead now. Awful good man to work for. Had to work, at that. Took a eight-pound rock hammer beatin' rock in th'road. And I worked at that ten cents a hour, and raised our children. That's all I'd get at the orchard when I went to work up here at this Grassy Mountain Orchard. They was three thousand apple trees up there. I lived up there with the boss for seven year—had th'land cleared, and I set out th'apple trees. That orchard now makes th'biggest and th'best apples anywhere in the state of Georgia.

"Took a hurtin' in my shoulders and things—I imagine it was prunin' and doin' so much—I don't know. It might a'been rheumatism. Doctors then called it neuralgia. But it hurt just th'same. Got to where I couldn't press th'pruners enough to cut a big limb. And I see'd I wasn't doin' no good that way. So I told Annie I was gonna' quit, gonna' quit work on the orchard. Go to work making liquor and have me a *home* before I quit or I was goin' to the penitentiary and stay *there*."

In Tiger, they settled into a twenty-four-foot-square chestnut log house. "That's a damned big one-room log house. It was covered flat, and every time it got cloudy anywhere in the world, we could be at home and we'd get wet before the clouds ever got here. Now if you can beat me in tellin' a lie on that, I'd like to know where you come from! And on this land here, broom straw wouldn't grow two feet high. Now, by God, I can grow corn all over it higher than you can reach.

"Anyway, then I went to see old man Duckett's brother who was in Cornelia, Georgia. I said, 'Mr. Duckett, I'm needin' some help and if you want to let me have it, fine. If you don't, you don't.' I was pretty high-tempered back then.

"He said, 'Brother Tom told me it didn't matter what you wanted nor nothin'—to let you have it. He said that if you don't pay for it, he would.'

"So I said, 'Well, that's mighty nice of you, Mr. Duckett, to go ahead and let me have it just on account of your brother said that. You don't know me.'

"He said, 'My brother does.'

"I said, 'Yeah, me and him's had a lot a'dealins' together.'

"'Well' he said, 'he told me that, and he said to let you have anything in the world down here that I had that you wanted.'

"I said, 'By God, I can tell you in a few minutes what I want. I want enough lumber dressed and fixed up to build a six-room house! And,' I says, 'I want windows and doors.'

"He went in there and figured it up, counted and everything and said, 'I'll have it up there for you day after tomorrow—$1,700 worth.' That was a big debt. I knowed I could make it though. I was well and healthy, and I knowed how to do. And I went right ahead and got it and the upper piece of land the same way, and now we don't owe a damned cent on nothin'. I paid some ever' month or two. I just kept workin', kept makin' liquor. [The law] would come in and cut [my stills] up. And I'd run off and leave'em. I'd come back and just pitch right in and get me another still if I didn't already have it—go in the woods and go right back to work.

"So I don't owe a penny on my land nowhere. I could sell it for a good price [to those] that's seen it but it's not for sale. One feller said anytime

PLATE 2   Ray McBride, Gary Turner, and
Simmie on the way to his still furnace.

PLATE 3   Simmie, Ray, and Gary at the
furnace.

I got ready to take $250,000 for it, cash, he'd just hand me th'money. He lives right down here at Tiger—he's got it, and plenty of it. He'd buy it just like it is. Th'land ain't never been measured—just guessed at it being fifty, sixty, might be sixty-five acres. Guesswork's all right if you can make it hit, but sometimes you don't know whether you're gonna guess it just right or not. I got six acres of good bottom land here. But I'm not able to tend it, nor nothin'. I'm gonna have it all turned in a few days. I can raise weeds without work—I can raise them without a bit of effort. That's what I'm gonna do with it if nothin' happens. I ain't gonna sell no land—I'm gonna keep it. We got a good home, and we don't have to sell it. I'm just gonna' live here th'rest of my days, and as long as I live and [Annie] lives, we'll both be here. We're gonna stay right here, for it's th'first land we've ever owned in our life, and it's gives us th'big head. We're gonna stay here!"

For Simmie, making liquor just made sense. He could rarely make more than ten cents an hour at regular work, and yet he had land and a house to pay for, and a family to support. With liquor, he could turn his own crop into a commodity that would bring him a dollar a gallon.

The fact that he did make some of the best around is attested to again and again by people who were in the area at the time. The difference between him and many of the others who made it, according to Simmie, was that he never made his only to sell, but to *drink*. He did make money from it, but he drank his share of it too. "You gotta be nice with your liquor—be clean with it and handle it right and don't work it too young. You work it too young and it makes the liquor taste bad and you don't get no turn-out. And then you've ruined it. You gotta make it at the right time.

"There's a lot of people who don't know how to make liquor. They ought to make it [as if it were] for *them,* but they're tryin' to make it for the money. But look here—that's not right. The thing people ought to do is first calm down and say, 'Well, I'm gonna make it honest, straight and right, and I'll live as long as I can and die when I have to.' That's what I say. I don't believe in makin' liquor to kill anybody, do you? I'd make liquor to drink, and if I didn't drink it, I could sell it to somebody and go to bed and not cry about it. I'd know they wouldn't be hurt.

"I made th'best line a'liquor that's ever been made in Rabun County. I tried t'make it honest. Tried t'make it taste as good as I could 'cause I loved it anyhow, and th'better it tastes, the more I could drink. And I've drunken lots of it. God, I wish I had some of that liquor now. I'd give a ten-dollar bill for a gallon of liquor I made then and sold for a dollar. I'd give twenty dollars for a *half* gallon! Directly, I'll go up [on the price] again!

"But too many people make it just for the money. They can kill you! I know, for some come in a damn a'killin' me. It cost me $487.00 to learn. I bought me a half gallon a'liquor up yonder. It cost me $6.00, and then it about cost my life. I didn't bother him; never did say a word about it because I wasn't able to. I was about dead. And I'll tell you how he made his liquor. He had four-foot-square boxes—vats I call them, you know—and he took old, beat-up car batteries and worked the beer off with them. Then when he got ready to run it, he had a bloomin' old thing—I don't know what it was, I never saw it. But I used some of the liquor. I give him $6.00 for a half gallon. I ain't never told his name, but I know where he is. Boy, like to have killed me. Doc Turner sent some to Atlanta and they tested it, and they said they was enough lead in that little bottle to kill six men. Damn, it didn't get me but it like to. Now I believe a man makin' liquor like that *ought* to be caught. I'd say it if I knowed it was my last word. Anybody in the world makes liquor like that should be punished. I had kidney trouble for a long time after that. Cost me $487.00 in doctor bills. Doc Turner said I was dead. Grover—that's my oldest boy—said I was dead. Another one of them said I was dead. But I wasn't. I ain't quite dead yet, that's th'truth. But it's dangerous.

"Too many that's makin' it just ain't got knowledge enough to know—don't understand it enough to make it right. And all they want to do is just push'er in and make out a great big bunch and get a handful of money. What's money worth to you? Not worth a penny. Money ain't no good to you. What are you going to do with all the money when you die? You know, I read somethin' one time, and it wasn't in *Grier's Almanac* either—you can't beat me! And look here. I read where money is the root evil of all sin. Ain't you ever read that in the Bible? It's in there. If I had read that, I'd show it to you. I ain't a preacher, but I could of been one. But I believe a man that makes it honest and right—I don't believe the law ought to be so hard on them. Of course, that's takin' up for my own self, but I'll do that anyhow as long as I live. I believe if a man can make it right, the judge ought t'let him make what he wants to for himself. Then if he does, I'll make that judge a drink too!

"Now it's just as honest work as anyone's ever done. You get out here and make liquor and see if you don't sweat. As far as me tellin' you what it's like or anything, you'd have to find it out for yourself. And I'd have to learn you first. You don't know a bloomin' thing about it, but *I* do. My father learnt me way back yonder when I was young—back when I was a nine-year-old."

Simmie and his father cut out the pieces for and made their own stills from sheets of copper. His father made it the old mountain way in a thirty-five-gallon pot with no thump barrel, wood for fuel, and a copper worm. Simmie continued the tradition after his father died. A typical recipe consisted of fifteen bushels of cornmeal, a bushel of homemade malt, and a half bushel of rye. He'd cook the meal (three pecks of cornmeal per stillful until the meal was used up), distributing the mash evenly in ten fifty-gallon wooden barrels, let it sit overnight, add a third more water the next day, and then cover the barrels and let it work off until it was ready to run. "When your beer gets ready to run, it's got a bitter whang. When it goes to gettin' a bitter whang, you better be a' makin' your liquor and that's the truth. Now the way I done it—I don't run backin's in my liquor. I take my liquor off when it breaks at the worm and run th'backin's. When I got a thump barrel, I'd have them backin's to put in it and not lose a drop of liquor nowhere."

He'd add an innovation here and there after it had proved itself, but he never moved beyond that basic style of production. The major innovation he accepted was the use of a "snail-shell" furnace in place of the more traditional bedrock style. He took us to see the furnace one afternoon [see Plate 3]. In this rare style, everything is the same as the bedrock furnace except that the flames, instead of wrapping around the pot from both sides and venting on the front, move around the pot through a spiral rock and clay flue and vent out the *back*. It uses half as much wood, and eliminates the discomfort of heat and flames venting into the operator's face.

"I was makin' liquor on government land so I wouldn't have to pay taxes on it, and the federal man who caught me said that [snail shell] was the prettiest still they'd ever seen. They oughtn't of tore it up, but the damn fools did."

Simmie never really tried to conceal his stills. "Tain't worth a Red. You've got to get to it yourself, and the damn law can get to it as good as you can. Thing to do is just keep everything quiet yourself. You don't have t'get out and strut your onions. Just leave your still out in the open 'cause if anybody's lookin' for it, they're going to find it anyhow. Keep your mouth shut. That's the best thing to do."

Of course, almost everyone knew Simmie was manufacturing. "Hell fire, I've had twenty-five cars right out here in my front yard of a Sunday, and all of'em buyin', and church goin' on over there across the road. I shouldn't of done it, but I was pretty bold."

The law knew he was making it too (one sheriff frequently did business with him), and although he was caught many times, Simmie remains convinced that each time he was caught, it was because an informer reported him—and not because the law necessarily *wanted* to catch him. He retains an intense, and typical, hatred for "reporters." "Nobody with a still place is gonna' harm [report] nobody unless you harm him first. After you harm him first, you better watch out—you're a mule up a bush.

One time they was a feller over here—he didn't love liquor like I did, but
let me tell you one thing right now, he loved liquor good. He'd even steal
it from me. And I sold him land up there, and then he went and reported
me. I don't like a reporter. I'd tell the world that; and he found it out
the next evening. He found it out and it was pretty rough finding. I just
told him he had twenty-four hours to leave. Never come back across that
bridge. Never. He went! If he didn't, just as sure as that old gun in there
would shoot, I'd a'killed him. Now fellers, you might not think I would,
but I got some pretty good old shells. They shoot too. I said, 'If you don't
leave here within twenty-four hours, I'll kill you just as sure as my gun will
kill.' He left. And he had a good idea!

"But they'd report you. That's what they'd do. See they'd get *money*
for it. Report you and then get money. Why, the officers knowed me just
as good as anybody in the world. They knowed I'd plead guilty to it 'cause
I knowed they knowed I was in there making it. I'd go down and plead
guilty to the judge.

"One time I had a brand-new outfit. Starting to make brandy there.
Thirty-six-gallon rig. Some of the prettiest copper—never had been set to
th'fire! Brand new. I'd just started makin' it and got it just nearly ready
t'put the cap on. And a feller lived right over there that used to come over
here and buy liquor from me and try to pawn his shotgun from me for it.
He never had money for his liquor, and so I got tired of it. I told him just
to leave his old gun at home and t'come and get the liquor and pay me for
it when he could. Well, he went in and reported it. Went down the walk
way down here and called the law.

"I see'd him cross my pasture fence up here. I had a big pasture—and
a wire fence around it. I see'd him cross my wire fence up there, and me
and one of my other boys was out down there just ready to put the cap on
it. And I see'd him cross the fence and I said, 'Claude, right there a'crossin'
that fence is the law's tailin'. We been caught now!' I knowed he was
a'runnin' with th'law, and goin' trying to catch people.

"I knowed I wadn't a'goin' with him. Anyway, there was pretty corn—
nearly roastin' ears. Pretty corn. So I says, 'You go down through that
corn patch and cross the creek and come out up there at Nelly's and
Harvey's.' That's one of my boys. I says, 'The law will be here directly.'
So I come on out and I picked up the cap. Some folks would [try to get
the whole still] but I knowed it was full and I didn't have time. I knowed
he'd be here.

"Well, he come on down here across th'fence to where the still was. So
I come on over here to th'house and I had some liquor in there and I
poured me out a pint of liquor and put it in my pocket, and I had a
ol' double-barrel shotgun layin' right behind the door here. And so I reached

up there and got my gun with three or four shells, shut up the doors here, and went right up on th'hill so's I could watch'em. Sat there, laid there in the sun and drank my liquor, and directly they come up yelling, 'Hey ol'Simmie! Hello ol'Simmie!' and knockin' on th'door. They didn't know I heard ever' word they said, but I wouldn't come to them. I knowed they'd carry me to jail and I didn't want t'go. So I just waited and then that night I stayed home here. I stayed here in the back room. See there's three rooms back in on this side here.

"So way in th'night my dogs started barking. I always kept a bunch of ol'dogs here. I waited awhile, and then the deputy sheriff and his daughter come down here and they just knocked on th'door. I was just a'layin' in there, and they knocked and knocked. I heard him say, 'I don't believe he's here. I think he'd a'come out.'

"I think to myself, 'You crazy as hell. I ain't a' comin'.' And so after awhile they gave me up a'bein' here and got in th'car and went on back.

"And th'next mornin' that feller that reported me, why he come on over here. He come at five o'clock. [Annie was] in there gettin' breakfast, and I was in there in th'bed. I heard his car crank up over there and I knowed he was a'comin'. I said to her, I said, 'Well, I'm not goin'.' I went in there and took me two or three swallers of liquor and then come back in here. Set my gun in th'rack behind th'door.

"So he come and said what he come for, and he said, 'Well, I come over here and I'll tell you what I'll do.' He said, 'I'll carry you up to town and you won't have to walk and if you want me to I'll see that you can get a bond.'

"I said, 'You looky here.' I said, 'I'm not a'goin'.' I says, 'I'll die and go to hell a'fore I'll go with *you*.' And I said, 'That's as plain as I can speak. I'll die and go to hell a'fore I go *one* step with *you!*'

"He says, 'Hit'll make it harder on you if you don't.'

"And I says, 'I don't give a damn how hard it makes it. I'm not goin' and you can depend on that.' I said, 'You go back up there and you tell the sheriff to send a *man* down here after me.' I said, 'If you try to carry me, me or you one is a'gonna die!'

"And he knowed it, and he went on up there and told the sheriff just what I said. And they said you could a'heard th'sheriff laughin' fer two hundred yards. Laughin' at his ol'deputy who wouldn't try to carry me.

"So that mornin' after they left, why I just pulled me out a jar and got me a drink of liquor and put it in my pocket and pulled out and walked to Clayton. The ol' jail was there at that time. And ol'sheriff he seed me a'comin', and he knowed, an'he come to the door and he laughed till you could a'heard him a long ways off. So he says to his wife—she was back in th'kitchen I guess—and he said, 'Come here! Betcha' don't know who I see a'comin'!' I went on up there and talked to'im awhile. And I said to'im—him just a'laughin'; it was funny to him that that man didn't try to catch me—I says, 'It's a nice idea he *didn't*. As much liquor as I've sold him and dealt with him, and then him go and report me and think I would come to jail with *him!*' And th'sheriff said that'd tickled him to death.

"I said, 'What I want to do, Sheriff, is make bond, and then I want you to do me an accommodation.' I said, 'You do this, and then some time or another you'll never lose nothin' by it.' I says, 'You accommodate me, and some time or another I can do somethin' fer you. You ask me fer help, and any way I can do it, you let me know and I'll do it.' I says, 'You let me come in here now and plead guilty to this and then pay you the [fine] on it and let me pay it off a'fore it gets to th'grand jury room. Then that man ain't gonna have a thing to say.'

"He says, 'I'll do that thing.'

"I said, 'Now you're talkin' to suit me.'

"And so he went and he figured up what it would be. He said, 'It would cost you forty-seven dollars.'

"I says, 'Now that's all right.' And I pled guilty to it, and it cost me forty-seven dollars. No hereafter about it. Just pay the forty-seven dollars and that was all. And I paid it and come on back home.

"And that informer was a'waitin' thinking when court come that he'd get to bill me and he'd get to be a witness. But he didn't know nothing about it. So that's the way I got out. Didn't need a lawyer or nothin'.

"But whenever I was found out, I wouldn't deny it, for I knowed they knowed me and I just wouldn't tell them I wasn't guilty for I was. It's pretty hard to lie when you know one another. But they'd never catch me [physically]—slip up and say, 'Oh now, Simmie, I *got*cha.' Hell, they didn't have me. I'd be across the hill! There wasn't no man on two feet could catch me. I never been caught and held but one time, and that was when I was fourteen years old. I got caught up yonder in North Carolina by my overall bosom. I used to sell that man liquor lots a'fore he got to be deputy sheriff. Catch dog I call it. And he run up and grabbed me and he said, 'Look, Simmie! I got you.' He weighed about two hundred pounds. I knowed he had me, but I was as stout as a mule then to my size. And I was mean enough that I didn't care. The ground was steep up in there. The mountains wasn't level like they are up in here. He was higher than I was and I jumped up and grabbed him by the shoulders. There was a rock cliff down where I was makin' liquor up there in Jackson County and I drug him off a rock cliff that was seventeen feet straight down. He didn't want to go, and, boys, he was hard to get down. When I got him down there I wouldn't turn him loose till I knowed he was gone. I pulled his shoulders s'fer back that I *knowed* he couldn't pull back. We both went off together and I was just a little in front of him, and when I hit the ground, why I whirled over on my hands and feet and I jumped up and ran off and left him. They was seven of them, and I got into a creek a'runnin' and I knowed the creek and I knowed the banks and I knowed there wasn't no man that could outrun me. I didn't care who he was. I never was afraid of no man runnin' and catchin' me fer I knowed they couldn't do it. And I got down there in a bear road and boys I *made* it bare—right on out across that mountain right through the lower end of the gate. It's a rough place, but I run home and got away. And I left from there and come back to Georgia!

"But I got caught lots of times. I've went to the penitentiary. Well, I didn't *go*. That's a story. I didn't go. They *carried* me! I had four cases again' me and I had to go. I was already under six months' probation and they caught me four more times.

"So I got put in jail in Clayton and the sheriff—he liked me and all that—and he said, 'Well, Simmie, it's about ninety days before court. I'll tell you what I'm gonna' do. Since they brought you in again last night, I should send you off. But I ain't a'goin' to. I don't aim for you to go off. I'm goin' to turn you loose.' Says, 'I'll just ask you one question, Simmie. Will you be up here when court sets?'

"I says, 'You know damn well I'll be here when I say I will.'

"He says, 'Yeah. I'd trust you anywhere.' And he says, 'Well, you can go home this morning. I can't let you make bond, but I'll open the door and you can walk out.'

"And so I come on home and stayed till court. When court come, I [went up then and saw there was a rough judge in charge]. So I went to th'sheriff again and told him I was goin' to forfeit my bond 'cause I didn't aim to be tried in front a'that judge that was up there—I knowed we was gonna' have another judge later, and I *liked* the other judge. The other judge, me and him was buddies. He liked his liquor as good as I did mine. And I wanted to get him to be my judge. So I told the sheriff, 'Now I'm a'goin' to forfeit my bond this time, but after court I'll come in here and pay th'forfeit off and then make you a new bond.'

"He said, 'O.K. Simmie, that's all right.'

"I said, 'I thought I'd tell you I was gonna' forfeit so's you'd not look for me.'

"He said, 'I ain't gonna look for you nohow.'

"I said, 'Well, I thought I'd tell you so you wouldn't think you had to hunt for me. I'll come in and make a new bond.'

"Then when next court came, my judge was in there and I went in and pled guilty. They had four cases again' me. And I had twelve months' probation again' me, and I'd served six of it out, then got into trouble—

meanness, I reckon. Them six months that was again' me—you can't pay
outa' that, and I knowed it 'cause I'd been in court enough till I was a
pretty good lawyer. I knowed they couldn't do it. Well my judge, then,
when I got to talkin' to him, he nol prossed two of th'cases. He said, 'You
pick out two a' them cases, and I'll have them throwed out—nol prossed.'
So I picked out two a' th'cases—the biggest ones—th'ones I thought'ud be
the worst—and let'im nol prosse them, y'know. Then I pled guilty to the
other three. Then he give me two months apiece on each one of them
three cases. Well, that made six more months, and I already had six
months. Then he said, 'Well, I'm a'gonna take this six months now, and
put it with that six months, an' Simmie, that's all you'll have—just six
months. And I'm goin' to see that you don't stay that.'

"They carried me to th'penitentiary. I went down there and stayed two
months and fifteen days and I was right back out here in th'yard.

"I didn't use a lawyer in court. I wouldn't have a lawyer in court.
That's the worst thing a man ever had. If they ain't nothin' again'y',
they'll send you t'the chain gang *anyhow!* I ain't never been in the chain
gang, but I don't see how I missed it! I've always been lucky at that.
When I got into trouble, I've always been just as lucky to get out as I was
lucky to get in. I got in and I got out.

"But I served that sentence and three others in the Gainesville jail—81
Maple Street. I didn't stay *in* jail, I stayed *under* th'jail—had a room
downstairs. Y'heard of people bein' put under th'jail? But I was just like
one of the boys, and got to where I never did have to have nobody to
stand for me, nor nothin'. I kept on comin' back. I had a heart attack
while I was down there once. Lasted two days and nights—come in a
damn a keelin'over. I didn't know nothin'. I was in ward number two—
I didn't have to work. I was sentenced not to work. Th'judge told'em to
fix it so I wouldn't have to work a lick at nothin', 'cause he liked me, and
I liked him. But I did help cut off tater roots one day there—ol'jumbos,
I believe they call'em. Why they was bigger'n any y'ever see. They'd grow
from anywhere to three, four, five hundred bushel of 'em. And they had a
great big canner over there—just cut th'roots off and throw 'em in there,
and boil'em and peel'em, and they'd come out canned! We canned three-
hundred-and-eighty gallon cans. They'd come out red hot and you got
t'wear gloves. Just catch'em—just toss them to another feller that'd be
a'standin' there. I done that all day one day, and the next mornin' I
went over there to hop up on the counter. The boss, he was long-legged
and I was going get acquainted with him. So I hopped up by the side of
him and I said to him, I said, 'Look a'here boss. Your breath sure smells
good to me this morning!'

"He said, 'What are you in for?'

"I up and told'im what I was for.

"He said, 'You set right here and if anybody comes here and asks you to do anything, you tell'em that I said for them to go to hell. You got you a buddy now!'

"So I set there and he said, 'I gotta go over there and straighten out a bunch. I'll be back directly.' Them fellers that passed me going to work would holler, 'Come on here, Free, and let's go to work!'

"I'd say, 'Go to hell! I ain't gonna work no more!' I never did strike another lick at work. Him and me got outta there and walked—seemed like a quarter of a mile. Went to a place—great big room—and it was chock full of pints and quart bottles of government liquor. See, they got a big distiller there on that farm and they made the liquor there. He went in there and he'd done took up with me by then, and he took a drink out of a bottle. I was a'wantin' to drink. So I said, 'Look a'here, boss! I ain't had a drop of liquor in two weeks. Longest I ever done without in my life.'

"And he said, 'Well, it's right here. You help yourself.' He said, 'I don't care if you drink *all* that.' He said, 'Me and you can't drink it all, but you're welcome t'drink ever'drop you can.' He said, 'I can't allow you to take one drop back only what you can carry with you.' He said, 'Fill your stomach plumb full and 'at's all I can let you carry.'

"I told him, 'All right, then.'

"He said, 'You be over here ever' mornin' between eight and nine o'clock.' And sure enough I was over there ever' mornin'. And we'd pull back and go to the place. After we'd stayed there a week, he wanted to give me a key so I could go in there and get it any time I wanted it. I said, 'No sirree. I ain't!' What if I was to go in there and get a drink of that liquor and someone was to come and overpower me and take a whole bunch?' I said, 'I won't do it, I didn't come down here to get into trouble. I come down here t'go home when my time is out.'

"He said, 'How long are you down here?'

"I said, 'Six months, but I won't be here but two months.' But I was. I was two months and fifteen days. But I got out easy and quick, I thought. I'll be damned if they wasn't plumb good to me. Know what they taught me how to do in there? Play horseshoes! I already knowed how to fight. I've always been quick to get mad and quick [to get] over it. I don't care if I get a whippin'. When I lived up here in the orchard, I come in many of a night with my eyes swelled closed. What did I care for it? Go right back and try it over. I'm one that wouldn't give up. I've been a tough little customer. Everybody'll tell you that!"

HUNTER

"I used t'turkey hunt a lot. Used t'coon hunt lots. And a way *back* yonder—that's since me and her was married—I used t'possum hunt lots. Had dogs that was just the awfullest things t'tree possums you nearly ever see'd. Well, back then, I *ate* possum. I thought they was as good a meat as I ever ate in my life. But later on I just got kindly weaned away from'em. I ain't eat no possum now in, I guess, twelve, fourteen, maybe fifteen years. But we'd just skin'em. She's the one knows how. She knows how to *do* it! I'd skin the possum, dress'im up good? Then she'd take and boil'im good and tender? Wash'im off in clear, cold water and cook 'im up till he got plumb tender? Then take'im out, put'im in a pan and put'im in the stove and bake'im good and brown. That was good eatin', now I'm a'tellin'y'. And she knows how. I guess she's cooked more wild meat than any ten women that's ever been in Rabun County 'cause I used to keep it here all the time. I was young and stout and able to do anything. I could hunt all night long and it wouldn't hurt me. I *enjoyed* it, you know. And I always wanted t'hunt by myself. I've always wanted to be out by myself just a'huntin'.

"[Before we moved here] we lived down in Habersham County, and I wanted to come to Rabun County to go a'huntin'. I didn't have but three

PLATE 4   Wig, Ray McBride, and Simmie in his cornfield.

dogs then. Just coon dogs, you know. Well, I come on over in here this side a'Black's Mountain in the Pollyanne Gap twixt Black's Creek and the Oakley Church. She'd always have me something cooked to put in my hunting sack t'carry with me to eat while I was out, and I'd always carry stuff for my dogs too. This one time I was gonna lay down there and wait till daylight 'cause I was going over in a pretty rough place (which I didn't care for the rough woods nor nothing); but I wanted to do that 'cause I'd coon hunted enough till I knowed when it was time t'get them! You get them after daylight—tree'em after daylight. Well, I come on over there. I lay down and went t'sleep—laid with my head on one of the dogs all night. Used it for a pillow, and it was a good'un too! And I knowed I was just as safe as I woulda' been at home about anything a'bothering me 'cause I had a *good* stock a'dogs—blue tick and redbone mix, and black and tan, and they was mean too—I mean they was mean enough for anything. Kill a snake or anything that came around. They'd kill it.

"Well, I laid there and waited then till I see'd daylight was comin'. I got up and eat me two or three bites—she'd always send me some coffee along for my breakfast—and I got my breakfast ready and I sit there and eat. And then I always had my little bottle with me—it had a little more in it then it's got now [looking at his pint of moonshine, laughing]. It's about empty now, but I'll put some more in it in a minute! I'd always carry it with me, you know, and drink what I wanted to and put it back in my pocket and go on.

"So I had two dogs never had been trained for coon hunting, but I knowed they had the stock in'em ready *to* train. I wanted t'get'em trained and I knowed how to do it—just take the dogs and go on and *go*. I got down in right in above old man Joe Brooks' place. He was a preacher—lived down right beside Oakley Church. And so I was in way above his house way up in there, and I knowed them coons was in there. So I carried my dogs and went on down in there, and I looked down in a little old branch and there was the tracks just coming and going like everything. And I knowed they was in there before, but when I see'd that, that *pleased* me! I went t'yellin' and callin' my dogs, and just as quick as they could get to me, they come to me and I said, 'Hyear! Hyear! Get in there!' Hollered to'em, you know; and they just fell off into the branch there and went t'runnin' and barkin' like they'd *always* run coon. They follered that branch gulley I guess a mile around there and treed up a white pine. It must'a' been nearly two foot and a half through. And you know the limb's on'em's so thickety you can't hardly see through'em, but th'sun was a'shinin' good by then. Well, I went plumb around the place, and it was in just above a great big high rock cliff where the pine tree was.

"Well, I went around there—go on that side and then come around on the other side—and I was fixin' t'leave. I tried to. Couldn't see nothing. I called little Buck—he was a small dog—but he wouldn't *quit*. I called him and called him and he wouldn't come to me. He was sittin' there with his feet up on that pine tree and barkin' up there, and I knowed then it was up there. I says, 'Well, I'll be doggoned.'

"Well, I didn't have nothing with me but an old dull ax, so I kinda started to come on home but I couldn't get him to quit. He was a'barkin' and a'barkin' and a'barkin'. I turned around and I went back up there and I said, 'Well, I'll look that tree over one more time.' And right down about the second or third limb there lay as big and pretty a coon as you ever see'd in your life. He'd got out on a limb and had his head turned back toward the body of the tree. Well, there I was. I didn't have no gun ner nothin'. And I didn't have no way a'gettin' him but that old dull ax. 'Well,' I says, 'I'll cut th'thing down.'

"I pitched in there, and honestly, I guess it took me two hours and a half, or maybe three. But I cut it down and it come right down over the top of this rock cliff where this old man had six barrels right in under there and the whole outfit where he was a'makin' his liquor up in under the rock cliff. And that tree went right down over the top of it and it turned a somerset and throwed the body part of the tree a *way* back down the mountain, and boy that old coon *left* there! The old man was at the house, but if he'd a'been in there it would'a scared him to death!

"My dogs never had knowed how to get in there and run, but I got a way where I could go around the rock cliff and I come down there, called'em, put'em after it, and they run then. I guess they run it a mile and a half—just went around and around that little old mountain there, and it tryin' t'keep ahead of'em, you know. And they'd never learned t'run like they ought to, but they was a'learnin' it *then!* I'd holler to'em ever' time I could, and that was pretty often; and so they kept on and it run I know nearly an hour till they treed it up a great big ol' forest poplar, and it on government land. And I says, 'Uh oh! No cuttin' this down here.' Back then they wouldn't let'cha'. Well, they won't do it *now*—let you cut down a tree. I wouldn't a'been able t'cut it down nohow. But I see'd that old coon a way up there on a limb, and I said, 'Well, *now* what'll I do?'

"So I pulled out and went down there to old man Aaron Wooten's house. I knowed him well. I went to him, said, 'Mr. Wooten? My dogs got a coon treed up there and I'd like t'get a gun and some shells and kill it. I'd like t'get'im.'

" 'Yeah,' and he says, 'Simmie, I'd like t'go wi'y' too!' He says, 'I'm a'goin' back up'ere wi'y'.'

"I says, 'Come on!'

"We pulled out and went back up there, and that little dog that I couldn't call away before? He was still sittin' there, but the other two had come to hunt me. That one's daddy was a wirebeard, and th'best tree dog you could keep. Mean little dog. And so we got up there and I says, 'Well, Mr. Wooten. If you don't care, let me have the gun and shells. I'll shoot it.'

"He said, 'Yeah, for that gun knocks me down nearly ever' time I shoot it.'

"I said, 'I don't care for a gun kickin'—not a bit.' And I got around and got t'where I could see it. I didn't want t'kill it. I wanted t'just cripple it and see m'dogs fight it. I liked t'see my dogs fight a coon. And the coon was bigger than my dogs.

"And so he had his leg a'hangin' over th'limb, you know. I told him, I says, 'Mr. Wooten, I'm gonna' shoot him in this left hind leg. I'm gonna' shoot him now and maybe he'll jump out.' I said, 'If he ever jumps out, these dogs'll catch him.'

"I shot him, and the old coon set there—he got up—he didn't care whether he come out or not. He set there. And where th'shot went in his leg and it was bleeding, he'd sit there and try t'keep licking that blood off'n his leg. He'd look down, and there was the dogs just a'takin' on. They knowed that he'd be down directly. We just kept waitin', and Mr. Wooten says, 'Simmie,' says, 'you're gonna' have t'shoot him again!'

"I said, 'Let's give him about two or three minutes,' I said, 'and he'll get mad and come down from there directly.'

"And sure enough, it wasn't but a minute. He just kept licking that blood, and that shot was a'hurtin' him too I know. So I said, 'Here! He's gonna' come down!'

"And Mr. Wooten got down pretty tolerable close to the poplar tree, and that coon, he turned and he come down head *foremost*—come down with his head down holdin' with his hind feet, y'know. And boy them dogs of mine, when they see'd him come down in sight, that's just all they wanted. And th'yellin'—you never heard the like. They wadn't no need t'tell them t'hush. They wouldn't. And that coon just jumped right on top of that little dog of mine, and boy from that they doubled up over and over. 'Course the other two was right with them then. And it wadn't but a minute till they had that coon dead.

"And from then on, that little dog made the best coon dog I've ever see'd in my life; and I've had some as good a dogs as any man ever could own. And *that's* what learned him, was getting him out and letting him know what he needed to do.

"And so I come on back home, and there was a family of people that lived near there that had registered coon dogs—great big old dogs. Mine looked like little feist'es. Wadn't nothing t'th'size of their dogs, y'know. And so the old man and two boys said, 'We want to go a'coon huntin', and we want you to go with us.'

"I said, 'Well, I'll go with you'uns *tonight* if you want to.' And that was after goin' out the night before! But I'd done got that big one, and they knowed my dog'ud *tree* one. Well, they got their dogs then and I carried mine right on back in there. We got in above this man's house, and I said, 'Well, now, we'll just have t'listen, for my dogs is gonna' go back where them coons is.'

"When we got there, it was done twixt daylight and sunup and we was all just walking a'old road. I said, 'Listen. I hear Buck.'

"And by that time, why they heared him then, and their dog barked. I forget what they called him, but he was a *great* big pretty dog—pretty a dog as you ever see'd nearly. But th'sun was way up then, maybe a half-hour high. We got over in there and my dogs [had] stopped at a big poplar stump. Buck was there barking, and the old man says, 'My dog's gone to a different tree. Which one of the trees do you want to cut down first?' He says, 'I *know* there's one there where my dog's barkin'.'

"I said, 'Well, my dog's young. I wouldn't *say* there's one in here, but I'm not goin' home till we cut down this poplar stump.'

"He said, 'Well, let's go down and get mine first.' There was a poplar tree with a hole in it. We went down and cut it down. I didn't do none of the cutting. The boys was younger and bigger'n I was, and then I was tired already from up in the night before. I let them cut it down, and it fell and hit the ground, and out of there went the biggest old gray squirrel you ever see'd, and right around the mountain it went.

"My dog run, but he turned *right* away from where the squirrel was and went back to where he had treed up that poplar stump. 'Well,' the man says, 'Simmie,' says, 'your dog must be right. I've never see'd a dog do like that in my life.'

"I says, 'Well, this is the second one he's ever treed, but,' I says, 'there's a coon up that stump.'

"We cut it down, and when we cut it down, two coons just barely grown run out. We shot one, killed it. I says, 'Wait a minute. Let's don't shoot *that* one. I want t'see the dogs fight it.' I says, 'I'll climb the tree.' So I clumb the tree up there and got me a stick and made him jump out, and the dogs, they killed it.

"But his dog was just mistaken. It wasn't a thing but a squirrel den. And that old man says, 'Well, I never have see'd the beat in my life. What do you reckon's the reason my dog did that?'

"I says, 'I don't know.'

" 'Well,' he says, 'what made your'n *wouldn't* stay there at that tree but come back to the poplar stump?'

"I said, 'He knowed what a *coon* was.'

"So we got both of them. I give them one and took one. Boy, now, we had a *good* time on that trip!

"There was a year or two that she'd go with me when we carried the mules and wagon. Me and her would go and camp out and like that, you know. We went one time right over here on Seed Lake, and I had a little old dog along with me. Now this was going *fishing,* and we *caught* fish. We went over there in above the Bedingfield place and we camped out. They all knowed me and her, and we was just welcome anywhere we wanted to camp out. I had my mules and wagon and everything. Stayed the night.

"So the next morning, I carried my little old dog out there and he got after a coon there; run about, I guess, three hundred yards when he treed. And I went up to him. Somebody'd cut a great big hole in a poplar tree there—it was holler—and he was little but he couldn't get up to that hole and he was wantin' in there. Well, I got up there to him and picked him up and pushed him over in there! After I got him in there, I was sorry I put him in 'cause it was an old coon and a bunch a'young'uns. And that dog wasn't as big as the coon, but he wouldn't holler. He was gritty. So one of the young coons run out of that tree and I caught him. Catched him alive. I brought him back to the wagon after I got my dog out of there. Then I had me a pet. He was pretty. I brought it home and raised that thing. It'd just come to me and run up my arm and run around my neck and from one shoulder to the other. Made a awful pretty pet. And a feller come down the road from close to where I was a'livin'. He was carryin' off a load a'hogs t'sell, and he had the *prettiest* old big'un there. I *wanted* that pig 'cause it was pretty. And he wanted to buy that coon. I said, 'I don't want t'sell the coon. He'll *miss* me.'

" 'Well,' he says, 'I've got some boys. They'll take care of him.'

"I said, 'Well, if you want to . . .' Said, 'If you'll let me have that pig in there that *I* like so good, I'll swap you that coon for that pig.'

"Sure enough, I did and he traded with me. I come on and made a great big hog out of that pig.

"I don't know *what* he ever done with the coon.

"Now I never shot a deer in my life. I went bear hunting, though, one time up there in North Carolina. Went way *back* yonder a hundred and fifty miles or more. We went up to an old bear waller place—me and Lawrence Nixon—and I carried a dog from here that I thought had all the nerve a dog *needed*. We got up there—you know it's laurel thickets and everything—and my dog came running back t'me with her bristles up and so scared she wanted to get behind me. By God, I was about half scared. Lawrence said she smelled a bear.

"So we went on walking along, and directly it went like a *mule* a'runnin' away. He says, 'My dog's got one a'goin' now!' And the dog wadn't a'barkin', but he'd scared a bear out of its bed.

"Me and Lawrence went up there, and they was two logs a'layin' together and one right across them? And right in between them logs is where that bear had been a'layin'. That was its bed. And so his dog went right on out across the ridge after that bear, and my dog come and stayed right *behind* me. I didn't care because I'll tell you that bear was makin' such a racket it sounded *dangerous*. Now it finally got away, and that's the only time I ever did go hunt for one.

"I'll tell y', they're a dangerous lookin' thing! I was over there right above Ellijay Post Office one time coon hunting, and I had a high-powered shootin' rifle. It'ud really shoot now! And so I was walkin' along by myself pickin' out a place to coon hunt—goin' up a little ridge—and I was slippin' along. Wadn't makin' no racket. And all at once I heered somethin' make a little racket. Didn't know what it was. I just stopped and was standin' there and lookin'. I had my eyes open, and I had *two* good eyes then! I wouldn't want to be in that country with the only eye I got now. And I looked, and there set a bear. He was settin' right up on the stump of a lind tree that somethin' had broke off. And me by myself way over there two mile from home. And I looked at that bear *knowing* I could kill it 'cause I knowed I had somethin' with me to do it with. And I stood and watched that bear—great *big* old son of a gun—wonderin' would I kill him dead. 'But now,' I said, 'it's a way over here, and I ain't able to get none of it home, and I'll just not shoot him.'

"Directly he come around—barely turned his head that way and sniffed like he was sniffin', you know. I couldn't keep from laughing at him doing that way [he sniffs twice], knowing that he couldn't get to me 'cause I had something that would kill him and I was quick enough with it too. And I seen directly he winded me, you know, and he come down that lind tree stump from where he was sittin', and I'll swear his claws went down into that straight up stump over a inch deep as he slid down. He just went walking on. I stood there and laughed at him a'walkin' on.

"I love bear meat, though. Best wild meat they is. I like that stuff. But I don't want one *after* me!

"And I used to hog hunt a lot. Used to keep a big bunch a'big hounds. I mean red bones and blue ticks—somethin' t'hunt *with*. So I used to be an awful feller to wild hog hunt. Just get right out in the woods and hunt by myself—me and my dogs. I'd always have seven or eight great big old dogs, and all I'd have to do was get back in there about where I thought the hogs was a'rangin' and holler and call my dogs to me like I'd see'd some. Stand there, and when I got'em all, say, 'Hyah, hyah now!' and holler, 'Sooey!' two or three times, and holler about them to go get it, you know, and they'd start going. Sometimes when I heered'em, they'd be a mile from me, but they'd have one bayed, and I'd go to'em then. I always carried my gun, and if it was one I wanted to kill, I'd just kill it. It was on government land. Anybody could kill'em that wanted to. And I liked t'kill'em and *eat*'em too! When I got one, I'd quit and come in home where I had a mule. I'd get him and go back and get my hog and bring it in. Skin my hog in the woods. Wouldn't scald it'r'nothin'. Just skin it, and then bring it in and eat it! I've had a lot of them too.

"But one time they was one on Rob Lovell Mountain. There's several different old house places over there where people used to live, and they'd all moved off and left all their old hogs in the woods. So the woods was pretty full of wild hogs, and they just didn't care who went and got'em. Th'government wanted'em moved out anyway. They didn't care if you killed'em, and nobody else didn't care, so I got my part of 'em. I could do that and I didn't have to buy no meat. I could have all the meat I wanted, and it was *good* meat, for back in them days the woods was plumb full of acorns and hickory nuts and mast, you know, that would fatten a hog. And I mean t'tell you you could get some good eatin' out of'em. It was *wild* hog, but I like wild meat anyhow.

"Anyhow, they'd been a hog in that country I know was anyhow twenty year old—older'n that 'cause he was a big'un. He'd sharpen his tushes—rub'em up on a pine sapling—way up there about three and a half foot high. He was a *big*'un. I know he was a big'un anyhow 'cause I killed him!

"But I had eight hounds then, and they'd fight anything. Mean. Well, Jeff Burton was livin' there, and he'd come up there and told me, said, 'Simmie, we scared up that old big hog awhile ago.'

"I said, 'Y' did?'

"He said, 'Yeah. I ain't jokin' you.' Says, 'Did, and it's as big as a cow!'

"I said, 'That sounds pretty good.' I said, 'You'ns want t'go with me and we'll go get him?'

"He said, 'Hell, yeah we do.'

"He had two dogs up there, and I had maybe a half a dozen. So we went on down there and he showed me where he scared him up at. I took them dogs and put'em to the bed. Called'em, said, 'Hyear! Hyear! Sooey!' Showed'em the way it went and they left.

"I said, 'Jeff, we got t'get to the top of that mountain so we can hear my dogs.' And I'm a'tellin' you right now, they run that hog two hours and fifteen minutes. Better than any fox race ever was in this *world*. Wasn't no breakdown in it. You never heard such a like. So I had my gun and Jeff had his'n. 'Course we didn't run together. We was just tryin' to keep in hearing of the dogs. If he'd a'bayed, that hog would'a killed ary dog I had before we knowed it.

"But those dogs was a'runnin' him, and I was a'runnin' t'foller. I was gettin' to where I thought he was gonna' cross the creek. I knowed where a ford was, and I was a'makin' for it. I got right up in there and I heard my dogs come in over top of a mountain—all six'r'eight of them in a bunch, you know—and here that hog was a'comin' right here. It looked as big as a cow to me! But I had my old gun and I just pulled the hammer back just as it hit the edge of the water and I shot it, and he stood right up on his two hind feet, and I *know* he was seven and a half foot high a'standin' in that creek. Then he just fell over 'cause I put th'shot right where I wanted it! That's 'cause I was scared of that hog. He'd a'*got* me if I hadn't a'shot him. You know, a hog'll cut you with them tushes like a knife!

"And I killed'im, and I jumped in there and cut his neck vein so he'd bleed in the creek. Left him a'layin' there.

"So just as I was coming back out a'th'creek, here come Jeff just as hard as he could run. He hollered from way up the hill, and I answered him, and so here he come, and me with the hog a'layin' there. He'd done quit kickin'. I'd done had his neck vein cut so he'd bleed good, y'know. And here Jeff come runnin' right up there and pulled his gun hammer back and he shot a dead hog right there!

"Well, then my son Grover had a A-model car, you know. We all got in the car and come back—we could drive the car pretty close to where the hog was. We snaked the hog to where we could get him and put him in the A-model. He was a great big'un. And I forget how long them tushes was where they come out of his head, you know, but I know they was the longest hog tushes I ever see'd in my life. And I forget how long he was from the end of his nose to the root of his tail, but I know his tail was twelve or fourteen inches long. Awfullest hog tail you ever see'd.

"So we come on and brought him home; and back up at the orchard up yonder, we had plenty of wash pots, tubs and ever'thing. We scalded him and cleaned him and we divided him up—give him t'anybody wanted him. I sold Lynn Blakely up here a ham and a shoulder of him because I had plenty and I decided I'd just let him have it. Boys, he went and gimme I think it was nine cents a pound for the ham. Now go buy you one and see if you can get him for nine cents a pound! So that was the biggest hog that had ever been killed in Rabun County.

"I brought a wild hog in here live one time and kept it for a brood sow to raise pigs from. Put her right over there in my hog lot.

[We asked Simmie how he brought it in.] "Drove her! Had her by the leg. Ain't you never driv a hog [laughing]? Well, you don't know how then. If you didn't know, you'd get eat up. It'd turn on you, and boy! You wouldn't be there no longer. It'd bite you. Wild hog'd eat you up!

"What you have to do is have you a stick and keep him going yon way, and if he starts back at you, be able to knock him down. You *better* be able 'cause if you don't they'll *bite* you! You have to have it tied with a rope right above the hoof here on the right hand hind leg here. There's no danger of it gettin' off. [We asked him how he got the *rope* on.] Didn't I have dogs that'd hold him? Good God yeah! There's a way a'doin' *anything*. I've had dogs right here since I've lived here.

"Anyway, I brought her here and raised I don't know how many bunches of pigs from her. I kept her for a stock hog eight or ten years."

VETERINARIAN

"I was a bad hand to go all over the country and do anything in the veterinary line for cattle, hogs, anything. I've got the name of bein' the best they was in Rabun County. Once a feller lived right over here and he had four hogs to be castrated, and Herman Hunter had two t'be castrated. Well, I was ready for one of mine to be castrated too, so when Herman asked me what I charged, I said I never charged a man a penny in my life, but I guarantee the hog'll live when I get through with him. But I says, 'I won't charge you nothing, but I'm gonna have one some of these days, and I want a little help to do that one.'

"They both spoke up and says, 'Simmie, we're ready any time you are.'

"So I said, 'Well, come over tomorrow and we'll fix it.'

"So this hog of mine was a registered big-bone Guinea. Weighed about 480 pounds. You know what's the truth? The meat from them makes the best gravy of any hog ever was 'cause the gravy's sweet and good all the way through. I'd fatten them and kill them and cure them out. You know how to do that? Kill your hog, let the heat go out from the meat and lay it down on a table and take your sugar cure and just rub it all over both sides of it. Then hang it up. I hung mine up over yonder in the crib—no sack or nothing. Just hang it up and nothing else'll ever happen to it. It stays good all the way through—makes some awful good breakfast eatin'. Used t'have a big old barn to do that in. Used t'have cattle and everything. Now I ain't got nothing.

"Anyway, I had this big hog to be castrated over in the lot. He'd come up to me. I could rub him. He'd foller me anywhere I wanted'im to. See, I'd kep'im ever since he was seven'r'eight weeks old, and he liked me and I did him. And he was a *big* old hog.

"And he had a long tail on him, and Fred says, 'I can hold that hog.'

"I said, 'Fred, now listen. I've handled more hogs'n ever you've see'd, and,' I says, 'some of as mean a hogs as ever you've see'd, and I'll tell you right now you can't hold that hog.'

"He says, 'I will.'

"I said, 'I'll bet you ten dollars you can't do it. By God, I'll pay you the money if you can.'

"Well, he come in and he wrapped that big old tail around his hand and he was gonna' hold him anyhow? And I'll tell y' what the devil done. He helt that hog till he pulled th'hogs tail in two! And th'hog went runnin' down the hill, you know, and I couldn't do nothin' I wanted to then.

"Next day, here come a feller—me and him used to hunt lots together— Harrison Crump come up here and said, 'Well, I heard you and Fred couldn't do anything with your hog.'

"I says, 'No, we didn't.'

"He says, 'I can help you if we can catch'im.' Says, 'I'll show you how easy it is done.'

"I said, 'Well, a man never gets too old t'learn. I'm ready t'learn.'

"And he come and he says, 'Well, how you gonna' catch him?'

"I says, 'Well, I've got a dog. All I have to do is tell him to get him. When he gets him, he'll *have* him.' He was a great big old half blue tick and red-bone. And I told him, I says, 'Get him, Spot!'

"And he just made a dive and got the hog by the ear. The dog come right back here again' th'hog's side, you know, and th'hog tried t'swing loose, but he couldn't.

"I said, 'Well, there he is, Harrison. What am I gonna' do now?'

"He said, 'Have you got a barrel?'

"I said, 'Yes sirree. Good sixty-gallon barrel.'

"He said, 'Well, get it.' Said, 'How long will that dog hold'im?'

"I says, 'The dog'll hold him till I tell him t'turn loose.' And he didn't believe it, but anyway I went up there and rolled down the barrel—brought it right by the side of him—and then me and Harrison got the hog and got his head sort'a started in there? And then I made m'dog turn his ear loose so we could push'im in that barrel.

"Now it don't look reasonable, but this is the truth. We got that hog in there and turned that barrel up, and Lord, the hog was way up higher'n the barrel. I had to reach way up there to get to'im. But he was in there, and it worked just that way. I castrated him a'sittin' right there. Then we put the barrel over and the hog got right up and I throwed him some corn and he went t'eatin'. But once he was in that barrel he had no chance t'sling his head or do nothing, and it didn't take me a half a minute then 'cause I was used to that. I was all over Rabun County in the veterinary

line of business. They'd come far and near for me. I never charged a thing
for it in my life. Never did. Didn't believe in it. My father always did people
like that. He wouldn't charge. And I never did. Never took a penny of
no man's money in my life for that kind of work, and I got a name of being
as good a one as has ever been in that line of business.

"One morning Joe Lovell's cow was tryin' t'have a calf and was in a bad
shape. Well, they sent and got two veterinarians to come, and they'd stayed
up nearly all night with the cow. Didn't do no good.

"Next morning, me and Jeff started to town—we was walkin' down
there towards town—and Joe come out there. Says, 'Mr. Free, I've not
had a chance t'see you nor ask you, but,' he says, 'that's what I should'a
done. Come and asked you first.' He says, 'I've had two veterinarians here
nearly all night, and m'cow looks like it's gonna' die anyhow.'

"I said, 'Let me look at her.' Me and Jeff walked out there and looked at
her. They'd worked and worked and didn't know *what* to do. And the cow
was a'layin' there just fixin' t'die. Would'a died. They'd even took th'calf's
legs off up here at its knees and *then* didn't know what to do and all of
them veterinarians. If they'd had any sense, they'd a'knowed t'push it *back*.
The calf's head was just doubled up—never could'a got out. Well, it didn't
take me long. I told'em I wanted a gallon a'warm water and a whole lot
of soap and a pan. I pulled off my coat, and rolled up my sleeves. I said,
'Here, that'll be *easy* done. We'll have that done before you know it.'

"Went t'work and we worked there about—I guess it took me about forty
minutes t'do what I done. It's what should'a been done the night before.
It's all in knowing how. Had t'push it back in and straighten th'calf's head
so it could come on out. Then after I got that done, I had to clean her
out and everything. That was to do. If you want one t'live, y'have t'be
decent with'em. Be nice to'em, you know. And so we got her up then. Had
to help her up she was so weak.

"But then I said, 'Joe, y'got any fodder?'

"He said, 'Yeah.'

" 'Good,' I said. 'Get the prettiest fodder you've got and bring it here to
this cow. And if you've got any cornmeal, get her a little cornmeal.'

"He run and got the fodder and I fed it to her. She was up then,
standin' up just eatin' like ever'thing. But I knowed about that on account
of watching my father so many times. You know, you can learn by seein'
other people do. And I saved that cow. He's told me many and many a
time since then that that was the best deal he ever had happen to him.

"And she came right on and made a good cow—aw, she already *was* a
good cow, awful good cow. But they had her bought and never had paid
for her. And this man had three or four children. *Anything* you can do to
help a man out when he's raisin' his family—help'em out, I mean, in milk

or bread or anything like that—I know it's good for anybody 'cause I've had to live like that myself. I've *lived* on milk and bread. Me and her, when she was able to take care of'em and milk'em, we'd never be without two or three cows. But back when I was raisin' my family—back in old Hoover's times—people was hard [pressed]. Ten cents an hour and *then* no work. I had to make liquor or do something or starve to death. I told'em I'd do anything before I'd starve. And, dern, I'd starve before I'd *steal*. I never *have* had to do that. But I've see'd the time when it begin to look pretty dangerous! I've sent my boys to school with one shoe of one kind and one of another. But it didn't hurt'em a bloomin' bit. Naw, it didn't hurt'em. It let'em learn a little hard times.

"But about that veterinary business, you've sort'a got t'know the nature of a cow to find out what disease she's got. They's a lot a'people don't understand how to take care of a milk cow or anything. If you know *how,* you know *how,* and if you don't know how, nobody can't tell you. You've got to kind'a learn. Self-experience is a mighty good teacher. My father learnt me how to do things.

"Like sometimes a cow gets what they call hollow tail. Now a cow ain't supposed to get hollow tail. Most of the time, if she has hollow tail she's had too much hollow belly! Now I'm gonna' show you how to cure it. You may think I'm a'tellin' you a lie, but it ain't. It's the truth. Take a cow's tail that already got a hollow place? Pull it up and take both fingers and mash that way? They won't be a bone in there. Maybe it'll be three or four inches before they'll be a bone in there. Well, you know what I do? *I* do. I say it's the present cure. You feel back up there where the bone stops at. Take your knife and just cut that tail smack off and throw it away. That's the present cure of a hollow tail. But *then* feed your cow, or next time you can't lay it on the hollow tail. The hollow belly'll kill her. She'd starve to death!

"Now if your cow had such a pretty tail that you don't want to cut it off, I'll tell you what you can do. You can split her tail just as far as it's hollow and put stuff in there and tie it up for two or three days and then come back and if it's still hollow, you better cut it off! You can always use a little turpentine in there, but be sure you don't fill that hollow place *full* of turpentine 'cause if you do, it's liable to go to th'cow's brain and kill her dead as a nail. But a little'll take the soreness out.

"I'll tell y', they's a whole lotta things that people don't understand. None of you'uns don't have no warts do y'? [Ray McBride shows him a wart on one of his fingers.] Is that a wart? Yeah. It feels like it. That the only one? You've gotta tell me the truth now. If you've got another'n, tell me the truth. If you don't, you won't get it done. [There is only one wart]. Do you want it to stay there, or do you want it gone? You haven't got no business with it, have you? Well, you won't have it long. I'll give you a nickel and you won't ever know when it gets gone. You needn't think about it no more.

"Now it used to be if your nose was bleedin'—about to bleed to death—I could stop it just like that [snaps his fingers]. But that's something I'm not allowed to tell you. If I did, then I might not be no more good from then on. They's just a whole lotta things I understand. They's a whole lotta things I *know*. It's th'truth.

"One time I had a dog get bit in the eye by a rattlesnake, and his eye turned white as cotton. I got me a half pound of lard and a half teaspoon of alum and give it to that dog and he never died. They'll eat that lard. They know it'll do'em good. And that alum—you needn't to worry about'em once they've got that in there. It'll be two or three days before the swelling goes down, but the dog'll be alright.

"Now I believe that'd be good for people. You know, alum's not poison. You could eat a half teaspoon full a'alum and it wouldn't hurt y'! It'll sure cure a dog. It'll keep a dog from dyin'.

"I'm afraid of snakes now. One bit me. Copperhead. Tushes over a inch apart! I was about half drunk when he bit me. That's the way I generally stay when I got anything to drink. And he just snabbed me. It was in a old log barn I bought when I first come here. And so when he bit me, the son of a gun run. It pleased me t'see him go! I *wanted* t'get him out of the way. I come on over here. They wasn't no porch here then. They *had* been a big porch there but a storm blowed off half of it. So I come back and set down on th'doorstep and I heered a car comin'. I was sellin' liquor at the time. Bootleggin'. And they come here t'*buy* it too! And I was sort of glad of it 'cause them comin' all the time is what caused me t'have what I've got now. If I hadn't a'bootlegged, I couldn't a'made it. And I'd sell it t'anybody that come. I didn't care who it was.

"So while I was sittin' there, I told my wife t'get me a pan a'coal oil—kerosene oil, but I call it coal oil—like we heat with. She did. And I was sittin' there squeezin' them two places there where th'tushes went in? You could see a little clear bubble come to th'top of that oil. I just rubbed it, and took me a drink along. I heered a car comin' up th'hill there. It come up th'hill and I had my hand down in the pan there, and my son-in-law come up and said, 'Lord have mercy, Simmie. What in th'world's th'matter?'

"I said, 'Nothin'. Damn snake bit me a while ago.'

"And he said, 'You want'a go t'th'doctor?'

"I said, 'I'm not in no hurry. Yeah,' I said, 'I want'a go, but I ain't in no hurry.'

" 'Well,' he says, 'we're not in no hurry.' He says, 'Get ready and we'll go.'

"I said, 'Well, don't rush.' And I had a little half-pint bottle in my pocket—it was nearly full—and I handed it to'em. I said, 'You'uns can drink this. I'm goin' t'get one t'carry with me.' I come in and poured me out a pint and stuck it down in my pocket. Pulled out and went up there to th'doctor's.

"I said, 'Look here, Doc.' I said, 'I'm goin' t'tell you now before you do *anything* to me.' I says, 'I was pretty drunk when the snake bit me, and,' I says, 'I had plenty a'liquor and I've been drinkin' liquor ever since, and,' I said, 'look here. I've got a full pint just to drink. Don't you give me no shot nor no kind of medicine that'll gee-haw m'liquor.'

" 'Why,' he says, 'Simmie, I ain't gonna give you nothin' to hurt you.'

"I said, 'You *better* not!'

"My hand swelled up, but never did hurt me a bloomin' bit. Stiff—I couldn't use it for I don't know how long. Swellin', you know. But if it hadn't a'been for that liquor, it would'a done me in.

"But that doctor laughed. Said, 'Simmie,' says, 'you needn't t'worry about yourself.' Said, 'All you've got t'worry about'll be the snake 'cause th'snake'll *die*. Said, 'You're so much poisoner than that snake was that that snake'll die!'

"I said, 'I don't care if he does.' And that's all they ever was to it. Got right over it. But I'll tell you now, you let a stick or anything move around where I can sort'a see it and I'm scared now. I used t'never be afraid of a snake, but you get bit and then you *will* get afraid.

"I was glad to see that one that bit me go. He went down to that damn waterhouse and I burnt the whole thing up. Boy, I got mad. Come to find out a big white oak log over there on the left side of the house had always been the holler, and that's where the snake den was. Way we found out was me and a girl we raised was washin' one day. We used to have to build battlin' benches—take the battlin' paddles and beat hell out of the clothes to get them clean—old-fashioned washin'. Me and her were down there at the washin' place where the reservoir is now, and we was down there battlin' one day; and I said to Diane, I said, 'Diane, come over here and help me turn this log over.' She was stout—strong—and young. I was stout too then —stout enough to move a log as far as that went. But she stuck her hand down here and we turned that log over and there lay an old copperhead right there that close to where she put her hand in there. A big'un too. And someone went and got my double-barreled shotgun and brought my shells. Well, I just took my time. I knowed what to do. I could see then—I had two good eyes then. I usually just put their heads off 'cause that's where the poison is, and I knowed how to get rid of th'poison. So I shot it in two. Now I'm gonna' tell you—these people might say it's a lie, but it's the truth —there was *six* little ones fourteen inches long crawled out of its mouth.

And them little son-of-a-guns would strike at anything they saw. They came right out here where she was supposed to have her mouth. She had swallowed them. They just came crawling out. They was fourteen inches long. Six of'em. You gonna' give me th'dog, huh? You think I got the world beat don't you? You don't believe that's true? Well, I wasn't lying. It's the truth.

"And this last summer, right behind where the chair's sittin' right now? Annie was sittin' over there in the chair you're in, and I was sittin' over here lookin' through the winder. We have to keep this door here shut on account of the wind. Comes from the northwest. And she says, 'I see a snake.' [It was inside the house along the living room wall.]

"I says, 'What kind is it?'

"She says, 'It's a copperhead. It's spotted.'

"I said, 'Don't you *move*.'

"So I went in there and got my gun; came back and set down over in this chair. And I couldn't get to find its head nowhere. But I see'd that I could cut it in two twice with that shotgun. And I thinks to myself, 'If I can make *three* snakes out of one, the head part won't get far!' I shot it. Shot that wire that runs to th'heater here plumb in two, and shot a hole plumb down through the floor, but I killed that snake! Don't like them much at all."

"I've been through a lot, but . . ."

"They ain't nobody ever been through as much as I have. And of all the trouble I've ever had in my life, I've never asked none of my folks t'help me one penny. I've never asked none of them for one brownie. They have to work to make a livin'. I'll get mine, and I ain't gonna' steal it neither.

"I've always lived on my own—since I was sixteen years old. Now I'm a'settin' here and I'm a'livin' at *home*. Got plenty to eat, and plenty to wear if I don't get out and get it wet!

"We had nine children. Two of'em died. It's lucky to have seven a'livin'! Back in old Hoover's time when we was a'raisin'em, it's a damn wonder ever' one of'em hadn't a'perished to death. But I always set my head to have enough to do with, and I never listened to nobody.

"My daddy—that's his picture right up there—never owned a foot of land in his life, and I always said I was going to. By God I did, and I got it, and I know who it belongs to. Ours. Nobody can come in here and tell me I gotta' move. Look at the money I've put out here, and I made it the best way I could. And I ain't stole none of it. And there ain't no damn

PLATE 5

man in this world can say that I ever took nothing that didn't belong to me. If a man accuses me of that, I'll shoot him sure as that gun in there will shoot. And it'll shoot! It ain't got a bit of sense. It'll shoot anybody I tell it to! No, I wouldn't be accused of stealing. It makes me so damn mad to have something around and have somebody come and steal it. If they need anything I've got, I wish they'd come and ask me for it. Then if I see fit, I'd let'em have it, and if I didn't see fit to, I'd just say, 'I ain't got no use for you.' That's what I'd say.

"No, never had to steal. I made it on liquor and damn good management. I've never listened to nobody since I was fifteen year old. Not even my wife. I've been a long-headed somebody. I don't listen to what nobody tells me. Well, I *did* one time. When I stayed out a'school t'go a'huntin', the teacher asked me why didn't I come to school? I listened to her. Then I told her I'd rather hunt. I got graduated from the second grade and didn't go no further. And I've hunted all my life ever since. Now I've got no dogs. I've got eight, but they ain't no *dogs*. I want t'show them to you directly. I've got five of the prettiest pups out there that's ever been. They're beagles.

"And now here we are at home. Got our own home and don't owe a penny. I've seen the time when it begin to look pretty dangerous! But you might know some of my boys. Lewis is a carpenter here in Clayton, and Grover runs the Quick-Stop down here in Tiger. He don't run it—he owns it! And then Harvey, he's a second-handed car man out in Clayton. That's my third boy. And my fourth boy's in Florida. They're all off now and a'makin' their own way and a'makin' a good livin' and I'm pleased of'em.

"No sir, I've been lucky. Been *plumb* lucky. T'be a'livin'. I've not done nothing t'hurt nobody. 'Course I wouldn't let nobody drag me around. That's one thing I've never done.

"I got a good home here. All paid for and don't owe a penny on it. Enough a'timber over yonder to make *fifty* houses bigger'n this one. All my children's married off. Ain't nobody but me and her here, but we have a big time. She can't get around and go much. She won't even go a'fishin' with me. She never *would* fish . . .

"But I've been a worker. I've worked as hard, I guess, as any little devil that ever lived. But I've enjoyed it. I've always lived and had a good time. Going to as long as I can. And I'm gonna' live just as long as I can see anybody else a'livin'. Now they needn't say nothin' about that!"

HIDE TANNING

I enjoyed working on this chapter because the people we interviewed were all so friendly—like Minyard Conner who gave us two coon skins and R. M. Dickerson who told us this story:

"Men used t'have stories they'd tell about dogs—about what their dogs would do in th'way of hunting one thing'r'nother. And Oscar Powell was a'talkin' one day t'get ahead of Lawton Brooks and his stories. And that possum dog—coon dog, especially—there's two of th'kinds that could always be just nearly perfect. And Oscar said he had a dog one time that you could just blow your horn and he'd come up. He'd know you was going a'huntin' when he heard th'horn blow. Said he'd come up, and you could take your board [to stretch the hide on] and just hold it out there and let him look at it, and said he'd go off into th'woods and he'd catch you a possum that'ud just fit that board.

"But said he lost th'dog one day, and he didn't know *what in the world* come of his dog. He never had done that before, and he always come back home; but he said this time he hadn't come back and he didn't quite understand.

"And he heard his wife a'talkin' in there tellin' about so'n'so that had come over t'their house t'borry an ironin' board. And said she went and got th'ironin' board and brought it out there, and they'uz standin' at th'door talkin'—she had th'ironing board up on her hip just standin' there talkin' t'th'lady—and said she looked out in th' yard there and that dog'uz actin' kindly funny. Said he'd look around, and look around. Then finally after awhile she said he just went off up thataway. Said she didn't think anything about it. But he never did come back.

"And Oscar said, 'You know, only way I ever figgered out—that dog never could find a possum'uz big enough t'fit that ironin' board and he's still a'huntin'."

From working on this chapter I've learned how to tan at least seven different kinds of hides in at least nine different ways, and I feel that I can do it all on my own. It's been a fun way to learn.

RANDY STARNES

Interviews and photographs were done by Ken Kistner, Curtis Malan, Mike Pignato, Joe Sabin, Kevin Speigle, and Randy Starnes.

EQUIPMENT

The equipment needed for removing hair or tanning was far from complicated. Almost any watertight container made of wood or cement or cast iron will do as long as it is big enough to hold the hide(s). Will Zoellner advised, "Don't use a steel drum, or tin. Something in the metal ruins the hide." Julius Speed used a cement vat large enough to hold simultaneously fifteen cow hides spread out flat. Others used boxes made of white oak boards. One man even buried his hides in the ash hopper and removed the hair from them at the same time he was dripping lye for soap.

By far the most popular container, however, seemed to be the "tan trough"—an eight- to ten-foot-long section of yellow poplar trunk two to three feet in diameter and split in half. One half is hollowed out (like a dugout canoe) with a broadax and foot adze, with four holes bored underneath at the two ends for legs, and a drainage hole bored in the bottom and sealed with a plug. The hairing or tanning mixture is mixed in the trough and the hide(s) submerged until they are done. The trough is rocked or agitated frequently to make sure the solution gets into every fold of the hide.

One also needed some sort of knife or scraper for scraping the flesh and fat off the flesh side of the hide prior to and after hairing and tanning. Harry Brown, Sr., filled this need easily: "I made me a little fleshing hammer. I just turned me over a buggy spring and took a file and filed me some little notches in it. You don't want it too deep, but you got t'go in that skin. There's a little thin layer between th'hide and th'skin, and if you don't get that off, you can't work it up."

For scraping or currying and smoothing the hide when it came out of the vats, some used a rough brush like a curry comb. Julius Speed made a log stand for currying and working. He put two three-foot legs in one end and let the other rest on the ground. Standing behind the raised end, he'd drape the hide over the log and curry it smooth.

Beyond this, all one would need would be the ingredients such as ashes, bark, mutton tallow, or neat's-foot oil, and so on, as will be explained later.

REMOVING THE HAIR

The first step employed by almost every contact we had in converting the animal skin to something useful was the removal of the hair. Most of them did this by first scraping the green hide free of flesh, and then soaking the hide in a mixture of hardwood ashes and water (about one shovelful to the

PLATE 6   Jake Waldroop

PLATE 7 A fresh coon hide has been soaking in a paste of hardwood ashes and water in this bucket for nearly a week. Now Jake fishes around in the bucket to find it.

PLATE 8 He finds it, raises it out, a checks to see whether or not the hair l started to loosen yet.

gallon) until the hair pulled free. The thicker and larger the hide, the longer—and the more ashes and water—it took. The process could last anywhere from two days to nearly two weeks. When the hair began to turn loose, the hide would be taken out, scraped clean, washed, worked as it dried out to keep it pliable, and then cut up into shoe laces or whatever else it was to be used for.

R. R. Singleton said, "We always had a log with a trough cut in it. Put your hide with hardwood ashes—hickory and oak mostly—and water in there, and leave it until the hair comes off. [Richard Norton recommended putting a thick layer of ashes on the hair side of a larger hide and rolling it up before putting it in the water-filled trough.] Then take all th'hair off of it and then take runnin' water at th'branch and wash all of that lye out of it. Then you take it and put it over a barrel'r'log and work it till it's soft."

Dan Manous used ashes, but rather than submerging the hide in the pasty ash mixture, he did it as follows:

"Back when I was a boy, I used to trap animals and catch'em, skin'em. Then I'd spread my skin out on a board. You could tack it down if you wanted to, but you didn't have to as long as you kept it spread out good. Then I'd take ashes just out of th'fireplace, y'know, where they burned somethin' like oak or hickory like you'd burn through th'winter season— good strong ashes like they used to use in these ash hoppers.

"Put th'hide hair side down, and put a good thick layer of those ashes on th'flesh side. Apply ashes all over it—not leave any of it naked, y'know. Then sprinkle it over with water until you get th'ashes good and wet, but be careful not t'wash any of th'ashes off. Let it stay there three or four days and nights, and when you go back, take ahold of some hair stickin' out and pull. You can tell when it's a'gonna' come.

"When th'hair's ready t'come off, you just turn it over, tack some little nails around th'edges of it—spread it out so you can get ahold of it—and scrape it with a knife or somethin'. All that hair will just come off.

"Then put it down in a bucket of lye soap. They made it in a liquid form back then. Just grease and lye. Later on they got t'makin' it where you could cut it into cakes, but they made it back then in liquid form. Put it in a bucket of lye soap and let it stay there about three or four days. Then you take it out and wash all that soap and ashes off of it—get it clean. And

PLATE 9   When he finds it has, he drops the ide into a bucket of rinse water to remove the hes and some of the hair.

PLATE 10   He then pulls most of the rest of the hair off by hand.

PLATE 11 Once the hair is off, Jake
the hide with a burlap sack.

PLATE 12 Now, using the edge of a
bar, he works the hide, scraping it back
forth across the top of the bar to make su
the hair is off, and to make sure it is sr
and clean.

PLATE 13 Then he wrings it out to remove
any remaining water, takes it to the house to
wash it well with soap and water [traditionally
he would have used lye soap], and leaves it in
the sun to dry, working it occasionally to keep
it pliable.

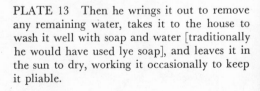

PLATE 14 Tedra Harmon (left), who makes banjos, uses groundhog hides for their heads [see banjo-making chapter]. He showed *Foxfire*'s Ray McBride how he prepares the groundhog skin for use. Here, he and Ray hold up the skin of a groundhog he has just killed.

PLATE 15 Tedra uses an automobile oil pan, lined with a plastic trash bag split open. He places the hide in, hair side up, covers it with ashes, and then waters it down, folds the flaps of the trash bag over it to keep it moist, and sets it in a nearby shed out of the heat of the sun. After the first day, he checks it every morning and afternoon to see whether or not the hair is beginning to pull free.

PLATE 16 When the hair will pull off the skin easily, he and Ray push the wet ashes aside and begin the long job of picking the hair loose. In this case, because of the warm weather, the hair began to come loose after two days of soaking.

PLATE 17 They work together until as much of the hair as they can pull off has been removed.

PLATE 18   When the hair is mostly removed, Tedra lifts the hide out . . .

PLATE 19   . . . and takes it to the nearby creek to wash it off well.

just keep workin' it then, and beatin' it over a stump or log or somethin', and workin' it with your hands till it gets dry."

Jess Rickman remembers that you could shortcut the whole ash process by simply taking the lye that came out of the ash hopper and wetting the hide down with that. That method, as he remembered, would take the hair off in about three hours, as would unslaked lime in water, according to Will Zoellner. Will's only warning was not to leave the hide in any longer than necessary (8–10 hours) or the hide would be damaged.

There were other ways of removing the hair too. Dan Manous told us, "With a wildcat, you can crack th'head, y'know—break th'skull—and take th'brains out of th'head and rub it all over that flesh side—just take your hands and rub it all over th'flesh side—and that will take th'hair off. It don't take long. If you can get it to a fire where you can just kinda' hold it up to th'fire where you can just warm it up—not too hot—just warm it up a little, that'll take effect and th'hair'll just drop off. It'll work fast—faster than them ashes.

ATE 20   He then takes it to the back h and, with a piece of scrap wood, scrapes y any remaining hairs from that center ion of the hide that will be used for the jo head. Then he puts it in a bucket of ng soapy water to soak overnight. This sts the action of any lye that may remain would continue to eat away the hide.

PLATE 21   The next morning, he removes a dried deer hide from the shed door. This hide will also be converted into heads for his banjos.

PLATE 22   In its place is tacked the soaking-wet groundhog hide. It will be left there until completely dry and stiff, and then stored for use. Just before use, he will cut out the head, soak it in water to make it pliable again, and tack it onto the banjo while still moist. As it dries, it will tighten on the instrument.

PLATE 23   He sizes up the deer hide and estimates that he will be able to get three good heads out of it—a good use for a hide that most hunters would simply toss away.

PLATE 24   Tedra also sometimes tacks groundhog hides on boards to dry. He tacks them so that they don't touch the board to allow air to get underneath them as well.

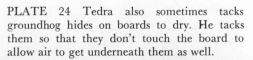

"Now I don't know if a groundhog brains'll do that, but I know a cat's will. Yeah. I've tried it. I've done that."

Builder's lime was another possibility. Harry Brown, Sr., said, "Use about a quart of lime to a gallon of water. [You can approximate because] if you don't get as much, it might take about a half a day or a day longer. If you get a little more, it'll get th'hair slippin' about a half day or a day earlier. You just keep checkin' it. Then take it out, clean and scrape it, and stretch it out as tight as you can and let it get almost dry. Then you finish workin' it dry. That's when y'get into work!"

Another contact told us he used to use soda, smearing it over the flesh side of the tacked down hide. No water is needed as the grease and fat in the hide will keep it moist. Leave it eight or nine days, and when the fat turns loose, the hide is ready to use.

TANNING WITH BARK

The majority of our contacts removed the hair from the hide first, using one of the methods described earlier, and then, if desired, tanned it by the following means:

In the spring of the year when the sap was up, they would strip bark off chestnut oaks (or "buck" oaks as R. M. Dickerson called them), and haul it to the place where the hides were to be tanned. Will Zoellner emphasized that a good time to gather the bark was on the new moon that comes about May 30. He said if you waited until summer to gather it, it wouldn't work nearly as well.

Then, using the bark either dried or green (we found people who did both), they hacked it into tiny pieces (and beat it with a hammer if they wanted to speed the process), placed it in the trough or vat, and added water to make an ooze. To this ooze, the hide was added and allowed to soak until tanned into leather.

For some of our contacts, the collection of tan bark for tanning hides became their living. Mr. Dickerson described how it affected his family:

"When I come down here in nineteen and nine, I'uz sixteen years old. And we'd been here two years when my father died. We had some land up in th'Blue Ridge Mountains there, and my two older brothers'ud go up there and cut down trees and skin th'tan bark and haul it down here and sell it. Take it down t'th'railroad station and load it on a car. Or they'uz people over here at Dillard'ud buy tan bark. Millard Grist bought a lot a'tan bark, and then he went into th'acid wood business. He'd buy tan bark and crossties and telephone poles.

"And they'd get up enough tan bark t'fill up a [railroad] car, and they'd ship it over t'Canton, North Carolina 'r'somewhere over in there, and then they'd beat that up.

"The way they done that, they'd cut'em a ring around th'tree about four feet long, and they'd just get around and cut that ring off—just take a ax and chop a little "v" all th'way around th'log [at the base], and then they'd come back and split th'top off—just take th'ax and go along th'top—and just get that bark loose between th'two rings they made around there. And then they'd put th'ax in there, or a spud (most all of'em had a spud but we couldn't afford t'buy one because they cost a right smart, and all th'money we could get we needed t'take care of our kids at home. There was three boys and two girls left at home, and all of'em just little fellers. I'uz th'biggest one and I'uz just sixteen and they'uz on down. So we didn't have enough money t'buy a spud). So they'd just put a ax in there, and if th'sap was pretty good they'd start up here and push th'ax down— one of'em 'ud hold th'bark and pull it over, and th'other'n 'ud push it down—get a great big slab a'bark off. And then they'd lay it up.

"Had t'cut th'tree down on th'ground [to get the bark]. They'd do that in th'summer time. Then they'd go back in th'fall of th'year, and if it'uz somethin' that'ud make a saw log, why they'd cut a saw log off a'th'body if it'uz a good body. If it didn't, why they'd work it up into firewood at home. And use it. So when th'sap was up and it'ud skin good, they'd have t'do th'skinnin' then. But 'long in th'fall they'd go back and work that tree up inta wood'r'lumber'r'somethin'. Wouldn't waste anything.

"And that tan bark'ud come off kindly round. Look sorta like a trough. Well, they'd take and lay it down and flatten it out, y'see. Maybe lay somethin' on top of it and weight it down. And by doin' it thataway, you could get a whole lot more loaded in a wagon than if it'uz rounded up. So they'd mash it down flat that way. Get'em a stack up, then lay'em maybe a big rock on there and let it lay there till it dried out. Then they'd go back and get'em a sled and put it on a sled and haul it down t'where they could get t'th'wagon. And they done that with steers."

For the actual tanning process, we found that each of our contacts, though using basically the same method, had his own tricks and variations. First we've let Julius Speed, who used to tan cow hides for his neighbors for a living, describe his method completely. Then we'll add variations at the end of the chapter.

Here's how Mr. Speed described it:

"You go through th'woods and y'skin th'bark off a chestnut oak. Then y'haul that in.

"Then you get your hide. I went and got hides. They [the people who wanted the hides tanned] generally always had th'cow skinned. Somebody'ud say, 'I have a hide I want'cha t'tan' and so when we got ready t'go t'tannin', I'd go and get it. [According to Mr. Speed, as soon as the cow or calf died, the neighbors would usually skin it right away, take the green hide, salt it down good on the flesh side and roll it up until it took the salt well. Then they'd hang it up on the side of the barn and let it dry out so that by the time he got it, it was usually dry.]

"You take them hides—they're generally dry—and then you soak'em about two or three days in the creek. And then take'em out, and then you put 'em in a vat and spread'em out and cover them with ashes is what we used to do—put ashes over'em on the hair side. And then you take'em out, and y'take a curry knife and y'take the hair off of'em. And then you take'em, whenever y'get'em haired, back to the creek and soak'em for about a week.

"And then you take'em out of the creek, bring'em back to the vat and spread'em out, and you hack up that bark that you skinned. You cut it up right fine. I set up many a day and hacked it up until I'd get enough to cover the [first] hide. Then I put in another hide, and do th'same thing until I got the remainder put in.

"Then about two weeks later, I taked it out and I'd put it on this horse and curry the flesh side of it—where all th'flesh was. Curry all that off. And hack up *new* bark and put it back just like I did th'first. And I'd leave it in there then, I guess, for a month.

"Then I'd take it out and I'd curry it again on that flesh side, and if it'uz colored good—I could tell, y'know, if it'uz colored all th'way through good or not. It'd look sorta like that [pointing to light brownish boots]. [If it was not tanned completely, it went back into the vat.]

"It'll get hard when y'take it out. You have to put it down and roll it up and work it till it becomes limber after y'take it out of th'vat. It don't take very long. I always just put it down on th'floor and just rolled it back'erds and for'erds."

According to Richard Norton, you could change the color of the hide depending on what kind of bark you used to tan it with. He said that after the hair had been taken off the hide with ashes, the men would beat either chestnut oak bark (if they wanted the hide to come out brown) or white oak bark (if they wanted it to have a yellowish cast). The bark, according to Richard, could be used either green or dried—it made no difference— and the ooze would be strong enough to tan with when it was a dark, coffee color. Rather than using a large vat, like Julius Speed, Richard's family used a small tanning trough and tanned only for family use. They would wash the ashes out of the trough when the hair had been taken off the hide, place some bark in the bottom, and then lap one hide in, accordion-fashion, with bark between each layer. Then water was added, and when the ooze was strong enough to begin tanning, they would watch it closely, agitating the mixture once in a while to make sure the ooze got into every portion of the skin. Then, periodically, they would change the bark to make sure the mixture stayed strong to the end. When the hide was tanned, they would take it out and work it. As it dried, they would rub oil into it so that it would stay pliant.

As Mr. Dickerson remembered the process, they would go ahead and tan the hide in bark ooze without taking the hair off first. They would skin the bark off while the sap was up, and then beat it into fine pieces with a hammer: "You heard the expression about the Devil beatin' tan bark? These old mountain people used t'take, fer'instance, some sorta' unusual sound, somethin' out a'th'ordinary, or some expression that was sorta' bewilderin' that you didn't quite understand? They'd compare that as to th'Devil a'beatin' tan bark." When the ooze was made, and the hide submerged, they'd test every few days to see if the hair was coming off yet. When it began to come loose, they'd take the hide out, take a rough brush, curry all the hair off, and then use the hide as it was for shoe leather, etc. He admitted that it was hard for him to remember exactly how it had been done, because he was young when his father was doing that work. "You'd get in th'way of them old people, and they would tell you to get out of th'way, and if you didn't get out of th'way, directly you'd be standin' up t'eat for about a week."

Will Zoellner agreed that you could tan the hide in bark with the hair on. He said that if you did it that way, though, you had to either burn the hair off with a blowtorch when the hide came out of the ooze and was dried, or pass the cut shoestrings through a fire to get it off. (Or you could just leave the hair on and use the hide that way.)

Most of our contacts disagreed as to exactly how long the process took. R. R. Singleton remembered that it took about two weeks to tan a small hide like a groundhog, but that a larger one took considerably longer. Will Zoellner said that you could speed up the whole process by boiling the beat-up bark and water until the mixture turned the color of indigo. After it cooled, you added the hides, and for cow and mule hides it would take twelve months for a thorough job. For smaller hides like wildcats and foxes, it would take only ninety days. Harry Brown, Sr., remembered most of the tanning being done in the fall, cow hides being left in the bark solution for the entire winter.

All agreed, however, that no matter how long it took, it was hard work.

When easier methods came along, according to Mr. Brown, "They quit this tan bark business because it's a lot of trouble to get out there and skin tan bark, beat it up; it takes so much longer."

OTHER WAYS TO TAN

The use of chestnut bark was not the only way of turning hides into leather. Other contacts remembered using a variety of different methods.

WITH BRAINS

Minyard Conner said that rubbing the flesh side of a freshly killed squirrel or groundhog or wildcat with its own brains, and then holding it up to a fire to warm it, would not only make the hair turn loose but would also tan the hide at the same time. He had done it often himself.

Will Zoellner also used brains, but somewhat differently. Once, when he killed a wildcat, he skinned it immediately and then rubbed its brains on the flesh side of the hide while the brains were still hot. He then folded the hide in half flesh side to flesh side, carried it home, and then took the hair off with ashes and water. When the hide was off, he dried the already tanned hide, rubbed it with Vaseline, and used it for a banjo head.

WITH ALUM

Julius Speed used to tan coon hides for shoe strings with alum. He took the hair off the green hide with ashes and water, washed it thoroughly, and then laid the hide out flesh side up and covered it with alum. The hide would be tanned and ready to use in about a week. Richard Norton described using the same method for wildcat hides.

Harry Brown, Sr., sometimes tanned using alum and salt. He used about four ounces of alum and two ounces of salt per gallon of water. He then let the hide soak in that solution three or four days. That turned it white and tanned it.

Will Zoellner also used alum, but claimed it could only work on thin hides that were easily dried—especially groundhogs. He claimed to have used an alum and water mixture successfully too.

A strong tea made with alum and oak bark would also work, according to Dan Manous, but he couldn't remember the proportions of the recipe.

WITH LARD AND FLOUR

Mary Green remembers that one of the best methods was to rub the inside of the haired hide with lard and coat that with a thick layer of flour. The hide would then be rolled up with the lard and flour to the inside and set away until the blood was drawn out and it "looked like it was done." Then it would be worked and oiled to keep it soft.

TANNING WITH THE HAIR ON

Julius Speed often tanned sheep skins by taking the green hide, scraping all the flesh and fat off, and salting down the flesh side. When the moisture from the hide had absorbed the salt, he shook off any excess and then covered the flesh side with alum. When the hide was thoroughly dried (about a week or so), it was ready for use.

R. R. Singleton used almost the same method for fox, deer and sheep skins, except that he used a mixture of half alum and half soda, and didn't bother salting the flesh side first. He simply rubbed the mixed powders into the scraped flesh side and let it dry for about a week. The mixture would work on either a green hide or one that had been dried for a week or so. He thought it was better, however, to do it while the hide was green. When the hide was dried, he would just dust any remaining powder off. It didn't have to be washed.

Harry Brown, Sr., rather than using either of the above, always used one bar of P&G laundry soap and six ounces of arsenic or lead. He'd chop up the bar into a small kettle, mix it with a little water to dissolve it into a mushy paste, and add the arsenic or lead. When it was pasty, he'd rub that on the flesh side and let it dry. It would preserve the hair side intact, but

PLATE 25   A bear hide being dried in the loft of a barn. The hair side is down, and the flesh side has been coated with a thick layer of alum.

PLATE 26 Hides were often removed from the animal whole, turned inside out, and stretched over boards to dry for shipment to fur companies. Here Lon Reid and *Foxfire*'s Robbie Letson hold a fox and a raccoon, skinned and dried in that fashion.

would turn the flesh side black. He used to mount deer heads for trophies in this manner.

Many people in the area used to simply dry hides with the hair on for sale to fur companies. They would use a long, thin board about two and a half feet long, six to eight inches wide, and tapered at one end (rather like an ironing board). The size would depend on the size of the hide being stretched. Then they'd skin the animal from the rear so that the hide was

PLATE 27   An old photo of Lawton Brooks with hides drying on boards.

PLATE 28   Minyard Conner dried hides on boards for use in making shoelaces or rawhide to repair harnesses. Here, he and *Foxfire*'s Ken Kistner slip the board out of a dried coon hide.

PLATE 29   Then, as Curtis Malan holds the board, he slits the hide up the middle . . .

PLATE 30 . . . opens it up . . .

PLATE 31 . . . and cuts a strip off the edge for use as a bootlace.

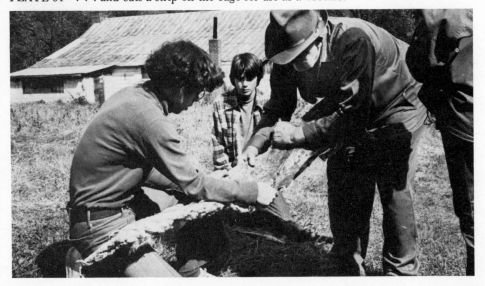

PLATE 32   After the lace is sliced off, he drives a nail in a post and draws it rapidly back and forth against the nail to remove the hair. For longer strips, he cuts in a circle and joins two strips together as described in this chapter.

PLATE 33   Ken and Curtis examine the strip of hide.

peeled off all in one piece, but inside out. This inside-out hide was pulled over the board so that the flesh side was exposed to air all the way around. The section of hide covering the head fitted snugly into the tapered end of the board.

The hide could also be skinned off flat (split the hide down the inside of the back legs to the crotch, and down the inside of the front legs to the breast bone, and then from the underside of the chin down the chest and stomach to the crotch and peel it off). Sharpened sticks would be set into the pouches of both the back and front feet thus stretching them apart and thereby stretching the hide out flat.

The hides were then simply hung up in a barn loft and allowed to dry prior to being shipped off to fur companies.

KEEPING THE HIDE PLIABLE

As hides dried after being haired or tanned and washed, they were kneaded and rolled to keep them pliable and soft. Many contacts told us of sitting around their fires in the evenings after supper working hides.

People had various methods to make sure they *stayed* that way. Will Zoellner rubbed neat's-foot oil into the hides to force water out and let the oil take its place. He claimed this would keep the hides good for twenty years or more.

Harry Brown, Sr., melted either mutton or beef tallow, mixed it with equal parts of melted beeswax, and rubbed this into the hides. The mixture could also be rubbed into shoe leather to keep water out of boots and shoes, and keep them soft for at least two months.

USES FOR HIDES

Some hides were sold. As Richard Norton said, "They used to buy hides in here of all kinds. Fellers came around buying skins of any kind that would make furs, y'know, like coons, polecats, possums and everything like that. They used them for coat collars, and that was another way for us to make some money back then."

R. M. Dickerson, the mail carrier at the time, remembered the industry vividly: "They'd let them dry and put'em in a sack and wrap th'sack around—tie'em up pretty tight and pack'em in a tow sack'r'cotton sack—and then they'd mail'em. I used t'be th'mailman around here, and I've brought lots a'packs a'hides in thataway. They'd sew th'sack up tight, and they'd have a tag, and they'd sew th'tag on there—or hook it on there with a copper hook—put their name on th'outside of it, and on th'other side'ud be th'name of th'company it'uz goin' to. Th'company always furnished these tags, and then they'd ship'em. I carried lots of'em. Most all of'em went t'th'Funsten Fur Company in St. Louis. Some of'em went t'Memphis. They'uz a few that shipped t'Chicago. I think Sears and Roebuck used t'buy hides.

"And they'd send out price lists—sorta like this junk mail we call now. They'd put th'prices on there: so much for a possum skin so big and so on; so much for muskrats, and then a coon, and then wildcats and foxes.

None of'em hardly ever bought a rabbit skin because their skin is not stable enough—not strong enough t'be worth much.

"And when th'price lists didn't come, they'd [the people in the community] come back and say, 'What'd y'do with m'fur list!' They'd wait for that. And they'd usually come out from this time a'year [October] along up till about February. You had t'wait till along in th'fall, and then catch'em [animals] through th'winter and let'em dry out, and then ship'em along that way up until spring. You couldn't hardly sell hides caught before maybe th'first of September. They wouldn't buy them. They had t'be in th'season when th'hides was good. Th'hides were green in th'summertime, y'see. And they'uz another angle to it. They'uz a huntin' law that y'couldn't hunt those things back in th'rearin' season. And th'fur companies, in order t'keep their business up, they wouldn't buy'em then so th'people would stay within th'law. And then, th'hides was just naturally better when th'fur come out in fall for th'winter season. It'ud all shed out and be thin in th'summertime, y'see, and there wouldn't be much hair on that. Feller didn't want a fur coat with no hair on th'collar! In th'winter, th'hair on th'animals'ud begin t'come out and thicken up. Durin' th'summer they'd be a'sheddin'."

But by and large, almost all the hides tanned were used around the farm. Most people tanned their own. When they got someone to tan for them, however, they generally paid that person with part of the tanned hide. Julius Speed, for example, said, "I generally divided th'hide as near as I could in th'middle; and whoever I got th'hide from, he got that half and I kept th'other half."

The hides were used in a myriad of ways. Here, in note form, are some of them.

FOR BELL COLLARS, HARNESSES, HORSE GEAR, SACK STRINGS, LINES, BRIDLES, AND HANG STRINGS:

Cowhide. Hair and tan in bark. Take strips and tie or staple the ends together. You could tie the ends together by punching holes in the wide strips and tying through the holes with thin strips.

FOR BANJO HEADS:

1. Groundhog. Remove hair with ashes; wash, stretch on banjo while moist. Can also tan if desired, but not necessary. [Also house cat, deer, squirrel may be used.]
2. Wildcat. Remove hair with brains. Stretch on banjo while moist.

PLATE 34 Ray Conner, Minyard's son, has coon hides tacked on a tree in his yard to surprise passers-by.

FOR RUGS, SADDLE BLANKETS, SADDLE CUSHIONS:

Sheep skin. Tan with hair on. ("When I was a little kid, they'd take them to th'field and put them in th'shade of a tree for small children t'lay on while they was workin'."—R. R. Singleton. "We had one for th'baby t'sit on on th'floor before it could walk. He tanned me one—a great big one—and you could wash that—wash th'wool with a brush"—Mrs. Julius Speed.)

FOR SHOE STRINGS:

1. Calf skin. Hair and tan in bark, and cut into strips of desired width.
2. Deer skin. Same as calf skin.
3. Groundhog hide. Remove hair with ashes and water, work until dry, and cut. Can also tan if wished, but many didn't bother.
4. Squirrel hide (the favorite of most of our contacts). Same as groundhog. ("Now if you want real shoe laces like you was talkin' about before, you use squirrel hide"—Mary Green. According to R. M. Dickerson, if you cut straight down the hide where the backbone was, you could get a string long enough in one piece to lace a shoe.) Can also use this hide to sew up shoes when they rip.
5. Wildcat hide. Same as groundhog. ("I like t'use it. It'll stretch, and it's soft and tough."—Richard Norton.)
6. Raccoon. Take hair off with ashes and tan with alum.

FOR SHOES:

1. Cowhide. Remove hair, tan in bark; use thick part for soles and thin part for vamps. Use maple pegs to tack the sole to the vamp and thread greased with beeswax to sew pieces together.
2. Horsehide. Hair and tan in bark. ("But it won't turn water like cowhide"—Richard Norton.)
With all the above, some didn't even bother to hair the hides. They just dried them, cut off strips, and either burned the hair off, or drew the strip rapidly back and forth against a nail driven into a post to remove the hair.

CATTLE RAISING

as told by Mack Dickerson

Seventy-nine years is a long way to look back. Mack Dickerson looks back over that many years and is able to share the many changes—some good and some bad—that have come to Wolffork Valley. Living near him, you find that he is a uniquely interesting individual. Mack is a bachelor (he says he likes being his own boss) and he has lived by himself for most of his life. He's quiet and keeps to himself, but once you take the time to know him, you discover that his has been a full and crowded life worth sharing with those who will listen.

Mack's family moved to Wolffork in 1835 when the area was still very much a frontier. There were only four other non-Indian families in the valley: the Keeners, the Carters, the Pinsons, and one which Mack can't remember. Mack's father bought the land Mack lives on now from Grandpa Keener in 1896, and then built the hand-hewn log house that Mack still lives in. Its chimney was made of bricks made of lime, sand, and red dirt in back of Gay McClain's place on Betty's Creek. Until the railroad came to the county, the post office for the valley was located in the Dickerson home.

When Mack was a boy, he made blowguns with which to shoot wild cherries, swam a lot, gathered wild chestnuts, hunted rabbit with his father, and helped his mother with their garden. He got his first toy—a little wagon—in 1901 and still remembers it vividly today because toys were so rare in the community. He also loved playing pranks on people. Once he and his brothers took the wheel off his cousin's wagon and hung it in the top of a tree. His cousin had two men hired for the day to help him get in his corn, and the men wasted half a day hunting for the wheel.

By the time Mack was fifteen or sixteen, he was catching wild hogs. He caught his first one in 1911 with his Uncle John Moore's bird dog. He'd feed the hogs all summer and then kill them in the fall and salt them down

PLATE 35

for meat for the family. "I done a lot of that mountain going. I always enjoyed that. That's one reason I kept hogs and cows in the mountains—have an excuse to go." Eventually he gave up fooling with hogs, though, and concentrated on cattle because hogs were so much trouble. "You know you can't make a hog go backwards? He'll get his head caught in a fence and choke. Only way you can make him go backwards is just take a club and hit him on the nose and he'll back up *then*. You can put a rope around a hog's neck and he never will back out of it. He goes forwards all the time. Tie him out and graze him—he'll stay right there. Put you a rope around his neck pretty tight and he won't know nothing about backing out of it. You just try it and see!"

Mack's father died of stomach cancer in 1914 leaving behind four sons and three daughters. Mack had to stop school at the sixth grade and work to help keep the family going. They had a close family, and there was a Christian atmosphere in their home. "I never heard my daddy say an ugly word in his life," Mack recalls.

Mack held lots of different jobs during those days: he worked on public works, as a clerk with the Atlantic Coast Line Railroad, and on farms all over the county. There were many days when he made only seventy-five cents a day.

Then came World War I. Mack volunteered for the Navy, and from

1918 to 1919 he served as radio messenger on the U.S.S. *Supply*. His ship was the first one to fire a shot in the war. When he was released, he came back home to the country. "I wouldn't live in a big city. All the noise and racket. I stayed in New York City twenty-two days one time. We tied up to the Ninety-sixth Street dock. It was the longest two weeks of time I ever spent. I just stayed over on that ship. You'd be out on Saturday evening— people just as far as you could see. I don't like that. I've been in all them big cities: Detroit, New York City, Philadelphia. And I've been all out in Idaho. Them old barren hills, and you don't see no trees. I get sick of that. There's old rocks a'sticking up and nothing *but* them. I just came back home."

Since there wasn't any regular work in the county when he returned, he did odd jobs. His farm buildings and fields needed repairs and attention. To get a little money, he hewed crossties for the railroad, cut acid wood, and worked in a sawmill. They were hard times, but Mack stuck with it, and today he owns twenty-five acres of pasture land, as well as a large piece of forest land on the side of a nearby mountain. And, of course, he has his cattle. "My cattle are what mean most to me now. If it weren't for them I'd be in the poorhouse. I sold $4,000.00 worth of cows last year. I

PLATE 36   Mack with Terry York.

PLATE 37   Mack gathers dried corn from neighboring fields each fall, has it crushed, and uses it for winter feed.

could work all day raising corn and beans to sell and it wouldn't pay out at all."

Those cattle take up most of his time now. The rest of his time he spends listening to ball games (or, during season, attending all of Rabun Gap's basketball games), cooking his meals, and just passing time.

To the kids from the magazine who visit him, he says, "Pay off your debts. Tell the truth. Don't have too much money or you'll get greedy. Have a good reputation. Do as you wish to be done by."

TERRY YORK

Interviews and photographs by Gary Warfield, Karen Cox, Terry York, David Dillard, Steve Smith.

The man I bought my bull from said that breed was over three hundred years old. Not many people have them. The man who sold me the bull brought him down from Cleveland where he'd bought it. He said used to they never would sell a bull and heifer together, so two agents in the Barnum and Bailey circus got together and bought one of each and brought them here. Call them Holland Dutch, or Swiss Belted.

Meanest cow I ever had was a Charolais. I wouldn't have another one. And her calf is the same way. Take this Charolais calf I got. I got six calves down here. All come around about the same time. And that little old calf is wild as . . . The others will just come up. I hadn't fed them but a little bit and they'd be around up here. I'd go out about feed time—I guess they're out there right now waiting on me to feed them—they just come on. And that thing—he won't come up. He liked to never come up and eat with them.

Another thing I found out. I used to be pretty lenient with my calves. I'd have four or five about the same age and go out to feed them and maybe want to put them in the barn or somewhere. Why, they'd get wanting to play, you know. Just like a gang of kids when you holler for them to come to the house for supper. They'll linger along behind, and the cows'll come. That's before they get big enough to eat, you know. Last winter it was muddy and bad like this winter. They'd go up there and the cows would come running to the barn, you know, knowed they was going to get fed. And them little old calves a'running and playing—just stay out. I got to putting my dog on them. Some dogs—I got one here—wouldn't run a little calf to save her life. But that shepherd my brother had up here, I can send him up there—tell him to go up there and get them calves. He'll go up there and run them in about three times. Then next time you go out there and call your cows—holler up at them—when *they* starts, them calves come *with*'em! Dog learns them a lot.

I had one yesterday out there—he didn't want to go in. Put that dog on him. He went t'bellering. That dog makes them beller and scares them. Calf'll follow that cow after you get him scared thataway. He'd follow her into torment if she'd go!

Mack has evolved his own personal approach to stock and his farm from years of observing others, and from years of trial and error. He says firmly that, "farming has improved 500 percent over what it was back in those days." Those technical improvements, combined with the polishing of his own techniques over the last forty years, have made his life now a comfortable, if not a wealthy one.

Things weren't always that way:

We used to plow with horses, plant with our hands, put manure out, work the corn, hoe it about three times with all the kids out in the fields, plow it about three or four times with an old slow mule. I never did plow with no oxen, but lots of people did. They didn't fertilize any back then. They just used manure. Back when I was a kid, they didn't anybody make a hundred bushels, I don't guess, here in this valley. Then they got to putting lime on and they got pretty productive. No fertilizer when I was a kid. We had no railroad back in them days. I never had seen a hundred pound of cottonseed meal till I was ten or twelve years old. Railroad come here in 1905 and got to hauling this meal. But before then we were hauling everything in and out of wagons.

Didn't know much about caring for stock. Fed calves flour for scours.

And hollow tail—my uncle ran cows in the woods. They'd get poor in the wintertime and he'd drive them in, and they was weak and wobbling everywhere, you know. And one of them got down, and he split her tail and put a little salt in it and wrapped it up. Said she got up after a while and come on in! He was an old-timer. They believed in all that stuff. Sometimes you *can* feel their tail [near the base] and it's just like it's been broke [but salt won't fix it].

And the hollow horn. Used to be all the cattle was horned in this country when I was a boy. And they'd take and saw their horns off with a hand saw. They'd half feed them through the winter and they'd be poor in the spring and couldn't walk and wobble around everywhere, and they'd saw their horns off! That's silly because *every* big cow that's got horns on that's hollow!

And I've saw people take a iron and get it right hot and drill a little hole in their head right in here up next to their ear. Said that was good for hollow horn!

There wasn't no meadows back when I was a kid—just corn fields. My great-grandaddy said he had *one* up here. He cleared up that old swamp ground and pulled the stumps out of it and cut it by hand. Stacked it. Didn't have no hay rakes. Never heard tell of that. They'd take and rake it up with pitchforks—cot it up, what we call cots—big pile of it. Then they'd get two little long skim poles and run under it and one man get between them and pack it out. Stack it then in great big stack for feed. Just put'em a pole in the ground and stack it around and around piled up against the pole, and just keep on till you run out the top. I've stacked hundreds of stacks like that. Twenty-foot pole, maybe. At least ten or twelve or fourteen.

Until the time stock laws that required all stock to be fenced in at the farm itself were passed, most stock ran loose in the woods and grazed on what they could find. Dairy cows were kept close to the farm for daily milking, but the others were taken.out in the spring, turned loose to range, and then gathered to be fed at home through the winter.

There was no pastures. Our cows were turned out. Lay around in the bushes. Had to chase them in to milk them. Get wet all over in them wet bushes. We didn't make hay. Just corn and fodder.

And we kept hogs. I let them run in the woods and eat the acorns. We'd lose a few back in the woods—never know what come of them. They'd die, some of them would. Get that milksick. Couldn't get home. It'd kill them. Or some were stolen by them too lazy to work. But not many.

We'd mark the stock's ears. Everyone had his own mark so he could tell whose was whose. Our mark was two swallowforks and a hole in the right. There was lots of combinations (see *Plate 38*):

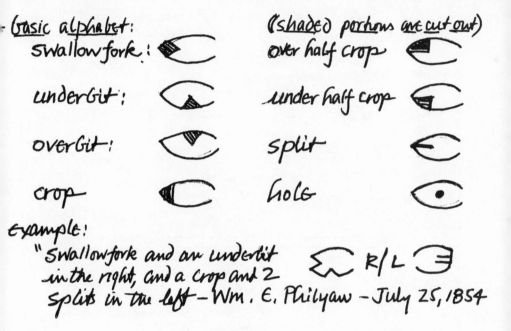

basic alphabet:
   swallowfork: (shaded portions are cut out)
                         over half crop
   undercut:
                         under half crop
   overcut:
                         split
   crop
                         hole

example:
   "Swallowfork and an undercut
   in the right, and a crop and 2
   splits in the left – Wm. E. Philyaw – July 25, 1854   R/L

PLATE 38

Some had some of the awfullest darn marks I ever heard tell of. Swallow-fork and underbit in the right and split in the left. Always marked the right and left. I saw a bunch of cattle in Atlanta down at a calf show way back in 1930, I guess—somewhere back in there. They said they come from Mexico. They had them cut all to pieces. I couldn't even *read* their mark.

We used to range our cattle in the mountains. Had an old cow here one time, and she was heavy with calf, and I was wanting to take the rest of my cows to the woods in the spring of the year. So I decided I'd just leave her here, and when her calf got up about a week or two old, why I'd take her on out there too. Chase them up in the woods. They don't ramble off much in the spring. Stay around pretty good. Thought I'd put a bell on her.

Well, I went up there to Tate City and backed up and turned my cow out and put the bell on her. She never had a bell on before in her life. And they got out of the truck and away she went t'running. That bell scared the calf too. Man, had a heck of a time. Calf got away from the mother, and I stayed around there and worried with her for about two or three hours, and that little old calf wouldn't come out to her. Finally, I believed I heard [the other cows] a way up there on the mountain. I went out to my other

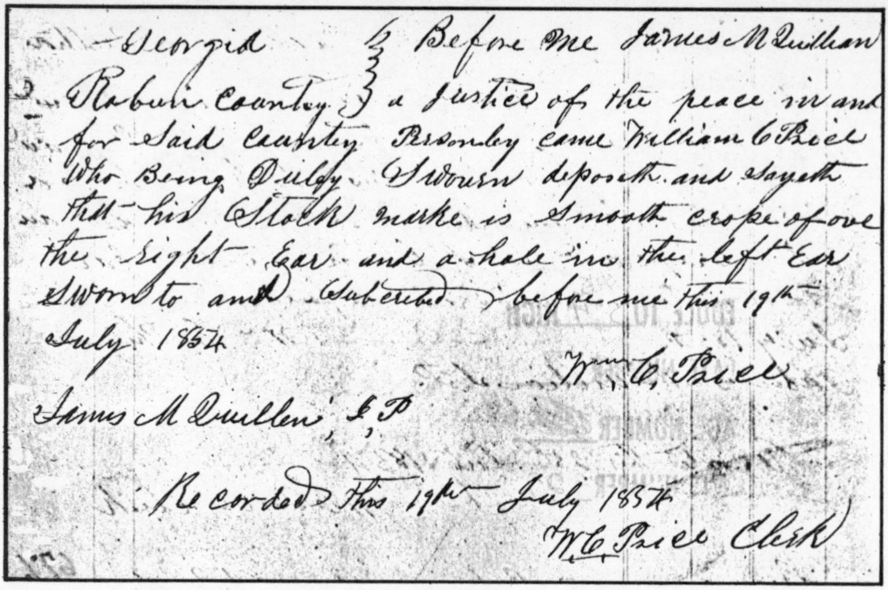

Georgia } Before me James M Quillan
Rabun County } a Justice of the peace in and
for said County Personaly came William C Price
Who Being Duly Sworn deposeth and sayeth
that his Stock marke is smooth crope of ove
the right Ear and a hole in the left Ear
Sworn to and subscribed before me this 19th
July 1854

                        Wm C Price

James M Quillen J P

       Recorded This 19th July 1854

                  Wc Price Clerk

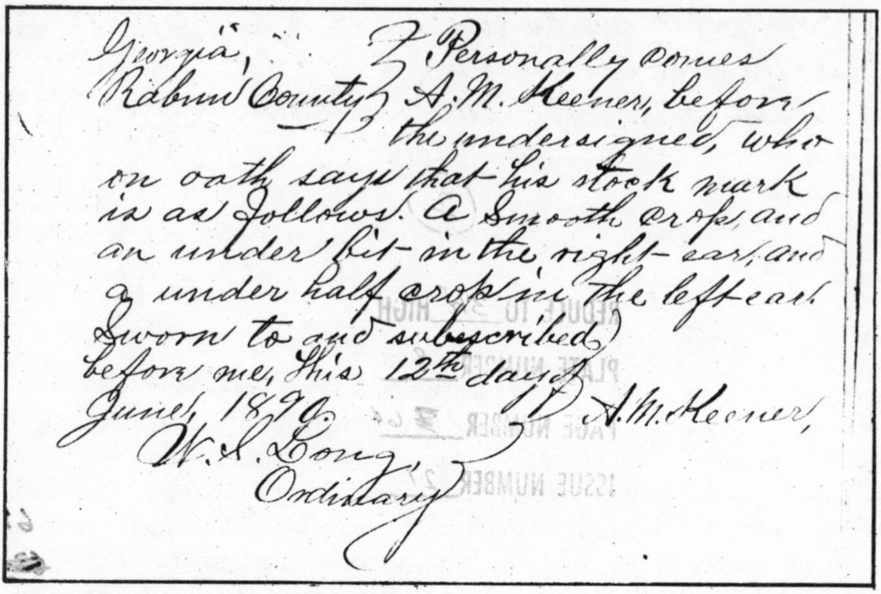

Georgia } Personally comes
Rabun County } A. M. Keener, before
the undersigned, who
on oath says that his stock mark
is as follows. A smooth Crop, and
an under bit in the right ear, and
a under half crop in the left ear
Sworn to and subscribed
before me, this 12th day
June, 1890

                A. M. Keener

W. S. Long
Ordinary

PLATES 39–40 Court records of livestock markings.

Georgia } Before me James M Quillian
Rabun County } a Justice of the Peace in and for
said county Personly came Jesse Lovel
Deposeth and sayeth that his stock mark is
a swallow fork in each year sworn to and
subcribed before me this 25th of July 1834
James M Quillian JP 13   Jesse Lovell

State of Georgia }
Rabun County } personally appeared before
the undersigned John W
Hollifield who being duly sworn says
on oath that his stock mark is a swallow
fork in the left ear and an an over-
bit in the right ear.
                              John W Hollifield
Sworn to and Subscribed before me
this 22nd day of December 1894.
                        H. A. Bleckley
Filed and Recorded }   Ordinary R. C.
Dec 22nd 1894 H. A. Bleckley }
           Ordinary R. C.

Georgia, Rabun County
          Personally appeared before
me H. I. Dockins who on oath
says that his stock mark is
a half crop on the top side of
the right ear and and a
half crop on the under side
of the left ear
                         his
                    H. I. Dockins
                         mark
Sworn to and subscribed
before the 8th day of Oct 1906
          Abt I James
          Ordinary

PLATE 40

cattle. Come back down there and he'd got with her then and I drove her on up the creek and she got in there with them. But boy that scared me. I couldn't find the calf nor the dog either. He'd run off and hid somewhere'r'-nother and just left her there, you know. But she wouldn't leave at all [with that calf gone].

Then, first black cow I had here—half Durham and half black—decided to take her to the mountains. She'd run one summer in the mountains as a heifer. Next spring I decided I'd put a bell on *her*. And there was a great big old ditch out there from the barn. And I put a bell on her a few days before I took them out, you know. And boy I never heard such jumping up and down and bellering in my life. She got down in that old big ditch and stayed all day. She'd happen to sling her head and wouldn't think and that bell'd ring and she'd take another trip!

They just have to get used to it.

You could get out in the woods, though, and salt them, and they'd hear you go to calling, and boy you never heard [the like] coming down off of them mountains just a'flying to get that salt. And if they was anybody else's with them, they'd come too!

Sometimes I'd team up with four others on Persimmon, and we'd put all of our cattle in together. Then we'd bring them in in the fall and separate them out. We done that up there at Big Bald one time, and I never did get as mad in my life. Grade Ledford went with me up there, and Eddie. I'd been the day before and I knew where one bunch was up there. Couldn't find the other. We pulled up over at the mountain, and Grady was going to drive them down the Coleman River. Me and Eddie was going over on what we called between the Bald and Shooting Creek in there, and separate all them out and bring them down there. Pick him up.

Well, we got them all separated out and walked down there—we was gone three or four hours, I guess—and he was going to meet us at what we called the Wheeler Fields. And we come down through there and the bells a'rattling and going on, and couldn't hear no tell of Grade nowhere. And we got down there and stopped, and after while he got to hollering a way up there on the side of Little Bald, and it about dark then. Him mad, too.

Got up there and he had a bunch of them in there. They was a lot of acorns that fall, and they was just going through them cliffs a'hunting acorns, you know. And he couldn't do a thing in the world with them by hisself. Had them here and here and there, and they was just a'going around them rock cliffs and over logs. We finally got them all surrounded up, and— I always used a walking stick up there—I flew in there trying to run them

PLATE 41   Mack with his Dutch-belted herd bull.

PLATE 42   Mack's dogs aren't just pets. They help him round up his cows and calves.

PLATE 43   Mack begins and ends every fall and winter day by toting a bale of hay out to the pasture for his cattle.

PLATE 44

PLATE 45

PLATE 46

downhill. And we had them all hemmed up there, and I was a'using my walking stick on them, and some of them pulled down the rock cliff there and slid plumb from here to that fence out yonder! We finally got them all separated in and got them all down there and had to leave them and go back the *next* day and get them.

But he'd been all that evening trying to run them out and never *had* got them down. It was five hours, I guess. Six. I could hear him hollering. He'd lost his dinner. And he had a rope and he'd lost *it!* We had some terrible times with this cow business.

Sometimes they'd get over on the Shooting Creek side and go as far as Highway 64. And that's a long ways. Head of Buck Creek. And they was bad to get down on Nantahala.

I had two and Kate [Decatur] Burrell had two up there the year the war ended in 19 and 45. You know we never got those cattle in till the sixth day of February! That was the year them forest [Forest Service] fellers had the little deer over there—they'd brought the deer in here. But they was there and had a little place fenced out and sowed in with rye for [the deer]. And they had some field glasses with them and saw some cattle up there on the side of the mountain. Said one of them had a hole in its ear. I'd been over there inquiring to him about them, and he sent me word that they was over there. And we pulled over there and couldn't find them!

They'd been three or four snow storms that winter up in there. We'd find their sign all around there. Finally that forest feller put them up down there. He was a'camping there looking after the deer, and he'd go home every weekend. Finally he got ahold of them and put them in a stall over there. Didn't have nobody over there to help him water them or nothing, so he finally turned them out. We went back one Sunday morning over there and tracked them. He'd had to turn them out that night since we didn't come—we were a long time about getting the word or something—so he'd turned them out and we took their tracks out up what they call the Curtis Branch. Found them up there and drove them home. Sanford Garland was at the post office looking for mail from some of his boys in the service and saw us go by and asked what we were doing driving cattle. I said, "We're just getting them in from taking them out last spring."

He went up there and looked at them. Said, "Them's fatter'n them I got at home, and me feeding them all the time! Wonder what that [Forest Service] feller'd take to run *mine* over there!"

You know them old big ferns? You ever see them out here in the woods? Ones that stay green all winter? That's what they lived on. And they'd get up under those cliffs out of rain and sleet.

But you could trust people then. I lost a few over there, but not many. People would send you word, and you'd do the same. Them old folks is all dead and gone now. All of them honest. They'd tell you where your cattle was at. Just worked through each other, you know. You can't trust nobody, nowadays. Or believe nothing they say, hardly. Ain't like them oldtimers.

Mack can feel things changing all around him. He's concerned about the energy crisis, but says, "I'd live it the same way I did, but I'd hate to live it over from now on. But, I'm ready to go back to wood anytime."

He's more concerned about people that are "too busy working just trying to make a dollar. It's good in a way, but a neighbor needs some help some time, and a feller hates to bother'em when they've got these regular jobs."

He is also deeply concerned about certain farming practices he sees now, and about the steady influx of new, part-time families that fragment the sense of community that once existed:

They've got so there's not many people farming nowadays, you know? Feller used to be his own boss—didn't have no one to come around to tell him what to do. I don't like to be bossed. Them fellers that you give a farm to [hire to work for you], you just as well to throw them in the river. You've got to work it out yourself.

I never did go into debt much. If I wanted a little money at the bank, I'd go out there and they'd give me however much I wanted in the fall, and then pay them back. If you borrow and they've got to sue you to get it back, then there ain't no use to go back [to them again]. Kinda pay your way.

'Course, land's got awful high now. These people come in here, buy it all up. They buy it here and just leave it trying to make a dollar on it. Don't *care* about the fellers that was raised here. Not a penny.

It's always been a funny idea to me. Bunch of people [from outside] bought up some land here and tried a cattle business. I went up and looked. They hired everything done. Never came around. I was up there one spring, and the cattle all poor and about dead. Calves around there that couldn't stand up. They didn't feed'em. Just let it go to the dogs. You can't *do* that. You've got to be there and oversee it yourself.

I knew a rich man that bought a summer home here. He took a notion he wanted to get into the cattle business. Talked me into going with him to an auction to buy a thoroughbred black bull. Then he talked more about dogs and hunting than bulls. Showed off his trophies. Give $600.00 for a bull and didn't even have a pasture or feed. Just had money. Man sold him his hay. Fed him in a mudhole. I never saw one around here nowhere yet that could hire people to look after [their stock]—and them good workers and everything—that could keep them up.

Now they're buying land for the investment. I'd like to see a lot of them stay out'a here. They're ruining our country. Come in here and post it.

That's the first thing they think about. We never used to think about posting nothing back when I was a kid. Never heard tell of posting land. And they come in here from the city up in here and drive their jeeps around, or buy land and try to get the old roads closed. You take these old roads—I don't care if nobody ain't been on them in fifty years—you can't go and stop them up. Take the road we got goes around up here on our mountain. Been using it for a hundred years—different landowners, you know. And some of them bought this land in there since then and wants to stop *that* road up. That was built when my grandfather owned the land and it's been there ever since I can remember. Now they want to stop it up. They just come up here and think they can just go and do everyway and keep you out.

Take what the government owns, and the outside people, and there wouldn't be much of Rabun left. Some of them may get ahold of this and not like what I say about it, but that's all right.

ANIMAL CARE

Today, farmers can specialize and raise hogs, chickens, cattle, or horses, or they can raise only vegetables or grains, without an animal on the whole place. But years ago, because families had to rely almost entirely on themselves for food, shelter, and clothing, raising, working, and eating animals was an absolutely necessary and integral part of farm life. In order to be nearly self-sufficient, which families had to be in the mountains, they needed a wide assortment of animals. They didn't have them as pets or for fun—they needed them to live and didn't have much choice. This is not to say that people didn't enjoy their animals, but they were very dependent on each other, and even the animals themselves were interdependent.

People fed the animals and the animals fed the people. For instance, the mules (or steers or horses) that pulled the plow to cultivate the land to grow corn, produced manure to fertilize the corn, hauled the manure out to the pasture from the barn in the wagon, hauled the mature corn in the wagon from the pasture to the barn for storage, and hauled some of the corn to the market to sell. They ate their share of that corn, too, and so did the hogs, ducks, chickens, sheep, geese, guineas, etc. It would have been difficult to raise any animals at all without one or more beasts of burden. In addition to the work and manure produced, the horses reproduced both themselves and the mules (with a little help from a neighbor's jack), and the steers, when too old to work, were fattened and eaten. I could go on for pages trying to clarify the relationships among the farmers and their animals, but I'll let you infer them from the people's own comments.

All the animals on a farm were kept for a definite reason—some animals may have become pets, but animals were not acquired as pets, and even a pet had to make itself useful, or it wasn't feasible to keep it. Dogs were kept for hunting, protection, and herding the other animals, such as sheep and cattle. Cats were primarily used to keep the rodent population under control, because rats and mice would eat almost anything they could get to. People kept ducks and geese primarily for their feathery down for pillows

PLATE 47   Carlton English feeding some of his animals. The goose adopted the cow on the left, follows her around the pasture, and sleeps with her in the stall.

PLATE 48   Ducks belonging to Marinda and Harry Brown's grandchildren, swimming in Brown's pond.

and feather beds and some also ate their eggs and meat. Chickens were very versatile; people ate the eggs and meat, sold chicks and eggs, and traded them for other goods at the store. Guineas, on the other hand, provided only eggs, and announced the arrival of anyone or anything. Few people had turkeys, which were raised primarily for meat. Goats, not common either, were kept for milk. Many families had sheep which were mainly kept for their wool. People would usually eat some of the young lambs, and sell or trade the ones they didn't need. Everyone raised hogs, because pork can be cured and kept without refrigeration. The hogs provided the family's main source of protein, and the sale of extra piglets also provided a small income. Cattle, too, were very useful. Cows provided milk, calves were sold or eaten, steers (castrated bulls) were used for work and transportation, and the cows and steers were fattened and eaten when they became too old for other work. They all provided manure to fertilize crops, and many people used the tanned hides for various purposes.

Mules and horses didn't have as many uses, but many preferred them to steers for working. They provided faster transportation as well as providing manure for the crops.

This chapter is not meant to be a manual of animal husbandry, but I think you will learn something from it. We also hope it helps you to better understand the southern Appalachian farmers of years ago. Each family's animals were vital to the family's survival, and people spent hours and hours during their lifetime around and about their animals.

Researched and photographed by Sheila Vinson, Janet Dickerson, Cathy D'Agostino, and Cathy Campbell.

GEESE

ESCO PITTS: [We ate geese eggs] but I didn't like'em—they're strong. We plucked geese, too. My mother'd hold a goose and pick the feathers just like she would a duck. You can get half a pillow's worth of feathers off a goose. Goose-feather pillows are *nice*.

Our house was up on pillars, and the geese could go under the house, or under the crib and sit there in severe weather. Now th'crib was up off the ground, and the geese usually stayed under there, because there were some cracks in the floor of the crib, and the corn sometimes would fall through the cracks, and the chickens and the geese both liked that.

DUCKS

JESS RICKMAN: Ducks never were any trouble—my mother used to keep twenty-five or thirty of'em. An' she made and gave all her children a set of feathers and a feather bed each.

Ducks'll thrive around and catch bugs and eat grass, and don't take too much corn except during the winter season when they'll eat a good deal.

With a duck, you have to start picking'em when they get full-feathered, and you have to watch and pick'em every new of the moon. They loosen up and aren't hard to pull off. If you let'em run over [the new of the moon], they're real hard to pull off and it's rough on the duck. My mother'd leave her other chores go, and pick her ducks and geese at a certain time.

Geese and ducks both are hard on your garden—they like tomatoes,

PLATE 49 Guineas in Carlton English's barnyard.

PLATE 50 Some of Carlton English's chickens.

watermelons, cabbage, and bean blossoms. There's not much difference in the way you feed ducks and geese.

Ducks'll have a few worms if they don't have a good-sized place to run around in.

ESCO PITTS: Now ducks are something we didn't bother with much—they make their own living. A stream went down by the house, and those ducks usually stayed in that stream up and down and around. We'd have t'feed'em a little, but you didn't have to feed them much—they'd make their own way.

My mother'd pick the feathers from the ducks and make feather pillows. That's the reason she had ducks.

We'd eat the eggs. Duck eggs are good, but my daddy wouldn't eat a duck—wouldn't let us kill the ducks.

[In order to pluck duck feathers], my mother put the duck's head right back under her arm, took a'hold of his two feet in her hand, and pulled the feathers th'wrong way [against the "grain"]. She could pick a duck in ten minutes, and get a great big pile of feathers. The ducks were used to it.

They didn't run away from her, and I think one time a year was all she picked'em. They'd have t'get full-feathered.

LON DOVER: People kept ducks to make feathers. We have some old feather beds and pillows now—they'll last fifty years. When the ticking wears out, you get some new ticks and put your old feathers in there, and they'll wear on and on.

Once in a while, people would eat ducks and duck eggs, but we never did.

The ducks would go under the floor of the house and roost. You had to feed them year 'round—the more you feed'em the more feathers they'll have. You just catch'em up by the feet, and pick their feathers. Sometimes people will tear the skin. You have to be pretty careful about it. If you don't pick'em they'll pick their feathers themselves. Pick about once a month—pick'em and drop'em in a bag. We just fed'em corn.

Once in a while a hog would kill one—if the duck was sick, the hog would kill'im and eat'im.

TURKEYS

JESS RICKMAN: We used to raise turkeys, just to eat and a few to sell, but we didn't have'em [eating] a lot and they got to takin' too wide a range around. You can't manage a turkey to do any good.

BEULAH PERRY: We took care of turkeys just about like we would chickens. They take a little more special care. They were weakling before they got grown—you had to take very good care of them. You couldn't let them get out early in the morning in the dew and get wet.

GUINEAS

KENNY RUNION: Lots of folks had guineas. They'd lay—I don't mean maybe. They'd lay from th'time th'bud swelled till way up in the fall.

Now if I had guineas here, I might find their nest on the other side of them trailers. They don't lay in the front door. They might go a mile. They make a noise you'd know if you were used to them.

I never heard tell of [guineas eating your garden]. I don't believe they'll bother nothing. They might eat the worms and bugs off of the vegetables, but they won't eat the beans or nothing like that.

ESCO PITTS: We had a few guineas—the eggs are the biggest things. Y'know, they lay a lot of eggs. They go in th'trees and roost—they wouldn't go in a chicken house. Finding them nests was a big job. They just go a way off, and first thing you know they've got a whole nest of eggs. We had t'feed them, too. They eat more than chickens. And they'll eat all the insects in your garden.

We ate guinea eggs. They're a prolific thing. They lay a nest plumb full of eggs. They'd hide their nests—you'd have to watch where they gathered a lot and you could find their nests.

We just had a few. A guinea can just get up and fly away, and they're a noisy kind of bird. They're always a'hollering, and the geese are the same way.

We lived three-four hundred yards from the road, and if any stranger came in through that gate, those guineas would go to squalling. They're just like a watchdog. They'd bite you. Guineas eat the bugs [in the garden]; they're good to keep any kind of insects off. They aren't half as bad as chickens [about eating up your garden].

CHICKENS

ETHEL CORN: Some people would have chicken houses for chickens to go in to roost, but some chickens would just run around and make their nest anywhere in the barns or anywhere they could and roost up in the trees.

The chickens were turned out where they could scratch. An' you know chickens liked that. You wouldn't think that there'd be any difference in the taste of the meat in those that they raised in these brooder houses, and in the ones raised in the open. But there's a wide difference; they're as good again. And we never fed laying mash'r'nothing like that to our chickens. They didn't get a thing but corn or rye.

Most of the chickens would lay eggs around the barn'r'around the building. Some would lay eggs up under the floor. Some would come in and lay'em on the porch. Just anywhere they could find to make'em a nest. Sometimes they'd make their nests up on the mountain. Part of the time you'd find'em and part of the time they'd be settin' before you could find them. When they'd lay their eggs, they'd go to setting. They'd come off the nest once a day, and that's all—come off to eat. And if you'd watch and catch'em there, then you could watch'em go back to their nests. But if they ever seen you watchin'em, they'd sneak away another way. They wouldn't go near their nest till you weren't around to watch'em.

[When the chicks were born], they'd keep as many of the roosters as they wanted and they'd kill the others when they were ready. If you don't have the roosters with the hens, the eggs won't hatch. [The roosters] are good to eat when they're young, but after a rooster gets grown, his meat has a tendency to be tougher.

Just nearly any kind of a wild animal will catch chickens—hogs, mink, weasels, possums, owls. Foxes are awful bad after a chicken.

Chickens will have cholera. And they have what's called the "weak leg." Their legs just get so weak they can't go. And they'll take the disease they call the "limber neck." It seems like their head just twists and jerks back ever' way. Why, I've killed as high as five or six big pretty hens· of Mommie's that had taken the weak leg and they'd kill'em and tote'em off to keep it from spreading.

BEULAH PERRY: We had a great big chicken house and a lot for the chickens made out of palings—you know, we didn't have wire back in those days.

We fed those chickens crushed corn or wheat.

We had a lot of chickens. In those days, it wasn't strange to go to somebody's house who had two hundred or more chickens. Once in a while, we'd get eggs up to sell, and my dad would take'em to town to sell'em, or maybe they'd sell two or three fryers t'get little things we didn't have on the farm.

Some of the times, we let th'chickens run around and scratch, but most of the time, you'd have gardens and chickens was bad t'get into the garden. They would eat th'worms off th'cabbage, but then they'd get to where they'd eat th'cabbage, too! We were so glad when Dad and Mom would let the chickens run out because if the chickens didn't get in there and pick them worms off, we would have to. We cut down the number of roosters— seems like they'd keep six or seven chickens to a rooster.

Polecats was bad t'come in and catch the chickens at night—the chicken house wasn't closed up real tight. My daddy would keep the door open unless things would get to botherin' them too bad. A weasel was bad t'get in th'chickens. They'd get in there and eat the chickens. The chickens would get sick—sometimes their heads would get sore. I don't know what caused that.

ESCO PITTS: We had a chicken house, where they roosted of a night, and where we'd set'em for hatching little baby chicks. It had a roof on it, poles for'em t'sit on, boxes around in the walls for the hens t'lay. You could close it up t'keep animals out, or when you wanted t'catch any of'em when y'wanted t'sell'em or anything. Of a mornin', we'd turn'em out. They had free range, anywhere they wanted to go. We would have t'feed them a little, but they'd scratch out a lot of worms, bugs.

In the spring after the warm weather started, my mother would grind up red pepper and feed'em—that'd make their comb turn just as red, and they'd go t'laying. That's where we got our eggs for our breakfast ever' morning.

PLATE 51   Fred Darnell's sheep waiting to be sheared.

Chickens didn't usually lay in the coldest part of the winter, but in warm weather, they start layin'. A good hen won't lay much longer than three years, then y'kill'em and eat'em or sell'em for meat. Most of the time, we'd kill'em and eat'em.

I remember a bald eagle came into our chickens one night and picked up a hen and carried it off. Those bald eagles, they're big things, and they used to be lots of them in our country.

GOATS

BUCK CARVER: We used t'keep goats—let'em run all over. We'd kill them an' eat'em, sell one occasionally, but we never milked'em. A mother goat was lucky if she could make enough milk t'give to a kid. We'd use that hide—we could sell it, tan it and make shoelaces out of it, or make a whip out of it. Our big trouble with'em was durn dogs. They'd come an' kill'em ever' once in a while.

They're easy t'take care of, an' hard to make sick. They'll eat anything; live off the wrappers off tin cans an' be fat, too. They're good in particular barbecued.

SHEEP

ANNA HOWARD: We had a lot of sheep—we got th'wool; we sheared'em washed the wool, carded it, spun it, wove it on a loom and made cloth. We had homemade clothes. I despised shearin' sheep. Had big old sheep shears. I've sheared many a sheep. Sheared'em in th'spring in the new moon in May. They had little lambs born in early spring. They was the sweetest little things I ever played with.

JESS RICKMAN: It's best to have a barn on account of the little lambs. My father used to have a barn out yonder about sixty feet long that he kept his sheep in. He had anywhere from fifty to sixty in the flock.

My father sold the wool—he'd ship it out to Greenville, South Carolina. It was lots of work if you used it at home. But we had to shear them. We'd get a table, and lay the sheep on it, tie their feet, and shear them. I guess it took twenty to twenty-five minutes but I'd average thirty minutes. The average sheep'd give us two and a half pounds of wool and the real large ones, about three pounds. We sheared them early in the spring, had to go by the weather, by the putting out of the leaves, and again in the late summer or early fall, in time for them to put on a new coat for the winter.

Sheep start lambin' in the first of February till way up in May. Everybody kept rams—one or two to fifty head. We'd eat the male babies mostly; they'd come in off the range about every two or three weeks and get salt, and Daddy'd pick out a nice heavy one to butcher. Most of the old people would kill a sheep, hog, and beef and have a big barbecue—mutton, pork, and beef.

[Sheep are apt to take cold, from] cold rains—pneumonia's what we called it. We'd keep'em fastened up in the barn in bad rainy times (to keep them from getting pneumonia) and we hardly ever had any with colds.

They'll get worms—the old people would burn hickory and give the ashes to'em, and I think they'd mix cornmeal with turpentine and give that to'em. But we weren't bothered years ago with worms like they are now. I guess they have a dozen cases to our one, because they don't run out on the wild range, and I believe that played a big part with keeping them healthy.

Wildcats and wolves and dogs are bad on sheep. The old people would put a bell on the sheep, and they said the wildcats didn't seem t'bother one with a bell on it like they did without a bell. My father never did, but he lost lots of'em.

They notched the ears of the sheep—something like a slit in the left ear and an undercrop, just a notch, cut out of the right ear. But my father's was just a cut off the tip to the end of the ear. Each man had a different mark. The old-timers all knew each other's mark through Rabun County, Towns County, and Macon County.

BERTHA DOCKINS: My daddy had no more than twenty-five or thirty sheep at a time. They ran loose until time for'em t'lamb, an' then they'd get'em up. They stayed out all winter, but he had to get out like he did the hogs—go feed'em. They huddle together in sheltered-like places in the winter. And then at shearin' time, we'd have t'herd'em down from the mountains.

I've held many a sheep for my mommy and daddy while they sheared the sheep. That's when they look so pitiful—when they get all that wool off. We sheared'em twice a year. They had spring wool. That was the prettiest. And then they had fall wool. We'd shear'em about October in the fall, because they wanted it to grow back before it got cold weather.

He'd bring salt, cornmeal and corn up to the sheep. He'd just put th'stuff down in piles, and they'd find it. And they'd be right there the next time when he went back.

It got t'where he couldn't hardly keep sheep. There was so many wild animals—wildcats and things that'd get'em, an' the lambs when they're young are easy t'get. They didn't used t'have diseases then like they do now. M'daddy just always counted on losing some ever' year.

ESCO PITTS: The sheep were taken care of just like the cattle. Sheep would range further away than the cattle, b'cause they didn't have to come home. But in the spring of the year, during the lambin' season, we had t'watch after them pretty close. Sheep would wander way off; they'd have t'come in in the lambin' season, take care of the small lambs, then they'd have t'be sheared when warm weather come. That's the way our mother made our clothes—with the wool.

They sheared the sheep one time a year. My mother would shear some, but Daddy done most of it. She could do it all right, but she was usually busy with her work in the house. She had t'weave the cloth to make our clothes, she had t'card it and spin it; she had a loom where she wove it, so it just kept her busy till the dead hours of the night t'get th'cloth that we needed. In the rough, just as you took wool off a sheep, sometimes you'd get five pounds of wool off of one sheep. Of course it wouldn't weigh that much after it's washed, cleaned, and carded. They were sheared and after the lambs got big enough t'follow, why we'd turn'em back out and let'em go. 'Course we'd have t'go look after'em ever so often, salt'em, keep'em tame, give'em a little corn. Then in the winter, we'd have t'bring'em in— we had a sheep house that they'd stay in of a night, and of a daytime they'd run out and browse around.

They's always what they call the bellwether—that's a male sheep that's been altered and he was generally the leader of the flock. Put a bell on him and they'd follow him anywhere he went. And my father had a ram or two.

Bobcats was bad t'catch little lambs. I don't remember us having any trouble with wolves, but the bald eagles would pick up a little lamb.

Sheep are pretty delicate animals, and sometimes they'd get poisoned, and you wouldn't know what'd poisoned'em, and they'd die.

HORSES AND MULES

ETHEL CORN: Horses were generally kept in the pasture fenced in for them, and they were kept in the barn at night. They fed the horses fodder and corn and hay. If you had a good pasture, when they weren't working, why you'd feed'em night and morning. If it was a good pasture, maybe you wouldn't feed'em but once a day. You'd just give'em corn. And if you were working them, you always fed'em three times a day to keep'em good and strong and in shape to do the work.

PLATE 52   Cathy Campbell feeding Marinda and Harry Brown's old mule, Kate.

PLATE 53   Billy Long's horses grazing in his pasture.

We always curried and brushed them down good. Some people would let a mare raise a colt every year. They generally bred in the spring of the year. And some people would work a mare on up till just a week'r'two before the colt was due. And then they'd quit working'em and wouldn't work'em after they had their colt till the colt was a couple of months old.

They'd stop the mare from working in order that she not be strained. They always let a colt nurse until it was about three months old; then they were weaned gradually. If the colts weren't weaned gradually, the mare had to be milked. And some of'em you couldn't milk—they'd kick your head off if you tried.

JESS RICKMAN: A draft horse is a large horse, and it's not raised here in this mountain country. There's a saddle type and a work type. For work, you need a heavy draft horse, weigh up to a ton. You've got to pet'em more to get along with horses good, have lots of patience and work. I'm gentle with'em—then I can get'em to do most anything for me. They won't stand knockin' around. We fed'em corn, oats, hay, and sweet feed—cane syrup mixed in with the corn and oats.

LON DOVER: Sometimes horses would founder. If you got'em hot work-in'em and they'd get to the water and drink too much and they'd water-founder. You have to watch horses awful close on that. It'd kill'em if you didn't do something.

A horse is greedy—he'll just eat anything. One time a man's horse ate some cane hay, gave him colic. That cane seed gave him the colic and he liked t'died—we sat up with him all night. That horse swelled up like he'd bust. He just lay there and he'd grunt, and he'd roll.

They also had bots—like a grub worm. A horse is bad to get'em, but a mule hardly ever has'em. They lay their eggs inside the horse and they hatch and grow in there. They get so many in there and after they get grown, they'll take hold of that horse an' kill'em. A man told me that I should take a pint of syrup and get me some pulverized sage and mix it with that syrup to make a quart bottle full. Then pour it down the horse and it makes them grubs turn loose down in where the food goes. He claimed the sage would kill the grubs when they turn loose of the flesh and eat the syrup.

Now horses and mules'll get milksick, and it'll kill'em just like it will cattle.

KENNY RUNION: You take a horse that's got distemper—I'll tell you what'll cure him up real good. You get a peck bucket and pour some hot tar in there. Put a hornet's nest in first and put the tar over it. Let it bleed a few minutes and when it quits, hold it right up against that horse's nose. Just put his nose down in the bucket.

Now there's one thing I don't reckon can be cured—that's the bots. They get right here in a horse's throat and eat through. If there's a remedy, I ain't never heard of it.

ESCO PITTS: A horse, especially, would take colic. Some wouldn't but others would. That's a disease of gas—just like if you have gas on your stomach. It'd bloat'em up and you had to drench'em. There was one remedy we used in those days that I don't see anymore; that was Japanese oil. Of course, if you didn't use anything, they'd get over it after a while, but they'd be down a'rollin' and be sick two-three days. I don't know just how they got it—maybe they just ate a little too much of something. Sometimes they'd just take it and you wouldn't know what caused it.

BUCK CARVER: Horses got sick ever' now and then. An' they had a heck of a lot of different diseases. They'd have lampers, bots, kidney colic. Now old man George Grist had a Virginia mare, called her Daisy, a real good old mare, and you could feed her one more ear of corn than she was used to, and she'd just almost die with that kidney colic. Old man Zack Dillard, no tellin' how many times he came over there. Now he'd take hot water and soap and a big old hose, and insert that hose in th'rectum and pour her full of that soapy water. Then he got'er up as soon as he could, and keep'er walking.

Now them lampers—the gums would go out underneath their teeth till they couldn't bite th'corn off of the cob. You'd have t'shell it. Well, y'take a good clean pocketknife and open their mouth with a hammer handle or something so they couldn't shut down on you—it usually took two people t'do that—and cut the gums. They'd split'em toward the teeth, y'know, and y'wasn't supposed t'go past the ridges in their mouth called bars, or they'd bleed t'death. They'd have t'do it ever' year or two, or maybe two or three times a year. I don't know what caused it—maybe too much blood up in their heads caused their gums t'swell. I've seen'em level with their upper teeth. They couldn't shell the corn an' couldn't hardly chew—an' they'd just swallow it whole an' get pretty durn poor if you leave them gums that way. Them whole grains act as a filler unless you crack'em.

Then there's another thing they call stringhalted. It was actually a strained tendon'r'a nerve and caused them t'limp or walk at an uneven gait.

A mule is a cross between a male donkey (jack) and a female horse.

LON DOVER: I always loved my work mules. You could plow the best with'em, and they work real good. Some of'em's nice, but some of them's mean. They'll kick. I had one that when you opened the door to the stall, she'd kick the facing off the door. If you wasn't watching, she'd get you. But once you got the bridle on her, she wouldn't kick. You could handle her anyway you wanted to. One day [my son came out to the stall to get her] and she kicked at the door facing, and he dodged her and got a pitchfork and got her right in the hams, and she just bowed up and never did kick no more. That broke her.

I kept mine shod all the time, and that made'em rougher. If they'd a'hit you, it'd a'killed you, but most of the time they're gentle.

ESCO PITTS: Of course we had t'keep mules at home. We didn't let them get out—put'em in the pasture at home. They didn't run out with the cattle. We usually had a use for them—plow the crops in the spring and during the summer.

Just had t'feed them the year round. In those days and times, people pulled the fodder off their corn and cut the tops. That's about all the roughage we had to feed the mules. We didn't have any meadows for hay; sometime we had to go down in the valley where they had some meadows, and buy some hay. Most of the time though, we fed'em on the tops and fodder off the corn. Of course, we fed'em corn for grain. Sometime we'd grow some oats and a little rye. We generally saved rye in th'fall of th'year, in September, in our cornfield, and that was pretty good pasture during the winter. Rye, you know, is hardy and the freeze wouldn't kill it out—it stayed green. But mostly we fed the mules corn.

PLATE 54 A jack which belongs to Frank Rickman. A jack and a mare horse produce a mule, which is sterile.

BEULAH PERRY: My father had some mules, no horses. In th'mornin' he'd curry those mules and then take a great big brush and brush'em good. He did that at least once a day.

Th'mules used th'pasture too when they weren't working, but not as much as the cows. We had t'feed them at least twice a day heavy, because they worked so hard. My father grew wheat and oats for the mules. And sometimes he'd feed that straw to the mules. If they wouldn't eat it too well, my father would make a little salt water to sprinkle over that dry straw, and they would like that.

One thing that stands out in my mind—mules had what they used to call colic. It was from over-eating or something, and they would get sick and the veterinarian or some of the older men that knew how to do it would make up a medicine and put it in a long-necked quart bottle, and one person would hold th'mule and th'other would put that bottle in his mouth till he drank all that medicine. It would look like it was doing'em so bad, but it wasn't—it was for their good.

Some of our contacts preferred keeping and working horses, others would rather have mules. They told us some of their reasons.

JESS RICKMAN: It takes a lot more caring for a horse than for a mule. The mule you can do most any way, and they'll get by. A horse requires a good bit of doctoring, but they've got a much stronger brain than a mule has, because you can teach'em to do different things and tricks that you couldn't teach a mule. A horse is more likely to have kidney trouble than the mule is. My father'd drench'em with spirits of nitre (ethyl nitrite spirit or spirit of nitrous ether) till they got straightened out with th'kidney trouble.

You can just rough a mule through on corn and a mule won't hardly eat enough to hurt him, but a horse will—they'll founder every time they get into the feed.

LON DOVER: Now horses, you have to take better care of them than you do a work mule. Everybody kept mules, and they didn't have many horses—mules worked as good again as horses. I never could get horses to work.

A horse'd go too fast for me—they'd almost trot sometime. You couldn't turn horses and mules out, you had to have a pasture for them. They'd be the first thing in people's fields. A mule is as hard again to keep in a pasture as a horse—you had to have a good fence t'keep a mule in. They used horses mainly for pulling buggies and riding. Now mules you could work good, but they wasn't fit t'ride hardly.

They had t'feed horses'n'mules till work time was done. Then they'd put'em in a pasture and let'em eat grass for a living. But you did have t'feed'em in the winter if there wasn't much grass. Fed'em corn and fodder, same thing as the cows.

ESCO PITTS: A mule was usually easier broke than a horse, and he was just a little easier to control, unless you had a horse of some aging and well-broken. They're very much alike, only a mule is stubborn. You couldn't make him do what you can make a horse do after he's well-trained. They'll work about the same. I believe a horse has got more sense than a mule. We didn't have any of those big work horses—just country-grown mules and horses—not the big, heavy draft type. We didn't need'em, because our farm just wasn't big enough to justify keeping them. They're big eaters, you know. Ours were small and didn't eat so much, but they'd do all the work we needed.

HOGS

KENNY RUNION: [They used to put bells on hogs.] I mean, good, big bells. I had a hog that learned your voice. He'd come from just as far as he could hear you. Some of'em would blow [through] a gun barrel and them hogs was just all over each other a'coming.

BERTHA DOCKINS: Back when my daddy raised hogs—and he had wild hogs all over the mountains—he'd go every week and feed them hogs corn. He carried it over his shoulder. He'd shell it and take a big bunch of corn— and if it was real bad weather, snowing, he'd go up twice a week. He always had four or five brood sows; he had over a hundred up in th'mountains when he died. He sold a lot of hogs—he didn't just grow them to eat. Now they'd put up hogs t'fatten nearly all summer. They'd put up a shoat in th'pen—'bout a hundred pounds—then kill'im in November.

Daddy'd pack his meat in a big old box, salt all over it, and let it stay there about two months, and he'd take it out then and wash it and hang it. Let it drip from November to about March, and he'd wash it and let it dry, and put it in any kind of a cotton sack, tie it up real good, and most of the time, just hang it back up.

He generally kept several male hogs. You see, hogs don't stay all in one flock. Maybe over here on this mountain, they'll be one bunch in a hollow; then maybe way over yonder a mile or two miles will be another bunch. They stray off a lot. They're worse than cattle. My daddy castrated most of the male hogs when they were little, before they got out of the bed. I believe it's six weeks when they turn them out of th'bed.

[Hogs have a lot of enemies] sometimes if they haven't got a real mean old boar hog, and something will get a'hold of th'pigs. And the mother has t'be tough, too. Wildcats, wolves, and th'fox are bad t'get little pigs. If there's little pigs out where people can't look after'em, foxes'll eat them pigs up—maybe one a day till it gets'em all.

The biggest disease bothering hogs was the hog cholera—they still have it now. They used t'do away with the ones that got it, but most of them died.

PLATE 55   Young hogs in Glen Dockins' hog lot.

BEULAH PERRY: Little baby pigs were always my favorite. My father'd keep four-five hogs—one to raise little pigs from, then two or three he'd kill each year for meat. He'd keep maybe two or three pigs, depending on how many hogs he had on hand and sell th'rest.

My daddy kept one male hog if it was a good breed—he'd always pick one of a good stock to sire the pigs. If he didn't get a real good one from th'batch of pigs, he'd buy one rather than keep one of his own.

The hogs we fed slop from th'kitchen, and shorts that come from th'wheat when it was made into meal. We kept a big slop can in th'kitchen all the time.

We had a hog lot, with a shed with a wooden floor, and every once in a while, my father would get in and clean that out, and in the wintertime, he'd put straw or leaves in there. You've got to take good care of your animals.

There were a few hog diseases. Th'hogs used to get worms, and my father would go to the veterinary who'd tell him what to do but I don't remember what that was. And back in those days, there was a lot of cholera got into the hogs.

LON DOVER: Hogs roamed the mountains, where there's all kinds of mast-chestnuts. The hogs'd get just as fat on them as they could be—fatter than they would on corn. And you could bring'em in an' kill'em right off the mast. But they claimed the blight killed off all the chestnuts.

If a family was large, they'd need t'kill six or eight hogs a year. They'd have maybe half a dozen sows, and sell some of the pigs. They'd have them all sizes and ages, and they'd keep enough so they could have a large hog t'kill, and the other'uns taking their place. Nearly everybody kept a male hog. They'd run outside, and not cost much t'keep.

Ever'body had their hogs in the woods, and ever' man had a different mark [which was registered]. You'd know your hog by your mark. They'd notch the ear. Me and my daddy had the same mark—crop and split in the left ear, and a split in the right. You did that when they were little. The sow would make a big bed for delivering her pigs, and you had t'get'em [and mark them] when they were little.

People had s'many hogs in th'woods they'd go ever'day and look after'em, and if a sow was gonna come in, they'd check on her pretty close, and people generally knew where they slept. They stayed out in the woods all the time. They was raised in the woods and didn't know nothin' else. You'd have to take corn up to feed'em in the wintertime. They'd root under that snow and leaves and get acorns under there.

Hogs was bad to get cholera—that kills'em. There's something used t'come into Towns County, called it black plague and that killed'em. That killed nearly ever' hog in them mountains. The hogs would die in the branch, and you couldn't drink the water. It worked different from cholera.

JESS RICKMAN: Hogs were smaller and had a nose about three times as long as the tame ones now—we called'em jug drinkers. They had the Russian type hogs. They lived off of acorns, chestnuts, and pine roots. They could uproot a small pine just rooting around it—they like those tender roots.

ESCO PITTS: The hogs ran out with the cows, y'know. In my young days, the chestnuts were in the woods—you could just rake'em up by the handfuls and hogs would get fat on them. It wasn't firm meat; it was too flabby. We didn't like it because it didn't make much grease, and it was flabby and spongy. They'd get fat off chestnuts but all you had to do was take'em off of that and bring'em in and feed'em about six weeks on corn and then you got good meat. It tastes good then.

When we wanted to put pork up in the fall of the year, we put the hogs up in a pen and fattened'em on corn and just anything. If we had excess Irish potatoes, we'd cook them and feed them those and take corn to the mill and grind it and make slop, and fatten'em on that—on corn and slop and scraps from the table.

We generally kept two or three brood sows and we'd have a dozen or two hogs, maybe two dozen small shoats. We had plenty of hogs any time we needed to kill'em, and sometimes we'd sell one, maybe to pay the taxes or something. Usually one or two males was all we ever needed [for breeding]. We'd pick the best one or two of the bunch, and alter the rest of them when they come.

A brood sow was good for about five years and then you could put her up and fatten her. Then you'd raise the young ones for breeding. There's always younger ones coming on. Sows have piglets twice a year. I've forgot the gestation period, but anyhow they'd have'em twice a year, usually in the spring and sometime in the fall. They would generally run out till snow fell on the ground, and I've known Daddy to go in the woods and find his sow that he was looking to bring pigs, and she'd have her brush pile built, great big brush pile full of leaves and everything, and you'd find her back in there under the snow with her baby pigs. He'd let the sow alone and feed her till the pigs got big enough to follow her and then he'd turn her in home and in a lot, and take care of her until the little pigs got pretty good size.

[The mother was mean when she had babies]; she'd bite you. Usually she didn't want you around. But she knew my daddy, and he'd feed her, and he could do more with her than any of us kids. But he couldn't get a'hold of one of them pigs just then. He'd lead her home by taking a bucket of slop and towing her home [when the piglets were big enough to follow her].

CATTLE

LON DOVER: They didn't have any other kinds of cattle, only the milk stock. They'd raise their own work cattle (oxen), raise them from the cow. People'd pay the fee for a bull—it'd be a couple of dollars at the most.

People would keep three or four milk cows—the bigger th'family generally the more cattle they'd keep. But they wasn't able to afford too many—and you could buy a good cow for thirty dollars. People would raise calves, sell the heifers or keep them for milk cows. Th'males they'd sell or eat, or keep for breeding purposes.

We'd raise corn for grain and fodder. That's all cattle had t'eat [in the winter]. And the people had the poorest cattle you've ever seen—they didn't raise hay like they do now, or have big pastures for'em to run in.

I've heard of milk cows living to fifteen years old, still give milk, but the milk ain't good—they generally raised calves when they got older. One time, my daddy bought one—I believe he gave $15.00 for it. Now she must have been eighteen years old. Didn't have no teeth. They just swallow their feed; then of a night, when they lay down, they chew their cud.

You knew a cow was sick if she quit chewing her cud. And if you doctored her and she got better, that'd be th'first thing she'd do. Cattle'd get poison ivy in the spring—they'd be poor and eat ever'thing green, and sometimes they'd get that poison ivy. It wasn't so bad; it'd make'em sick t'their stomach, and they'd stagger just like a drunk man, and you'd give'em something and they'd throw it up. We generally use coffee and raw eggs t'make'em throw up the poison ivy. And there's an old thunder berry that has seed on it, and if they get that, it'll kill'em nearly every time.

Whenever cows had the hollow head, their nose generally would drip and run. The disease would eat the soft inside out of the horn, and the horn would feel like a shell. I reckon it hurt. I've sawed their horns off—whenever they had hollow head. It'd heal up if you sawed the horns off.

ETHEL CORN: Steers have a forked hoof. The way they'd shoe a steer—their shoe was in two pieces—they'd be a piece put on the front to give'em a better hold in pulling. They were wide but in two pieces.

Sometimes, it would maybe be a year or more before they'd wear their shoes out and they'd have to be re-shoed. If you don't keep shoes on'em when you're workin' em, it splits their hoofs and makes their feet tender and they can't pull as much as they can with shoes on. It's all right not to have shoes on'em when they're not being worked.

PLATE 56 Glen Dockins' cattle. Notice the bell on the cow on the right and the two steers in the background.

Now, there were a few horses worked that was never shod, but they was so mean they'd kick and they was afraid for you to mess with their feet.

ESCO PITTS: We had as high as three cows one time, but usually two was about what we had because we didn't want'em to come fresh at the same time, and we'd have milk all the time. There were eleven of us—we were raised on bread and milk and butter and syrup and meat.

People didn't have good grass pastures then like they do now. We had to wait until way late in the spring before we had any grass, and so we had to feed the cows. We fed them quite a bit—nubbins and fodder and shucks and tops. Nubbins are small ears of corn, too small to make seed or to go to meal. We just sorted out the small ones that the cows could chew and sometimes they would be a little too big and we'd chop'em up with the hatchet, put a little cotton meal on'em and sometimes my daddy would go down in the cotton country and bring back a wagon bed full of cotton seed hulls. A cow would give more milk off of cotton seed—just the whole seed. If we didn't get the cotton seed, then we'd get the cotton meal.

It would take about three weeks to go down to the cotton country with a yoke of oxen and he generally took a load of apples and cabbage and produce that we had grown on the farm and took it down there and swapped it for what we needed.

Oxen were the same [kind of cattle] and we worked them. Had t'give'em grain when you worked'em—corn and oats.

You could work a steer a long time before he got too old. Generally, my daddy would trade with somebody for a young yoke. Oxen could plow, bring in our wood, bring in corn. When we wanted t'haul heavy loads, we'd put the oxen to the two-ox wagon.

People made beef out of oxen. They weren't tough. An old animal after you fatten it, is tenderer than a young one.

The veterinarians will laugh at a fella for saying a cow has hollow horn, but usually, the cows would get droopy and they'd get to where they wouldn't eat much and they'd go to fallin' off. We'd take and cut their horns off and put disinfectant on there to keep flies from bothering them. They'll heal up and get all right so we thought that was what was the matter.

Sometimes they'd get hidebound and you had t'take and loosen their hide by hand—on the spine. Just get a'hold of the hide and lift it up, go all along and loosen it up. I've seen my dad do that. I wouldn't know what causes hidebound. The cows usually get in too thin a condition, not enough nutrition, and they get poor and they don't have enough circulation and enough fat on their bones, and the hide gets bound down in there and it gets droopy, but that wasn't very often. It did happen though.

Now and then the cows would eat this mountain laurel and sometimes they'd get poisoned. We'd feed'em strong coffee, pour strong coffee and lard down'im and that'd generally kill that poison. You'd have to give him about a quart of that. We'd mix it while it was hot and melt the lard, and pour it down'em. You'd have to get the cow right by the under jaw and stick their head straight up, and get a'hold of their tongue and just pour it down'em. I've drenched many a'cow by myself.

BERTHA DOCKINS: They always had a stable for the cattle. An' they'd feed'em good an' turn'em out on nice days. That's during the cold weather. If th'milk cows didn't come in, they'd go and get'em. The dry cattle, weaned calves, they'd stay in th'mountains in th'warm weather. Th'people would go maybe once a week to see how they were and take salt to'em. They had bells—if they had four or five cattle, one of'em would have a bell. If it was a big bunch, maybe fifteen or twenty, they'd have two, three bells. And they could hear the bells when they wanted t'find them.

[Cows had notches in their ears]. My daddy's notch was a split on th'right and an underbit on th'left. Everybody had a mark, y'know, and they registered'em at th'courthourse. If anybody was t'get a'hold of a stray cow, they'd know who it belonged to. My daddy's cattle wasn't a special breed, most of'em was mixed. Back in old times they mixed'em—not like they are now. He usually had some Jersey in his milk cows, so they'd make good yellow butter.

My daddy usually always kept a bull with his milk cows. And when he put'em out in th'woods, he turned th'bull out with the heifers—put'em in th'woods in th'spring. Mostly, the cows had their calves in th'spring—nearly always. You had t'go out in th'woods to get the cows or they'd have their calves in the woods. My daddy kept kind of a record of it, and he always knew about th'time they was gonna bring their calves. So he'd go out and drive'em in, and put'em in the pasture where he could look after'em.

Most of th'time, my daddy would keep the calves and get some growth on them, then sell them. He'd let'em grow till they got up two, three years old, then he'd sell'em. In th'fall, he'd drive them all in, and pick th'ones he was gonna keep. The fattest ones he'd sell at th'market for meat. He walked'em to th'market at Tallulah Falls.

He used t'kill some of them, if he took a notion, in the fall of th'year. He'd say, "Well, I'm gonna have me a good beef this winter." And he'd put it up and he'd feed it corn twice a day for two, three months; then he'd kill it. He said that corn made the meat sweet. They cured it and wrapped it in this cheesecloth, hung it in the smokehouse. They call it dried meat, jerky out in the West. We ate what we could fresh, and dried th'rest.

My daddy always kept a pair of oxen—we used t'ride in the wagons. Oxen are th'same as beef cattle. They castrate'em and make steers out of'em—th'bulls, you know. And then they learn'em to work. A yoke of oxen have t'be three or four years old before they begin training them. Then they drive'em—put that yoke on and let them go with it on for a while. Next thing, they'll put a little log to'em, just a little light one till they get'em used t'pulling; then they'll put a bigger log; then they'll put'em to th'wagon. It takes a while t'get'em trained. They live maybe sixteen, seventeen years. My daddy always kept a young yoke—he'd be training them while he was workin' th'older ones. When the younger ones got up t'where he could work'em, he'd turn th'old ones out. They'd get out in th'woods and get fat and he'd sell them for beef.

ANNIE PERRY: When cattle get sick, they'll eat ivy sometimes. Now you folks know what ivy is. It grows on bushes. We have ivy, rhododendron, and laurel. Sometimes animals get t'where they don't want nothing t'eat but that. And then it makes'em sick. And then t'get'em over that, you get you some sweet milk, tablespoonful of soda (baking soda), and a little salt. Put it all in that pint of sweet milk, shake it up, pour it down'em. He'll be sick then, y'know. Then they vomit and it makes'em better.

BUCK CARVER: In the winter, most people's cattle was in a lot or a pasture somewhere close to th'house. Last time we ever let ours run out was the late twenties or 1930. And they was milksick up in that country somewhere. I remember one summer three or four people had got it. Their cattle had got it somewhere in the woods. Now a milkcow that's a'giving milk, it don't bother her a bit; it comes out of the milk. You can tell it— it's where the milk won't foam, and it looks like spots of grease on top of it. If the cow is dry, or a male animal eats it, it'll kill'em as dead as eternity. You can pour plenty of liquor to'em if y'got it t'waste. Sometimes whole families got that and nearly died. Milksick is something that's in the ground, and it's most usually found in deep, cold hollows, most usually on north ground.

CATS

LON DOVER: People had lots of cats. They'd keep the mice down—they wasn't really pets. People'd keep'em in the barn, and they'd get mice, but you still had to feed'em once of a morning.

JESS RICKMAN: When I was comin' up as a kid, everybody had a big cat-hole, a notch sawed out of the door, and the cats'ud go and come in an' out.

PLATE 57   A hound dog belonging to Carlton English.

DOGS

BEULAH PERRY: My father and mother's brother were big hunters—coon-hunting, possum-hunting, and rabbit dogs; and sometimes there'd be ten or twelve dogs at our house. The dogs had a big shed t'stay in—they didn't stay in the house. I was the one who had t'make bread for th'dogs t'eat—they didn't hunt much of their own food.

LON DOVER: You never see a dog now that's any 'count to tree coons or possums or anything. People used to train'em from a pup on up, train'em with older dogs. They were mainly hunting dogs, but a few people had pets. Had to feed'em good.

JESS RICKMAN: People used to keep more hunting dogs and stock dogs than they do now. They had what was called the old brindle cur, good to catch wild hogs with, and they had hounds. The old blue-speckled hound would do the trailin' and then they had a half bulldog and half cur to go catch and hold'em till you could tie'em.

ESCO PITTS: We just had one dog at a time. One was a snake dog, and he'd kill rattlesnakes. Ever so often, you'd hear him bay a rattlesnake and you could always tell whether it was a poisonous snake or one that wasn't poisonous by th'way he'd bark. He knew the difference. When I was a boy at home, our dog never did get snake-bit.

PLATE 58

PLATE 59

BANJOS AND DULCIMERS

Trying to trace the history of the banjo as a musical instrument is one of those tasks that can quickly make you want to tear your hair out. Though hundreds of articles have been written on the subject [a fine bibliography is available from Joe Hickerson at the Archive of Folk Song in the Library of Congress], many are contradictory and filled with speculation. On one fact, however, nearly all are in agreement: that America's favorite folk instrument was brought to this country from Africa and Jamaica by Negro slaves in the eighteenth century. Thomas Jefferson, for example, in his *Notes on Virginia* (1782) mentions the "banjar" as being the chief instrument of the American Negro.

How did it get to Africa? Pete Seeger speculates that the Arabs may have brought it to the African West Coast [*How To Play the Five String Banjo,* third edition, published by the author in Beacon, New York, 1961]. We know that instruments like it in the Near and Far East (the sitar and sarod, for example) have been common for nearly as long as records exist, and stringed instruments with skin heads and wooden shells are known to have existed nearly 4,500 years ago in Egypt ["The Five-String Banjo in North Carolina" by C. P. Heaton; *Southern Folklore Quarterly,* Volume 35, Number 1, March 1971, page 62]. What paths the instrument followed through these countries, however, is simply guesswork.

At any rate, the instrument did make it to this country, where it began to undergo (and survive) an amazing amount of experimentation and popularity, despite a popular white belief that all banjo players and fiddlers were certainly bound for Hell. "Thick as fiddlers in Hell" is an expression still used in our part of the mountains.

The first banjos to come to our coast "had two, three or four strings (of horsehair, grass or catgut) and a hide stretched across a gourd. Cats, possums, raccoons, sheep, snakes and other assorted creatures supplied the skins

PLATE 60

PLATE 61

for the early banjo heads" [Heaton, page 62]. An article by C. J. Hyne in the December 15, 1888, issue of the "Boys Own Paper" [reprinted in the March 1974 issue of *Mugwumps*] says, "With rapid strides it improved in form. First a wooden hoop, and then a metal one; first a rough skin for the drum, then the best parchment; first nails to hold it on, then neatly-made tension screws. At one time the strings were made of anything that came handy; now they are formed from the 'intestines of the agile cat.'" That was in 1888. Since then, the number of variations that have been tried that we *know* about would dwarf those of Hyne's experience.

Usually cited as the most important development in the history of the instrument itself was the addition of the shorter "chanter," "drone," "thumb," or fifth string. Here again, facts are hard to come by, but many historians credit Joel Walker Sweeney, a Virginian who was a professional blackface minstrel, with the addition sometime between 1830 and 1845. His original banjo is now in the possession of the Los Angeles County Museum. Arthur Woodward writes of Sweeney and the acquisition in the museum's Spring 1949 quarterly [Volume 7, Number 3, page 7]. The article says, in part: "In 1890, Mr. F. J. Henning, a teacher of music and a skilled banjo performer, learned of the existence of Joel Sweeney's original banjo . . . He entered into negotiations with the family and secured the old instrument . . . [It] is made of a dark, reddish colored hardwood. The head is of stained leather, fastened on with tacks. There are no strings. Scratched in the wood, still faintly visible, are the initials 'J.S.'" [One Sweeney banjo will be found documented in this chapter on pages 165–66].

Though all banjos prior to 1880 were fretless [Heaton, page 64], demand for fretted ones by minstrel banjoists at that time caused several manufacturers to put them on the market. Though their popularity lapsed in the early 1940s, players like Earl Scruggs brought them back, and today the five-string, fretted banjo (often with a plastic head) is again king.

Our interest in the banjo really began when a whole new group of students at our school began to learn to play it riding the crest of still another surge in its popularity. We knew almost nothing about it—not even where to begin to look for information. Now, two years later, we feel we've made a good beginning, and everything we read confirms that. In the Heaton article, for example, the author quotes Louise Rand Bascom, who, in 1909, described the North Carolina mountain banjo of that day for the April–June issue of *Journal of American Folklore:* "The banjo is home-made, and very cleverly fashioned, too, with its drum-head of cat's hide, its wooden parts of hickory (there are no frets)." As you read the following articles, you'll find that to still be true in some cases.

Heaton continues by quoting an article about Frank Proffitt that appeared in the October–November 1963 issue of *Sing Out:* "As a boy, I recall going along with Dad to the woods to get the timber for banjo-making. He selected a tree by its appearance and by sounding . . . hitting a tree with a hammer or axe broadsided to tell by the sound if it's straight-grained. . . . As I watched him shaping the wood for a banjo, I learned to love the smell of the fresh shavings as they gathered on the floor of our cabin. . . . When the strings was put on and the pegs turned and the musical notes began to fill the cabin, I looked upon my father as the greatest man on earth for creating such a wonderful thing out of a piece of wood, a greasy skin, and some strings." You'll find many echoes of that here too. In fact, three of the banjo makers represented here are from Proffitt's home county.

We found four major head styles, all of them represented in this chapter: the all-wood head; the all-hide head; the wood head with the hide center; and the commercial head held on with brackets. Likewise, hoop styles and neck styles have great variety. In fact, there is so much variety in banjo construction that it would seem as though *anything* goes as long as it "rings." Stanley Hicks, for example, showed us a banjo his father made out of a cake box. It worked well.

What we've done is to pick out seven banjo makers that represent the major styles we located. Their own instruments are documented here, as well as old instruments they may have owned from which they perhaps borrowed patterns or ideas. It was, and is, fairly common, for example, for an instrument maker to adopt a neck style from one banjo, a hoop style from another, and a head style from yet another, and put them together with his own wrinkles and ideas to form an instrument that is uniquely his in the best Sweeney tradition of borrowing/inventing.

Then, to conclude the chapter, Robert Mize, a dulcimer maker of genuine skill (he's made over seven hundred of them) describes his method of dulcimer making in detail.

And on top of all that, you'll also find fine diagrams by Annette Sutherland, one of our student staff members, which depict two of the banjo styles and additional details of the Mize dulcimer.

It's taken us a long time to put this material together, but we think it's been worth it. We hope you will too.

BEW WITH RAY MCBRIDE

ERNEST FRANKLIN

Last February, we drove up into North Carolina to visit with Ernest Franklin who, we had been told, would be a good person to talk with about instruments. He came out onto his porch as we lurched up his single-track, rutted dirt driveway. The weather was cold, and misting rain.

His house is an old log cabin chinked with red clay that was later boarded over. It has a single fireplace and a porch that extends along two sides. Firewood is stacked out back. His two dogs looked us over and acted as if they wanted to bark or run up and jump on us but were either too old or tired to try. One of them slowly lifted himself to his feet and half-heartedly wagged his tail just to let us know he was there.

When we explained to Mr. Franklin why we had come and who had sent us, he grinned and waved us in. We followed him inside, greeted his

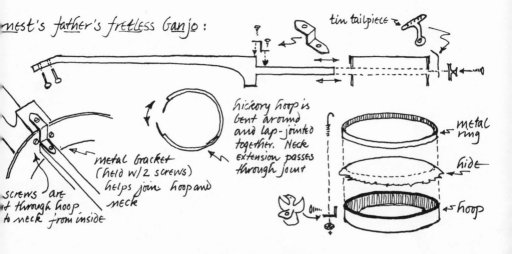

nest's father's fretless Banjo:

tin tailpiece

hickory hoop is bent around and lap-jointed together. Neck extension passes through joint

metal ring

hide

hoop

metal bracket (held w/2 screws) helps join hoop and neck

screws are put through hoop to neck from inside

PLATE 62

PLATE 63

PLATE 64

PLATE 65

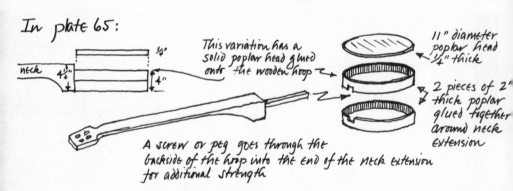

In plate 65:

½"
neck 4¼"
4"

This variation has a solid poplar head glued onto the wooden hoop

11" diameter poplar head ¼" thick

2 pieces of 2" thick poplar glued together around neck extension

A screw or peg goes through the backside of the hoop into the end of the neck extension for additional strength

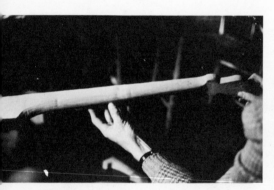

PLATE 67

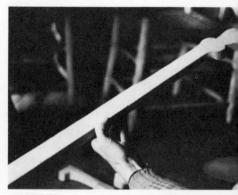

PLATE 68

PLATES 67–68   Two views of the poplar neck that Ernest Franklin is roughing out for a second type of banjo not based on his father's design. There is no tail extension— the neck will be mounted directly to the side of the hoop as shown in *Plate 69*. The wood is seasoned at least three years before being sawed out. Once sawed, it is worked down with a drawing knife, pocketknife, and wood rasp. Note the indentation in the side of the neck for the fifth-string peg.

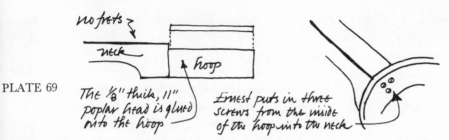

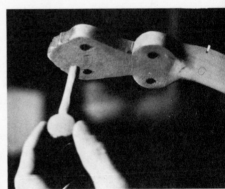

PLATE 69

no frets →

neck

hoop →

*The ⅛" thick, 11"
poplar head is glued
into the hoop* —

*Ernest puts in three
screws from the inside
of the hoop into the neck* →

PLATES 70–72 In *Plates 70* and *71*, note squared place on hoop where neck will
be attached. The hoop is cut out of a solid piece of well-seasoned poplar. He takes out
the center with a brace and bit. In *Plate 72*, note how a slot is sawed into the neck
at the base of the peg head, and the wooden finger bridge or nut set into the slot. Holes
for the strings are sawed into the peg blocks first, and the pegs are whittled out around
the holes.

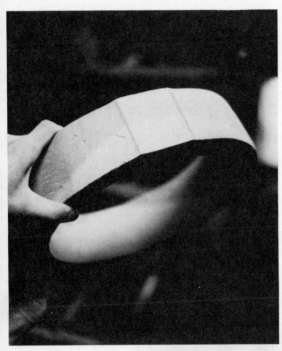

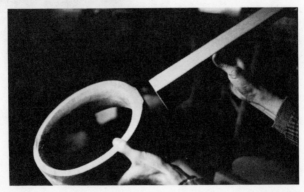

PLATE 72

PLATE 71

dogs as we passed, and met his mother. He told us to sit down just anywhere. We settled down in a living room heated by the fireplace, lit by a
kerosene lamp, and decorated with various family photographs, a picture
of Jesus, an advertisement for Buck cigars, and the word "Love" in blue
block letters above his bedroom door. His friendliness was overwhelming.

We asked him to tell us about his banjos. "Well, I'll tell you, the first
one I ever made—you've seen your wooden cigar boxes? Well, I made one
out of a square wooden cigar box. I didn't have no patterns or nothing to
go by. I just thought that up myself."

Later, using a banjo his father had made as his pattern, he produced
another one using a rasp, a pocketknife, a saw and a drawing knife. Instead
of using a hide for the head, however, as his father had done, he glued on a
wooden head. I had never heard of that being done before, but I later
found out that some of the other *Foxfire* editors working on this chapter
had found a second man nearby, M. C. Worley, who used wooden heads
also.

"It's got a finer, mellower tone than that there," he said, pointing to my
factory-made banjo. We asked him if a different type of wood would

change the sound. "Yeah, I imagine if a man had spruce pine it would sound better."

We asked questions for hours, sitting in his tiny living room and later walking over the farm. Slowly we began to realize what a story could be here for the future. His grandfather (whose old log house still stands on the property) had made fiddles, so he had tried that too. Many of the tools his grandfather and father had used (a shaving horse, for example) are stashed away in corners all over the farm. Every outbuilding holds its collection of family history.

Each time we asked a question about his instruments, he headed for the attic or bedroom and soon produced another battered banjo or tool or pattern or piece with which to answer us. We had the sinking feeling that if we only knew the right questions to ask, we could trigger a flood of stories hidden away behind the walls. Next time, perhaps.

When we asked him why he didn't use frets, he laughed. None of the old ones he had seen had had frets. Besides, "It's pretty tedious getting them in. You got to be spaced just accurately or it won't chord right. I tried one or two, but I never did get them right—they'd dischord—so I just made mine a plain neck."

None of the instruments he was making were finished, and he didn't have a completed one around either—as soon as he gets one finished, it's bought—but we finally got enough pieces stacked up on the living room floor to get the following information about his technique.

RANDY STARNES

Photographs by Randy and Don MacNeil.

PLATE 74

M. C. WORLEY

"Old people back in them times used to make everything they used. Make their chairs and tables and everything. Made everything they had to have. When I was a young man, I made the whole outfit for one of my cousins to go to housekeeping in. Bed, all the furniture . . ."

M. C. Worley also remembers that nearly every family had a banjo. Both his grandfather and father made them. His father used the skin of a housecat for his heads. "I'd rather skin a polecat than a housecat. They're the stinkinest things I've ever seen." Like Tedra Harmon, he'd take their hair off with ashes.

Many of the old banjos Mr. Worley remembered seeing had hoops bent out of single strips of hickory. The hickory splits were either put in a form

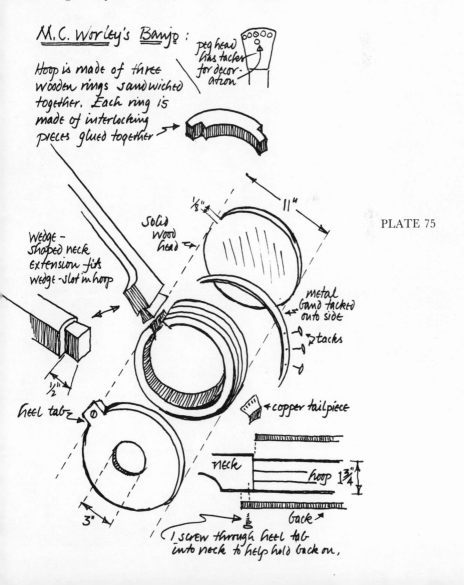

M.C. Worley's Banjo:

Hoop is made of three wooden rings sandwiched together. Each ring is made of interlocking pieces glued together

peg head has tacks for decoration

PLATE 75

Wedge-shaped neck extension fits wedge-slot in hoop

Solid wood head

⅛"

11"

metal band tacked onto side

tacks

½"

heel tab

copper tailpiece

neck

hoop 1¾"

3"

back

1 screw through heel tab into neck to help hold back on.

PLATE 76

PLATE 77

PLATE 78

PLATE 79

green and left thirty days to dry and cure, or the cured wood was steamed and then bent into shape. The old necks he remembers had a long tailpiece that went all the way through the hoop and out the other side so the strings could wrap around it. There were no backs on the banjos, and the heads were hides that were either tacked on or held in place by a wooden ring that slipped down over them. He also remembers seeing wooden heads that had a four-inch circle of hide in their center.

His first banjo was a cigar box. "It rang pretty good, too." As he began to make them regularly, he moved away from the old patterns and began to experiment. He tried out an all-wood head, for example, and liked it.

PLATE 80

PLATE 81

PLATE 82

PLATE 83

Then he changed the hoop style and added the back even though he doesn't think the back helps the sound at all. He just likes the way it looks.

And he began to run into others who were experimenting too. One man he knows, for example, saws rings out of aluminum kettles and uses those for hoops. Now he tries something different on almost every instrument he makes. The one pictured in *Plates 75–77* for example, features a decorative metal band, tacks, and a green half moon colored on with a crayon. "I just put that on to be different. Just figured it out myself," he laughs.

He tries his hand at instruments other than banjos, too. He once made a guitar completely out of metal except for the wooden sides. And he fashions out fiddles, mandolins and dulcimers when he tires of banjo making.

Mr. Worley never goes to craft fairs, or makes an effort to advertise. He sells his instruments by word of mouth; and during tourist season, he sets them on the porch and, "people pass by and see them and come in." It's an unsteady living, but it keeps him occupied—and inventive.

DON MACNEIL

Photographs by Don and Jeff Williams.

TEDRA HARMON

Mike Clark, the Director of the Highlander Center near Knoxville, told us about Tedra Harmon, thinking we should meet him, and so we arranged to do just that. We got to his shop on time, and as we stepped up onto the porch, we could see him sitting inside, waiting for us to get there. It was rainy and cold outdoors, so he had his oil heater lit and had the shop warmed up for us. From the minute we stepped inside, we felt welcomed.

Inside his workshop, hung on the wall, he keeps the necessities for making his banjos: saw blades, rasps, squares, gunstock finish, etc. In one corner there is a fox hide stuck up next to a walnut gun rack that has deer hoofs for gun supports. The fox hide still has the hair and the head attached, and Tedra plans to make a cap out of it. He tanned it himself by turning the flesh side out and coating it with a thick paste of baking soda and water and leaving it for twenty-four hours.

In another corner of the room hang three of his banjos, including the first one he ever built. His workbench is stationed in the middle of the room, and on it, among the tools, were placed pieces of a banjo waiting for a skin head. Instead of completing it, he had left it disassembled so we could see and photograph the various pieces. Although he makes banjos only for a hobby, when we asked him how many he had sold, he replied, "It'd take a truck to haul them."

Teora Harmon's Banjo: *[for complete measurements and additional details, see plates 172, 173, 174.]

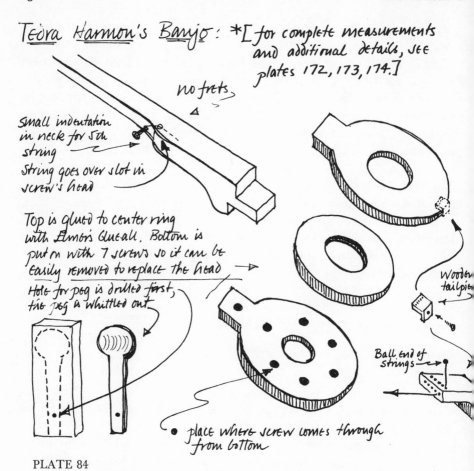

no frets

Small indentation in neck for 5th string
string goes over slot in screw's head

Top is glued to center ring with Elmer's GlueAll. Bottom is put on with 7 screws so it can be easily removed to replace the head
Hole for peg is drilled first, the peg is whittled out

Wooden tailpiece

Ball end of strings

• place where screw comes through from bottom

PLATE 84

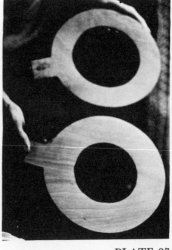

PLATE 85

PLATE 86

PLATE 87

tting the hide :

Tedra chisels out
a notch in the hoop
to tack the hide into, then
cuts off the excess

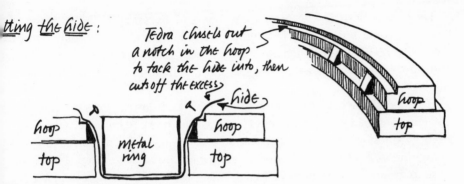

First the banjo, without the back, is turned top down on a counter.
Then the damp hide is pushed down into the hole in the top and hoop, and
pinched into place by the metal ring, and then tacked into place and trimmed.
Then the back is screwed into place, and the banjo set aside to let the hide dry
and tighten into place

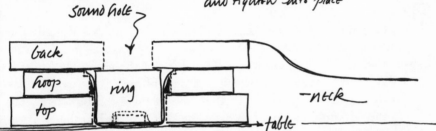

When hide is first put in, and is still wet, Tedra sets a small wooden
disc under it (dotted line inside ring) to create just enough slack so
that when the hide dries and tightens up, it won't split

PLATE 88

PLATE 89

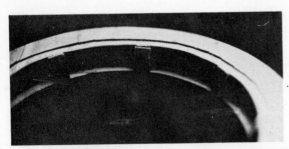

PLATE 90

Tedra was born in the mountains—he still lives on the same piece of land his parents settled on. He taught himself how to make and play banjos. He made his first one when he was thirteen, constructing it from poplar and putting it together with brass bolts. Since then, the hide has only been replaced once.

He's one of the few men we met who makes his instruments totally without commercial heads or pieces. He uses skin heads which he gets either from groundhogs and deer that hunters bring in, or from animals he has hunted himself. Once he was hunting and ran into a rattlesnake: "It was as close as from me to that stove there. I was sitting down there looking for squirrels when it went to singing. That racket was all over everywhere. I looked, and there that thing was coiled, his head up about that far [a foot]. Pointed right at my face. I leaned back and took my shotgun to him and took off his whole head. I was so nervous I could hardly get up and walk." He now has the rattles from that snake mounted on the peg head of one of his banjos.

After getting a hide, he tans it himself. He sets the hide in a trough with the hair side up, and puts two to three inches of ashes over that. Then he pours water over it until it comes up over the top of the ashes. He leaves it for three days, and by then the hair will pull right off unless the weather has been too cold for the lye to work. In that case, it takes a little longer. He then tacks the skin up on a board to dry. The skin is tacked so that it is up off the board enabling air to get under it and allowing the skin to dry quickly and thoroughly.

When the skin is dry, and he is ready to put in into a banjo, he soaks it in salt water overnight, washes it in strong soap, and lets it soak for five minutes in warm water. He puts it in the banjo wet, and it tightens up as it dries. If the skin is put in too tightly, there is a danger that it will rip as it dries out. To keep this from happening, Tedra has invented a gauge, which is just a round disc of wood about a half-inch thick, and smaller than the diameter of the hole for the hide. The gauge is placed on the table, and then the banjo is placed, top down, so that the head hole is centered around the gauge. As he puts the hide in, this pushes up on the skin and creates the right amount of slack. It tightens up perfectly every time. He prefers deer or groundhog skins because they are the toughest. "You can whop a man over the head with one and still not bust the hide." Complete directions for Tedra's method for tanning hides can be found in the hide-tanning chapter.

Tedra sticks to the traditional mountain way of making his banjos. He makes the entire thing out of wood except for the head, strings, and screws. He likes hardwoods best because he thinks they create a better tone. He carves out his pegs with a pocketknife and then sands them smooth.

Often he makes them out of walnut. He makes his bridges, tailpieces, and nuts the same way, favoring walnut and curly maple.

He takes pride in his work, and enjoys not only making banjos, but also being helpful and generous in the true mountain fashion. He's the one, for example, who told us about Stanley Hicks. When we expressed an interest in meeting him, Tedra told us to come back in two days and he'd have an interview set up by then and take us there himself. He was good to his word—he set aside an entire morning to take us to Stanley's shop and then waited patiently until we had finished. That kind of generosity is rare nowadays.

He remembers his childhood days with more affection than many: "Back then was the peacefullest times they ever was. I wouldn't mind seeing it go back to that." He's hanging onto as much of it as he can—his banjos are proof of that.

RAY MCBRIDE

Photographs by Ray and Steve Smith.

STANLEY HICKS

Stanley Hicks could have kept us entertained for months—if any of us had had the time. That, of course, is the frustrating thing about the kind of work we're in. We seem to be always on the move.

Stanley and his family live on the top of a ridge far back in the mountains. From his little shop comes a stream of fine banjos and dulcimers, all the result of orders he gets from across the country, even though he never advertises his work through the many craft guilds and co-ops in the hills.

He learned how to make banjos from his father. Banjos, and lots of other things, for his father was one of those tremendously inventive mountain men we wish we had had the chance to meet. He made his own tools—many of which still hang in Stanley's shop: a plane with a reworked file for a blade, a croze with a piece of a saw blade for its cutting edge. And with those tools and his imagination he made wagon wheels, chairs, churns, barrels, tubs, tables, baskets, cabinets, and corner cupboards. A piece of steel with two slots cut into it and driven into a log is what he dressed his white oak splits with. Drawing the splits through the slots in the steel smoothed them and trimmed them to uniform widths. Stanley even helped his father hew out and build log cabins. He remembers it all.

His mother was industrious too. She made soap, for example. Her ash hopper was a hollow log set on end with a spout cut in the bottom to one side and a screen strainer. She boiled hog innards and the lye from the hopper together in a pot to produce their soap.

And they made molasses, using a horse-drawn cane mill they had to crush the cane. "My grandma got her arm ground off in one. She was feeding cane and got it hung in there, and they didn't know nothing about running the mill backwards to get it out, and they cut her arm off. Took it off right there [between her elbow and wrist]. You know, that was rough!

"Dad used to make ladles and spoons and forks [out of wood] and pack them across the Beech [Mountain]—put him a sack full and put them on his back and walk'em out. Be gone, maybe, till late of a night. And then we used to peel tan bark and haul it with a old yoke a'cattle t'Elk Park. We'd leave—take an old lantern—and it'd get cold sometimes, and we'd get in the wagon, and the old steers' tongues would hang out about a foot. And we'd take a load of tan bark out there, and then we'd camp that night and get back in the next night.

"Sometimes them steers would cough and sull up. And sometimes they'd lay down and turn in the yoke. One'd be turned that way and one this'n. They went and sulled up on him once, and he went t'get some mud. He'd take and make up mud and pack it around their noses and *then* they'd come up. He wouldn't beat on them, but he'd pack this around'em. I kind'a got ill at it myself, and while he was gone, I took and rook up leaves and rook it up right in here on their hind ends and took a match and lit it. And they come *up*, son! And they left with sled and all and run away with it plumb down to th'John Walsh's Mill!

"And Dad come back and wondered what happened, and I told him I *guess* they wanted water . . .

"We dug up most of our ground. Right there's an eye hoe that I used

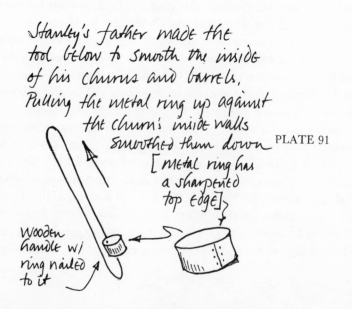

Stanley's father made the tool below to smooth the inside of his churns and barrels. Pulling the metal ring up against the churn's inside walls smoothed them down [metal ring has a sharpened top edge].

PLATE 91

Wooden handle w/ ring nailed to it

when I was a kid. He'd get an old yoke a'cattle and get'em broke, and times was so hard that when he got'em broke, somebody'd buy'em off him for fifty dollars. Forty or fifty for two. And then we'd have to go dig our ground up [by hand].

"And we went to the Beech and cut haw—it's just a little old bush—to get our shoes. Mother made our clothes. We gathered galax, peeled cherry, all that. Got about eighty cents a pound for the haw, and about three cents for the cherry. Get about thirty-five cents a day. They used it for medicine —sell it to one of these here that buy herbs. See, they wasn't no jobs until Whitings and Ritters [sawmills] come into this country in 1928—somewhere's along there. I worked for them two years for a dollar a day. They cut timber. And the first work I done was on the WPA building roads. We had t'build'em by hand. Take a drill, you know, and drilled'em ourselves. Hammered [the drill] and turned it, you know. One turned it and another hammered it, and then we'd take a teaspoon on a little old handle and dip the dust out. Then they put the dynamite down in there.

"Time off, me and my brother was courting. Had to walk about twelve miles each way. One time we was going to see our girls up there, and they was a trail that went through a big bottom. And me and my brother was going through there and here come a buck sheep and hit just turned him a flip-flop. And he hollered and it hit me but I got aholt of it. And ever' time I turned it loose it'd knock us down. Big buck. We kept a'holding it— I'd hold it a while and he'd hold it a while. He'd go a piece and then I'd turn loose and run and time I got to him, he'd catch it and hold it.

"Well, we was there in the trail, and here come an old man through there, and he said, 'What are you boys doing?'

"And I said, 'Will you care to hold this sheep till we get out here and get our rope?' I said, 'We've run it till we've give out, and we left the rope out here catching it.'

"And he said, 'Yeah. I'd be glad to.'

"Well, me and my brother give him th'buck sheep, and then we went over the ridge into the river and then hid. And he turned it loose, and when he turned it loose it just turned him a somerset. And he'd look around one way, and then he'd grab it again. Well, directly he got him a rock and got it right between his legs like that and he beat that thing till snot come out its nose; and turned it loose, and boys, it went through th'*field!*

"And for a long time I see'd him—run on him, you know. And he'd look at me and look at me. One time he says, 'Ain't you th'feller that got me t'hold that damn sheep?'

"I said, 'I don't know. Why?'

"He said, 'By God I'd a'killed you boys,' he said, 'if I'd a'got ahold of you.' He said, 'I see'd what you done.'

PLATE 92

"I said, 'Well, a man *has* to do *something* to get out'a th'way.'

"He said, 'I may whip you yet.'"

"And that's been five or six years. But we was courting. You'd have to walk for miles to see anything, and then, hell, you'd have to run your girls down atter y'got there t'*catch*'em. Hell, they'd run. Now, then, they're running the boys!

"But I helped my daddy make banjos. I don't know at the cats I got for him [for the hides]. But people got fond of'em. I had the best cat dog that could be got. I'd turn him loose and have my club tied right here [in a loop on his pants leg], and that dog would go to a house. I had him trained. He'd come to this house and run this cat away from there and take it to the woods and tree it. And I'd go climb the tree and motion about

PLATE 93

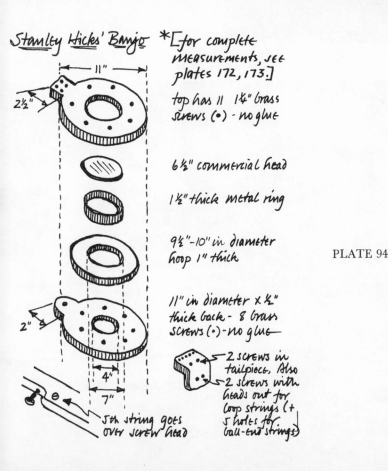

Stanley Hicks' Banjo

*[for complete
measurements, see
plates 172, 173.]

top has 11 1¼" brass
screws (•) - no glue

6½" commercial head

1½" thick metal ring

9½"-10" in diameter
hoop 1" thick

PLATE 94

11" in diameter x ½"
thick back - 8 brass
screws (•) - no glue

2 screws in
tailpiece. Also
2 screws with
heads out for
loop strings (+
5 holes for
ball-end strings)

11"

2½"

2"

4"

7"

5th string goes
over screw head

PLATE 95

PLATE 96

PLATE 97

<u>When Stanley uses a hide</u>:

①

②
← needle

. Hide is trimmed, and a wire ring the diameter of the 7" hoop hole is laid on top

. Metal ring pushes damp hide into hole

2. As in photos (where newspaper represents the hide), hide is sewn around wire. Thread is pulled tight, but stitches are big/loose
4. Back is clamped into place and banjo set aside

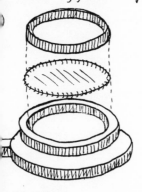

④ Note that wire ring fits just outside metal ring so that hide gets bound tightly - pinched into place

Back		4" ho's
Hoop	metal ring	7" hole
Top		6½" hole

Hide

PLATE 98

FOXFIRE 3

two or three times to it, and if it jumped, he'd catch it and hold it till I got down. He wouldn't chew it up. I had him trained so he wouldn't *chew* it! And then I'd get down and finish it off. I'd take'em in a sack and slip around through the woods so nobody wouldn't see me. I couldn't tell you how many I *have* took in.

"But they got fond of'em. Back *then* they didn't care, you know. They'uz too many cats anyhow, and they didn't care much. But they just didn't want t'see you come t'th'*house!*

"I wouldn't get th'last cat a man had [laughing]. When I got down to one, I'd leave it fer'im!

"But I've been making banjos for about twenty years. That's my hobby. I ain't worked on a job in about six years. Kidneys went t'th'bad and I just do this for a hobby—and then it helps me out [financially]. And then I farm. My wife works every other day at the hospital.

"You have to be careful at this. I make my instruments to play. Sometimes I get a western one—that's what I call it if I get something in there and it doesn't work. Then you have to take it out. That's the western type. I've took out some. Before I'd send you one, I'd take'em *all* out and make'em right [if I had to]. That's what I make'em for is to play'em. You've got to check'em out, and when you get a western one, you've got to change it!

"They was a boy here one time—young like feller—and said, 'What you get for them?'

"I said, 'Sixty dollars.' [Both Stanley and Tedra get about $100.00 apiece now.]

" 'God,' he says, 'I'm a'going home.' Said, 'I can get rich.' Said, 'I can make one of them in a day.'

"I said, 'Y'can?'

" 'Yeah, yeah.' Said, 'I can make one a day.'

" 'Well,' I said, 'when you *get* that, you come and let me know. I need to know how you do it. I need more money.'

"He never did get *nary one* together. Worked at it about four days and laid it down and quit.

"I sell mine myself. They come here [from a co-op], and I told them I just made mine for hobby and if I wanted to give somebody one, I'd give it to him. I don't have to take their price and sell it to you. He said, 'Oh, we'll get you a lot more money!'

"I said, 'Who gets the money? Me or you?'

" 'Oh,' he said, 'we get a certain percentage of it.'

" 'Well,' I said, 'you'll have t'go some'eres else.' "

In his work, Stanley is painstakingly careful. He refuses to be pressured. Of course, the other thing that slows him down is that every few moments,

PLATE 99

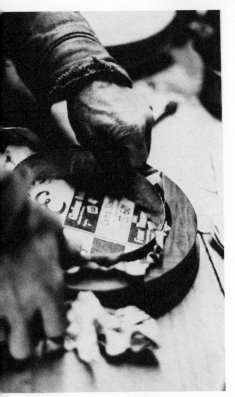

PLATE 100

he stops to tell another story—like the ones following, told as he was sawing slots for the frets on a dulcimer fingerboard. If he had to stop telling stories, he'd probably have to stop making instruments also, for the two are inextricably linked . . .

Be about like one time they was an old man had a boy who was crippled. Been crippled for years and couldn't walk. Come two old Irishmens along, and they was wanting something to eat, and asked something to eat, and the man said, "Well," said, "my wife has t'take care of the crippled son." Said, "She ain't got much time."

PLATE 101

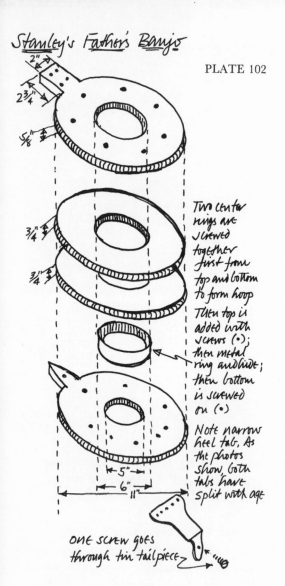

Stanley's Father's Banjo

2"

2 3/4"

5/8"

3/4"

3/4"

5"

6"

11"

PLATE 102

Two center
rings are
screwed
together
first from
top and bottom
to form hoop

Then top is
added with
screws (•);
then metal
ring and hide;
then bottom
is screwed
on (•)

Note narrow
heel tab. As
the photos
show, both
tabs have
split with age

One screw goes
through tin tailpiece

PLATE 103

PLATE 104

PLATE 105

Said, "What's the matter with'im?"

"Well," said, "he's been crippled for years."

"Well," said, "we'll cure him if you'll give us something to eat. We'll cure'im."

"Well," said, "alright."

PLATE 106   PLATE 107

PLATES 106–108   As Stanley does, his father used to sew his groundhog or cat hides around a ring using thread cut from a squirrel hide. He had a log trough into which he would put four or five hides at once, with ashes and water, to remove the hair. His banjos were all five-string, fretless, and made mostly of poplar, although he also used maple and chestnut. He smoothed the wood with the edge of a piece of glass, or a rasp. They sold for $2.50 each. The banjo has been modified to hold commercial pegs.

PLATE 108

PLATE 109

Old Irishmens, they went in and got'em something t'eat, "And now," he said, "you'll have t'cure my son."

Said, "We'll cure'im. Put him in a room where he can hear us at." So they put him in a room by hisself, and the old Irishmens got one [right beside]. And got'em a butcher knife apiece, and they started then a'whettin': "R-r-r-r-r, whetty-whet-r-whet whetty-whet r-r whetty-whet-whet." Said, "Sharp enough t'cut his head off?"

Said, "No, not quite."

Boy had raised up, y'know. Watched'em through a crack.

"R-r-r whetty-whetty-whet." Said, "Sharp enough t'cut his head off yet?"

Said, "No, not hardly."

Well, they looked through the crack and he'uz almost raising up in the chair. And they started again: "R-r whetty-whet whetty-whet r-r whetty-whet whetty-whet." Said, "Sharp enough t'cut his head off yet?"

"Yeah," he said, "I think we're sharp a'plenty." Said, "Jerk th'door and let's go get'im."

They jerked the door open, and he run out the other, and as fer as I know he's still running yet! He just cleaned the door hinges off and got out of there!

That's the way this is [sawing frets for his dulcimer]. R-r whetty-whet!

I guess a man would feel kindly funny, you know, them whetting on knives! They said that was true . . .

Then they was two more Irishmens going along the road and looked up in a tree and saw a boomer. Said, "You go get a pot t'cook it in and I'll have it caught when you come back."

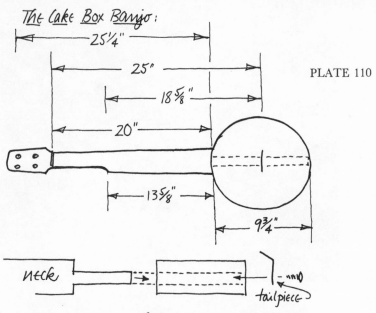

The Cake Box Banjo:

25¼"

25"

18⅝"

20"

13⅝"

9¾"

PLATE 110

neck   tailpiece

One screw goes through tailpiece into end
of neck extension. A 4½" sound hole
is cut into the bottom of the cake tin

PLATE 111   PLATE 112

PLATE 113

PLATE 114

PLATE 115

Well, this old Irishman, he took off t'get'em a cook pot. And he got his pot and went back, and th'other Irishman's layin' down in th'road with blood runnin' out of his mouth. And he looked at him right straight and he said, "You must'a been awful damn hungry," he said, "t'eat it raw!"

He'd made a jump y'know, to get where the squirrel was at, and his legs wadn't long enough and he'd hit the ground!

After he showed us the banjos, Stanley brought out a game he had made (*Plate 116*).

PLATE 116

PLATE 117

PLATE 118

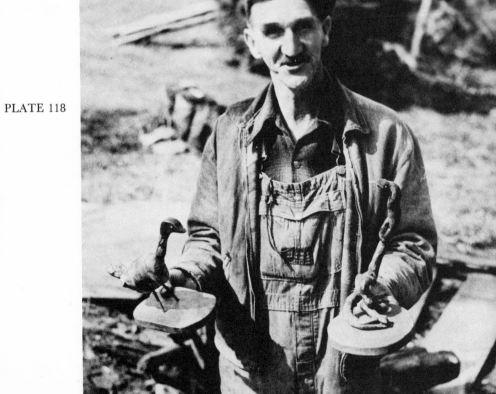

PLATE 119

"We used to make these [pecking birds]. See, here it goes! [As he swings the paddle and the birds peck, he sings/chants the following]:

> Chicken in the bread bowl peckin' out dough.
> Granny, won't your dog bite? No, chile, no.
> No, chile, no.
> Chicken in the bread bowl peckin' out dough.
> Granny, won't your dog bite? No, chile, no.
> No, chile, no. No, chile, no.

"Watch 'em, now! Watch'em. Watch'em. Now, this'n here [pointing a slower one out], he got beat up and we had t'remodel his tail. Y'see him? He looks a little bit *rough*. Now they's supposed to be corn in here, but I ain't put any in yet. That one's a little lazy [pointing at another]. 'At's a rooster. He's just a little lazy, boys. Now them hens is smart, y'see? Now watch him. He's a little ill there!

"But they's a lot of things that way you make, you know, just while you're beatin' around at it. I've got a snake. And, let's see, where's my 'moisture' at [a paddle with a rough head and a crayfish claw nailed to either side (*Plate 117*)]. And I've got me a bird at the house. My wife, she wouldn't let me keep the moisture at the house. And that bird and snake, I just picked up roots and made them. I'll run down t'th'house and bring'em up here and let you look at'em!" (*Plate 118*).

RAY MCBRIDE

Photographs by Ray and Steve Smith.

LEONARD GLENN

Leonard Glenn went to school with Tedra Harmon, and they still live almost within shouting distance of each other. He farms tobacco and sells an instrument once in a while to bring in an income for the family. His son, Clifford, also makes banjos and dulcimers.

On the day we visited him, it was rainy and cold, and although we had never met him before, he invited us in and showed us two of the banjos he had made. The one we were most interested in was the one made in the same style as those Tedra and Stanley Hicks made. Glenn got his pattern from his father who made banjos fifty years ago. His father used squirrel hides for the heads because they were thinner than groundhog and deer, and he felt they had better tone. Glenn did the same until recently when he started buying cowhides out of which he could get at least three heads.

When he was using squirrel hides, he'd put them fresh in a vat under about an inch of hardwood ashes and water. When the hair loosened, he'd

PLATE 120

scrape the hides clean, wash them thoroughly, and put them in the banjos immediately.

He could cut out the pieces for the head, the neck (for which he preferred cherry or walnut), and put in a skin in one day. He'd cut the pieces out with a band saw, and cut out the holes for the head and the sound holes with a jigsaw. Finishing work was done with a rasp, wood file, and sandpaper. Pegs were cut out with a jigsaw and then shaped with a pocketknife. Rather than trying for a high gloss, Glenn preferred simply to rub in a wax for the finish.

He's sold many instruments—some of them ones he didn't really want to sell. He'd set the price at two or three times what he thought they were worth to discourage buyers, but someone always came along with a checkbook.

RAY MCBRIDE

Photographs by Ray and Steve Smith.

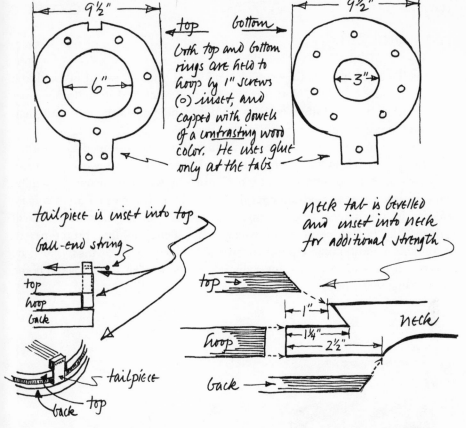

top   bottom

9½"   9½"

6"   3"

both top and bottom
rings are held to
hoops by 1" screws
(o) inset, and
capped with dowels
of a contrasting wood
color. He uses glue
only at the tabs

tailpiece is inset into top

ball-end string

top
hoop
back

neck tab is bevelled
and inset into neck
for additional strength

top →

hoop →

back →

1"

1¼"

2½"

neck

tailpiece

back   top

PLATE 121   The banjos that Leonard Glenn makes are similar in construction to those of both Tedra and Stanley (three wooden rings, a metal ring to hold the head, no neck extension, etc). There are several differences worth noting, however, as shown.

PLATE 122

DAVE PICKETT

Dave Pickett is thirty-one years old and was born and raised in Davidson County, North Carolina. Both his great-grandfather and grandfather were blacksmiths, and his father was a machinist and gunsmith—all with their roots in the same county.

Dave has always been restless, searching for the livelihood that suited him best. He tried farming—he was raised on a farm, has worked a team of horses, and raised tobacco and grain—then he took two years of machine work in trade school, and later returned to school and earned an Associate Degree in mechanical engineering. He worked seven years in technical writing, the last three years of which were spent building prototypes of textile air conditioning equipment from engineering drawings. Now he makes banjos and folk toys for a living, has a garden, and makes home brew. Finally he's happy.

PLATE 123

The posts are set so that every 4th one passes through a lap joint to help strengthen it

Dave's 3" high, 11" hoop is made of 8 separate, lap-jointed pieces of a hardwood like maple. The pieces are glued together in matching pairs, and then the pairs are glued together to form a perfect

PLATE 124

circle. Then the whole hoop is turned and finished, and the posts and brackets set, and the hole cut for the neck extension (tail). There are 31 posts and 30 brackets (the 31st post is where the tailpiece is set at the neck's tail). They are spaced 1 1/16" apart

PLATE 125

PLATE 126

PLATE 127   Dave has his pieces figured out so carefully that he can get every wooden piece he needs out of one 40″×3″×3″ piece of stock.

PLATES 128–130   These plates illustrate another hoop style that Dave has used in the past.

PLATE 129

PLATE 130

PLATE 131   PLATE 132

PLATE 133   PLATE 134

PLATES 131–134 The pattern for the side of the neck is traced off on stock and cut out with a band saw (*Plates 131, 132*). Then top is traced off and cut (*Plate 133*). A slot is cut in the top of the neck to hold a steel rod that acts to counter the tension of the strings. The fingerboard covers the slot (*Plate 134*).

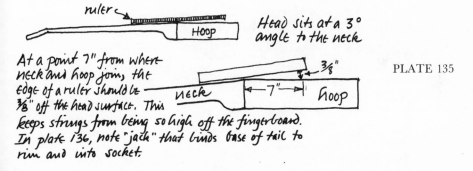

PLATE 135

ruler

Hoop

Head sits at a 3° angle to the neck

At a point 7" from where neck and hoop join, the edge of a ruler should be 3/8" off the head surface. This keeps strings from being so high off the fingerboard. In plate 136, note "jack" that binds base of tail to rim and into socket.

neck   7"   hoop   3/8"

Dave got started making banjos entirely by accident. He had always wanted to learn to play one, but he couldn't afford to buy one. A man he worked with came to him for some help in figuring out how to turn a banjo rim, and he got involved in the project and decided to go ahead and draw out diagrams for a complete instrument. He worked on them for a year polishing and perfecting every angle and joint, and then he built one. It was an impressive success.

He originally planned to build just that one, but people kept pestering him to build one for them also, so he finally quit the engineering job, opened a little shop with several other craftsmen in Winston-Salem (they

PLATE 136

PLATE 137

PLATE 138

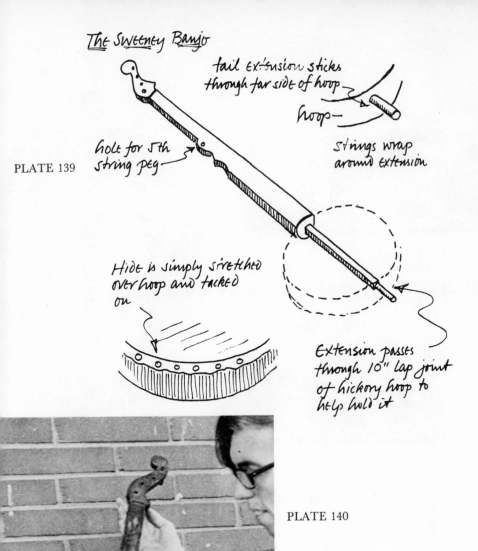

The Sweeney Banjo

tail extension sticks through far side of hoop

hoop

strings wrap around extension

PLATE 139

hole for 5th string peg

Hide is simply stretched over hoop and tacked on

Extension passes through 10" lap joint of hickory hoop to help hold it

PLATE 140

PLATE 141

PLATE 142

PLATE 143

share the rent and tools), and stuck strictly to banjos and folk toys. He guarantees the toys such as limberjacks, for a lifetime.

It took a lot of moving around to find satisfaction but it turned out that none of the jobs he had tried during his restless period were a waste of time. He used his knowledge in engineering to design one of the finest banjos we've ever seen. Being raised on a farm he knows how to—and does— produce enough food in his garden to feed his family. And using his skills in machine work he can manufacture almost every part needed for his instruments.

He sells the finished banjos for about $300.00 apiece (unless the customer specifically requests him to design and make parts such as the tailpiece and fingerboard himself instead of using commercial ones. In this case, the price goes up). It sounds expensive, but even at that price, Dave is lucky if he comes out making fifty cents an hour:

"I haven't made a fortune, but I haven't starved, either. What more can a person ask out of life. The main thing is I enjoy what I'm doing. I believe in enjoying what you're doing. I come in at 8:30 or 9:00 of a morning, and you're liable to find me here at 10:30 or 11:00 at night because I *want* to work; not because I have to. If things go bad, I just lock the door and go squirrel hunting or fishing. You set your own schedule. I have no one working for me. Everything I produce is totally from me. No outside help. Main reason is that I'm kind of a bad person to work for. People just can't do the work like I want it done. I've tried to have a few people help me, but all they can do is assembly work. As far as making the parts, there's just no way. Why pay somebody to do it and then have to do it over?"

He is always experimenting, improving and working on new ideas. Dave now plans to try his hand at something he gets many requests for—an old-style fretless banjo. It will be easier to build—and thus not as expensive—as it will have fiddle pegs instead of commercial ones, and it won't need the metal reinforcing bar in the neck—the fretless banjo is tuned lower and so the tension on the neck is less.

But if what he's doing now is any indication, the quality will still be flawless.

RAY MCBRIDE

Photographs by Ray and Ernest Flanagan.

DAVE STURGILL

Dave Sturgill's roots in Piney Grove go back to the time of the Indian. Unlike many of his ancestors, however, he spent a large portion of his life away from the mountains. After he graduated from high school during the Depression, he began to wander, covering the country from New York to San Francisco. "I got my education by traveling, and of course one of the things I was interested in, even then, was music, so I carried my instrument and played in clubs to make a little money."

In 1938, he wound up in Washington, D.C., went to school for a year, worked for the Western Electric Company, and then moved to the Bell Telephone Company. He stayed with them for twenty-nine years in Washington, and was a general engineer in switching equipment when he left. He was fourteen months away from retirement, he had a wife and sons, "But my heart never left the hills. This was where I always wanted to be. There were riots in Washington then, and these hills looked so good every time I came down here that I finally came down here and stayed." He

PLATE 144

Sturgill Mountain Banjo Kit

Plate 146 shows the pieces that come with the Sturgill kit, as well as an [example] of the finished banjo the kit produces. There are several variations here [incorporated from traditional instruments Dave has seen, such as those in [following plates) that we have not previously noted : the thin hoop, for example, [fits into corresponding grooves on the inside of the top and back. [Note] also that the commercial 6" head is held into place by a wooden ring, which is [in turn held in place by 5 wooden blocks nailed or screwed into the underside of the top. [Note] also the tailpiece — simply 3 brass brads driven into the top. The strings hook [into their heads. Design and cut your own sound holes. Has fretted fingerboard.

[Here are the] diagrams that come with the instructions in the kit:

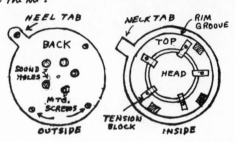

PLATE 145

PLATE 146

PLATE 147

PLATE 148

PLATE 149

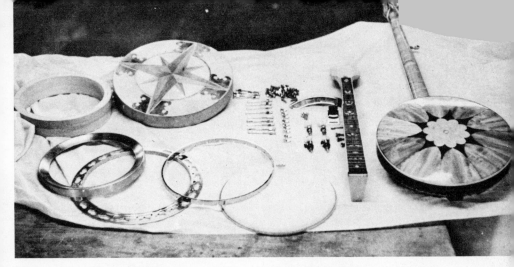

PLATE 150 The component parts of the most elaborate Sturgill banjo laid out. They include a fully inlaid resonator.

worked for a while in a small musical factory in Nashville that was foundering, then left, came back home, built a shop and dug in. His two sons, meanwhile, had been doing some wandering of their own—one worked for the Evans Steel Guitar Company in Burlington, North Carolina, for a while—but they, too, were circling closer and closer to home. Now they're Dave's partners in what has turned into a thriving business in guitars, banjos, mandolins, and dulcimers. Neither Dave, Danny nor John has ever regretted the move. As John said, "Being born in Washington was an accident I couldn't help. I never did count that home. I spent all my summers down here. Now I'm here to stay."

Recently Dave went to Washington to attend a dinner celebration that Bell was sponsoring. He ran into a friend there whom he had worked with, and they began to talk about the move he had made. Asked Dave, "Who was president of this company when you and I started to work for it?"

The friend said, "I'm not sure," and thought for a few minutes. "It was either Mr. Wilson, or . . ."

As Dave tells the story: "I knew who was president at that time because I'd made it a point to find out. So I reminded him which one it was. I said, 'Now that wasn't even thirty years ago, and you're not even sure who the president of the company was when you started.' I says, 'Think about this a little bit. Twenty years from now, there won't be anybody working for this company that will know you or I either one ever worked for it. But,' I says, 'a hundred years from now, they'll be people who will know I made musical instruments.' "

Dave is convinced that the move away from Washington saved his life—and his spirit. "When it gets down to a question of security, the only security you can possibly have on this earth is what your Creator gives you. It

PLATE 151

PLATES 151 and 152   The walls of Dave's shop are filled with instruments they have made—everything from mandolins and fiddles to guitars and banjos.

PLATE 152

PLATE 153   The evolution of the banjo from its simplest form to the Hicks-Harmon-Glenn variety to the most modern, complex form worthy of an Earl Scruggs.

Plates 154–171 illustrate four varieties of banjos which Dave has in his collection. They are documented in the following four groups and in the "Dave Sturgill" section of the comparison chart (*Plate 175*).

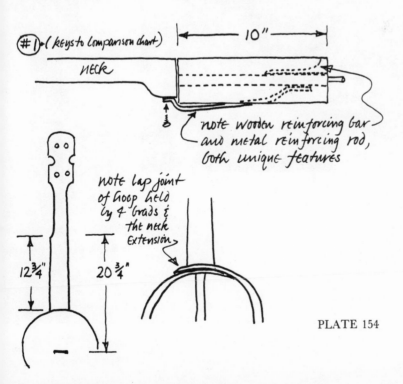

(#1) (keys to comparison chart)

← 10″ →

neck

note wooden reinforcing bar and metal reinforcing rod, both unique features

note lap joint of hoop held by 4 brads & the neck extension

12¾″   20¾″

PLATE 154

PLATE 155

PLATE 156

PLATE 157

PLATE 158   PLATE 159

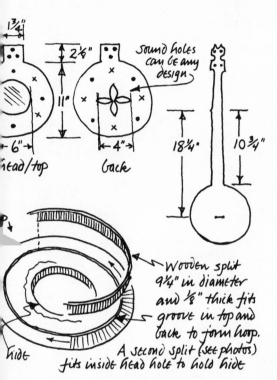

1¾"

2⅛"

11"

6" ← →

head/top

sound holes can be any design

4" → ←

back

18¾"

10¾"

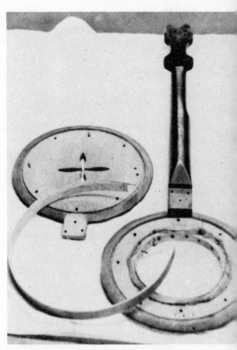

Wooden split 9¼" in diameter and ⅛" thick fits groove in top and back to form hoop. A second split (see photos) fits inside head hole to hold hide

hide

...op split meets at, and is attached to, neck. ...gs held the top and back together inside ...t hoop. In paired diagrams at top left, • ...dicates where peg went in, × where it came out. ...ote sloped, beveled edges on top and back

PLATE 160

PLATE 161 PLATE 162

PLATE 163

PLATE 164

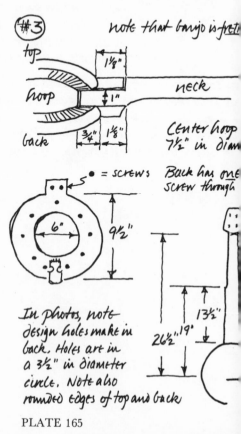

(#3)   note that banjo is fret...

top

hoop   neck

1⅛"

1"

back   ¾" 1⅛"   Center hoop
                          7½" in diam...

● = screws   Back has one
              screw through

6"   9½"

In photos, note
design holes make in
back. Holes are in
a 3½" in diameter
circle. Note also
rounded edges of top and back

13½"
26½" 19"

PLATE 165

PLATE 166

PLATE 167

PLATE 168

doesn't come from anywhere else. He can take it all away from you just like that, or he can give it back to you. I don't have to worry about health insurance because I figure He's going to look after me. So I gave up life insurance, health insurance, pension—all the rest of it—but I have absolutely no regrets. Smartest thing I ever did as far as I'm concerned, because I know now that if I'd stayed there, I'd be dead. I was getting ulcers and high blood pressure. My heart was bothering me, and several other things. And all that's gone now. None of it's bothering me. I'm actually in better health now, five years later, then when I left there. I certainly don't regret leaving all that behind. And nothing would ever get me back into it, I'll tell you. Not again.

"I'm not saying you should go completely back to Nature. That's not the answer either. They talk about the good old days. Well, I was raised in those, and I don't want to go back to oil lamps and outdoor toilets. That's a little too much. But there *are* things that are a lot more important than how big an automobile you've got, or how big your bank account is. I was into it up there. An hour and a half fighting traffic every morning to get downtown. An hour and a half fighting that traffic every evening to get back. I'd be a nervous wreck every time I got on the job, and I'd be the same way when I got home. And, boy, I started asking myself every day, 'Why? Why? What in the world am I fighting this for?' "

Dave's time away from the mountains, as well as the fact that the original grant for the land he now owns was made to his four-times great-grandfather and there has never been anyone but Sturgills and Indians on it, has made him passionately committed to his land and people:

"The picture that's been drawn of these mountains down through here has been wrong—so much of it—through the years. When I was with Bell, I had several assignments up in New York City. I'd be up there sometimes for two or three weeks at a time, and those people would find out where I was from—that I came right out of the edge of the Smoky Mountains down here in the Appalachians—and they would call me 'Hillbilly.' They'd get a big kick out of it. And I'd say, 'Yeah, but there's one big difference. You can take any boy out of those hills and turn him loose in New York City and he'll get by. But take one of you fellows down in the hills and turn you loose; you'd starve to death.'

"But the picture most of those people had of those mountaineers was pure Little Abner. Now that's where they got it from—the comic strips. And that's the truth today, even. Ninety per cent of the population, they think of everybody down in the mountains in terms of Little Abner. They don't realize it's not that way any more.

"We had some people come in here last summer when I was writing

Note the modern variations
added to this traditional
        basic design

Any design on
back for sound
holes is sufficient
Note decorative heel
tab raised by sanding
away surrounding wood.

Note fretted finger
board is inlaid, and
glued in place on
top of neck. It
does not fit flush
with top surface of
top, as in many
others

Note designs cut
into top and peg
head

PLATE 169

PLATE 170

PLATE 171

this history of my family. One woman I corresponded with was from Portland, Oregon. Her ancestors had come from here and she was very interested, and she had some information that I didn't have. She passed that on to me, and we incorporated it into the book. But her daughter came by here last summer and called and introduced herself, and she said she wanted to come down and take a day and visit. And I told her I'd be glad to meet her, to come on down. And so she came on in here into the shop, and the first thing she said after she introduced herself was, 'Tell me something. Where is this Appalachia I've been reading about and hearing about all my life? The picture I've always had about this country was little shacks and people sitting around on the porch.'

"And I said, 'Well, I could take you to a few places like that, but we'd have to hunt for them. They're pretty scarce, and they're still a few here, but . . .'"

Dave, and most of the true mountain people, have humorous stories tucked away about outsiders that have come in looking for REAL mountain folks. We have more than a few ourselves. And the humor is often touched with a sense of anger. Dave told us his favorite:

"I'll tell you the best one I heard of all. Up at Laurel Springs where there's a motel, service station and so forth, a couple of years ago this big car from Pennsylvania pulled in there to get some gasoline. And the man and his wife got out—middle-aged couple—and they were straight-out tourists all the way, with the colored glasses and the shorts, the camera, the whole bit. So while the man was putting gas in the car, the woman came around and started talking to him. Says, 'Where can we go to see some real genuine hillbillies? This is the first time we've ever been down in here.'

"And he says, 'Well, lady,' says, 'I'm sorry,' said, 'you can't see any now.'

"She said, 'Well, why?'

"And he said, 'Well, it's out of season.'

"And she says, 'Well, I don't understand.' Says, 'What do you mean it's out of season?'

"And he says, 'Well, they're all up in Pennsylvania teaching school!' "

As a young boy, Dave made his first banjo because he wanted one and was too poor to buy it. He took a plywood packing crate, set it in the creek until it came apart, and then wrapped a strip of its thin wood veneer around a five-gallon can and held it in place with rubber bands until it dried to form the hoop. Then he whittled the neck out with a pocketknife.

His interest in music came naturally. His mother could play instruments, as well as his grandfather and great-grandfather on her side. In addition, he had an uncle who liked music so well that he cleared a half-acre of land down on the river, kept it mowed, and built benches in between the willow trees. "There was a little sandy spot there where they used to land the boats. And us kids twelve, thirteen and fourteen years old, we'd get down there and play and dance and sing until three in the morning—and sometimes it would go longer than that. Dancing on the ground. He'd take wood down there and pile it up for us—always kept wood down there—and he'd build a fire and sit down there and listen to us play."

Now Dave and his sons make mandolins, guitars, fiddles (he's made nearly thirty-five and restored over 200 himself), dulcimers, and, of course, banjos of all types. At one end of the scale is the mountain banjo kit that they sell for $35.00. The pattern for the kit came from an old mountain banjo that was much like those that Tedra Harmon and Stanley Hicks now make except that it is fretted. The kit includes instructions as well as everything that is necessary to make one yourself from the pieces of yellow poplar (all routed, marked for holes, etc.) to the fret wire, strings, tension blocks, nails, screws and the plastic head.

At the other end of the scale is the one-of-a-kind, staggeringly beautiful

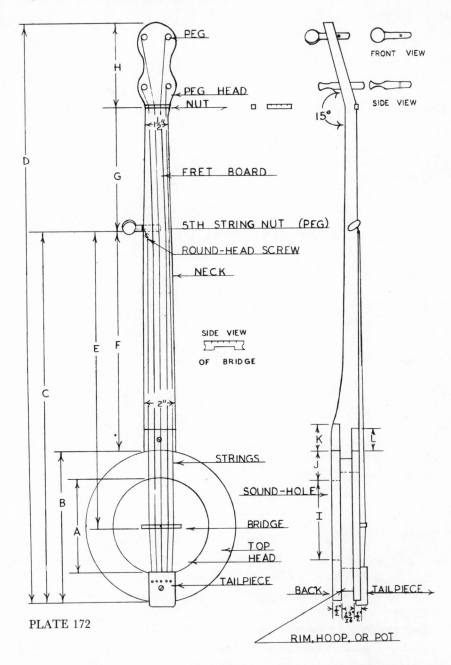

PEG

PEG HEAD
NUT

FRONT VIEW

SIDE VIEW

15°

FRET BOARD

5TH STRING NUT (PEG)

ROUND-HEAD SCREW

NECK

SIDE VIEW
OF BRIDGE

STRINGS

SOUND-HOLE

BRIDGE

TOP
HEAD

TAILPIECE

BACK

TAILPIECE

RIM, HOOP, OR POT

PLATE 172

	A	B	C	D	E	F	G	H	I	J	K	L
TEDRA HARMON'S BANJO	6	$9\frac{1}{2}$	23	36	$18\frac{1}{2}$	$13\frac{1}{2}$	$7\frac{1}{2}$	$5\frac{1}{2}$	5	2	$1\frac{3}{4}$	$1\frac{3}{8}$
STANLEY HICKS' BANJO	$6\frac{1}{4}$	$10\frac{1}{4}$	26	37	20	$15\frac{1}{4}$	$5\frac{3}{4}$	$5\frac{3}{8}$	$5\frac{3}{8}$	$3\frac{1}{4}$	$\frac{5}{8}$	$2\frac{1}{4}$

PLATE 173

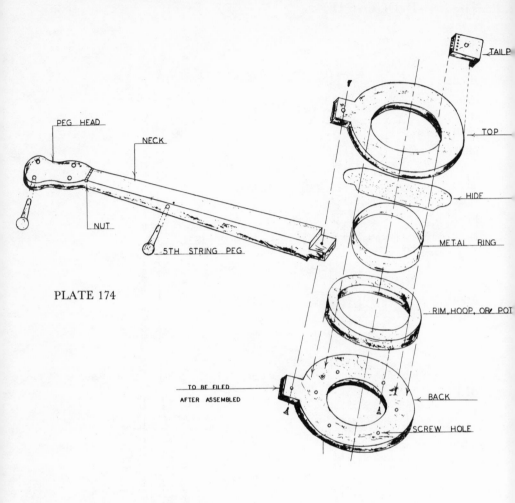

PEG HEAD

NECK

NUT

5TH STRING PEG

PLATE 174

TO BE FILED
AFTER ASSEMBLED

TAIL P

TOP

HIDE

METAL RING

RIM, HOOP, OR POT

BACK

SCREW HOLE

custom variety that he and his sons turn out for special customers willing to pay up to $1,500.00 for one of the finest banjos money can buy. With engravings and inlay, these instruments are works of art far too complex to detail here.

Dave has done a good bit of experimentation in his time, and has whittled his choice of materials down to a few favorites. If he were to make banjos with animal hide heads instead of commercial ones, he would prefer housecat. He has a banjo hanging on the wall that has a cat hide in it that is forty years old and still rings well. And he has also heard of catfish skin being used, and he imagines that would also be good as it wouldn't be as subject to humidity as the other hides are.

For wood, he likes yellow poplar (his choice for the kits) because it is strong but resilient, vibrates well, and has good tone. A favorite neck of his is red oak. And for head sizes, he's found that on the mountain-style banjo, a six-inch head with a half-inch-thick top and back rings the best.

I could tell that Dave was really happy now making instruments for a living. It shows in his work, and it shows in his face.

While we were there, Dick Finney, a man Dave grew up with, came over. Both were born on the same day, January 21, 1917, and had played together since they were young. Dick uses the second guitar Dave ever made, and Dave is building him a new one now. They played for us, Dave on the banjo and Dick on the guitar.

We played the tape we made of them all the way home.

RAY MCBRIDE

Photographs by Ray and Steve Smith.

ROBERT MIZE, DULCIMER MAKER

Robert Mize was born and raised in our county, and he still has enough folks here to have good reason to make the trip down from Blountville, Tennessee, with some regularity. Nowadays, when he comes through, he stops by, and more often than not he brings along a new dulcimer or two—just finished—and either he or one of his children winds up playing it for us.

Several months ago, he stopped in as the result of a request we had sent him via one of his nieces some two years before to give us a hand putting together an article on his method of dulcimer construction. He offered to write the article for us, and we accepted.

It's an honor for us to have his directions, for he truly knows what he's doing—one of the reasons why he's a favorite craftsman member of the Southern Highlands Handicraft Guild. He's made more dulcimers than anyone we know. Each one is sequentially numbered, and as he packed up his newest one after showing it to us on his last visit, we noticed its number on the end of the box: 666.

The mountain dulcimer is an instrument whose origin is somewhat a mystery. And after having read several articles and opinions of others, I still know very little about where they come from. I believe they have always

A COMPARISON OF STYLES:

	Head	Back	Pot (Hoop, Rim)	Neck + Frets	Hooking Neck / Pot	Tailpiece (Apron)	Nut + Bridge	Pegs
Ernest Franklin	father's = groundhog or cat. Covered whole pot. Held on with metal ring and brass posts. his = 11" x ⅛" poplar glued onto pot.	father's: none his: none	father's: hickory split put around frame and pegged. his: Solid poplar sawed out, or three rings of white pine and/or poplar sandwiched, glued together.	father's: 1 solid piece sawed out and shaped with a drawknife and rasp. Has extension. Poplar, maple, or black walnut. Fretless. his: 1 solid piece - no extension. Poplar. Fretless.	father's 2 screws at base of extension, 1 at end through tailpiece. Also glued + metal bracket his: 3 screws and glue.	father's: tin held on with 1 screw. his: tin	father's: any hardwood. his: same	father's: hand carved out of hardwood. his: friction pegs hand carved of wild cherry, maple or birch. Drills hole first; then whittles peg out from around it. Dislikes walnut as heads can wring off in time.
M.C. Worley	Solid wood - ⅛" maple veneer from a furniture factory. 11" diameter. Crayoned green quarter moon for decoration.	approximately ¼" thick piece of cedar with 3" sound hole and short heel tab. Glue + 1 screw.	3 rings (each made of interlocking pieces) sandwiched together and glued. Metal strip for decoration. Favorite woods: cherry, cedar, walnut, curly maple. 1¾" thick	Solid piece of walnut shaped with drawknife. Fretless. 25" scale (nut to bridge).	Dovetailed end fits into slot in hoop. Held with glue + one screw through back's heel tab. Top also glues onto top of dovetail end.	copper tacked onto hoop.	any hardwood	One hardwood. Peg head has upholstery tacks for decoration
Tedra Harmon	Wooden ring (9½" x ½") with 6" hide in center of groundhog or otter. Likes walnut, maple, chestnut, mulberry - Has 1½" x 2" long neck tab	Wooden ring (9½" x ½") with 5" sound hole. 1½" heel tab. Same woods as head.	Wooden ring (8¼" x ¾") Hole in center slightly larger than one in head. Same woods - sometimes varied with wood in head and back for color.	Solid piece of walnut - no extension. Also uses maple and chestnut. Fretless. 25½"-26" scale. Sometimes varied with head woods for color variation.	Top glued to center ring and sometimes 1 screw is placed in neck tab. Back screwed onto center ring and sometimes a spot of glue on heel tab.	⅞" thick walnut	walnut or some other hardwood. Likes curly maple bridge.	walnut friction pegs. (or another hardwood).
Stanley Hicks	father's: Wooden ring 11" in diameter w/ 6" hide of groundhog or house cat. 2¾" long neck tab x ⅝" thick. #2: metal cake box lid 9¼" in diameter. his: Wooden ring of walnut, cherry or maple 11" in diameter w/ 6½" hole for commercial head or groundhog hide head. Neck tab ½" thick x 2½ long and 2" wide.	father's: 11" diameter hardwood w/ 5" sound hole. ⅝" thick. Heel tab 2½" long x ½" wide. #2: bottom of 9¾" diameter cake box w/ 4½" sound hole. his: 11" diameter wood (walnut, cherry, or maple) x ½" thick x 4" sound hole. Heel tab 2" long x ½" thick.	father's: 2 wooden rings ¾" thick screwed together. #2: cake box (metal) his: walnut, cherry, or other hardwood ring 1" thick x 9½" diameter with 7" hole. Also likes chestnut.	father's: solid poplar with no extension. fretless #2: poplar with extension. Fretless. his: black walnut or other hardwood - no extension. Fretless.	father's: neck tab and heel tab screws plus glue. #2: Screw into end of tail extension. his: neck tab and heel tab screws (4 and 1). No glue.	father's: tin held with screw #2: tin w/ screw his: walnut or some other hardwood.	father's: #2: his: walnut	father's: hardwood (later modified to hold commercial screw pegs. #2: hardwood his: hardwood
Leonard Glenn	Hardwood ring 9½" in diameter with 6" head of cowhide set in. 1½" long neck tab	Hardwood ring 9½" in diameter w/ 3" sound hole. Heel tab 2½" long.	Hardwood ring w/ 6" hole. Metal ring to hold hide as in Hicks/Harmon banjos.	Likes cherry and walnut. Neck has bevelled notch to hold top more securely. Fretless. 25¼" scale. 13¾" from thumb screw to edge of top	Neck tab and heel tab screws (2 and 1) with a little glue on tabs.	inset into head. Hardwood.	Hardwood.	whittled out of hardwood.

Dave Pickett	Fid: commercial 11" head held on by a metal band and metal posts and brackets. Sometimes also uses 12" head. Sweeney: 12" hide tacked onto outside of the hoop.	Fid: none Sweeney: none	Fid: 8 lap-jointed pieces of hardwood glued together. Likes curly maple or walnut. Cuts 3/4"-1" thick, mixes sawdust with glue so joints will take a finish; turns rim down to 1/2" on lathe. Adds sleeve guard. Sweeney: Hickory split lap-jointed into a circle.	Fid: solid piece w/tail or extension sawed out with band saw & shaped. Has frets - commercial or hand-made fretboard glued on. 27" scale. Walnut or curley maple. Sweeney: 1 solid piece with long extension. Strings wrap around end of extension. Fretless.	Fid: metal socket-piece holds end of tail. Another metal piece holds base of tail to inside of hoop. Sweeney - extension plus glue.	Fid: metal with design. Either commercial, or designed and fashioned himself. Sweeney: none	Fid: Either commercial, or fashioned to his own design. Likes bone. Sweeney: hardwood	Fid: commercial metal geared pegs. Sweeney: Hardwood
Dave Sturgill	Kit: 6" commercial head set in wooden (poplar) top held by wood ring and 5 tension blocks. #1: Hide stretched over 10" ring and tacked. #2: 6" hide set into 11" wooden top held by wood split tacked to inside of the 6" hole in the top. #3: 6" hide set into wooden top. #4: commercial head set into wooden top.	Kit: wooden, with sound holes drilled in a pattern. #1: none #2: same as kit #3: same as kit #4: same as kit - raised decorative heel tab.	Kit: 1¾" x 31" 3-ply laminated hardwood strip that fits into grooves in top and back. Nailed into heel of neck, and glued. #1: Hickory split lap-jointed. Neck's tail goes through joint. #2: Hardwood strip as in kit. #3: 7½" in diameter wooden ring. #4: wooden ring.	Kit: solid poplar - no tail. Has fretted fingerboard. #1: Wood - long tail - extends through hoop & strings loop over. Fretless. #2: Wood, no tail, Fretless. #3: Wood, no tail, no fingerboard but fretted. #4: Wood, no tail, has fretted fingerboard.	Kit: Heel and neck tab, nailed or screwed, glued. #1: Neck tail, plus metal rod and wooden reinforcing block. #2: Heel and neck tab, screws. #3: Heel and neck tab, screws. #4: Heel and neck tab, screws.	Kit: 3 brass brads. Strings loop over heads. #1: none - strings loop over neck's tail. #2: thin metal strip screwed into top just below head. #3: metal - loops over head - 1 screw. #4: inset metal strip	Kit: wood #1 wood #2: wood #3 wood #4: wood	Kit: whittled wood. #1: whittled wood #2: whittled wood #3: whittled wood #4: whittled wood

N.B.:

1. String pressure holds bridge in place on head. Scale can be changed by sliding bridge.
2. Resin on wooden fiddle pegs can increase friction to increase holding power in peg head.
3. The longer the neck, the lower the pitch, and vice-versa.
4. To find fret spacing, Dave Pickett uses the following formula: measure distance from nut to bridge (scale). Then figure $\frac{1}{17.830}$ × scale, and that gives correct distance from nut to first fret. Mark on fingerboard, subtract that answer from your scale, and work the problem again multiplying by the new scale figure. That gives spacing for next fret - etc.

PLATE 175

been here in the Appalachian area. One thing I do know is how to build them. In this section, I will try to explain some of the steps and procedures used in making them. Of course, there is more to it than this, and after over six hundred, I am still learning new tricks.

There is no standard-sized or -shaped dulcimer. Every maker has the one he likes best. I use the same general pattern and vary the type of wood, or number of strings. Kentucky, Mountain, and Appalachian are all names for the plucked dulcimer, which may have any number of strings. Mountain people call them "dulcymores" or "delcymores."

The dulcimer we refer to is the plucked dulcimer and should not be confused with the hammered dulcimer, which is a forerunner of the piano. The hammered dulcimer has many strings and is played by striking the strings with small wooden hammers.

The word "dulcimer" is derived from the Latin word "dulce," and the Greek word "melos," which put together mean "sweetsong" or "sweet tune." This truly describes the dulcimer, as it is a soft-voiced, personal-type instrument which can be easily tuned to the range of your voice. This makes the dulcimer a natural for playing hymns, ballads, and folk songs. Like the five-string banjo, it seems to be an authentic American musical instrument.

I was born and raised in Clayton, Rabun County, Georgia, and never saw nor heard of the dulcimer until the late 1940s. Some of the craftsmen of the Southern Highland Handicraft Guild began making them, using old ones for patterns. Their popularity has been growing ever since, especially in the last few years, with the revival of the folk music and handicrafts. I don't know if anyone owned or knew of dulcimers in Rabun County before this time.

Many different woods may be used. I make a combination of wormy chestnut, butternut, gum or sassafras for the top, and all other parts from black walnut. I also make them using cherry for all parts, or curly maple. Bird's-eye, or highly figured maple, is very difficult to work. It is also heavy.

The combination of a hardwood on back and sides, with softer wood for top, gives a good mellow sound, and the contrast of two woods is pleasing to see. Cherry on back and sides, and California redwood on top will make a soft tone. Butternut and walnut are also good. I use a lot of wormy chestnut with walnut. The color, grain, and worm holes make a nice looking top, and also a good tone.

Different woods will affect the tone of the instrument somewhat, although the size and shape of the sound holes have very little effect, except for looks. I use an "F" shape, like in a violin, for most of mine: but I do make heart, diamond, or other shapes when requested to do so.

I have used many different woods, such as apple, red elm, oak, sourwood,

PLATE 176

PLATE 17

PLATE 17

PLATE 17

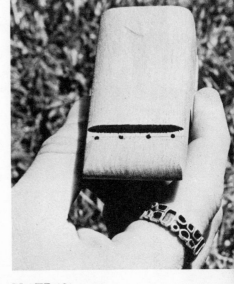

PLATE 180   PLATE 181

PLATE 182

gum, pecan, cedar, beech, birch, sassafras, chestnut, butternut, walnut, cherry, maple, and others. Most of these were only to see what they would look and sound like. If you stick with black walnut for the back, and butternut, gum, chestnut, or poplar on top, you can get good results. Curly poplar of the deep purple color makes an exceptional dulcimer. The wood is not as important as the construction, and each instrument should be better than the last.

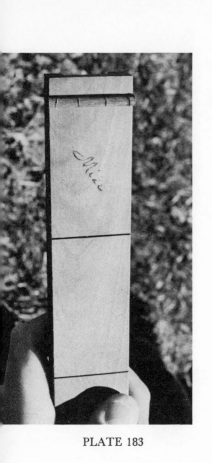

PLATE 183

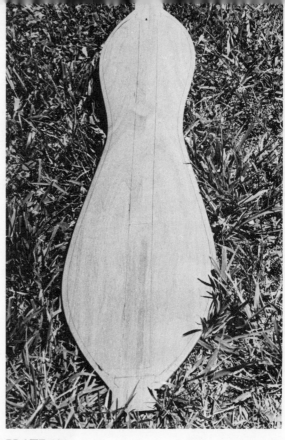

PLATE 184

PLATE 185

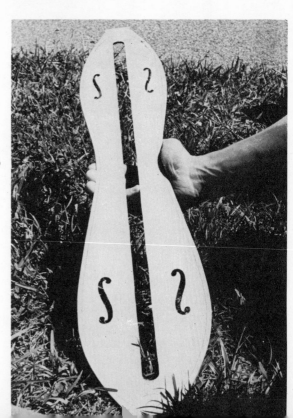

PLATE 186

PLATE 187

The dulcimers I make for sale are made as nearly like the old traditional ones as I can get them. No fancy inlays of exotic woods, no veneers or plywood, just good, dry wood like that used by the early craftsmen. I do not use metal guitar-tuning keys, but make wooden keys from Brazilian rosewood. I use modern techniques, glue, and finishes.

All wood used should be kiln-dried unless you are sure it is thoroughly air-dried, to control shrinking and cracking in low humidity. As we cannot control the environment around the dulcimer, we try to protect the dulcimer from the extremes of humidity. Our modern homes get very dry in the wintertime and air conditioning keeps the humidity low the rest of the time.

I apply two heavy coats of sanding sealer lacquer, then two coats of finish lacquer, hand rub with steel wool after each coat of lacquer, and wax with a good paste furniture wax. A dulcimer must be a good musical instrument, and if it looks good also, so much the better, but musical quality comes first.

I will describe and make a four-string dulcimer of wormy chestnut and black walnut, in the shape generally known as the elongated hour glass. We will make all parts, rough sand, assemble the parts, trim, finish sand, apply the finish, hand rub, wax, string, tune up, and, hopefully, play.

THE PEG HEAD

As this is to be a four-string dulcimer, we will select a piece of black walnut 8" long×1½" wide×2½" thick. The shape of the peg head is traced on the side, and the shape of the peg box is traced on the top. The peg box is ⅝" wide and about ⅞" deep, and long enough to accommodate four tuning pegs (*Plate 177*). To make a five- or six-string dulcimer, just make the peg head and peg box a little longer to get the extra pegs in there. I drill part of the peg box with a ⅝" drill, then finish cutting to shape with a chisel. Once the peg box is finished, saw slots in the end to receive the sides and cut the notch for top and fret board (*Plates 178, 179*). Cut the peg head to shape last, so you will have straight and square surfaces to cut notches and slots accurately (see diagram on page 206).

THE PEG END

The peg end is also made of walnut, the same width as the peg head. The length of the slots, where sides fit, must be the same as those of the peg head, as this determines the depth of the sound box. Cut slots for the sides

PLATE 188

PLATE 189

PLATE 190

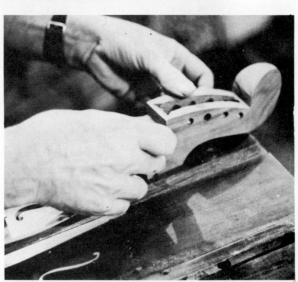

(*Plate 180*), a notch for the top and fret board, and cut a notch on the back side for strings (*Plate 181*).

I have tried to lay out each step or saw cut in the proper order to give you better control for safety and accuracy, so please follow these steps. You may wind up with a difficult cut to make and no safe way to do it. You should then start over with that part and do it again.

THE FRET OR FINGER BOARD

This piece is the most important and critical of all the pieces. The distance from the string nut, near the peg head, to the bridge on the other end, must be exact. The frets must be placed exactly at the right place, or the notes will not be true. This distance or spacing of frets can be figured mathematically, although I do not know the formula. I have a master pattern of a fret board which was given to me by a master dulcimer maker. I go by this, and am most particular about its construction. The quality of the fret board determines the quality of music of the finished dulcimer. A beautiful dulcimer with a poor fret board makes an expensive wall decoration, as that is all it is good for. Remove some of the wood from the inside of the fret board, or hollow it out, to make the sound from the frets and string pass more easily to the sound box (*Plate 182*).

Keep the top of the fret board perfectly flat from one end to the other. If it is not flat, when you press the strings down on a fret, the string will touch the next fret also. This will deaden some of the sound and make the string buzz. Be sure the frets are seated solidly in their slots; raise the bridge a little, or even file a high spot off the fret to stop the buzzing. Sometimes it becomes necessary to remove all the frets, scrape and sand the fret board straight, and replace the frets to get it to play again.

Use regular guitar frets from a music store, cut to the proper length. Make saw slots with a thin coping saw. Make a saw slot in scrap wood, and file down the side of the blade until you get a thin slot that is a nice tight fit for the fret (*Plate 183*). Again, take care in making the fret board, as this is the most important part of a dulcimer (see *Plate 209*).

THE BACK

Take a piece of black walnut $3\frac{1}{2}''$ wide$\times 30''$ long$\times$about $1''$ thick. Try to find one with as much grain or figure as possible, as we will bookmatch two pieces to get a nice design on the back. Run this blank across a jointer or planer to get one surface smooth and flat. Square both of the edges. Make a pencil mark on one edge at a slant. By lining up these marks, you can arrange the cut pieces in the same position as they were in the original board. Set the rip fence on a bench saw for a $\frac{1}{8}''$ cut. Place the blank on edge and cut two $\frac{1}{8}''$ pieces. By using the pencil marks, get these two pieces in the same position as they were cut, then open them up like a book. Note the pattern of the grain. If it's not the best, close the "book" and turn it over and open it again. Always look at the inside of the book, as these two surfaces are the only ones that will match. Now joint and edge glue these pieces together. This is called "book-matching" or a mirror image. Reinforce this glue joint on the inside with thin pieces of wood, with the grain direction 90° from the glue joint. This should give you a piece of wood $7'' \times 30'' \times \frac{1}{8}''$ from which the back is made.

THE TOP

Select a piece of chestnut or whatever you wish to use and cut and glue a $7'' \times 30'' \times \frac{1}{8}''$ piece as you did for the back. Place the top blank on the bottom with the two bookmatched sides on the outside. Trace the shape and saw these pieces together. By keeping the top and bottom in the same position as they were cut, you do not have to worry about the contour of both sides being the same, as the top and bottom will match. Sand the inside and outside of these parts. Cut a slot in the top under the fret board (*Plates 184, 185*). Also, fix the position where sound holes are to be cut in the top. Make a pattern from paper or a thin, flat piece of plastic, cut the shape you want, place it on the top, and draw the design. Use a jig saw or coping saw: drill holes in the top, insert the blade through this hole, and cut the sound hole to the traced shape. Take care in cutting these holes. Finish the shape with a sharp knife. Get the shape of the sound hole right, as it is going to be on the top of the dulcimer and it is always the first thing noticed if it is not right.

The sides are cut from the same wood as the back. Start with a piece 30'' long and a little wider than the slots in the peg head and peg end. Dress this piece on a jointer to get it smooth. Slice a thin piece off with a bench saw—a little under $\frac{1}{16}''$—so it's flexible. Dress down the blank, and saw another side. Make three or four sides, always dressing down the thick blank, as the cut sides are too thin to dress on a machine. We now have all the major parts made and can start assembly.

ASSEMBLY

Clasp the top and bottom together as they will be later. True them up, then trim, sand, and finish the edges. Round off the sharp, square edges. Do all the sanding of the parts before putting them together, as it is easier

PLATE 192

PLATE 191

to get at some pieces. Leave only a light final sanding for the end of the process.

Be very careful from now on, as you are building an instrument you want to be proud of. Keep everything clean; work on a soft rag. A bad scratch or a mistake is hard to overcome at this stage. Remove all excess glue now, or at least mark around a glue spot for removal later. If the glue is not removed, it will make a light or white spot in the finish.

Cut the frets to length, fasten them in the fret board, file and putty the holes, and finish the fret board now (*Plates 186, 187*).

Place the completed fret board on the top at the proper place and cut the top to the exact length of the fret board (*Plate 188*). Glue the peg head and peg end on the underside of the top (*Plates 189–191*). Apply glue

PLATE 193

PLATE 194

PLATE 195

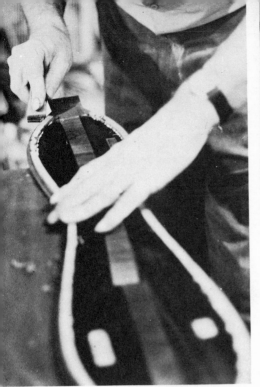

PLATE 196

PLATE 197

PLATE 198

PLATE 199

PLATE 200

PLATE 201

PLATE 202

PLATE 203

PLATE 204

PLATE 205

PLATE 206

to the fret board (*Plate 192*), and clamp it on the top (*Plate 193*). Use small brads (½×20 brads) to fasten the top and fret board and allow the glue to set. Any good wood glue will do if you give it enough time for curing, and remove any excess glue carefully.

Place the top on the inside of the back and mark the position where the peg head and peg end are to be attached. On the inside of the top and bottom, draw a mark from end to end about ³⁄₁₆″ in from the sides (*Plate 194*). Make four glue strips about ⅜″ square with closely spaced saw notches cut in one side (*Plate 195*). Glue these flexible strips on the inside of the marks of the top and bottom (*Plates 196–199*). The sides are glued to them later.

Glue the top and bottom together and let the glue set (*Plate 200*). Cut the sides to the proper length and width, and pre-bend them by holding the back side to a source of heat and bending by hand (*Plates 201–202*). Use just a little heat, as too much will make the side brittle.

Glue the sides in place (*Plates 203, 204*).

Trim, sand, and stain if needed (*Plate 205*). Take a lot of time and get everything just right now. There are a number of ways to do the finish, depending on the amount of gloss you desire.

Lacquer, varnish, urethane, or shellac, with sanding and steel wool rubbing between coats is good. You can use only wax, or some of the penetrating oil finishes will give a flat finish. When I build in volume, I spray on the lacquer and then wax by hand.

A standard violin peg hole taper or reamer is used to taper the holes in the peg head. This tool can be found in some music stores or at a musical instrument repair shop. You can use large violin or viola pegs or make your own of rosewood or other hardwood.

Make the string nut and bridge, glue it in place, and bore the holes for the strings in the peg end and pegs.

For the first three strings (nearest you), use an E or first guitar string, ball end. For the fourth string, use a G or third guitar string, ball end. This is a wound string and is the bass string of the dulcimer. If you use banjo strings, use two first strings, one third string, and one fourth string, which is the bass.

Tune the first and second strings to G, below Middle C, on a piano. Tune the third string to Middle C, and tune the fourth string to C, one octave below Middle C, on a piano. This is a major tuning. Pick the melody by noting the first string only. Strum the other three strings; they are the drone strings and make the same tone all the time.

Making a dulcimer is not an easy job. You will have to make some of your tools and clamps. You will also have to figure out for yourself how to do

On this page, Robert Mize has been generous enough to share with us the crucial patterns for the dulcimer he makes. They are reproduced here actual size - they have not been reduced at all. Cut apart the three pieces of the pattern, and join them at the dotted lines (put line "A" against line "A", line "B" against line "B"). Mark off the frets exactly as they are here, or the dulcimer will not note properly. The fret spacing is the only crucial part of the instrument. Design the rest to suit yourself...

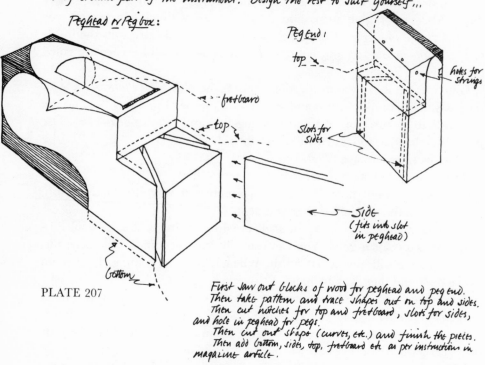

PLATE 207

Pegheads or Pegbox:

Peg End

top

holes for strings

fretboard

top

Slots for sides

side (fits into slot in peghead)

Bottom

First saw out blocks of wood for peghead and peg end. Then take pattern and trace shapes out on top and sides. Then cut notches for top and fretboard, slots for sides, and hole in peghead for pegs. Then cut out shape (curves, etc.) and finish the pieces. Then add bottom, sides, top, fretboard etc as per instructions in magazine article.

PLATES 207–209 illustrate the plans for a Robert Mize dulcimer which appeared actual size in an insert in *Foxfire* magazine. Space has forced us to reduce this insert, but a copy of the original may be ordered from *Foxfire* for $1.

certain steps. Take plenty of time and think out each step as you go along. Do not worry about getting all the dimensions the same as those I have given here; the only thing that must be exact is the finger or fret board. Make the rest to suit yourself.

ROBERT MIZE

Photographs by Warren Gaskill.

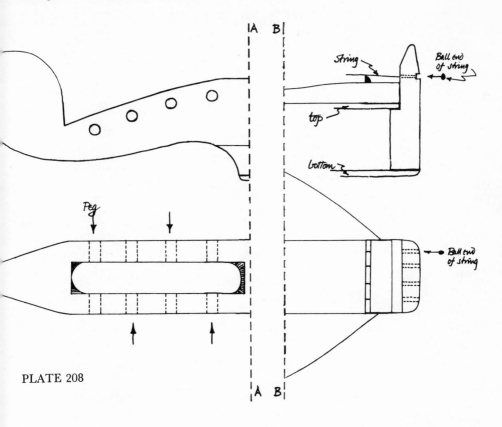

PLATE 208

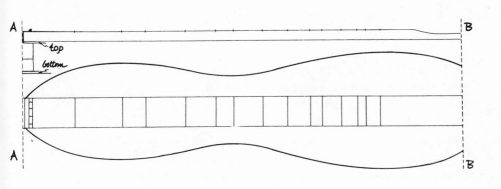

PLATE 209

PURPLE MARTIN GOURDS

People in years back put up martin houses to entice the martins to stay on their place during the summer to chase off chicken hawks. Bryant McClure told us: "My mother had purple martins long ago and they were not for catching insects, but to keep the hawks away from the chickens. They'll fight them. They'll fight a crow. If a hawk comes around, these purple martins will gang up on him. They'll chase him out of the country."

The primary reason people erect purple martin gourds or apartments now is to keep flying insects away from their gardens and from around the house. People who have them say they can sit outside late in the evening in the summer and not be bothered by mosquitoes or gnats.

Lester Davis says, "I guess the martins help me a lot because they eat all the bugs and insects. Martins will cover a large area eating insects, mostly mosquitoes. They'll be up in the elements all day long until nearly sundown. You can see them dive like a jet airplane. A lot of people like martins, especially around ponds."

To prepare a gourd for a martin house, a large round gourd with a short neck should be used. A round hole, two inches in diameter, should be made in the side of the gourd. Then small holes should be drilled in the bottom so that rain water will drain out. Drill two small holes through the neck of the gourd for a wire to be run through to hang the gourd by.

Mr. McClure told us how he got started with his martin houses. "When I decided I wanted to get purple martins, I bought an expensive setup— apartments, aluminum pole, and all that. I guess for two years I didn't get a martin. Two came and sat on the little deck, but flew away and never came back. I asked Bob Hooper what went wrong, and he said, 'You've got to have gourds.' Gourds must be their natural houses. I got gourds. I sent to Georgia and paid seventy-five cents apiece for them. I put them up and the next year I got martins.

Articles needed:
One galvanized pipe - 20-21 feet long; one and one-half to
two inch diameter
One galvanized pipe - 3-4 feet long; two to two and one-half
inch diameter
Two crossarms - 2x4; seven to eight feet long.
Ten to twenty gourds
Bag of cement

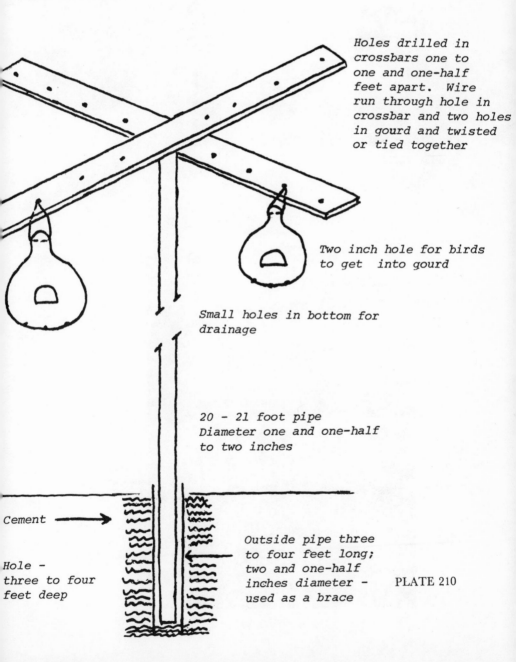

Holes drilled in
crossbars one to
one and one-half
feet apart. Wire
run through hole in
crossbar and two holes
in gourd and twisted
or tied together

Two inch hole for birds
to get into gourd

Small holes in bottom for
drainage

20 - 21 foot pipe
Diameter one and one-half
to two inches

Cement ———→

Hole -
three to four
feet deep

Outside pipe three
to four feet long;
two and one-half
inches diameter -   PLATE 210
used as a brace

PLATE 211   PLATE 212

PLATE 213

PLATE 214

Mr. Davis told us that he raised his own gourds. Ask for seeds for martin gourds. [NOTE: We have recently received word that seed companies like George W. Park Seed Company, Inc., and Hastings Seed Company sell not only dipper gourd seed, but also a special variety ideal for martin houses.] "I don't have any trouble. I like to plant my gourds in fairly rich soil where they'll grow good. I want to get a good growth. I plant my rows about twelve feet apart and my hills in the rows about twelve feet apart. I'll take my shovel and dig a square about three or four feet out, fill it with fertilizer and rake it nice and smooth. I plant my seed in that in early spring." Mr. Hooper suggested a mesh fence for the vines to grow up on, so that the gourds could hang down. This helps them to grow straight. Don't pick the gourds off the vines. Let the vines die, and after the first frost, turn the gourds over so that they will dry out on both sides. Pull them off the vines after they are completely dry and hard—about December or January. Then they are ready for holes to be drilled in them and the seeds cleaned out of the inside of the gourds. Both these men save their seeds from year to year. Then they select the year's crop of short-necked, big, round gourds. Gourds may be reused from year to year, but as they get battered, replacements are necessary.

"In preparing houses for the martins, you should always clean the gourds out and put sulfur in them to keep down mites . . . about a teaspoonful to each gourd. Mites get in the feathers of the martins."

Put the gourds on a pipe or pole, about twenty feet high. The gourds are put up in February and taken down to be cleaned and stored after the martins leave in late July or August. Nylon cord is recommended by Bob Hooper to tie the gourds to the crossbars on the pole [see *Plate 210*], as wire breaks easily when the gourds are blown by the wind. The martin houses must be erected out in a field or clear area in the yard, away from trees and buildings. The martins don't want to be anywhere that a cat or snake could get to their nests. Martins won't even light in a tree. They do not present the usual problem of birds near the house because they carry their droppings away in little capsules.

Mr. Hooper told us many interesting things about the martins. They have several poles with gourds in their back yard and sit out in the evenings watching the martins fly in and put their babies to bed after feeding them. They wake the Hoopers in the mornings with their chatter, and the Hooper family feels as though some of their children have left home when they depart in August. We asked if they thought the same ones ever came back, and they said that they really do think so. They seem to know their way around so well. Mrs. Hooper said that when she hangs clothes on the line, they perch on the electric wires and chatter. When she goes in, they fly off until she or some other member of the family come back out in the yard. They they come back to visit again.

About the only time they light on the ground is when they are building their nests and then only to pick up leaves and twigs. They like to line their nests with green leaves to keep the nest cool. They will come down for crushed eggshells if you put them out on the ground in the open. That is about the only thing you can feed them off the ground. They do most of their feeding in the air, low to the ground in the mornings and climbing higher all day long, then back near the ground in the evenings.

The martins send out scouts in early March. They can be seen around for two or three days. Then they leave and after several weeks, the scouts come back with others. By the twenty-fifth of March,' about ten pairs will be around a set of gourds. Each pair usually likes to occupy two gourds— one for the parents and one for the young. They stay only long enough for their young to hatch and be able to fly. It takes about three weeks for them to hatch, and they start building the nests about the first of May.

The purple martin is about the size of a dove in the air. If the sun shines just right on the male, he is purple. Mr. McClure says that one morning you wake up and realize the martins are gone. It's such a lonely feeling.

There is no way to keep them here after late July. They stay just long enough to raise their young; then they go back to South America until the next spring.

BARBARA TAYLOR, ANNETTE REEMS

Photos by Tom Carlton.

DIPPER GOURDS

In the past, many people found that the gourd could be used in different and useful ways. They used gourds to make holders for women's sewing notions, to store lye soap after it was made, and as small types of bowls or dishes for decoration or to put odds and ends in. One of the best uses of the gourd was as a dipper at the well or in the house for drinking purposes.

The scientific name for a dipper gourd is Cucuribita foetidissima (perennis) and a couple of its common names are calabash and siphon gourd.

Not very long ago Suzy set up an interview with Lawton Brooks who grows his own gourds and had said he would cut us out a dipper gourd when we came. I was really glad I was involved with what went on that afternoon; the main reason being that it was my first visit to Florence and Lawton's, and I just enjoyed spending that part of the day with them. When Suzy and I arrived there, we talked awhile as Suzy has known them for a long time. Then we discussed the process of growing gourds. We went on out on the front porch while Lawton talked and made the gourd into a dipper. In an hour or so, we ended up with the gourd finished and ready to be used for drinking.

ROY DICKERSON

LAWTON: Gourds're a thing that has to be planted early, but if frost touches them, it'll kill'em. You've got to get a gourd planted early. Now the way I get mine, and the best way I think to do this is to plant'em the last of March in pots. And then they come up in them pots; well, when they come up, they'll just grow up a long stem in the shade and two little ol' leaves will grow up about [six inches] high. But just let'em alone and then you take them out there and you can transplant them. You can set'em out

PLATE 215 Lawton Brooks offered to show us how to make a dipper out of a gourd.

PLATE 216 The gourds themselves ripening on a fence in Happy Dowdle's back yard.

PLATE 217 Lawton first chooses where the hole is to be cut, and then rings the spot with a pencil line.

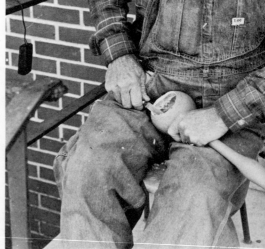

PLATE 219 Slowly he trims down to the line itself.

PLATE 218 Starting in the center of the penciled circle, he begins to cut through the gourd's shell with his pocketknife.

PLATE 220   Next he scrapes out the spongy
inside and the seeds, and saves the seeds to
plant next spring.

PLATE 221   Then he trims up the edge . . .

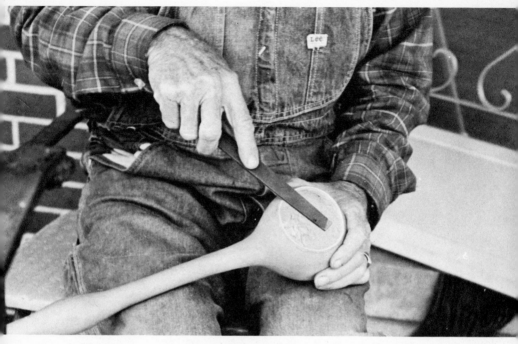

PLATE 222   . . . files it smooth . . .

PLATE 223   . . . and goes to the sink to try
it out.

wherever you want to, when you think there ain't going to be any more danger of frost. Now down at [Suzy's] place, you've got a perfect place 'cause you're nearly at the frost line. It wouldn't hit that way like here in these low places, 'cause you're just about above the frost line. And if you get down there, you can grow'em; you've just got to grow some next year. I'm gonna pot a bunch of'em for you. Pick you a good place and I'll come help you put up your wires; I'll get your wire. You just furnish the place, and me and you'll grow us a bunch of gourds.

They like a pretty good soil. They like a little clay in their soil but they need pretty good soil to grow. Manure's good [for fertilizer]; just regular ol' stable stuff.

They have to have support to [grow specifically into a dipper gourd]. If they lay on the ground, they're liable to grow in just any direction. [A fence for support] wouldn't have to be too high if you just keep the vine up on the fence. You know how they took to my clothesline up here—they'll just go from one to another, and they'll get around. [The gourds] just tie themselves to a fence or anything they can climb. Wherever the vine touches, it attaches itself. Then it goes a little further and ties itself again. You'll have to break them loose, because they've done tied themselves—the wind won't blow'em down.

Sometimes a vine will blight, but not bad enough to hurt. I've never had any insects bother me. If them ol' gourds stay there and they mash down into the ground, the seeds will come up in another year volunteer. They'll mix if you get'em too close to the cucumbers—it'll be so bitter you can't eat'em. Now I tried that out. I had my gourds on the lower part of my fence. And my cucumbers were way up here, but the vine runs down that way, y'know, and they didn't go all the way to the gourds. Anyway, we couldn't use them cucumbers; they was the most bitter things I ever ate. They was the prettiest cucumbers, but we couldn't eat'em. They were so bitter we just let them lay there. It didn't bother the gourds. It'll make the cucumbers bitter-like; cross pollination is why it happened. I don't know about squash; I never tried them.

You ought not to plant [the gourds] any closer than six foot apart. That gives them a chance to go one way and the other, or cross over each other. [Just plant them] along the edge of the fence; they'll take a runner and go by and hit something, anything, and climb it. Now this man that raised them in Atlanta gave me this gourd here. He planted one by his woodshed and out in a field he laid him a pole in the fork of the apple tree, and that thing went right on up the apple tree and crossed over to the other one and filled'em both up. They was hanging that close together. By gosh, I bet my pick-up [truck] could of been filled up twice. That's the prettiest sight I ever seen in my life from that vine. That goes to show you there would have been about a thousand if it all would have been counted. So you can't tell how many you'll have; it's according to how they get started, and how they turn out, and the season they get planted.

It takes them a long while to mature and get ready for the frost; frost keeps'em from rotting. Just let them hang till it frosts on them, or two or three good frosts. That hardens their shell better. Now [that man in Atlanta] hadn't picked his [gourds] till 'long in the winter and them apple trees was hanging full.

Leave about three inches shank [when you pick them]; break it off near the vine and leave the rest on the gourd. When you pick'em, you should set'em in a dry, cool place, in the air. Let them settle one or two months, and the seeds get hard and everything. They should be dry enough to rattle. When he gets dried out good and hard, then you can make your dippers. They're green growing, but turn kind of yellow when mature.

There's a type gourd they call a martin gourd. This is for the martin bird. They've got another great big one they call a half-bushel gourd. They grow more like a pumpkin. The old folks used to use'em around the house to put something in them for a waste basket or a sewing basket. They'd use the big gourd for it. Just cut the top off and clean'em out. It makes a good one; they'd last from now on. Just like a dipper would last from now on. Old people, when they made their lye soap, they'd use them to make their soap in and store it. And they've got a blamed gourd they make a dish out of. It grows kinda like a dish and it's got a ring around it. You cut out the ring and that ring makes a lid.

FLORENCE AND LAWTON BROOKS

Here I was, a VISTA volunteer, a Yankee from Connecticut in a strange place, very uncertain as to whether or not I wanted to stay. Who should I find but Florence and Lawton Brooks. They immediately adopted me, worried about me, fed me lots of collard greens and pound cake, and took me fishing. They revealed the mysteries of sauerkraut, cured hams and bee gums, introduced me to their friends, made me feel more at ease and less of a stranger. When I married, they adopted my husband, even though they can never remember how to pronounce his last name. And when I made my first garden—a pitiful one—they acted like it was one of the best.

Florence and Lawton greeted me with open arms, and opened up their world to me. I love that world, treasure it, almost wish I had never known another, and am concerned for its delicate existence. A lot has changed for me since I first came here, but Florence and Lawton have remained constant.

Now I'd like to share them with you.

SUZANNE ANGIER

"Always somethin' around to entertain ya', by gosh, if you's on the outside."

FLORENCE: Y'never get lonesome livin' out in th'country. I could always look out th'window and see th'mountains, maybe a deer, the cattle a'walkin' around.

PLATE 224   Lawton with Cathy D'Agostino and Cathy Campbell.

LAWTON: Cattle and deer a'walkin' around, birds a'hollerin', foxes a'barkin'. You never get lonesome up there. I used to live up Coleman River. I really enjoyed it too. I enjoyed these mountains more than anything in the world. I enjoyed to see the wild game and stuff that I could see, just set up on my porch, an' I'd always nearly go out there anytime, set down awhile, an' I'd see some kind of wild game walkin' around; a turkey here, groundhog. Florence and I enjoyed it fine till she commenced havin' asthma. I'd like to be back in the woods. Pretty water, good clean country, woods t'be in. I don't like this inside business. I'd rather be out anytime. That's the reason I always took farmin'. I never did want no inside job. I'd rather be out in the country. Clears m'thinkin' or somethin'r'nother. There you can see somethin' a'goin' on all the time outside. They's always somethin' a'goin' on all the time outside. You never get in a place where you don't hear nothin'. When did y'ever sit down an' ain't heard a thing in the world? Always somethin' around to entertain ya', by gosh, if you's on the outside. Y'never get lonesome out there.

FLORENCE: I like to hear cowbells ring at night. People used to keep bells on their cows, y'know. You get out an' you could hear all sounds of them. Some of them'ud be little, some of'em 'ud be coarse, some of'em 'ud be kind of music-like. You could hear the little ol' bells go "ding, ding," an' then you could hear a big ol' coarse one—hear all kinds. They go, "ding, ding, ding, ding," just like someone's heart a'beatin', just as reg'lar, all th'time.

"There wouldn't have been any people left on Nantahala."

FLORENCE: We used t'have picnics for ever'body way on up th'river, an' th'only way we had of going was on that train. They'd have big old flat cars, and benches made on'em for th'people t'sit on, an' we went up there one day to a picnic, an' started back, an' th'brakeman an' th'engineer an' ever'body got drunk. An' you talk about comin' back down that track, well it was th'awfulest thing in th'world. 'Fraid it was gonna wreck an' kill everyone of us. A wonder it hadn't. It was several miles—twelve, fifteen, maybe twenty. A long ways up there. Somebody ought to have whipped them trainmen when we got it stopped. It would have killed a pile. Well, everybody over there would have been killed. There wouldn't have been any people left on Nantahala, 'cause ever'body went. We didn't leave nobody at home.

PLATE 225

PLATE 226

PLATE 227

LAWTON: We had old wooden wheel wagons—saw a big old black gum tree down, black gum won't bust—an' then we'd saw that wheel about [four inches] thick. Take a crosscut saw an' throw it down to it. All right, then we'd take us a big old auger an' bore us a big hole through that, an' there was our wheels. Then we run us a axle through there, an' right behind these (front wheels) we tied us a rope onto both ends of th'axle t'guide it. We built us a frame, then we'd put us a piece across here to nest our feet on, then make us a seat back here—you just set there an' guided it. An' you couldn't wear them wheels out—they just wore an' wore an' wore an' wore. Sometimes th'wagon was s'heavy it'd take two or three of us to get it to th'top of th'hill. But, boy, you talk about going down—we'd all git on an' by God, we'd take a good ride. *Right* down the hill we'd go.

FLORENCE: And we walked laurel bushes. They was a laurel thicket close to our house that you could walk around an' around an' around all day an' not touch th'ground just like a squirrel. Just hold to the branches an' walk from one branch to another. An' down under there it was s'pretty an' clean; just laurel leaves where they'd fallen down.

We'd make our own guns for Christmas; get iron pipes an' drive 'em in logs, put gunpowder down in there, put a piece of rag down in there, y'know, for a fuse, put a little kerosene oil on that, an' put that on fire, so while that was burnin' y'had time t'get out of th'way. One time my brother made one too big an' it hit th'edge of th'porch an' tore th'edge of th'porch

PLATE 228

off. My brother had taken a can of powder (which he shouldn't have done) down on th'railroad track where they'd been a'blastin' rock. It didn't shoot nothin' out of th'pipe, that ol' pipe just blew up—golly, when that powder went off, the whole thing—why, it just split that ol' log all to pieces. If it had went up on top of th'house, that old iron pipe would have come down through th'top of th'house. Boy, Dad stopped our gun shootin' right there.

An' then they'd get old rags an' roll them—make great big balls out of them, put kerosene oil on that an' put gloves on an' get out an' throw'em from one t'th'other, an' catch'em an' throw'em back. An' them afire!

LAWTON: We'd play blindfold and please an' displease—it'uz a little ol' thing. A gang of us'ud be sittin' around and one [of us] would be up all th'time. Well, if I was th'one that'uz up, I'd ask you if you were pleased or displeased. If you'd say you're pleased, I asked what pleased y'. An' you could say, "A'settin' with so an'so I'm pleased." If you're displeased, I'd say, "What will it take t'please you?" Well now you might say you'd be pleased if so an'so would get up an' go over an' set with a certain person, or for that person to get up an' set with another. Whatever you put on'em they had t'do. If they didn't do that, why they'd black that person's face. If y'played it, y'had t'play it out, but it just goes on around like that. Sometimes we'd make a person get out an' walk plumb around th'house in th'coldest time in the weather.

FLORENCE: We'd play fox an' dog. Get an old Sears and Roebuck catalog, tear it to pieces, go off a'strewing it through th'woods. We'd let him get started about thirty minutes an' then a whole bunch of'em trail that, y'know. He'd be th'fox, y'know, an' a whole bunch of us'ud be th'dogs. Sometimes he'd take us five or ten miles over them mountains, in those rabbit places, briar patches.

But then when th'fun started was when we had a big snow, an' we had a lot of'em. We'd get out right after it quit snowin' an' make our tracks with a long, big ladder. We'd go way up in th'holler an' we'd make our tracks down through there, an' it'd get packed down. Well, we'd get up there an' you talk about flyin' down through there, now we did. Four or five of us on th'ladder, Mommy right up there with us. I guess it was five or six steps, an' my older brother was a brakesman. He was in front an' had a big old stick t'put under one of the runners. Well, he got down there an' jumped th'track, started through a briar patch an' ever' one of us rolled off in th'snow but him, an' he just got scratched all up.

LAWTON: [Buford Long] had a bow an' arrow, an' I had one. Well, we was out a'killin' birds an' I took me an umbrella stave an' I cut off a

piece about [five inches] long, an' I filed it sharp an' drove it into this
sourwood arrow I'd made, an' I fixed him one like mine. Well, these birds
lit up in this nut tree. I said, "Now wait a minute till I get m'arrow ready."
Well he just hauled off an' shot right up through there an' scared'em all out.
That made me mad an' when he did I jus' turned around an' shot'im
right there in th'jaw. It went under his jaw there an' went between his
teeth an' stuck in his tongue—enough to make his tongue bleed. It'uz lucky
it hit'im there. It might a'killed th'poor ol' boy. God, he just fell an' commenced hollerin' an' it'uz as close to his house as from here to that door
yonder, an' his mammy, she come to th'door—she was a'sweepin' th'house
—an' here she come with th'broom. Said, "What's the matter?"

Buford said, "Lawton shot me!"

God a'mighty, she chased me to that river—I didn't have time to tell her
th'details or nothin'. I took off, her after me with that broom. I jumped
that creek [but] she couldn't cross th'creek, an' I went on home. I felt bad
about it. I hated it, but me an' him played together right on after that. Hit
swelled up a bit—his jaw did—but not much. They give me a whippin' at
home. Buford's mother went an' told them about it, an' they gave me a
whippin'.

FLORENCE: Can you remember th'first picture show you ever went to,
Lawton?

LAWTON: Yeah, th'first one I ever remember was at Hayesville. They
showed it on a wall—no sound. Just people runnin' around here an' there.
An' I thought it was somethin' awful seein' them act a fool like they was.
I don't remember what it was about. They was no sound, an' they just
showed'em runnin' around. I'll never forget that.

FLORENCE: First one I ever saw was in th'barn loft. It was before
we were married—great long barn they put th'screen up back there, an'
we all sit at th'other end. They wasn't many people over there. That was
th'best place we had t'do it except for th'school house, an' th'teacher
wouldn't let'em go down there. She thought it was silly. I can't remember
what it was, but they was T-model Fords a'racin', goin' around fast—
couldn't hear a thing—just see'em.

"I seen that thing; I went wild about it."

LAWTON: This ol' boy, he had this car, an' they wasn't many of them
around in th'country. Cars was scarce. He had this thing, made just for

two t'ride in. They wasn't no fenders over th'wheels, y'know. Just a body an' a seat here, an' the wheels out there by themselves. I seen that thing; I went wild about it. An' I wanted it. I kept on my daddy, an' he'd always give in an' buy me what I wanted. An' I kept on at him, an' he said, "Now, son, if I get you that thing, th'first thing you'll do with it is get killed with it. I don't want t'get you nothin' you'll get hurt with." An' I kept on. Well, one day he told me, he said, "Well, son, if you go out to that man about th' car, I'll pay for it."

So I peeled out across th'mountain, went over to his house, an' he told me what he wanted for it. I come back an' told m'daddy, an' he wrote me a check, an' told me t'take it to him. I went back then an' he brought me back in th'car. Well, we had a big ol' shed at the farm where I was t'keep th'car. Well, the drip off th'shed roof made an ol'rut there. I'd get out there. The car had one of those little old gas levers. [I'd] pull th'gas lever down t'go, an' I'd ease up to that rut, an' I wasn't givin' it enough gas an' it'd stall. An' I'd have t'get out an' crank again. I fooled with it about a hour, an' finally I got mad an' I said, "I'll get y't'go in this time— I'll keep y'a'goin'." So I never thought about when I took my foot off th'clutch, it'd jump in high gear. When y'have your foot on th'clutch, it's in low gear, an' when y'take it off it jumps into high gear. So I got back out there up to th'rut an' it'uz about t'stop again, an' I just jerked th'gas lever plumb down. An' that thing just jumped over th'rut an' into th'shed we went, an' I'd forgot an' jerked m'foot off th'clutch, an' it hit high gear an' hit th'back end of th'wall, an' it just took all of it down.

Then it took off through th'cane patch an' I got scared, an' I gave it a cut [with the steering wheel] an' when I did, it turned up on its side and I went off on m'hands and knees into th'cane patch. It tore up a whole lot of his cane. Made Daddy mad! He come in, he says, "Son, I want you t'get shed of that devilish thing, it's gonna' kill y'. I told you it would. I want you to sell that thing."

That was right after I got it. So had t'go sell th'old car then. I kept it around there awhile, but I never did drive the blasted thing after that.

"Sleet'r'snow, we had t'go."

FLORENCE: Sleet'r'snow, we had t'go. There wasn't many people there, an' th'school was just a two-teacher school, with small school rooms, an' just taught through the eighth grade. Now we didn't even have no home-work in school—while th'teachers were doin' other classes, why we'd have th'time to do our studying an' get our lessons done. Didn't have no such thing as report cards. We started in th'fall an' went till up in th'spring.

LAWTON: There wasn't no such thing as a bus—we had t'walk. I walked four miles each way. That's eight miles an' y'had t'take your dinner with y'—carry it in a poke.

I never did like school. I paid the devil for not likin' it. I went wrong there. Th'teachers, they was rough, some of'em. Why, one 'bout knocked my ears off—the way they'd hit y'—boy, that hurt! She'd come by if we wasn't a'doin right, if we wasn't lookin' at a book'r'somethin'. She'd go down one aisle, maybe you wouldn't see her go down there, an' she'd walk around an' see what you was doin'. Well, she'd come around behind me an' I wouldn't know it. An' she'd hit me up side the head with a ruler—it felt like somebody broke it, y'know.

I remember one teacher who was a real nut—I don't know where she was from—not from our country. She'uz rough. She'd make us stand up on one foot up there in front of all of'em—on th'stage, y'know, an' you had t'stand there. She wouldn't let you put your other foot to the floor. An' then she'd make a ring on th'wall, an' you'd have t'stand with your nose in that ring so long. She'd do that t'punish us . . . for talking, fightin', one thing an' another. I always liked t'talk an' have fun, an' ever' dadblamed time I'd cut up, I'd get a whippin'. They'uz some girls sat at the desk right in front of me, an' I'uz always aggravating them, an' they'd tell th'teacher, an' she'd make me stand up on one leg with m'nose in a circle on the wall, an' she'd whip me sometimes, an' she'd try t'beat m'ears off with a pencil.

FLORENCE: At school, we had a man teacher—he was my first teacher, an' I liked him. Then another man came. Th'first one died. An' this other man come t'teach—that'uz th'last year I went. I'uz supposed t'have went through th'eighth grade that year, an' after we like t'run over that teacher, I'uz afraid t'go back so I stayed at home. That's th'time we stole th'lever car. We'uz a'ridin' down th'track right in front of the schoolhouse an' like t'killed th'teacher. He tried t'stop us an' got in th'middle of the track an' waved his arms, figured we'd stop. But we fooled him, boy, we just barely missed him. I was sittin' where y'put th'brakes on, an' all th'kids a'sayin', "Florence, don't stop. Don't stop." We went through there pushin' those handlebars up an' down, up an' down, as fast as we could. We nearly ran over that teacher. He shouldn't a'got in th'middle of th'tracks if he didn't want to be run over. Now let me tell you, if we'd a'hit him, we would have jumped th'track, gone into th'river, an' killed him an' us, too. But just thought, "You crazy thing, you, standin' there." But he finally got out of the way.

An' I never went back to school after that! The other kids went back an' they got a whippin'—they ought'a got me out an' give me one. I'uz chicken. I should'a gone right back with'em an' a'took my whippin' with th'crowd. I see that now. Poor ol' Dad. I think he'd of died, but he never did know that. If he'd a'knowed, I'd a'got a whippin'. You know, we were mean in a way—we took ever'thing as it come. We didn't mean t'do no meanness, we was just havin' fun. So I quit an' got married an' got educated anyways!

"Oh, hoeing corn. How I hated that th'worst of anything."

LAWTON: Back when we'uz comin' up as kids, th'kids didn't do like they do nowdays. We had certain times that we'd play an' certain times we didn't. If we worked good all week and everything, why we'd get a hour off on Saturday evening. We'd get out an' have a big time durin' that hour; seemed like it wasn't over five minutes till that hour was up. It was something t'look forward to. Then on Sunday evenings we got t'play till time t'do th'milkin', feedin', like that. We'd play till as late as we could, then we'd go home an' you'd never seen such workin' in your life t'get th'work done up 'fore dark. If you didn't do it but one time, they wouldn't let us have no play time for a week'r'two off Saturday and Sunday evenings. An' days that you wouldn't get to play at all, you'd just have t'sit around there an' watch th'other kids play. Well, I'd a'ruther took a whippin' an' a'got out there an' played any time. But they wouldn't do that—they knowed what hurt us worse than a whippin'.

I'm honest. I do believe that children growed up happier then. I'll tell you the reason why. What kids did get, they enjoyed it. They didn't [usually] get nothin'. But if they got any little ol' thing, they really enjoyed it. Now they get so much they don't enjoy nothin'. You can't get'em enough for Christmas an' things like that. We didn't get anything. If I'd a'got a tricycle I wouldn't a'swapped it then for the best Cadillac that ever drove up here today, but I didn't get it.

My habit was huntin' an' trainin' an' foolin' with dogs. I thought more of my dogs than anything else. I got more kick out a'my dogs than anything. An' huntin'—rabbit huntin'—me an' my dogs got a kick out a'that. That's what we done when I could get off enough. But most of the time when I went, it'd have to be a'rainin'. Now if it'd been raining all day I could go. If it wasn't raining, we had somethin' to do. We didn't just go out and say, "Be back directly," or "I'm gone." We went when they said we could go. We didn't go till they did. An' they'd give us so long to stay then.

Oh, hoeing corn. How I hated that th'worst of anything. Right out in that hot sun one row at a time an' you get in a big ol' field an' just go along as slow as you have to go a'hoein'. You couldn't build no time. Hoe all day and you wouldn't get as far as from here to there. All day and then just think about the days and days y'had t'go to get to that upper end of that field. An' it had to be done. Ever' stalk of it had to be hoed an' cleaned up around. I despised that worse than anything out in that hot sun. Oh, yes, they's agreeable with us, good to us. But ever'body just believed in kids working ever' day. They didn't believe in no playin' going on. Yes, sir, they whipped us if we didn't do what they said do. We got out an' had to work a little if they had to go off'r'do anything like that. When they come in, everything—milkin', feedin', an' ever'thing—had to be done. Wood carried in an' ever'thing. See, they burnt wood an' it had t'be piled on that porch'r'wherever it was—the stovewood box. The stovewood had t'be in that box. If it wasn't, boy, we got tanned. We all had a job apiece to do.

FLORENCE: Gosh, we did work. I never did work much outside, I usually done th'housework while ever'one else worked outside. Kept me pretty busy in th'house. I done th'cookin' an' house-cleanin' ever since I was about eleven or twelve. I'd tell Mommy to let me go an' her stay in th'house. She'd say, "No, you're like a chicken out there scratchin'. You'll do more in th'house." There was five children, an' Mommy and Daddy— a pretty good bunch.

LAWTON: The best advice my parents give me I didn't follow all up like I should. It'uz goin' to Sunday School and t'church, an' stayin' away from bad crowds, 'specially when people're drunk. They didn't want me about people like that a'tall. An' that was good advice. I didn't obey it all the way—I should. They didn't tell me nothin' wrong. If I'd a'done what they said, I'd a been a lot better off.

"When we moved out we didn't have a durn thing t'move."

LAWTON: I was twenty-three, an' Florence was nearly sixteen when we got married. I had t'tell a lie an' get two more fellows t'tell a lie.

FLORENCE: I was just a few days lackin' of being sixteen.

LAWTON: I took two boys with me, had t'have witnesses with me, t'get m'license. Had t'go t'Hiawassee an' get it. I lived in North Carolina, but had t'get m'license in Georgia, an' went to Georgia t'get married. See, in North Carolina—they're tight on y'in North Carolina—had t'go through a whole lot of this ol' red tape up there, an' in Georgia you didn't have t'do nothin' only get with it. I got these old boys t'go w'me. My first cousin, he was a'sellin' licenses up there, clerk of th'court'r'something, so he knowed me an' he says, "Now, Lawton, I don't believe [Florence is eighteen]." He just told me what he thought.

I says, "Well, I do. She's eighteen years old."

An' these two ol' boys with me said, "Yeah, yeah." One of'em said, "Well, I've knowed her ever since she's a baby. She's eighteen years old." An' they never even seen her. So we fooled around, I finally paid m'license. Eighteen was the age, but I got m'license just the same.

Well, ever'body wanted to see us married. I knowed ever'body, y'know, an' ever'body knowed me. An' they always ganged around with me all th'time. I told'em I'uz goin' to th'Georgia-North Carolina line [at Hiawassee] to get married. Just across th'line—we had to be in Georgia t'do it. So they thought I was goin' up to ol' man Pendle's. He lived just across th'line up here at th'main highway. So ever'body thought that was th'place. They said they had people strung up here, horses, wagons, buggies, said they'd never seen th'like just all up an' down th'road, waitin' till we come. But we went th'old dirt road an' went up t'th'other Georgia line, an' got in th'preacher's house right over the line, an' he married us an' we'uz out. We'd been back an' forth in no time, an' they spent all day waitin' over there.

We had a big dance the night before, an' they'd all come t'th'dance at th'house. Now, boy, you talk about people—they couldn't get in th'house —on th'porch, th'yard was full, they was ever'where. You've never seen as many people show up as we had there. But we had a time!

Lived there at Hayesville [when first married]. Lived with m'daddy at the home place. But we didn't stay there long—I wanted t'see how it would be t'get out by ourselves. We rented us a house for a dollar and a half a month, an' I could work it out with him. I had t'work three days f'that dollar an' a half. When we moved out we didn't have a durn thing t'move. Everything was a'moved out when we moved ourselves—they wasn't no trouble a'movin' then.

We had nothin'. Nothin' but a bed.

FLORENCE: We had a big bed an' a little bed. Your mother left us a big bed, an' your daddy gave us a little bed. An' I had some sheets an' pillowcases that I'd saved up. An' we had a old table that th'leg had been burned off an' your daddy fixed it for us. We carried our water, washed in a four-pound lard bucket.

LAWTON: An' didn't have a thing t'cook with—cooked on th'fireplace.

FLORENCE: An' had a lard bucket for a washpan. Couldn't buy a washpan. That's how hard times was.

LAWTON: I was farmin'—I worked on th'farms around there for people. You could get a job, but they didn't have no money t'pay. Now they could pay you in meat'r'anything you could use, but they didn't have no money t'turn loose. No farmer did.

FLORENCE: We worked t'get tops of fodder t'swap for a cookstove. Well, we had some chickens Mother and Daddy had give us, an' we raised some more chickens, an' whenever they got big enough t'sell we got us a stove pipe.

LAWTON: An' it was just ten cents a joint, an' we couldn't get thirty cents, by golly.

FLORENCE: But did we have fun! Y'know, we enjoyed it a whole lot better than we do now.

LAWTON: We had more fun. We cut tops and pulled fodder t'get th' stove, then raised fodder t'get the pipes.
    Back then people didn't raise hay like they do now. They didn't have no machinery t'cut and bale hay. Some of'em may have had a little meadow they'd cut b'hand an' rake it up an' stack it up. But most people took th'fodder and tops from their corn, an' they'd stack it up an' use that for feed through th'winter.

FLORENCE: Lawton, tell'em how much wood you said it took t'cook a pan of biscuits with that stove.

LAWTON: Well, I'uz a'devilin'em about m'stove, just a little bitty stove an' a little ol' door opened on each side of it. It'uz th' least little ol' stove. I told'em I could take two corn cobs an' a chip an' have a good fire. Florence made up th'biscuits over there, an' I sat on this side, an' she'd just pass'em through th'stove, an' I'd set'em on th'table on the other side. As they come through they's already done. I had th'most fun out of that stove. I'uz studying about that thing th'other day—I'd give a hundred

PLATE 229

dollars for that thing if I could find it. I ain't seen no more like it. I think it cost seven dollars new.

Now that's th'way we started.

FLORENCE: Had four dollars an' a half in money when we started out, t'buy flour (the miller'd give us half a bushel of meal when we started), shortnin', sugar, salt, soda, coffee.

LAWTON: When I was a'farmin', I'd get up at five in the mornin'. Well, th'first thing I'd do is start feedin' an' milkin'. I'd get that done while Florence was a'fixin' breakfast. I'd come in an' m'breakfast'd be ready—we'd have eggs, biscuits, jelly, ham.

FLORENCE: Sometimes we'd gather up some corn, cut it off th'cob an' fry it for breakfast. Fry chicken an' potatoes, too.

LAWTON: Then I'd put my mules to plow, or to th'wagon to get wood. Maybe I'd haul corn out of th'field. Maybe I'd go t'town for something. Then when I'd come in for dinner I'd feed m'horses'r'mules—throw them in some corn—they didn't get no hay at dinner. Put'em in th'stable with their gear on, an' I'd go on in an' eat my own dinner. Then I'd go right back to what work I'd been doin'. When I come in at night I'd put m'mules up an' ungear'em. Go to th'house, get m'milk bucket an' milk an' feed an' water th'cow. When m'chores was done, I'd head in f'supper.

I played the banjo a lot—that's the way it was with me an' Florence when we moved out—that's th'way I made some of m'money the second year there [in Hayesville]. Why, we'd make some money. I'd make ten or eleven dollars, sometimes as high as fifteen. These big shots there in town, they'd have their dances at th'hotels an' things, an' these big shots would just pitch money out, whatever they wanted t'give. We picked up the money an' divided it just before we left. We played at people's houses, too. They'd take a notion to have a dance on th'head of Tusquitty'r'any-where, we were there. Gosh, that helped out—that was th'only way we could of lived.

FLORENCE: I'd go an' dance while Lawton was pickin'. Never did get t'dance with *him* though—he'd have t'make music. Sometimes they'd come after we'd gone t'bed—nine'r'ten o'clock. Why, we'd get up out of bed an' go play until after midnight. But sometimes I'd get mad because

PLATE 230

they didn't let us know before dark, an' I wouldn't go—I'd go over to Lawton's daddy's an' sleep.

LAWTON: I like t'go to a place where you can have a good nice time. Goin' t'them dances was lots of fun—that's about all th'fun they was goin' on. They wasn't no ballgames nor nothin' t'go to. Go to a good square dance. Usually everybody'd stay pretty sober an' ever'thing went off smooth.

FLORENCE: We didn't go out on many picnics'r'nothin'. They'd have Decoration Day at a certain time of th'year. Everybody'd go out for Decoration Day an' have a dinner on th'grounds'r'something like that. An' th'rest of the time th'only thing we ever went to would be a corn-shuckin', or a pea-thrashin', or a singin', or a candy-pullin', 'r'somethin' like that. They didn't have ballgames or such as that.

"We went through some hard times. No money."

LAWTON: We stayed [in Hayesville] for—well, we made two crops— two years. We'd raised our own garden and corn and all that. From there we went t'Aquone t'stay with Florence's mommy and daddy. An' there was a rich lady lived down there, Miss Mattie Bates. She had a big place down there, big house, big yard and a flower garden. Nothin' but a big ol' flower garden. She wanted me t'work for her. An' on th'railroad all people could get was a dollar a day. An' she give me a quarter an hour. An' I'd get on m'hands and knees an' crawl all over th'yard, ever' piece of wild grass'r'any kind of grass with seed, I'd had a pair of scissors, I'd have t'clip it off an' put it in a bag. An' she'd have me carry it across th'road so it'd never come back toward her place. But then her health got bad an' she left there. After she left, I went to work on th'railroad.

We went through some hard times. No money. They's people's supposed to have had lots of money. Well, prob'ly th'big shots did. But they'd swear they didn't have a dime—they wouldn't turn none of it loose. They'd like you t'work, but you'd have t'take y'pay in something you could eat, like meat, corn, anything like that, but when it come to money, you couldn't get none. Once in a while you'd get a little job where you'd get eighty cents a day. I've worked many a night all night long for eighty cents. It'uz snowin', rainin', ever'thing. An' I worked on th'railroad—had t'work ten hours for a dollar. An' I walked—well, I'd have t'leave way before daylight—to th'top of th'mountain; then when I come back from work I'd light m'lantern in th'gap of th'mountain an' go back home—I had t'have light t'see. We was workin' on th'railroad. If it rained an' you couldn't work, they'd dock you. If it rained fifteen minutes, you was docked. That was back in Hoover's days—the worst depression ever been on us.

If you couldn't go one day, somebody else had your job. You'd better go. They was people cryin' for work, a'beggin' for work. Tramps'ud come along by your house beggin' for a piece of bread. They'd never missed a day of work before, an' now they was travelin' huntin' jobs. Couldn't find'em. They wasn't no jobs. Just worked a little now an' then, maybe make a quarter'r'fifty cents a day. I knew this old boy who was workin' on th'railroad, he told me he was leavin', an' he told me to put in my application an' said, "I'll tell'em about you, an' give a good recommendation." Shore enough, I got th'job for a dollar a day. It'uz just a loggin' railroad. It was about eight mile t'work over th'mountains. So that was eight mile one way an' eight mile back—I had t'walk that much an' build ten hours too.

They wasn't hardly no money t'work for. An' I was stouter than a mule an' could've worked anywhere if I could a'got a job that'd pay me a little money. Many a time I just felt like givin' up an' quittin'. I'd get so disgusted. I thought many a time, "Well, now, I'll just shoot myself." They wasn't no light in th'way I'uz a'doin'. But I'd just keep on goin'. Sometimes I'd get so disgusted where I couldn't see what was ahead'r'what was behind.

Let me tell you somethin'. I once heard a fellow say, "Oh, I'd starve before I'd steal." I ain't gonna say that. Because if I see I'm gonna have to, I ain't gonna wait until I get so durn weak I can't carry nothin'. When I go, I'm goin' while I'm able t'get it. An' get away from there *with* it.

"Good God, before y'could bat y'eyes it was done there."

LAWTON: I've caught wild hogs—I dog-baited'em; they's a'watchin' th'dog, an' I went around an' got'em by th'hind legs. I got a friend's ol' shepherd, an' he got after one of'em, he's a'runnin' off in th'branch, an' he commenced actin' like he was gonna get'im, an' I tried t'get that dog t'catch'im, an' he wouldn't do it—he'uz afraid of it. It got t'watchin' him. Well now I thought, "If I can get in th'back above'im an' slip right down on'im, I can catch'im. I just come down th'branch right on him, an' when he was watchin' the dog, I just made a dive for both his

PLATE 231

hind legs, got up and picked him up off th'ground 'fore he started t'turn around. When he did, I kicked'im in th'side of th'head, then I commenced going back'ards with'im. I drug him to th'house back'ards. I fattened'im in a pen an' we eat'im. Wild hogs got more lean about'em, more bacon. They taste better. I'd rather have one that never seen a grain of corn or no dog food; I'd rather have one right off the mast as t'have'im after y'feed'im.

FLORENCE: Dad used t'have [a mad dog]. Ever' time he'd take a runnin' fit, run right through the house, come right in an' jump on top of th'bed ever'time. An' we had a big washin' of clean clothes layin' on th'bed, had just brought'em in, an' that rascal would come in there an' jump right on top of them clothes. An' there's th'washin' t'do over again, an' that's just a'scrubbin' them on an ol' board as hard as you can. No easier way of washin' them—we ought to have killed th'dog!

I don't know [what caused it] less it's caused from worms. But he was a healthy-lookin' dog—fat. The slobber'ud just come out of his mouth when he had a fit, but his nose an' ever'thing was just clear as it could be. You know, if Lawton'uz out in th'field with him, he'd tree Lawton ever'time. He'd put Lawton up a bush or on a fence or somethin'. After he got him up there, he'd just keep a'goin'. But he'd head right toward Lawton, an' Lawton afraid, an' he'd run up a bush'r'anything he could get to. Lawton didn't know what th'dog might do. Must of been somethin' in th'hot weather, don't you reckon? Sometimes Lawton'ud have to walk along th'top of th'fence post; but that was a big ol' dog, an' I fancy he could've reached him on th'fence posts if he'd a'wanted to bite him.

LAWTON: Then one time a tornado come across that mountain. Just looked like a snow a'comin' across th'mountain, a'comin' down. Good God, before y'could bat y'eyes it was done there. An' at Hayesville, I was a'plowin' down below m'daddy's house, a little ol' field, there was an old log barn there. They was about four'r'five stalls t'th'side of th'barn—

PLATE 232

took a big barn t'have that many stalls t'each side, y'know—so m'wife came down there, an' brung me a drink of water out there, where I'uz plowing, on the fifth day of July. It was a'thunderin' bad, but I just thought it was a little ol' thunder shower, back across th'hill.

So she said, "Well, I b'lieve it's gonna rain, I better get me a bucket of water here at th'spring." An' she started back, an' was just across th'bank when I just happened t'look up an' I said, "You better get back here, look up there." An' it just looked like th'whole mountain was all fire, just a big fog a'rollin' like that, an' she run back t'th'barn, an' I run m'mule in the'barn in th'hallway there; an' there was another man happened t'be workin' up on th'hill above, he run down there. An' I'm a'tellin' you th'truth, th'minute that thing hit, it blowed them logs. I was a'leanin' up against th'corner, just a'standin' there, an' I felt the barn a'startin', it commenced pushin' me. There was a big corn crib right there, an' a big ol' locust post about [ten inches] big up t'th'corn crib. An' I thought when that barn started if I could jump an' get a'hold of that post I could hold on. An' when I made a jump for that post, th'post left 'fore I could get a'hold of it. An'it blowed me 'bout as far from here across th'street out there. And a big oak tree, awful big old white oak tree four'r'five foot through, it just pulled it down. When I hit th'ground that tree hit me; I'uz a'layin' under it, an' that kept [the tornado] from hittin' me.

They wasn't no rain. They was just sticks, ever'thing in th'world. There were all these cuts an'blisters on my face where the gravel an' stuff had hit me. Well, quick as it got light enough I went t'crawlin' back t'see where my wife went to. I just knowed she'uz done killed. An' I looked back when it let up a little, an' I seen that th'barn's gone. I knowed she was too. But I crawled back up there, an' she'd started out till this man grabbed her an' held her, an'squatted down, an' it just blowed th'logs up there about that high over th'top of their heads. Never left a log or nothin'. We never did know where th'barn ever went to. Never did find it. I just knowed she was gone till when I seen that man a'holdin' her there.

Then th'rain come after th'tornado. They's always rain comes after it, and we got in [an empty house nearby]. Somebody'd moved out of it, an' they'uz a bed in there, an' it was cold—that's the coldest rain—seem like it'uz ice in that water, so we tore up that old bedstead, built us a fire an'dried off in there.

These tornadoes, they just come, maybe won't hit a thing here, an' it might dip down right out here an' not leave a cussed thing for a mile an' a half. Then it may just rise up all at once an' just rise right over your house.

"I've seen lots of changes in my life."

LAWTON: What about th'difference between now an' then? Now if you could live back in them days and just see what we've seen an' what way we had t'do. There's so *much* difference. People'd never believe they'd been a time like that now.

FLORENCE: Sometimes I just wonder if there was times like that. I know they was, but th'way it is nowdays, so many ol' cars an' ever'thing to go anywhere y'want t'go. *Then* you couldn't go no way without ridin' in a wagon or ridin' a horse or walkin'.

LAWTON: I've seen lots of changes in my life. I'uz just wonderin' if I could live as long again as I have, what kind of a world we'd be in. But I just know the world is different from what it used t'be. Back then, when people had more time, they thought lots more of each other than they do now. Yeah, they did, they thought more of people than they do now. They's lots more people than they used to be. Now that's got lots to do with it. Oh, just lots more people. They goin' s'fast, that they ain't got time to take up with you. They ain't got time to take up with me. They goin' so fast. An' that's what makes th'difference. Used to be all ever'body had was time. They had plenty of time. They would stay all day with you if they wanted to—they could stay all week if they wanted to. They had all th'time. They didn't have nothin' t'say like, "I've got to be there to-morrow," or "I've got to be there in an hour," or "I've got to be out there." They wasn't no jobs like that. They wasn't no work like they is nowdays.

  Back then, they wasn't no such a thing as a car—you couldn't hurry. If you wanted t'come see me an' I lived here an' you lived in Hiawassee, you'd have t'start early this mornin' t'drive a wagon over there. Well, I couldn't come back that night or I wouldn't get t'stay none. I'd have t'go spend th'night with you. I'd have t'come back th'next day an' let m'stock rest that long. An' you wasn't in no hurry when you started off. Seems like now if you can't go t'Atlanta an' back in th'same day, God, you way behind. You ain't got time t'fool with it. People livin' s'fast you got t'keep up with it in order t'stay up with things. You got t'be fast t'keep up with it. You can't slow down like we used t'do. I can't either.

FLORENCE: We used t'walk across th'mountains—start early in th'mornin' till nearly dark t'see Lawton's daddy, carryin' a baby. Walk.

Twenty-two mile. We'd stay a day or two t'rest up, then go back home. But we enjoyed it.

LAWTON: I'll tell y'what—people enjoyed life better then than they do now. Because ever'body thought s'much more of each other. You never met a stranger; you never met anybody who thought they was any bit better than you neither. You never found people like that. If you got down sick, people'd come askin' about your eating supply, too. If you didn't have it, here'd come somebody with a shoulder of meat, somebody with a middlin' of meat, somebody with a ham—throw it right down there on your table. See that you had somethin' to eat on. An' then expect no money for it. Now tell me now who's gonna come up there when you're down an' throw you a good country ham down on your table—without any money. Now you show me one. Not never expectin' t'get a dime out of it. We never expected t'get a penny out of nothin' we done like that. We done it because we *loved* th'people, an' the people loved *us*. That was just a habit that we had.

They's a lot of changes. They's as much difference in people now as they is in day an' night. People don't care for people no more like they used to. Used t'be if anybody got sick in th'community, why people'd go see about 'em, not just pass'em by. If you lived in our community, even if you was seven or eight mile away, when we heard you'uz sick, we'd go see about you. If you had a crop, we'd go an' see about it. See about crops, take care of your animals, get you out of th'rut while you'uz sick. Then when you get up, maybe I might get sick, an' then you'd help, come in with wagons an' mules, gather corn, haul hay . . . anything I'd need t'do would be done for me, just like you'd do it for yourself. An' nowdays you can get sick an' people ain't gonna go see about you t'ask how y'are, let alone do anything for you. You'd freeze t'death 'cause they ain't gonna get you no wood.

People loved people better in them days. I know so. People cared for each other more. Nowdays they're livin' too fast. They ain't got time t'take time with you. That's true. That's as true as it can be. Because I'uz raised up that way. When I'uz comin' up as a boy, I'd go an' plow corn all day for a man, an' you know he wouldn't even offer t'pay you a dime. An' if I'uz behind in my plowin', he'd send his boys, 'r' come hisself, bring his horses an' get right in there an' plow for me two-three days, then just go on home. Wouldn't have no pay. Yep, people used t'help each other. An' when anybody got sick, they never lost anything. Suppose you'd put in a big crop, an' y'get down at corn-gatherin' time, wasn't able t'gather your corn up. People went in there with six'r'seven wagons, why, I've seen seven neighbors workin' in a field at one time. Why, they'd gather fifty acres in two days by hand.

FLORENCE: An' y'go t'church, Lord, have mercy! Oh, they went t'church all th'time. They went an' wore their overalls, their ever'day shoes. You go to town to this church here with a pair of overalls on, an' see what they say. Oh, they'd laugh at you.

We'd go t'church, maybe several of them come home with us. I've seen it when we had so many people go home with us that the steers couldn't pull'em up th'hill, an' part of'em would have t'walk up th'hill. An' I've seen it when we couldn't all get on th'wagon. They'd go an' spend th'night, then th'next day we'd all go back t'church t'gether.

LAWTON: Go to a meetin' an' see five or six ol' steer wagons tied around up in th'woods, y'know. They's more people then, seems like, that went to church than they do nowdays.

Nowdays you can go to church, an' if you ain't got no money t'pitch in, you may just as well stay home. They don't care whether you die or not if you ain't got somethin' t'throw in th' dadblamed pot. Back in them days, they wasn't no pot t'pass around nor nothin'. If a man had anything t'give the preacher, they'd give him somethin' t'eat.

Believe me, we was happier then than we are now. You knowed what you had was your'n, an' nowdays ever'thing is movin' on so fast you don't have time to enjoy what you have got because you'll see somethin' th'other man's got an' you'll be a'wantin' it, an' be a'studying now just how in th'world am I gonna get a'hold of that now. Y'see so much stuff—I think that's confusin' people more than anything. Th'world's goin' s'fast. Y'see s'many things you want an' you want to keep up with th'other fellow. We don't enjoy life like we used to when things were hard.

FLORENCE: They's so many people now that's livin' s'high they think they's better than th'poor people.

LAWTON: Yeah, but that ain't a'helpin' them a bit in the whole world, not in the sight of the Old Master. I don't care how high they live nor nothin' about it. When he leaves here, he's goin' just exactly like I do. He come here without a durn thing, he's gonna leave without nothin'. I'll tell you that. I don't care how much he's got. If you have millions of dollars, then you don't take a dime more than I take.

Nowdays, you have to have money to live. When we was first married, we didn't have none no way. We growed what we eat. We didn't go hungry. Now, remember, we didn't go hungry. An' back when I'uz raised up, my daddy had plenty of land an' some money in th'bank.

I believe that too much money makes people unhappy. You can't be happy with too much money. Because you're studying about what t'do with it, an' if th'gover'ment's gonna take it away from you, an' what-not. You're studyin' about that a whole lot. An' if you make a whole lot of money, you want'a make some more t'go with it. An' seems like th'more you make, the more you want t'make t'go with it; just t'add a little more to it. Seems like that's th'way that people try t'live nowdays. You keep tryin' t'stack it just a little higher. An' that makes them strain themselves an' worry themselves. They worry lots—people does—about their money. They worry more than a fellow like me does, 'cause I ain't got money. I ain't got nothin' t'lose. If I had two-three million dollars I'd be a'wonderin' now, who's gonna get it, what they gonna do with it when they do get it, an' which one's gonna fight over it.

I'd rather have friends as money. Anytime. 'Cause if I had a whole lot of money, an' if you didn't like me, I couldn't get you to do a thing in th'world for me. You'd say, "I don't need the money. I ain't got the time; I got to do this; or I got to go over yonder." But, if you were my friend, if you were really a friend, an' I asked you to go do something, you gonna do it. Ain't no ifs and ands about it. When a friend asks me t'do somethin', I'm gonna do it for a friend, when money wouldn't get me t'do it.

"I wished I had just one little rock from that old chimbley."

FLORENCE: They had more different things where Lawton lived than where I was raised. I was really raised in the sticks. Even now it's still way back. We went over to the old home place one time. It looked so different, though—everything gone. I said I wished I just had one little rock from that old chimbley. We'll go back over there next summer, see if I can find one. Ought to be one—th'old chimbley's got t'be layin' around somewhere. They may have scraped it all off and covered it up. Th'garden growed up, it didn't look right. That used to be a big cleared field up that mountain. Now it's all growed up.

Interviews by Mary Chastain, Eddie Connor, Laurie Brunson, Jimmy Enloe, Mary Thomas, Barbara Taylor, Julia Justice, Beverly Justus, Rebecca Hill, Kathy Long, Russell Himelright, Greg Strickland, Craig Williams, and Ernie Payne.

GINSENG

From the Himalayas to the Blue Ridge, and for as long a time as distance, ginseng has been a favored medicine. The American ginseng (*Panax quinquefolium*) is very similar to its Asiatic relative. It has a stiff stalk holding two leaves, each leaf five-divided like fingers on a hand, and vaguely resembling those of the horse chestnut. A small umbel of insignificant yellow-green flowers is followed by red berries. It takes two years to come up from seed, and if a plant has been injured, it might not send up a stalk until the following year. It is slow-growing and long-lived if left alone. The aromatic roots are the part used for medicine, although occasionally tea has been made from the leaves.

It was once found in rich bottom lands from Canada to Florida. William Gillespie wrote, "It is most common in beech woods." Another writer said, "It grows mainly in well-drained upland hardwoods, mixed stands of maple, basswood, butternut, and rock elm, or on the shady side of deep gullies where there is a transition in timber and the vegetation mixes." William Bartram, traveling near Keowee, South Carolina, wrote, "It appears plentifully on the north exposure of the hill, growing out of the rich, mellow, humid earth, amongst the stones or fragments of rocks." Associated plants have been listed as maidenhair fern (*Adiantum*), baneberry (*Actaea*), spikenard (*Aralia racemosa*), blue cohosh (*Caulophyllum*), yellow ladyslipper (*Cypripedium*), and the "little brother of the ginseng," the goldenseal (*Hydrastis canadensis*).

Our native ginseng first came to the attention of Europeans when Father Joseph Lafitau, who had been a missionary in China, recognized the similar American plant growing near a Mohawk village in Canada. He set up ovens and had the Mohawks gather and cure ginseng for the Chinese market. By 1717, it was being brought from as far away as Green Bay, Wisconsin, by the Fox Indians, and shipped to Hongkong via France. In

PLATE 233   A cultivated ginseng patch.

PLATE 234   A four-pronged bunch.

1784, the Empress of China sailed for Macao with a load of ginseng to exchange for tea, ginger, silk, and camphor. Also in 1784, George Washington wrote, "In passing through the mountains, I met a number of persons and pack horses going over the mountain with ginseng." In 1793, André Michaux wrote that ginseng was the only product of Kentucky that could be transported overland to Philadelphia.

By 1798, John Drayton of South Carolina said, "It is so much sought after by the Cherokees for trade it is by no means as plentiful as it used to be in this state." Ginseng gathering had begun to be a way of life for many pioneers. A man could go "sang hunting" and return with a fortune; or in those perilous times, might never return at all.

The early colonists not only gathered ginseng for sale, but used it in tea to encourage the appetite or strengthen the digestion, especially of elderly persons or puny children. Ginseng plus black cherry and yellowroot made a potent tonic, especially with the addition of some home made whiskey. An early herbal suggested gathering ginseng root and steeping it with chamomile flowers for fainting females.

Colonel Byrd, in his *History of the Dividing Line,* wrote, "To help cure fatigue, I used to chew a root of ginseng as I walked along. This kept up my spirits. It gives an uncommon warmth and vigor to the blood. It cheers the heart of a man that has a bad wife, and makes him look down with great composure upon the crosses of the world. It will make old age amiable by rendering it lively, cheerful, and good humored." Many early settlers dug ginseng root for their own use and never thought of selling it. By 1800, several patent medicines on the market featured "seng," or "sang-tone." Dr. McMasters of Michigan wrote, "Ginseng is a mild, non-poisonous plant, well adapted to domestic as well as professional uses. In this respect, it may be classed with such herbs as boneset, oxbalm, rhubarb, and dandelion. The medical qualities are known to be a mild tonic, stimulant, nervine, and stomachic. It is especially a remedy for ills incident to old age."

With some domestic sale, as well as a continuing foreign market, "sanging" became a business in the rich deciduous forests of the American heartland, and on the slopes of the Catskills, the Poconos, the Alleghenies, and the Appalachians.

It was inevitable that some would try to cash in on such a profitable and easy crop by cultivating it. Thus there was a craze for ginseng gardens from 1889 through 1905, with centers in Amberg, Wisconsin; and Chardon, Ohio. Later New York state and then Michigan became the centers of ginseng production. Ginseng was planted in beds shaded by lath slats, or under wire covered by fast growing annual vines. But growers found it took seven years to produce roots large enough to market, and then the roots lacked the quality of those gathered in the wild. Garden plants were subject to a variety of wilts, blights, and rots, and a whole garden could be decimated in a week. But even though they were a gamble, ginseng gardens continued to appeal to many who wished to make an easy fortune.

However, the most money continued to be in gathering wild ginseng. Around 1922, someone wrote, "Grandma B. took out the back seat of her Model T and filled it with ginseng and sold the load for $1,100. They dried the roots on shelves behind the stove." As ginseng disappeared in more settled parts of the country, sang hunting in the Appalachians continued. Maurice Brooks wrote that it was one of the few crops that could be sold for cash with which to pay taxes or buy a new gun or hound dog. The sang hunter would go off into the mountains or woodlands with his special sang-hoe made of rigid steel with a narrow blade. The average-sized wild roots weighed up to six ounces when dug, and an expert sanger could grub out two pounds in a day. As they dried, usually from the cabin rafters, it took five pounds of fresh root for each pound of cured or marketable root.

The conservative sanger only dug roots in the fall of the year and carefully replanted the seeds, or the rhizome extension called a "quill," or "bud." To keep ginseng from being completely killed out in an area, some sangers would carry seeds and plant them in other suitable locales. There were, however, those greedy individuals who gathered sang at any time of the year, and did not hesitate to rob a neighbor's patch. Sang hunters would try to find out where their competitors had success, and in turn would keep their own finds a secret. By 1913, Horace Kephart, in *Our Southern Highlands,* wrote that ginseng had been exterminated in all but the wildest regions.

After the war in Korea ruined most Oriental ginseng lands, the sale of ginseng roots reached a new peak, the price rising to $35.00 a pound for wild roots. Sangers scoured the country for roots, and dealers made and lost fortunes on ginseng sales. The price is still high, and while some ginseng is being brought to dealers from Illinois, Missouri, West Virginia, and Kentucky, the bulk now comes from North Carolina, Tennessee, and Georgia.

MARIE MELLINGER

"One of these days, there ain't gonna be no 'sang."

Ginseng is slowly dying out. Since people first discovered that "sang hunting" could be a profitable hobby, they have been digging it more and more with less and less regard for its safety. Now, because of its scarcity and the increased demand for it, the price dealers pay hunters for the dried roots has skyrocketed to $65.00 a pound.

There is much confusion here as to exactly what happens to ginseng once it is shipped out of the country, but many of our contacts remember it being used in the mountains in teas and other home remedies.

"They buy it in China," said Wallace Moore. "You know, when the President came back from China, it was on the television that that old main guy over there drunk ginseng tea every day? And he had *three* women. I never have drunk any tea. But now I'll tell you one thing. You can be in the woods and take a stomach ache or the old hungry colic, and you can just chew up some of the fine roots and swallow the juice of it and it won't be five or ten minutes [before] your stomach'll be just as easy as you please. I've had that to happen different times."

Buck Carver said, "You can take the roots that are dry and take a sausage mill or something and grind'em up and drop a pretty good little handful down into your vial of conversation juice [moonshine]. Take this ginseng and liquor and pour out just a small little amount of that in a tea-cup and set it afire. Strike a match to it, you know, and it'll burn. And I mean burn it good. And then turn it up and drink it. It's an awful bitter

PLATE 235   A pod of berries ready for picking and planting.

PLATE 236 Harley Carpenter picks a cluster of ripe berries for replanting in his patch.

dose to swallow, but if it don't do you some good you better get to a doctor and pretty durn fast. It really is good for that. And it's also good for female disorders. Very good, they tell me, for that."

Lawton Brooks laughed about a remedy he remembers seeing: "Now it's a bitter kind of something. They used to take ginseng and three or four herbs all together and put it in a quart of whiskey and shake it up and let it sit there awhile and then they'd take'em a drink of it every day. And they called it 'bitters.' And I guess it *was* bitter, for that ginseng'll make it bitter, I'll tell you that! I'll *bet* it was bitter! They didn't tell no crooked tale about that being bitter!"

Alice Lounsberry's *Southern Wildflowers and Trees* (Frederick A. Stokes Company, New York, 1901; page 364) says:

"Its true value lies, as we know, in its curious rootstock, long famed as being a cure for almost every sort of ill, and an antidote for every poison. Even the word panacea is believed by many to have been derived from its generic name. In China, where it has been largely cultivated and also exported from that country in immense quantities, it is still regarded as being possessed of properties more powerfully stimulating to the human system than those of any other drug."

Whatever its uses, its popularity grows yearly. Now new demands are being made for it from people interested in organic foods and medicines. As such, it is being written about in publications like *Mother Earth News* and *Organic Gardening*.

Because of its growing popularity, we interviewed a number of people in our area who hunt it or grow it or both. Many of them have been working with it since childhood. It rapidly turned into one of the most fascinating articles we have done recently, for each man had his own favorite stories, his favorite places to hunt and dig, and his favorite methods for finding and raising it. For many of them, the lure was not so much financial as it was just the fun of working with the plant itself—more a hobby than a livelihood. Their enthusiasm carried us along with them.

I really had a great time interviewing these people, and I think they had as much fun talking about it as I had listening. I'd like to give special thanks to Mr. Billy Joe Stiles and Margie Bennett, who helped me get a lot of information on ginseng, and also Suzy and Pat, who took Steve and me on most of the interviews.

CARY BOGUE

THE PLANT

Ginseng (*Panax quinquefolium*) is a plant that grows widely throughout the Appalachians, and does well in many other parts of the country. It rarely grows to more than a foot and a half or two feet in height, and has long, serrate, tapering thin leaves. At the summit of the stem, "prongs" branch off, each ending in a cluster of five leaves. From the summit, at the center of the plant, a smaller stem grows straight up and ends in a cluster of flowers or berries depending on the time of year.

The tuberous root, which grows at right angles to the stem, ranges in size from a half inch to sometimes eight inches in length depending on the age of the plant and the growing conditions. As Wallace Moore said, "The first year it comes up, why its root's not half as big as a penny match stem and maybe not but a half an inch long."

Roots from the older plants are the more valuable, of course, because they are generally larger and weigh more. Good sang hunters dig only the older plants and leave the younger ones for another year, telling how old the plant is by counting the number of prongs it has. Though this is sometimes an inaccurate yardstick, it is all they have to go by. "It comes up a three-leaf," Lake Stiles told us, "and then in a year or two, maybe it'll turn into a two-prong bunch. It'll stay a two-prong for maybe two or three years, and then it'll grow into a three-prong, and from a three-prong into a four-prong if it stands long enough. I have dug a few five-prongs,

PLATE 237 *Foxfire* editor Richard Page (right) makes notes as Harv Reid watches his grandson, Donnie, find and dig a clump of sang.

but not often. Sometimes after it gets four-pronged, that stem [in the center of the plant] will run on up there and instead of having seeds on that stem, they'll be some more prongs come out on that, and the seed stem on top of *that*. That's called a double-decker. You don't find many of those anymore."

The seed usually takes two seasons to germinate. If planted in the fall, for example, a little three-leaf plant should come up in eighteen months if it is going to germinate at all. In the fall, the leaves turn a bright golden yellow, the berries turn bright red and drop, and then the plant dies back to ground level to come up again the next spring. A more accurate measure of age is the "age stem," a small, knobby extension of the root from which the stem springs each season. Wallace Moore described it this way: "When it first comes up, the top'll come right out of the top [of the root]. And it'll put a little bud right beside that [where the base of the stem connects to the root] for next year's stem. And it'll just do that right on up through there going from one side to the other. It puts a bud on every year for it to come out the next year. And where the stem come out this year, when it dies it'll leave a little notch [where the old stem breaks off] right beside that bud. Then next year that bud'll come out on the other side of the stem, and *it'll* leave a little notch when it dies. You can count those little notches if it's a big enough stalk to where you can see them. Now where it's small—

just little bitty one and two-prong bunches—you can't count them because they're so close together. You might take a magnifying glass and count them, but you can't with your naked eye. I have counted it up to fifteen and twenty years old where you could count on the stem, but lots of times it's older than that. You count on the stem where the bud comes out, you know.

"I've dug it with the age stem three and four inches long. Maybe two-thirds of the way down, it'll be so little you can't count it. But maybe up here after it got up maybe an inch or two long [in root size], it would put out a feed root on that stem and maybe it would be in richer ground then. Well, that would step your top up—throw a bigger top out there—and then it'd go to having notches on there that you could count. It's according to how rich the ground is and all. Sometimes you can dig a little old one-prong bunch and it'll have an age stem on it'll be maybe a half-inch or an inch long and *still* be a one-prong bunch. But sometimes you can dig a one-prong bunch and it'll have three great big leaves on it—and it the first year that it's come up. It's according to the ground it grows in and how it suits it.

"Now the root a lot of time'll have ridges around it. But there's no way of telling how old it would be that way. [Many people believe that you can tell the age of the plant by counting these ridges, but we could find no support for that.]

"And that root, you find it in all kinds of shapes. I found a root one time looked just like a . . . well, just like the cross did. In drying it, it got split, and I took and put a straight pin in it and pinned it back together and shipped it. I never did hear nothing more about it. But it looked just like the cross."

At first the inexperienced sang hunter may have some real difficulty spotting the plant in the woods as many low-growing plants and ground covers (Virginia Creeper, *Parthenocissus quinquefolia,* for example) have similar leaf clusters. Minyard Conner knows from experience: "Well, now, the Indian turnip's got a big pod of red berries and looks just like it, and it gets red at the same time as ginseng. But that root's hot. It'll burn you up. [Take a bite of that and it'll] make you whistle all day! And I'm sure you boys have all picked spignet in place of ginseng; you know, see some spignet and say, 'There's some ginseng.'"

"That old five-leaf poison vine'll fool you the worst of anything," believes Lawton Brooks, "'cause it's got the same yellow till you get right up at it and go to looking. But ginseng's got more of a *gold* color than anything. Ain't nary another yellow in the world just exactly like it. But that other stuff'll fool you off at a distance. You'll think you see a bunch and you'll go up there and you've found the wrong thing!"

Sometimes the confusion takes on hilarious overtones. Lake Stiles still laughs about the time two members of the administration of our school were out looking in the fields for some marijuana they thought some students had planted, found one of his ginseng patches, and sprayed it all and killed it.

And Wallace Moore said, "My daddy-in-law used to call it 'rattle-root.' It's a three-pronged stuff, and it resembles sang quite a bit off at a few steps. But if you know sang, you can tell it just as quick as you get around it. A man that's hunted it and is well acquainted with it can tell the difference just as quick as he sees it."

The same need for experience applies to the dealers who buy the roots from the numerous hunters. The high price that ginseng has always commanded has encouraged many to start their own cultivated beds near their homes, but dealers claim they can always tell the difference between the cultivated and wild roots, and since the wild roots are believed to be more potent, they bring almost double the price. Dealers have to be sharp, for people are forever trying to fool them by mixing the two kinds of roots together. The number of hours that have been spent trying to figure out whether or not they can really tell the difference, and if they can, how they do it, must be in the thousands. It is generally agreed, though, that the cultivated ginseng grows faster, and thus has a bigger, smoother root than that which has grown in the woods and not been tampered with.

"You can cultivate that stuff," said Lake Stiles, "and it won't bring you half as much as wild ginseng. They can tell it. They can tell it just as quick as you look at that stuff. If it's cultivated, it makes a great big root. If it's wild, it's just a small root. But you can't get by with cultivated sang with a man who knows what he's doing."

Wallace Moore shares the same fear: "I have beds, but I don't fertilize them. I just plant it back up in the woods so it grows like the wild. Now you can put chicken manure around it. That'll really make it grow. But of course you might be able to tell it was cultivated then by the growth on the big stem, 'cause it would grow faster, you know."

Buck Carver has experimented, but carefully: "Right now is one of the times I need to be up there raking leaves and putting on—you've got to mulch that stuff. Now if you put it back twelve to fourteen inches from [the plant], Turner Enloe says this chicken litter'll make them roots grow like nobody's business. But you put it up close and that'll kill it right off the bat. I never throw fertilizer on mine. Except one time I thought I'd try one stalk and see what effect it had on it, and I carried a little handful of fertilizer up there and singled out a stalk and throwed that fertilizer around it—just a complete circle around about four to six inches away from it, I guess—and it done fine. It done all right.

"And I don't know—I just imagine—I've never tried it for it's too expensive a thing to experiment too durn far with, and it's too hard to find to just go on and run the risk of killing it out, you know; but I thought a few times—maybe in the wintertime—[I'd] just throw a little fertilizer right lightly over that cover of leaves that you have on it, you know, and see if that'd help it any. But I don't know. You get to doping it up too much like that and the first thing you know, if you have enough to sell, you're selling cultivated sang for about less than a half [the price]. Cultivated sang grows so much faster and don't have the ingredients in it and the medicinal value that the wild has. The wild has nothing but fertilizer from the earth, you know. It's natural. And where you put artificial fertilizer out there to make it grow faster and make it produce bigger roots faster—more poundage and everything—then you cut the grade of it. It don't have the strength the wild sang has. It just don't have it."

Minyard Conner is cautious, and refuses to dig around the plants in his bed and loosen the ground up for fear the roots will grow big and white and, "They'll look at it and say, 'That's cultivated sang.' "

Lawton, too, shares a healthy respect for the dealers' ability to tell the difference. "I can't figure out how them people know that cultivated sang. Now if I take me some back in the mountains and plant it, I believe I can fool'em. Now you go out here where you grow it, and you cultivate it and tend to it. Now I don't know what kind of fertilizer it would call for, but that might look cultivated. But I believe if I could get me some roots and go back in these mountains and find me a place where nobody wouldn't happen to find it and let it go about four years, I could show a man a nice patch of ginseng, and I don't believe they could tell the difference—it a'growing out there wild. Just stay away from it and let it alone. Set it out when it's right small. I believe it'd grow up wild and they couldn't tell the difference.

"But you have to be careful. I don't know. Don't ask me how they know. Maybe the root gets bigger when you tend it. But they sure can tell, 'cause we tried it with some one time. Put some [cultivated] in with some wild and they could tell that some of it was cultivated. You can't fool'em. A good buyer, you can't fool'em on cultivated sang.

"They like the wild sang the best."

FINDING AND RAISING GINSENG

Many people have started sang patches of their own. Some of them intend to dig the roots and sell them periodically to have a continuing supplementary income from year to year. Others just grow the plant for the fun of it, and because they like to have it around.

In an attempt to find the best spot on their land for a patch, many of them have invested a good bit of energy observing where it grows best naturally and then trying to duplicate those conditions. The problem is that it seems to grow fairly well in a wide variety of conditions, and so there is a good bit of conflict as to what makes the best site.

Wallace Moore has found it just about everywhere, and so when he starts a patch, he just chooses some good, rich, lightly shaded ground and lets it go at that: "It's bad to grow out here on these little dogwood ridges. And that's usually poor ground, you know, and a lot of people won't hunt out there for it. They say it's got to be down in these hollers and in this rich ground. But you find a lot of it on these dogwood ridges. And then it grows on north sides, mainly, but it'll grow up on these south sides if it's rich.

"You can find it under grape vines, and walnuts—black walnut or white walnut, either one—and basswood. And it'll grow around pine, but it's not a place for it to spread like some tree that [attracts birds] that scatters the seed. And it has to have a certain amount of shade. It'll grow right out in a blackberry thicket—in a briar thicket—and in these rich places in hollers. But it's got to have a certain amount of shade, you know. Not too damp. I never found any in a swamp. The only sang I ever found was out on a dry branch bank or up on these ridges on a dry holler or somethin'r'nother like that. It'll grow pretty close to water, but I wouldn't think it'd grow where it's awful soupy."

Lake Stiles has his own favorite places to look: "I've dug it in places where the sun hardly ever hit it. You'll really find more of it in real dark coves and dark ground than anywhere else. And west or north ground. You don't find much of it on south ground at all. It'll grow in dry places, but it prefers damp, dark places. It makes a lot bigger stalk."

Buck Carver agreed with the common belief that north ground is best for it, "But I've found it on every side of a durn mountain except the inside, and I didn't go in there! Right up there on that mountain, for instance; it's all in the north side among them cliffs. But I've also found it on the south side, and I've found it on this west end here. And I find it on the east end up yonder. 'Course that's northeast. But it grows better in dark, rich north coves under walnut, or lind. You find some walnut out in the woods, start looking for ginseng 'cause it'll usually be there. It's got to have shade. The leaves hold the moisture in the earth."

Lawton Brooks says, "It wants dark ground and deep coves. Where a lot of poplar grows—in those coves—is good. You've been squirrel hunting and come across one of those coves where a lot of poplar grows? Now you don't find it where there's pine and oak and stuff like that in those coves. You ain't gonna find no ginseng. You'll find your ginseng in where poplar and stuff like that grows. And you can't find it out on these ridges. You hardly ever find it on ridges because it wants dark, damp coves where there's more shade than anything else. It don't like sunshine too good.

"Now you can grow it if you've got dark ground to grow it in, and shade. You don't want it out on a hillside where there's any clay or anything. It won't do nothing there at all. You've got to have it in good, dark soil right in a cove where there's a lot of poplar and stuff grows—and this other old kind of lind tree, and these old cucumber trees. You've seen them. Now you can grow ginseng in coves like that. And it grows on the south and north sides too. I know by going up on the head of Bettys Creek. I dug some on both sides of the mountain up there. But it was in the dark coves."

Good sang hunters have their own code of ethics. They dig roots in the spring only if they intend to transplant them into their own beds. Aside from that, they dig only in the fall when the berries are ripe. The bigger roots, they sell. The smaller ones, they move. The berries are either planted back on the same site, or are taken home to be planted there. Breaking this code increases the scarcity of the plant and puts them all out of business, so even though scarcity has driven up the price paid for the roots, it hurts them all in the long run.

"The only time to dig it," says Lake Stiles, "is after it matures—after the seed turns red. That's the only time it should be dug. But half the time people will pull the seed off and take them home with them and maybe destroy them and not plant them anywhere. Before it's dug, if they would pull the seed off and scatter them back out on the ground where they find it, there'd be plenty of it. I don't know why, but there's not many people will do it. A few will.

"There's also some who will go, as quick as it comes out in the spring, and start digging it [to sell], and that's the wrong thing to do. [I was at a dealer's once and some people came in] and they'd started digging this stuff early in the spring as quick as it got through the ground. And the little stem that they'd broke off when they dug it was still on there. That showed it was dug before it was ripe. If it's dug in the fall when it should be dug, that stem will fall off. It will not stay on that little root. If it's dug in the spring and summer, that little top stem will stand up and dry on that root. That looked like a . . . put me in mind of a porcupine! When they put them on the scales, them little white ends a'sticking out there. That proved it was dug too early. They said no, but I've fooled with it all of my life. I know better than that.

"And it should never be dug its first years of growth. Then it's just a little bitty three-leafed thing, and the root on that is not much bigger than a toothpick. It ought to be from a three-prong on up before it's dug [to sell]."

Buck Carver has worked for years to find the proper way to get the berries he has brought in from the woods to germinate: "Now a lot of mine, I think, died up here from lack of moisture. I put leaf mold on them several inches thick, but it wasn't hardly enough. It takes the berries eighteen months to come up. The way it transplants itself out in the woods —the berries fall down in the leaves, you know, and leaves fall from the trees on it, and it lays in there, but one spring, it comes up.

"And you can't plant them berries too deep or they'll rot. I planted over a hundred berries—a hundred and four, I believe it was—out there between me and Turner. It was good and shady, you know. I said, 'Turner, I got a little old bottle of berries over there at the house. I'll plant them there, and if they come up, I'll divide the plants with you.' And he said, 'Yeah, plant them in there.' And I planted them durn things and they wadn't a durn *one* of them come up.

"You've got to plant them just *barely* under the ground and then throw the leaves on there. Lord, I guess I've got two hundred berries I'm going to plant up there this time, and like a dummy I've sit around here all this time and never put a leaf on [the bed]. I may do that this evening while I've got it on my mind.

"If you transplant them, you put a good piece of stem with it. You know that little bud right down at the base of that stem? That's your plant for next year. It don't make a whole lot of difference, but I'd rather have that little stalk on there. But if it breaks off down to the root, it's all right. Put it in there and plant it. I have planted *pieces* of roots and they've come on all right. I cut some of them digging them, and I planted the pieces and they've put out little old feeder roots and come on all right. They've made some sang.

"Then when you dig it to sell, you can sell it green, but you get about a third the price. Wait till the last of August when the berries start getting ripe before you start digging. And plant them berries back! If you dig it while it's maturing, that root is just as pithy as it can be; and when it dries up, it'll be a little bitty old swivelled up thing. It won't be slick and firm and hard. It'll be puffy and spongy first, and then it'll be full of wrinkles. And time after the berries start getting ripe, why, it'll retain it's weight a heck of a lot better. You can get a shoe box full of the stuff in the summer time while it's pithy and full of sap and it won't weigh nothing. In the fall of the year, that sap starts going back down, you know, and your sang'll dry up good and firm and hard, and it don't take it too long. I've dug a few roots of it in the summer time—maybe to have a few to chew on or something— and it'll be just as pithy as the dickens. I don't think it's got as high a medical value, either, while it's soft that way. I don't believe it does.

"A feller oughtn't to dig nothing less than a three-prong for the market no way. And a lot of *that's* got a pretty small root."

"It's getting scarcer all the time," said Lawton Brooks. "It sure is. When I'm out digging and find a bunch of seed, I *always* plant them back. Lots of people, though, they just grab them up and take the seed with them and maybe never plant them. But I always cover them seed back in the leaves. Scatter'em around. Then in a year or two, a man can go back to it and dig some more ginseng right in the same territory.

"Don't sow the seed too deep. When the berries go to dropping down, then take your berries off and sow them—just put them on the ground. That's the way they come when it's wild 'cause birds and things scatters them. That's what scatters the blasted berries in the mountains. And then sometimes they fall off and they get in the leaves, and the rain and snow and stuff'll wash them around in under the leaves some way or another and they come up. I've dug great big bunches, and they'll be four or five little ones right around under it. I know that's where the seed fell off and come up.

"And when you plant a root, find rich dirt and just scrape the dirt away a little. Don't break the little feed roots off or it won't come up. And don't worry about cold weather. I know one thing—it won't freeze out. It's a thing that won't freeze. I've seen it knocked over on top of the ground in hard winter, and you know in them north coves where the sun don't hit you *know* it stays cold in there in the winter time. But it comes up every year."

Wallace Moore was full of advice about digging and moving sang: "Ever since I've been big enough to follow my daddy in the woods, why we've dug sang and hunted it. It's not as plentiful as it once was. It's getting scarcer'n what it was. There's so many people now that'll dig the little one and two-prong bunches. When you dig those little one and two-prong bunches, it's not got a chance to come up right. They don't have berries on them. Sometimes a little two-prong bunch'll have maybe one or two berries on it. But you let it alone and it'll put on another feed root up on the top a lot of times, and then it'll shoot up a big top up there and put on ten or twelve, maybe fifteen berries. A man shouldn't gather it under a three-prong bunch.

"And always put the berries back. I always have. My daddy always did, and that's what I've always done unless I had some I wanted to take and sow—have a bed, you know, that I wanted to take and put berries and little roots in. Why then, sometimes I'd save a few of the berries; but I always— nearly always—put part of the berries back where I dug it up. You've got to. It'll eventually die out if they ain't something done. It's getting so much more population now than they used to be.

"But a man shouldn't dig it before the berries begins to get red, and that's along about the last of August. Before then, your berries is not mature. They're still green. Now my daddy always told me that a berry has got two seeds in it. An average size sang berry has got two seeds in it. And one of them seeds'll come up—like you plant it this fall and it'll come up next spring. And the other berry'll come up the next spring—eighteen months. Now that's what he's always told me. He's always growed it and had it and fooled with it all of his life, and that's what he's always told me.

"Now the very best time to dig it is after it comes the first frost. From then till the leaves falls off of it. It's a bright yellow then, and it's a different cast of yellow from anything else in the woods, and you can tell it just as far through the woods as you can see it. But it's a short time to dig it in then. You ain't got long to dig it.

"When you dig it, you've got to scratch and get the dirt away from the roots and get it out. You can scratch down to where you can get ahold of it and catch hold of it and pull it and pull all the main part of the root out—unless it happens to be a quick crook in it or something. Then it'll break. But if it's just a straight root, you can catch and pull it, but you'll lose every bit of your little feed roots—the fine stuff. It makes it look awful *rugged*. You've just got a old big stubby root. If you take just a *little* more time and get all those fine roots out, then boy, it really makes it look good.

"Just dig out from around it. Well, you take on the mountainsides lots of times, the ground's loose, you know. You can just take your two hands —just run them down in the ground and just might' near lift feed roots and everything out at one time. But a lot of times it's in hard ground, too, and you've got to take a stick and prize and work and dig it out. Most sang diggers uses sticks. Some of them uses a little old something like a garden mattock, you know, like women use around in their flowers. Right light where they can use it in one hand and dig. But the majority of sang diggers just use a stick—just run it down under there and put one hand down here at the top of the ground and prize down on it, you know, and you can break a pretty good little tree root; and just lift the dirt up and that loosens it, you know, and you can just lift it right out.

"Now I've got out here in Mr. Tom Grist's pasture, and I've got out over there sometimes right early in the spring when it first comes up before they turn the cattle in there and dig it then and bring it over here and transplant it. Sometimes it'll grow on, and sometimes it'll die down. I guess if a body took enough pains with it—took and watered it like you would when you set out tater plants—it would probably live and grow right on that spring. But I always just take and bring mine in and set it out, and if it lives [that spring], it lives; if it don't, why, it don't. Most of it'll come back the next spring anyway. I usually use a haverpoke. It's just a satchel with a strop goes across your shoulder—swings down on your side. And that don't skin up your roots so bad. If you put many of them in your pockets, you know, and you crawling around through the woods under logs and over logs and that, you skin all your little bitty feed roots up and they won't grow then. I usually just take mine and just dig it and stick the root right down in the haverpoke and leave the top sticking up and bring the whole thing back in and transplant it. That's better than berries. Even with a two-prong bunch, look how many years you're ahead of yourself there. At least three. And if it's not rich ground, maybe five or six years—maybe ten years ahead of yourself.

"But I bring it all home, and scratch a hole down just a couple inches below the topsoil, put it in there and cover it back up. Now you can take the bud out of a big bunch—where it's got a little fine feed root on it, you know, which it's bad to have; most all big sang has got a little feed root or two on it—and you can dig all those little feed roots out on that bud and break it off and reset it and it'll grow and make another bunch. Put feed roots, bud and all.

"And it'll come up every year if they don't nothing knock the top off or bother it. It'll come up the next year. You can dig it this spring when it first comes up and take and transplant it and lots of times the top'll die and you won't see no more sign of it that year. But then the next spring the majority of it'll come back up. Sometimes it won't. It'll dry up if those

PLATE 238   Minyard Conner's shaded sang patch.

PLATE 239   Minyard Conner showing Cary Bogue and Steve Waters his cultivated sang patch.

feed roots don't take ahold or something, and it won't come back up. Or you might have it too deep. It can't be too far under your topsoil."

Minyard Conner has a bed of ginseng under a shed tacked onto the side of his garage [see *Plates 238, 239, 240*]. As proof that the sang needs moisture, he points to the drip line from the garage roof: "See where the water's run off the shed here? It's growed so much better around here." He always either plants the berries he finds back, or brings them home and plants them just under the ground in his bed. In the woods, "Pick them and just sling them everywhere where they'll be hard to find! Put two or

PLATE 240   Minyard Conner dug one small
plant from his patch to show us the size of its
root.

three back where you dug, but sling the other ones. Leaves'll cover'em
up."

Minyard is one of the few men we talked to who believed that it might be
possible to make a living out of ginseng: "If you had a acre of ginseng, and
you dug a quarter-acre every year, that's all you'd ever want. Yeah. Make a
living on it. Set it out close together. Dig a quarter-acre every year. Now
wouldn't that be nice?

"But what about if you got up some morning and looked in there and
your whole [bed had been dug]. You'd feel sick at your stomach *then,*
wouldn't you?"

ENEMIES

Sang has a number of different kinds of enemies ranging in size from mice to men. Mice, squirrels and many birds eat the berries. Moles eat the roots. A blight attacks the stem and leaves; and people sometimes dig the roots at the wrong time of year, or transplant them incorrectly.

The berries, ripe in the fall of the year, tempt smaller animals. Lake Stiles said, "Little old woods mice eat them. I've had thousands of them climb up on that stem and cut the seeds off and sit up there and eat them."

Wallace Moore agreed: "Squirrels'll eat them. Rats is *bad* to eat them. And pheasants is bad to eat them. That's what the hunting book calls grouse, but we always called them pheasants. When mast is especially scarce, squirrels'll get into them. They eat the berries. And rats'll climb right up the stem of it and cut that little old seed pod off—cut it off to where they can get the berries, you know."

Worse than squirrels and mice are the moles which eat the roots and thus kill the plant. Almost everyone is afraid of the damage they can do because it is permanent. Wallace Moore said, "Moles is awful bad on sang. They'll eat the root, a mole will. If you ever plant it in a bed, you don't want to plant it in a straight row because a mole, if ever one time he finds a root here, he'll just take right out and he'll just take right out the row until he eats it all up. The only thing I know that you could do would be take this coarse wire—half-inch mesh or something like that—and just dig down deeper than a mole would run and fence you off a streak with it is the only way I know that you could keep a mole out of it. They usually run right close to the top of the ground, you know, 'cause he's got to bust up to get through. I started to fence my bed off up there one time—me and my wife did—and got some wire, but it run into too much work!"

Buck Carver is also afraid of moles. "Oh, boy. Dad jim they just love them roots like nobody's business. They'll eat them. Maybe I can get a mole trap or two and set around that patch and have better luck with it. I just haven't give it the care and attention that I ought to have."

Blight is one of the more mysterious enemies. No one seems to know what causes it, or whether or not the damage is permanent. Every single contact suspected that too much sun was the real culprit, but they differed widely as to whether or not they felt the roots were harmed.

Lake Stiles said, "Blight on lots of other things will kill the roots, you know. But now as far as ginseng, I don't know whether or not it'll kill the roots or not. I have some ginseng up here that has lived through the blight for two years. I don't know whether it'll live through another year of it."

Buck Carver told us that the blight had hit his bed the last three years in succession. "Last year I got a whole bunch of fresh roots and berries and planted a new patch and hope to have it come right on better this time. That blight made scabs on the roots, and eventually it'll eat the root up."

Wallace Moore described it vividly: "The leaf looks like you'd put hot water on it. It just turns black and just looks like it's cooked. It hit mine year before last, and I went and dug part of my bed. I was talking with Lester Davis and Buck Carver and them, and they said, 'Well, wouldn't never do no good after the blight hit it. Said it shedded them feed roots. Little feed roots come off of it.'

"Well, I never said much about it. I just listened to them talk, mainly. I had a big bed and it really had the blight. And I come on home and me and my wife got talking about it. I said, 'Well, I just as well go dig what I can find of that in my bed 'cause if them feed roots comes off, it ain't going to do no good nohow.' And I went up there, and it hadn't hurt the root a bit in the world. Only just the tops dead. The little feed roots was on there. But I went ahead and dug a whole bunch of mine. But all that I missed come up the next year and put berries and all on last year. But now *this* year the blight hit it again, and boy it really hit it hard too." Wallace is just waiting to see what will happen this spring.

People, of course, are another threat entirely. They either dig the plant in such a way as to endanger the species, or they can find a patch that a man has in the woods and clean him out in an afternoon. Sometimes they have even been known to sneak into a man's yard when he was away and dig all that he had in his bed. We talked to several people that had had that happen to them at one time or another, and they were understandably bitter about it. One man told us, only half in jest, that he protects his with a shotgun now.

Wallace Moore, who has no beds near his home, was more philosophical about loss: "I wouldn't want to catch nobody in a bed that I might put out around my home here digging it on my own property, but if you've got a bed out here on government land and somebody gets into it, why, it's as much his as it is yours. Ain't nothing you could say about it without causing a row about it, and ain't no need in causing no row about it.

"I had a *big* patch in between here and Mud Creek Gap up here—people around here knows it as the Homer Sawmill—Homer Grist and them had a sawmill up there. Big flat rich place, and it's on south ground, but it's rich and flat. Just a poplar thicket. And I took and sowed sang all in there, and I'd take and dig up little roots and scatter them around in there. And _____ got into it and cleaned it out about two years ago. I never have said nothing to him about it. He never has mentioned it to me and I never have mentioned it to him. As much his as it was mine. Only I planted it and he got it. That's all.

"Now I get in these little out of the way places where there's not anybody hardly goes, you know."

So growing ginseng turns into something of a perilous way to make a living, but at the prices they're paying now . . .

DEALERS

When it comes to the actual buying and selling of sang, it seems almost as though there's a contest of sorts going on; something along the lines of a "let's see who's going to beat whom this time." Sellers claim the dealers short them in weighing the roots. Dealers claim the sellers are trying to cheat *them* just about any way they can (by mixing cultivated with wild roots, for example). It goes around and around.

To some extent, the dealers are certainly right. Usually operating as middlemen out of their own homes and with their own capital, they're taking a certain risk anyway. Then they must face sellers like the one who shall remain nameless who told us: "I dry it [to sell]. You can put it anywhere to dry. You can just put it in the house and it'll dry, but it won't dry fast. I usually put mine in a car body. You roll all your glasses [windows] up, you know; leave your glasses all rolled up and put it in the back there where the sun'll shine through that glass and hit it? It'll more'r'less cook it. It'll dry that outside so fast that the inside won't be dry, but still the outside'll be hard. That makes it weigh heavy. You don't lose so much weight. That's the way I've dried mine, now, for the last four or five years."

Another contact, however, sees dealers as ripe to be beat since they're cheating too: "That one dealer won't talk to you much. He's got secrets he don't want to give away, I reckon. I've seen five or six thousand dollars' worth of sang in there at a time. He gets price quotations from New York at least every other day, and knows just how much to give for that. He's a shrewd trader. He'll talk you out of a few ounces and you standing there *looking* at him.

"Me and Byron Kelly one time went over there and carried some to him and he got to telling us about how he had certain days he'd go down to Bryson City and buy sang, and then certain days he'd be in Sylva and buy sang. And a lot of them Indians and half-Indians [from the Cherokee reservation near Bryson City, North Carolina], they'd dig the dickens out of that stuff. They ain't supposed to get it in that park in the Smokies, but they've got ways they can slip in there without the Park rangers knowing about it—and they's *plenty* of sang in them Smokies. So he said he was buying there in Bryson City one day, and he said they was just lined up. Big line of people. And he had his little old scales there and he'd just weigh that stuff. Quick as one man was out of the way, he'd grab the next, throw in on the scale, figure it up, pay him off, gone. And he said they was a tourist standing there watching. And after while, when the rough got over, this Florida man stepped over to him and said, 'I been a'standing here watching you for an hour or more buying and weighing, but there's one thing I still don't understand, and that's how you can do it so fast and still be accurate.'

"Well, that dealer looked over at him and said, 'I just weigh it pretty close, and then I give a little or take a little. And usually I take!' "

So who's beating whom? Hard to say. And really probably inconsequential in the long run. In the old tradition of horse trading, it all evens out. Meanwhile, the reputed sharp eye of the dealer adds pages to the folklore surrounding the plant.

"As big a root as ever I dug . . ."

Sang hunters, just like deer hunters, coon hunters, treasure hunters and fishermen are full of stories. Phrases such as, "One time me and . . . ," or, "The biggest root I ever found . . ." lead usually into tales of triumph or exceptional good fortune.

"One of the biggest roots," said Buck Carver, "I ever found in my life— now if you happen to find one on a little red ridge, it'll usually be a darn good root [because] it grows slow and it grows big—I was a'searching for it in a little cover right over there forty years ago, I guess. And this little dark holler, it was still on north ground but it had got up high enough to where the earth was beginning to get red, you know—red clay. And right on top of that darn ridge there was a stalk—it wasn't more than twelve inches high I don't guess—was broke over, was laying with the top pointed down the hill. And I straightened it up; I don't know whether something run again' it and broke it over or whether the weight of the pod of berries had broke it or what. Maybe the wind blowed it over. And I flew loose to digging that darn thing and it was the biggest root I ever got in my life over that small a top.

PLATE 241   A box of dried ginseng roots as delivered for sale to a dealer near Sylva, North Carolina.

PLATE 242   Buck Carver with a handful of roots he dug this fall.

"And then me and _____ was digging some over there in a cove near Mulberry one day. We'd been down in the nicest little flat you ever seen there; north ground, and dark and rich. Found just a few small bunches. And we come up over a bluff right up where we could look down over, and I looked back down there and away up in the air stood a ball of berries as big as a golf ball, looked like. And I said, 'Good God, do you see what I see?'

"And he said, 'What do you see?'

"And I said, 'I think I see the durndest stalk of ginseng down there that I've ever found.'

"And I pointed the berries out to him and he said, 'Do you reckon that *is* sang?'

"I said, 'Won't take us a minute to find out.' And we walked back down there, and surely it was. And we'd stomped all around it, you know, hunting for low, short sang; and it was so durn high we just overlooked it there. I forget how many berries they was in that ball. Seemed to me like it was just a few over a hundred, and nearly every one of them with two little berries in it. You know most of it has it thataway. Most of it has two berries to the pod.

"The oldest one I ever dug had about twenty-seven of them wrinkles on that stem. Now I talked to a Greek about that—that was back in 19 and 34 when I was talking to this Greek—and he told me that he had one with two more rings on it than that, which would have been twenty-nine. But he said them kind of plants was very few and far between. Now where I got this root with the twenty-seven wrinkles on it was where my grandfather lived at one time in a place called Pine Gap Cove way up on Darnell Creek, and he had planted out a garden of the stuff. And I was over there in the summer of '34 and found a few stalks of it. And when the berries got ripe, I went back over there and planted the berries back and dug the biggest stalks. And one of them was the one with the twenty-seven wrinkles on his stem. And he had a heck of a root too. I don't know. I don't guess there's any of that sang left there anymore."

Wallace Moore has found as many big ones as anyone around. "As big a root as ever I dug, I dug up here a year or two ago. I don't remember the weight of it, but it was bigger [around] than my pipe [bowl], and nearly eight inches long.

"And I've found some double-deckers. They'll come up and they'll be a big bunch of berries here, and then right in the middle of that, they'll be another little stem run up and have a smaller bunch of berries on top of that. And they usually got little leaves around that. But you don't find it too often. That's about as big a one as I've ever found. I don't know how old it would have to be. It's got to be in awful rich ground. A young bunch might make a double-decker after it got up big enough to have berries on it if it was in rich enough ground, but it would have to be in awful rich ground. The only ones that I've ever seen—and I never have seen many of them but I've seen a few—was in awful rich ground—usually loose, rich ground.

"But we was bad to hunt. Me and my daddy used to set in up here on the head of Wolf Creek and we'd hunt plumb around Bettys Creek through here. And back then we'd walk and come up Keener Creek and drop across in on the head of Bettys Creek and hunt all day, and then go back in home by night.

"One time me and _____ was hunting. And I kept a'climbing higher on the mountain. He had his little boy with him that day. And I kept getting higher—wanting to get on up towards the top. And he said, 'Oh,' said, 'we're getting too high, we're getting too high.' Well, we wasn't finding any—just a bunch here and yonder scattered around. But it was good, rich ground, and I just kept a'wanting to get on up there because I knowed that so many people that'll dig down in these coves won't get up around right under these tops and up in these roughs. And lot a'times it'll be rich above these roughs a ways, you know.

"And about the time we got up into the edge of the roughs, why, I found,

I believe it was seven bunches on one rock—little flat place on a rock kind'a like this room here, you know. And I come right around under the rock, and I seen a little one-prong bunch and one or two little two-prong bunches right up just by the side of the rock. Got to looking, and I thought well, now, them *seeds* has got to come from somewhere. And I just turned around and looked up in that little flat place and my face was right up in it! And I believe it was seven bunches if I ain't mistaken. It was right up in that one little flat place in that rock there. And then on out up on the rock, the dirt wasn't over a inch thick, I don't guess. Well, you could just take and lift the dirt up off the rock, you know, root and all, and just pull the root out from in under it then.

"And he come on up to me. I told him about it. Well, they was going around below me just on out in front of me, and I whistled at them and they kind'a come back. And his little boy begin wanting t'get a drink— wanting some water. That suited [his father] pretty well anyhow because he was wanting to get back down in the cove further. They wheeled and took back down. I told'em I was going to get a little higher and see if I couldn't find some more up there. So I just turned right back around the way we'd come, but I was way in *above*—right around through the roughs—I could see up on the top of the mountain from where I was at part of the time. And I dug over a pound right around through there [along] with those scattered bunches I'd dug that morning.

"I got away back around under the side of the mountain out there in the roughs, and I heered them down in the cove right below me, and I looked and I seed them and hollered at them—asked them if they was finding any. And they said they wasn't. And I said, 'Well, come on up here. They's plenty of it up here.' They come on up there and we dug on back around till it was time to come out that afternoon—which wasn't very long after they got up there. An hour or two, I guess.

"But there's so many days you put in that you don't find that. That just happened to be a lucky streak there."

Buck Carver claims that there are lots of places back in the woods where people have set out berries, and then either moved away or forgotten about them. They're there now for anyone to find. "Lord, there's patches of it planted back in them woods that people have planted in unsuspecting places [and never gone back to].

"Nearly everyone hunts on north ground in dark coves, you know, and lots of times a feller plants it back, he'll plant it on south ground. That's how come it's in Laney Cove there on Kelly's Creek.

"In 1937, we was making whiskey up there at the east end of them cliffs in what was called 'Stillhouse Cove,' and I come down there one day to see about the beer and see how near ready to run it was, and I dug several roots and got a good pocket of berries, and I went right out through the Gap—Stillhouse Cove Gap—between Kelly's Creek and Mud Creek and down in the head of Laney Cove there—some good dark rich earth there, and walnuts growing in that earth too. So I crawled off in down below the road and reached up and transplanted them roots that I dug up and planted out that bunch of berries. And I checked on it pretty good there for several years, and it was coming along fine. And then I forgot it.

"About twelve years ago, I was making liquor over on Kelly's Creek and stumbled onto the durn stuff walking out the road one day. And I thought, 'Well, good God Almighty, what in the world are you a'doing here?' Big old stalk, you know. Big ball of red berries. And another step, another big one or two. And, 'Oh, yeah. Heck, yeah. I remember now. I planted you here!'

"So I dug a root or two—I didn't try to dig it for market [but] I ought to have—and I forgot it again then.

"About three or four years ago, one of my wife's son-in-laws said something about that patch of sang over there—did I know it was there. I says, 'I ought to know it's there. I *planted* the durn stuff. And I went over there that fall to dig some of it and put in my garden here, and some feller had been in there just ahead of us and he'd dug all the big pretty sang they was there that he could find. And there'd be the tops down on the ground, and big balls of berries. He'd never planted the durn berries back.

"Well, sir, that made me so durn mad I couldn't hardly see. I gathered every durn berry, and went to digging the little stuff then. Dug every durn thing I could find and brought it on over here and transplanted it in the garden.

"But now it don't all come up every year. I went back over there for two or three falls and found more. You can't get it all. I don't care how much— that Raven Rock Mountain there has been sanged to death as far back as I can remember. When I was eight years old, I went to digging sang on that mountain, and I've dug it off and on ever since, and they's *still* some there that ain't been found. I went up there this fall for a little while one day and found several roots and brought them and the berries in here and planted them in that garden."

"The biggest one I ever found," said Lawton Brooks, "was a five-prong bunch. Had the biggest root on it that I ever saw on one. [The plant] was at least up to my waist. I was a'standing, and I didn't know too much about it then. My wife's brother, he knows it, and he was letting me help him look for some. And he was digging it. He gave me a top to go by, and I was a'looking at the top and then a'looking to see if I could see anything like it. There ain't nothing else like it if you ever get used to it. Now I can find it. I can spot it just anywhere. Anyway, I was standing there, and there was a big old wad of berries as big as my fist there, a'sticking right up by my side, and I commenced hollering for him, and he come up there and said that was the biggest bunch he ever seen. So he dug it for me. I let him get it out. He was afeared I'd break it. So he dug it for me and I took it on down there to the store, and that old man gave me a dollar and a half for it. Now that one root would bring a man ten or fifteen dollars because it's about sixty-five dollars a pound this year. It's higher than it's been a'being.

"Now as good a patch as ever I got into was that one that I found over in North Carolina. I got about forty-eight dollars worth that I dug and I wasn't over two hours. That's as good a patch of wild as ever I found in one place, and I didn't cover no territory. I didn't dig any further than from here to that filling station out yonder [about a hundred yards]. I just went backwards and forwards across the holler for a little piece, and I went up next to where the cliff was, and then I looked back down and I'd missed some and I went up, found some, and I went back down, and I come out. There might have been more below than there was above, but I ain't been back. But hadn't a'been nobody there in years digging no sang there. They'd a'been sure—they couldn't a *kept* from digging a whole lot in there. And I ain't been back. That's the reason I been wanting to go back so bad now. If I could get back in that place over there now and take my time and spend a couple of days over there, I could get a *pile* of that blasted stuff 'cause I know some places over there—them old hollers I used to hunt in when I was an old boy and lived there—I hunted in there all the time. I *know* where them old hollers is. I could get in there and I could *find* some ginseng.

"I like to hunt it, myself. It's interesting. You get to hunting for it, it's *interesting,* boys. You just take a liking to it. Same way by bee hunting. I like to bee hunt. I ain't got no use for them when I find them, but I just like to find the bee trees. I know where four or five bee trees is now. But I wouldn't get stung for *all* of them. I'm afraid of them cussed things. They run me crazy!

"But that sang's turning yellow right now. The berries are ripe right now on it. I ain't felt like it or I'd be going. Right now's the best time. Yes, sir. The berries are red as they can be. There's people in the woods today somewhere'r'nother hunting it like the devil right now, I'll bet you. I've talked to several said they've been out. They go and camp out—stay a week at a time back in the woods and just do nothing but get up every morning and start again. Hunt a new territory every time. But I can't climb the mountains like I used to or I'd be right out there with them. I get out of breath too quick. But if I had the air, I'd be right out there with them, climbing around them rough places."

If ginseng is getting scarcer in the mountains, and it seems to be; it still hasn't diminished the number of people who hunt for it. They all have their stories—and their dreams. As Wallace Moore said, "One day I dug a big haverpoke full out of each of my beds and *then* didn't dig it all. Boy, that's a pretty sight to see where it's out like that. Or run into it. Walk up and see big wads of berries just scattered all over the side of the hill and in the holler. Well, I reckon it's about every sang hunter's dream—everybody that's ever dug the sang or fools around with it any—is always a'looking for a patch where he can dig maybe two, three hours, three, four hours, or a half a day in one patch. Everybody you see: 'Boy, if I could just find a patch where I could dig a half a day, I'd be all right!'

"But *them* patches are scattered."

SUMMER AND FALL WILD PLANT FOODS

This chapter continues, and concludes, a section begun in *Fox-fire 2*. In that book, we discussed wild plant foods that could be gathered and eaten in the spring. This chapter does the same for those of the summer and fall.

All the plants mentioned grow easily in, and are native to, our part of the mountains, *and* were used traditionally in the ways noted. Any recipes that turned up whose actual use we could not verify with our older contacts were simply left out of the chapter.

Although the recipes call for the use of sugar, honey or sorghum are both acceptable substitutes, except for fancy cakes or light pastries. Some rules of thumb follow: 1) *Both* honey and sorghum may be used with preserves or canned fruits such as apples, peaches, and pears. The preserves will taste better and sweeter than if sugar is used, and less of each can be added (sweeten to taste). 2) Honey is excellent in breads and other yeast doughs. 3) Sorghum is best used in dark cakes such as apple cake, and will impart a ginger or caramel flavor. It is also good for sweetening apple butter—sweeten to taste and then add cinnamon or other desired spices.

Once again, we have been aided by Marie Mellinger, who has checked our information and added the proper botanical names, and by Carol Ruckdeschel, who has provided us with drawings of many of the plants.

CANNING AND PRESERVING

Making jams or jellies became popular after glass jars became available for canning and preserving. Before that, fruits and berries were dried or made into strawberry or peach leather. Drying fruits and berries called for patience and a great deal of sunlight, or an oven large enough to hold trays of fruit.

In the early days of jelly-making, the mountain women did not have Certo or Sure-jel, and used green fruit along with the ripe to make jelly "jell" or thicken. The tart little wild crabapples were often added to blackberries or blueberries. A fruit acid also was made up for this purpose by dissolving 1¾ ounces tartaric acid in three cups water. Pour this over three quarts mashed, sour-tasting fruit, and let stand twenty-four hours. Strain the fruit, and add one pound sugar to each pint of juice, stirring constantly until the sugar is dissolved. Bottle the juice, but don't seal the jars tightly for several days. This juice (two tablespoons in each batch) may be added to juices that need more tartness to make jelly. Or make a blackberry acid by adding one gallon blackberries to a quart boiling water. Let the berries stand six hours, then pour off and strain. To each quart juice, add one ounce tartaric acid. To each pint of this juice, add 1⅓ pounds sugar. As soon as the sugar dissolves, bottle the juice and seal the bottles with paraffin. Add these juices to berry juices to make jelly when acid is absent in the berries.

Mrs. Cora Ledbetter gave us these directions her mother and grandmother had used for making jellies.

"Fruit for jelly should never be fully ripe; some fruits must be almost green. There are exceptions to this rule, but very few. It is important in jelly-making that the fruit be used in the proper stage of ripeness, as no amount of cooking will make jelly of over-ripe fruit, and if too green, the flavor of the fruit is lost. It is also necessary that good, sound fruit be used to make clear, firm jelly. A porcelain kettle is always best, but a brass kettle (if it's kept bright) or a new tin pan will do.

"When the fruit is being cut, it should be kept in clear water until ready for use; then it should be taken from the water, placed in the kettle, and covered with fresh water, as the fruit is apt to have colored the first. Keep the kettle covered, and steam the fruit until it's perfectly tender, as you wish to get the juice from the fruit without breaking or mashing it more than is necessary. When ready to strain, pour in a jelly bag; hang it up and let it drip; don't squeeze.

"It is best to boil the juice a few minutes before adding the sugar. Speed is necessary if the natural flavor of the fruit is to be retained and the jelly is to be bright and clear. The jelly should "make" in twenty to thirty minutes from the time the sugar is added, and it should be skimmed all the time it is boiling. The best way to tell when it is ready is to drop a little from the spoon into a cup of cold water. If it goes to the bottom and forms a ball, it is ready to be taken from the fire. Another way to test its readiness is to let a small quantity cool on a perfectly dry surface; if ready, it should form a jelly.

"After pouring the jelly into the jars or jelly glasses, let them stand in the sun several hours. Then place papers, dipped in brandy, on the jelly and cover, or use paraffin or tins.

"Never cover the jelly jars with the tins until the jelly is thoroughly cooled, otherwise the moisture from the warm jelly will cause the tops to rust. The jelly should be kept in a dry place.

"To clarify jelly, beat the white of an egg and put it in the juice when the sugar is added; when it boils up as if it would boil over, take it from the fire and pour in a tablespoonful of cold water. After the ebullition ceases, put it on the fire again. Repeat this, then strain through a jelly bag, return to the fire, and let it boil until it jellies."

To can berries, select those that are ripe and firm. Put them in jars filled with cold water; have the rubbers on the jar lids and place the tops on loosely. Place the jars in a can, or any deep vessel, in which a heavy, folded cloth or rack has been placed. Fill the can with water to within an inch of the top of the jars, put it on the stove, and let the water in the can boil three minutes. Tighten the tops of the jars, remove them from the heat, and let cool. When cool, tighten the tops again. A cup of sugar may be added to each half gallon of berries when they are first put in the jars. Care should be taken to have them well sealed before packing them away, and they must be kept in a cool place.

BERRIES AND FRUITS

White mulberry (*Morus alba*) (family *Moraceae*)

The white mulberry was introduced to this country at an early date to help promote the silkworm industry. Silkworm culture never became very successful, but the mulberries remained, spreading naturally throughout the area. It is a small tree with shining leaves, rather rough to the touch and varying in form from whole, ovate to mitten-shaped to deeply cut or incised. Greenish catkins in early spring are followed by whitish or pinkish fruits of a rather insipid taste. Birds love them and a white mulberry tree will attract numerous bird species. The fruits are considered edible, but inferior to those of the red mulberry. Dried white mulberries were used as a substitute for raisins or figs.

Red mulberry (*Morus rubra*) (family *Moraceae*)

The red mulberry is a small, spreading tree rather common in the mountains, and often found around old homesites. Leaves are ovate, roughly hairy above, and softly hairy below. The fruits may be dark red, purple, or black. They have always been used for pies, preserves, jams, or jellies, and also make good wine.

Jake Waldroop told us that "mulberries ripen in June, about the first part. They're a long-shaped berry, usually an inch, or even two or three

PLATE 243   Red mulberry

inches, long. The trees have a pretty blossom of a pinkish color. The mulberries are practically all red."

Mulberry candy: crush mulberries and mix with ground walnuts. Make small balls and roll in sugar.

Mulberry pie: cook mulberries, and drain. Mix with two beaten eggs, one cup cream, and ½ cup sugar. Fill a pie shell and bake.

Wild gooseberry (*Ribes cynosbati*) (family *Saxifragaceae*)
    (dog bramble, dogberry)

The wild gooseberry is a small shrub found in the rich coves, and on the rocky ledges and outcrops of the mountains. It has semi-trailing, very prickly stems four to six feet long, and slightly hairy three- to five-lobed leaves. Small yellow flowers are followed by reddish striped, prickly berries that are very sweet inside. Gooseberries were hard to find but prized for jams and jellies when available. Spiced gooseberries were served with roast fowl on special holidays such as Thanksgiving and Christmas. They also make good pies and preserves. Cultivated English gooseberry, which has berries of a greenish color, sometimes persists around old house or garden sites.

Allegheny serviceberry (*Amelanchier laevis*) (family *Rosaceae*)
    (sarviceberry, sugarplum, shadbush, juneberry, currant tree, sarvis)

The service berry is an understory tree of the mountain woods. It has smooth gray bark, and rather crooked branches. Leaves are narrow and smooth, with slightly toothed edges. The flowers appear very early in the spring with the new leaf buds. Each individual blossom has five long white petals radiating from a greenish center. The red-purple berries are edible and sweet with a pleasant odor.

Serviceberry (*Amelanchier canadensis*)
    (sarviceberry, lancewood, Indian pear, May cherry)

The Canadian shadbush grows on the higher mountains. Leaves are ovate, and the young leaves have a reddish color. The flowers are slightly pink and blossom with the opening leaves, somewhat later than the Allegheny serviceberry. Both trees are called "service" berries because their flowering branches were picked and carried into churches for the Easter service.

Berries of both species are equally good and are prized for sauces and pies. They can be canned, dried, or eaten raw. They should be picked before they are fully ripe.

Jake Waldroop told us a lot about serviceberries. "They ripen in June. They're good food for turkeys, squirrels, bears—practically all wild game love to feed on sarvis. They're a pale reddish color. Some sarvis trees will get very large. I've seen sarvis trees over a foot through. Most of them, though, are the size of your arm. You can't harvest the berries without hacking down the tree or getting somebody to climb up and bend the limbs over. The berries grow in a cluster. There'll be just whole wads of them. The sarvis trees grow back in the wilder mountains, back down the Nantahala River, around under Albert Mountain, Standing Indian, Ridgepole, along Laurel Creek and all those places. Sarvis trees grow along the water courses mostly. Sometimes you find'em up on the mountainsides.

"The berries are just wonderful for pies. And you can just bend down a limb and stand there and eat till you almost tear yourself apart. They're sweet, got a good flavor. The sarvis can't hardly be beat for anything that grows wild in the mountains.

"The sarvis is a hardwood tree, almost as hard as any timber that grows. You can't cultivate them. They grow in the wilder country. They're the first thing that blooms in spring of the year."

All of our contacts agreed that it was hard to get the berries before the birds do. They're high up in the trees and their red color attracts the birds.

Serviceberry pie: heat one pint ripe berries and ⅔ cup sugar and pour into a pie shell. Bake in a hot oven. (You may substitute serviceberries for blueberries in pie recipes.)

Serviceberry flan: three cups berries; ½ cup sugar; ¾ cup flour; 1¼ cups milk; pinch of salt; one tablespoon vanilla. Beat milk, sugar, flour, vanilla, and salt together. Pour half of the mixture in a baking pan. Heat one minute. Add the berries, then cover with the other half of the mix. Bake one hour at 350°.

Muffins: Add serviceberries to cornbread or corn muffins.

Black raspberry (*Rubus occidentalis*) (family *Rosaceae*)
    (black cap, thimbleberry)

The black raspberry appears as a native in cool mountain ravines, but is most common where it has escaped from cultivation and has naturalized in old fields and gardens. This black berry has very pale, long, arching canes, and finely cut, very soft green leaves, whitish on the underside. The fruit is small, usually purple-black in color, but sometimes appears in a pale yellow form. It is very sweet when fully ripe and highly esteemed for jelly or jam. Berries were often dried to preserve them for winter.

There are several varieties of these berries, all good for jellies, jams, etc. If very light jelly is desired, the pink or white varieties should be used, and the berries gathered just before they are ripe. For jam and dark jellies, very ripe berries should be used. For preserves, gather the berries as for jelly. Ripe fruit is also desirable for wines and cordials. Fresh berries should always be used.

The leaves of the black raspberry are rich in vitamin C and were often dried and used for tea. Place several leaves in a cup of hot water and allow to stand ten minutes, then strain and serve with milk and sugar to make the tea.

Mrs. Mann Norton told us, "I like wild raspberries better than I do the tame ones. They've got lots more flavor. They used to be on our place up at the farm and we would go out and pick an eight-pound bucket full."

It has been suggested that they taste best eaten fresh with sugar and cream, but they also made a good berry drink. To make this, put berries in jars with vinegar, seal, and let stand one month. Strain through a sieve and put the juice in sterilized bottles. To use, dilute with cold water and sweeten with sugar.

Raspberry jelly: take ½ gallon berries and boil them in one pint water until thoroughly cooked. Strain, and to one pint juice, add one pound sugar. Boil until it jellies, and pour into jars.

Raspberry preserves: gather the berries when they are almost ripe. Put ½ gallon in a porcelain kettle with one pint of water. Boil ten minutes, or until the berries are tender. Drain off ⅔ of the juice, add one pound of sugar for each pound of berries, and boil until the syrup is thick. Put in jars and seal while hot.

Raspberry pickles: wash ½ gallon fresh, almost ripe, berries. Place them in self-sealing jars with a half teaspoon each of cloves and allspice, and one stick of cinnamon. Boil 1½ pints of good apple vinegar with a half cup of sugar and pour over the berries. Seal while hot.

Raspberry vinegar: put two gallons ripe raspberries in a stone jar. Pour a gallon cider vinegar over them, and let stand twenty-four hours. Drain, then pour the liquor over a gallon fresh berries and let stand overnight. Strain and add one measure of sugar for every measure of juice. Boil and skim. Bottle when cold.

Wineberry (*Rubus phoenicolasius*) (family *Rosaceae*)
(commonly called red raspberry in the mountains, strawberry-raspberry)

This berry was originally introduced from Japan, but has escaped from gardens and naturalized in the mountains. The wineberry has very long trailing, or arching, canes, with orange-red hairs along the stems. The tri-divided leaves are velvety to the touch and whitish on the underside.

White flowers with five petals are followed by bright red, translucent berries that taste delicious. They can be substituted for black raspberries, dewberries, or blackberries in any desserts.

Jake Waldroop described the wineberries. "They grow on a long, green vine, sometimes fifteen or twenty feet in length. The berry has a pretty round face, and is sorta hollow in the middle. They just about top them all for pies, preserves, and jellies. They really are good. There aren't too many of them around anymore. Where they build roads through the mountains or clear off a patch and don't cultivate anything, that's a good place for them to grow. Raspberries grow in bundles."

Aunt Lola Cannon says, "A wild raspberry is real red—the most beautiful color. They make a wonderful jelly because they're so tart and a beautiful jelly because of the color."

Dewberry (*Rubus flagellaris*) (family *Rosaceae*)
The common dewberry is found in many habitats, from open woods to old fields and roadsides. It has long runners that creep along the ground and may be prostrate, or may send up shrubby shoots. Leaves are usually divided into three (sometimes five) sections, and turn a rich purplish-red very early in the summer. Berries are solitary, round, shiny black, and very seedy, but very good for jelly.

PLATE 244   Dewberry

Southern dewberry (*Rubus trivialis*)

The southern dewberry appears on road banks and in fields, with flat, creeping branches that extend up to twenty feet from the parent plant, and root at the joints. Leaves have five leathery leaflets with prickly leaf stems. The flowers are solitary, large, and often pink. The berries are good to eat, but seedy.

Florence Brooks told us, "They make a jelly with a flavor that you'll never forget. You don't need to add anything extra to make them jell. You pick them, wash them, cook them, and strain out all the seeds. You take a cup of sugar to a cup of juice, or a lot of people put two cups of sugar and three cups of juice. Boil it till it rolls.

"Before there were canning jars, jelly was just put in glass jars and a lid on it. Sometimes my mother took beeswax and a white cloth. She melted the wax and dipped that cloth down in it and put it right over that jelly. That'll keep it from molding, but if jelly molds, it doesn't hurt it a bit in the world. All you have to do is run you a spoon around it and get the mold off."

Dewberry frosting: cook berries and strain. Use one cup juice to one cup sugar and boil until it's thick. Add one beaten egg white and beat until it can be spread on cake.

Dewberry pie: one cup sugar; 1/4 cup flour; dash salt. Fill a pastry shell with dewberries, sprinkle the mixture of sugar, flour, and salt over the top. Dot with butter and bake.

Blackberry (*Rubus argutus*) (family *Rosaceae*)

The common blackberry is found in old fields, under power lines, and where roads have been cut into the forest. It has very thorny stems which are either high and arching, or low and sprawling. The leaves have five leaflets and are a deep rich green in color. The fruit is black, juicy, and a prime favorite. Berries are eaten plain, or used for pie, jellies, preserves, cobbler, juice, wine, cake, and bread. Charlie Ross Hartley often saw them dried on strips of chestnut bark in the sun. They were then kept in sacks hanging from the rafters. When needed, the berries were soaked in water before their use.

All blackberries are rich in vitamin C, and blackberry leaves have been used for food. Mrs. Mann Norton said: "Brier leaves should be used when about an inch long, before they get tough. Wash and cut, boil and season, as you would any spring greens, or mix with lettuce or creases."

Blackberry leaves were also carefully dried for tea, used as a gargle, or swallowed to cure "summer complaint." A mixture of dried leaves and honey was a good medicine for a sore throat or thrush.

Blackberry cobbler: use one pint blackberries, sugar to taste, a small amount of butter, and enough biscuit dough for several biscuits. Cook the blackberries until they come to a boil. Add the sugar, then some butter, and cook until thick. Roll out the dough, cut as for biscuits, and drop into the blackberries. Roll some dough very thin, cut it into strips and place on top of the blackberries. Bake until the crust on top is brown.

PLATE 245   Blackberry

Blackberry syrup: one quart berry juice; one pint sugar; one teaspoon allspice; one teaspoon cinnamon; one teaspoon cloves; one teaspoon nutmeg. Mix ingredients and boil for fifteen minutes. Use over pancakes.

Blackberry flummery: one quart blackberries; 1¼ cups sugar; dash cinnamon; ½ cup hot water; dash salt; two tablespoons cornstarch. Mix berries with water, sugar, salt, and cinnamon, and cook to the boiling point. Reduce heat and cook slowly until liquid begins to look slightly syrupy. Make a paste of cornstarch and three tablespoons water. Stir into berry mixture, cook until slightly thick. Serve cold.

Blackberry roll: biscuit dough; four cups blackberries; ½ teaspoon cinnamon; two tablespoons melted butter or margarine; half cup honey; half cup sugar. Roll dough to ⅓-inch thickness, and brush with melted butter. Combine ½ the berries with cinnamon and honey and spread them over dough. Roll as a jelly roll. Place in a large, well-greased pan. Surround with remaining blackberries and sugar. Bake at 425° for thirty minutes. Slice and serve from the pan.

Blackberry jelly: one quart berries crushed in a pan without sugar or water. Cook slowly eight minutes. Strain; measure; bring to boiling point. Add 1½ cups sugar to each cup juice gradually, so the boiling does not stop. Bring to a brisk boil, skim, and bottle.

Blackberry cordial: boil the berries until they will break into pieces, and strain through a bag. To each pint of juice, add one pound of white sugar, a half ounce of mace, and two teaspoonfuls of cloves. Do not use ground spices. Boil for fifteen minutes. When cold, strain, and to each quart of juice add ¾ cup of whiskey. Bottle and seal. Another recipe: Wash the berries and place in a tin vessel, with a teaspoonful each of cloves, allspice, and mace to each gallon of berries. Cover with brandy or whiskey, and let stand four or five days. Strain and add three pounds of sugar to each gallon of juice. Let it heat until the sugar is dissolved. Bottle and cork while hot, and keep in a cool, dark place.

Blackberry wine: cover the berries with boiling water and let them stand twelve hours. Strain and add two pounds sugar to each gallon juice. Put in jugs, taking care to keep the vessels full to the brim, so that as the juice ferments, the scum which rises may flow off. Jugs should be refilled every morning with juice from a smaller vessel kept for this purpose. Continue this for four or five days; then stopper the jugs loosely, and after ten days cork tightly. This will be ready to bottle and seal in four months. Instead of using hot water, as directed, one may squeeze the juice from the berries, and proceed at once, using one pound sugar for each gallon juice. For dry wine, wash and squeeze the juice from fresh, ripe berries. Pour the juice into jugs; keep them full to the brim for four or five days so that the scum may flow off, replenishing each day with juice kept for that purpose. This will be ready to bottle and seal in six months.

Jake Waldroop's recipe for blackberry wine: Gather six to eight gallons of wild blackberries, wash them well, and put them in a big container. Mix in five pounds of sugar, and then cover the top of the churn or container with a cloth, tied down so air can get in but insects can't. Let the mixture work for eight to ten days.

Then strain the mixture through a clean cloth, squeezing the pulp so that all the juice is removed. Measure the juice you have. For every gallon of juice, add one and a half pounds of sugar. Let it work off. When it stops (when the foaming and bubbling have stopped on top), strain it again, measure the juice, and again add one and a half pounds of sugar to each gallon of juice. When it finishes working this time, it is done and can be bottled. Jake keeps his in an earthenware jug with a corn cob stopper.

He makes grape wine the same way.

Blackberry nectar: select sound, ripe blackberries. Add the berries to 3 cups good vinegar in a crock or large jar. Cover the crock with cheesecloth and let stand three or four days, stirring daily. When ready, strain without crushing the berries. Measure, and add one pound sugar for each pint juice. Boil gently for five minutes. Put in bottles or jars and seal. When serving, dilute with water and crushed ice. Use less sugar if a tart drink is preferred.

Blackberry shrub: gather the blackberries, wash and select so that there will be no sour or imperfect ones. Cover with apple vinegar (two years old) and cook until soft. Strain, and sweeten the juice to taste; boil down until it is about the consistency of thick syrup. Bottle and put in a cool, dark place. When serving, use three or four tablespoonfuls to a glass cold water.

Allegheny blackberry (*Rubus allegheniensis*)

This is the blackberry of the high mountains, whose blossoms and fruits appear late in the season. Canes are five to ten feet high, but almost thornless. Each of the five leaflets has a dark red leaf stem. Berries are long, shiny black, and sweet when fully ripe.

PLATE 246   Mountain blackberry

Swamp blackberry (*Rubus betulifolius*)

Swamp blackberry is found in thickets in low, wet places. It has high arching canes, five-part, dark green leaves, and very thorny stems. The berries are black and juicy, but rather sour to the taste.

Sumac (*Rhus typhina*) (family *Anacardiaceae*)
(shumate; lemonade tree)

A small tree of the mountains with crooked, velvety branches. Leaves are woolly-hairy, with 9–13 leaflets, which turn brilliant red in late autumn. Flowers are in large green clusters, followed by woolly red berries. The very similar smooth sumac (*Rhus glabra*) has stems and smooth leaves, and leaflets which are pale on the underside. The very acid red fruits are used to make a pleasing summer drink. Someone told us, "The berries are rather sour, but can be eaten plain. They can be used in jelly to add tartness."

Sumac lemonade: crush berries; cover with boiling water; steep until well colored; strain through a cloth; sweeten with sugar or honey and serve cold. Prepare and serve at once, for the prepared lemonade will not keep. The lemonade not only tastes good, but is said to relieve fatigue and reduce fever.

Sumac and elderberry jelly: boil one pint sumac berries in three pints water until there is one quart juice (boil one quart elderberries in three pints water until fruit is soft). Mash. Strain juice through a thick white cloth. Mix, add one cup sugar for each cup juice and cook into jelly.

PLATE 247   Sumac

Buckberry (*Vaccinium erythrocarpon*) (family *Ericaceae*)
  (mountain cranberry, deerberry, currant berry)

The buckberry grows on the higher ridges and along mountain trails and old roadways. It is a small shrub, three to five feet high, with green leaves and reddish stems. The leaves turn a reddish-yellow early in August. The small, reddish, bell-shaped flowers turn into shiny black berries, very tart, but pleasing to eat. They are a good thirst quencher when hiking in the mountains, or are good in pies or jelly and can be substituted for blueberries or huckleberries in any recipe.

PLATE 248   Buckberry

PLATE 249   Kenny Runion with buckberry.

Jake Waldroop told us, "Buckberries usually grow on high ground. They're a dark blue and pretty well the same size as blueberries. They grow in thickets—blueberry thickets. They get up about three feet high."

Florence Brooks suggested eating them with milk and sugar. "For a pie, clean and wash the berries and stew them with water and sugar—about a pint of water to a quart of berries. Then sweeten them to taste. If you want a dumpling pie, just cut the dough into squares and drop it into the stewed berries while the berries are boiling. I like to put my berries in a pan and cut the dough in strips and put them on top of the berries. Bake the cobbler in the oven."

Squaw huckleberry (*Vaccinium stamineum*) (family *Ericaceae*)
(gooseberry, dangleberry, tangleberry)

This is a spreading shrub common in oak-pine woods with very pale, gray-green leaves. The white, bell-shaped flowers are very pretty and hang down from the ends of the branches in the early spring. The glaucous green fruit hangs from a slender stem, hence the name "dangleberry." The berries are very sour until the time when they are fully ripe, late in the season. Few people enjoy them raw, but they make excellent sauce, jelly, and jam. Jake Waldroop told us that you hardly ever see gooseberries back in the north coves. "They're usually on the south ground, on the ridges and in flat woods. They're a round berry and there are white and red ones. The wildlife feed on gooseberries. They grow where you can pick just wads of them by the handful. When they bear, a bush will just be bowed over with them. You hardly ever see a gooseberry bush thicker [in diameter] than

PLATE 250   Huckleberries

my thumb. They grow pretty tall and thick, and ripen mostly in September."

Sauce is made by cooking the juice or pulp with an equal weight of sugar. Serve cold.

Florence Brooks said that "some people like to stew them and eat them with cake. To stew them, you pick them and clean them like you do blackberries. Add sugar to sweeten to your own taste. Eat on pound cake, plain cake, any kind."

Fanny Lamb said, "Gooseberries are good to use in pies—like you would make a huckleberry or strawberry pie, or anything like that."

Gooseberry pie: mix two cups berries with 3/4 cup sugar and cook until thick, mashing berries. Make a plain biscuit dough. Roll it out and cut into one-inch-wide strips. Pour berries into a pie plate, place strips of dough crosswise on the berries, and bake at about 450° until the crust is brown.

Sparkleberry (*Vaccinium arboreum*)

The sparkleberry is a tall shrub or small tree found on rocky ridges in open oak-pine woods. It has a gnarled trunk, and very shiny, almost evergreen, oval leaves. It blossoms profusely in early spring, with very sweet-scented white, bell flowers. Berries are wine-red to black and rather dry and insipid. It is said they can be used for jelly or preserves, but they need plenty of sweetening.

High bush blueberry (*Vaccinium corymbosum*)

The high bush blueberry grows to twenty feet high in rich woods or rocky hillsides, usually in deciduous forests. It has smooth green elliptical leaves. Flowers are pinkish. The berries are blue and small and rather sour. They were often dried for winter use.

High bush black blueberry (*Vaccinium atrococcum*)

Another tall bush found on rich hillsides and in mountain coves. The twigs are hairy, and the leaves slightly toothed. Flowers are white and the berries are black. They are very good to eat, but are seldom found in large enough quantities for jellies or jams.

Low blueberry (*Vaccinium vacillans*)

This is the common blueberry of the mountains and piedmont, low-growing and colonial, found in open pine woods and along roads and

PLATE 251   Low blueberry

PLATE 252   Blueberry

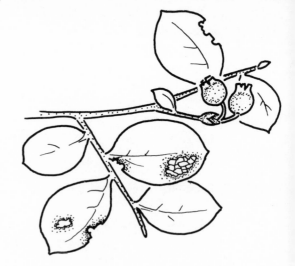

trails. Greenish-pink bell flowers appear before the leaves in early spring. The berry is the familiar, good-tasting bright blueberry, prized for cooking. It can be dried for winter use.

The difference between blueberries and huckleberries is more than that of color, for there are blue huckleberries and black blueberries. In general, huckleberries each contain about ten large seeds, while a blueberry has many tiny seeds. Huckleberry leaves have glands that can be seen if a leaf is held up to light or examined under a pocket microscope.

Blueberry cobbler: cook berries for fifteen minutes over medium heat with one cup sugar. For dough, use two cups flour and two tablespoons shortening. Roll the dough out thin, cut into long pieces, and place on top of berries in a pan. Let boil. Place in oven until crust browns.

Stewed blueberries: one quart of berries sprinkled with sugar. Cook gently without adding water.

Blueberry juice: cook berries; strain. Add dash of cinnamon or lemon and drink hot.

Hot blueberry sauce: simmer blueberries with cinnamon, nutmeg, sugar to taste, and a dash of lemon. Simmer until berries pop. Serve hot.

Blueberry dessert: one quart blueberries; two cups biscuit mix; 2/3 cup milk; two tablespoons melted butter; two tablespoons sugar; 1/4 teaspoon cinnamon. Cook berries and drain thoroughly. Roll out dough, brush with melted butter, and spread blueberries over surface. Roll up and place seam side down in a greased baking dish. Bake in a hot oven (425°) about twenty minutes.

Blueberry fritters: mix up biscuit dough, add one well-beaten egg, sugar to taste, and one cup blueberries. Fill a small kettle with grease, melt, and drop in two or three fritters at a time, turning until they're brown. Dip out and sprinkle with sugar.

Blueberry crisp: four cups blueberries; 1/3 cup sugar; four tablespoons butter; 1/2 cup brown sugar; 1/3 cup flour; 3/4 cup quick oats. Put berries in a baking dish, and sprinkle with sugar. Cream butter with brown sugar, blend in flour and oats with a fork. Spread over berries and bake.

Spiced blueberries: five pounds blueberries; six cups sugar; two cups weak vinegar; one tablespoon cinnamon; one tablespoon cloves; one table-spoon allspice. Tie spices in cheesecloth. Boil sugar, spices, and vinegar for ten minutes. Add berries, simmer ten minutes. Seal in hot, clean jars.

Bilberry (*Gaylussacia frondosa*)
   (huckleberry)

Bilberries are shrubs found on high, dry ridges. They have olive green, leathery leaves, resin-dotted on the underside, and pink flowers with open-ing leaves followed by dark blue, rather dry berries. Bilberries look much

PLATE 253   Bilberry

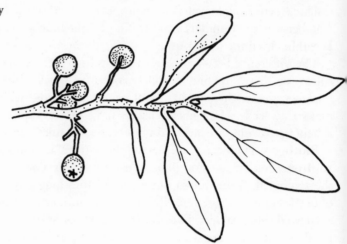

like huckleberries, but they have a white color that gives them a "frosty" appearance. They're good raw, and in pies and jelly.

Huckleberry (*Gaylussacia baccata*)

This huckleberry is a small shrub, which grows to four feet and has reddish stems and leaf stems. The leaves are shiny green and resinous. Flowers are reddish with the opening leaves and are also glandular. Berries are very shiny black, seedy, and very sweet.

Dwarf huckleberry (*Gaylussacia dumosa*)

Dwarf huckleberries grow in large patches, joined together by running roots. They are six to twelve inches high, with almost evergreen leaves. White flowers appear in early spring with the new leaves. The berries are black and very sweet. Box turtles often collect the entire crop.

Huckleberry is the common mountain name for all species of *Gaylussacia* and *Vaccinium*. They are also called wild blueberries, or buckberries, and are very similar to tame blueberries, but are a little larger, darker and more sour. They are eaten plain, with cream and sugar, or used in pies, preserves, jelly, or wine. They can be dried for winter use by spreading them thinly on a tray and placing them in the sun each day until dry—they should be ready in about a week. Store in tight containers.

Florence Brooks suggests adding a little rhubarb to huckleberry jelly. "I just don't believe huckleberries will make without Sure-jel or a little something sour added." Huckleberries may be put up in any way that dewberries are, but they require less sugar than other berries.

Huckleberry jam: wash the berries, put them in a kettle with a little water, and boil until tender. Add ½ pound sugar to each pound fruit, and boil thirty minutes or until quite thick.

Huckleberry jelly: boil the berries in very little water until very tender; strain, and boil the juice five minutes. Then measure and add one pound of sugar to one and a half pints of juice. Return to the fire and boil twenty minutes. Jelly should always boil fast.

Huckleberry pickles: the huckleberry may be pickled just as the dewberries are.

Huckleberry puffs: one pint huckleberries; two cups flour; two teaspoons baking powder; one level teaspoon salt; two eggs; enough sweet milk to make a batter a little thicker than that used for cakes. Grease six or seven teacups thoroughly with butter. Fill them half full with the above mixture; place in closely covered steamer and steam one hour. The puffs will come out perfect puff balls. Serve with sauce. Puffs are spongy and absorb a great deal. Other fruits or berries may be used.

Huckleberry cake: one cup butter; two cups sugar; three cups flour; four eggs; ¾ cup milk; two teaspoons baking powder; one teaspoon vanilla; one quart huckleberries. Cream butter and sugar; add eggs. Add milk and flour alternately, then add baking powder, vanilla, and berries. Bake in loaf pan in moderate oven (350°) forty-five minutes to one hour. Serve with butter and sugar sauce (light brown sugar) or eat as is.

Elderberry (*Sambucus canadensis*)
   (elderblow)

The elderberry is a tall shrub found in waste places, along streams, and in old garden spots. It has large leaves with many smooth, green leaflets. Often

PLATE 254   Elderberry in flower

PLATE 255 . . . and mature.

numerous stalks come up in a group. Bark is rather light brown and warty. Flowers appear in large, flat, fragrant clusters (*Plate 254*), followed by small, dark wine-red to black berries (*Plate 255*).

Elder flowers were brewed into a tea, said to be a blood purifier, or used as an alternative for aspirin, relieving pain and inducing sleep. The flowers were also brewed with chamomile or basswood to make a wash for the skin.

Flowers are also used for fritters or wine. Elderberries are used for cold drinks, wine, pies, preserves, and jellies. BERRIES MUST BE COOKED BEFORE USING as they are dangerous to some people if eaten raw.

Rufus Morgan told us that "we have the purple elderberries in this section [of the country]. People use them for preserves and elderberry wine. If you climb up in the mountains in the higher elevations, especially in the Smokies, there is a red elderberry with a white blossom—it's a different shaped group of flowers, like a pineapple, but smaller. The purple elderberry blossom is flat on top. They both have the white blooms, but the fruit of the purple elderberry is different."

Jake Waldroop says, "They're most everywhere. They're a small berry and they grow in a cluster. They usually ripen in August. They say elderberries make the finest wine, although I never made any. They make good jelly and preserves."

Aunt Lola Cannon's grandmother made elderberry wine. "She was a practical nurse and midwife. I believe she used it to give to people with rheumatism, lame joints. When she went to deliver a baby, she gave this wine to the patient."

Lawton Brooks told us that he does make wine out of elderberries. "You just put them up like you do all the berries. Put them in your churn or something like that. Then you let them work off [ferment]. Put a little sugar in them and let them work off good. Then you take them up and strain that. Add a good bit of sugar to them that time, and put them back in the churn again, and let them work off again. I don't know exactly how long it took us to make that stuff. I got drunk on it—stayed drunk for a day or two. That was such a bad drunk that I've never drunk any more elderberry wine. It liked to have killed me."

Mountain people used to make fritters out of the blooms by dipping them in a thin batter and frying them in grease.

Elderberry pie: make a crust using one cup flour and one tablespoon shortening. Roll it out thin, place in a pie pan and cook the crust before you put berries in it. For the pie, use one pint elderberries, one tablespoon cornstarch, and one cup sugar. Put them in the cooked pie crust and bake thirty minutes at 325°.

Elderflower flapjacks: remove the stems from two dozen flower clusters. Wash flowers in one quart water with four teaspoons salt. Mix with a pancake batter and fry. Sprinkle the pancakes with sugar.

Elderberry drink: cook berries with sugar. Strain and serve cold.

Elderflower fritters: dip flowers in hot fat. Sprinkle with sugar and eat.

Elderberry wine: use five quarts of berries to six quarts of water. Mash the berries and let stand in a crock two weeks, stirring every day. Strain. Add as much sugar as you have juice. Let stand two weeks and then bottle.

Elderberry jam: eight cups berries; six cups sugar; 1/4 cup vinegar. Crush and measure the berries, then add sugar and vinegar. Boil until thick. Pour boiling into scalded jars and seal.

Elderberry-apple-orange jam: one quart elderberries; five cups sugar; one lemon; twelve large cooking apples; three medium-sized oranges. Cook apples until mushy. Add the berries, oranges, and lemon chopped fine. Grate the rinds of one orange and the lemon. Mix together with sugar and boil thirty minutes.

Steamed elderberry pudding: four cups berries; two cups sugar; one teaspoon lemon juice; one tablespoon butter; two cups flour; four teaspoons baking powder; one teaspoon salt; 3/4 cup milk. Sift dry ingredients and work in the butter. Add milk and mix well. Combine sugar, berries, and lemon juice and mix these with the batter; pour into a buttered baking dish, cover tightly, and steam forty-five minutes. Serve with cream.

Possum haw (*Viburnum nudum*) (family *Caprifoliaceae*)

Possum haw is a large shrub found in wet places—in swamps and along streams. It has oval, shiny green leaves and flat clusters of sweet-scented white flowers. Its fruits are very seedy blue berries.

PLATE 256   Possum haw

Black haw (*Viburnum prunifolium*)

Black haw is a large shrub or small tree, which grows in open, rocky woodlands. Its leaves are ovate and finely toothed. Flowers appear in flat white cymes followed by black berries.

Both the possum haw and the black haw are extremely seedy, but can be used for jelly. They are sometimes combined with wild grapes or elderberries. Some say that the viburnum fruits are best gathered after a frost.

Possum haw jelly: boil berries, strain, add sugar to taste, and boil again until thickened. Combine with crabapples, if desired.

Black haw sauce: one quart berries; ¾ cup honey; two tablespoons lemon juice. Crush the berries, strain, and cook with honey and lemon juice for ten minutes; then chill and whip.

Figs (*Ficus carica*) (family *Moraceae*)

Figs persist as bushes around old houses and garden areas, freezing back every winter in the mountain areas, but sending up new shoots again in the spring. Its twigs have an acrid, milky juice that is poisonous to some people. The flowers are very insignificant, but when ripe the figs are very good to

PLATE 257   Fig

eat. The fruits have a large sugar content, and can be dried or frozen. Some say they should always be picked in the early morning. Figs have been used not only as a source of food but also in home medicine for boils, sores, or pulmonary and kidney infections.

Fig preserves: put figs in a pan, and add sugar until it covers the figs. Let them sit overnight, then cook slowly until the juice boils to a jelly. Put in jars and seal.

Preserved figs: one pint figs; ¾ pound sugar. Cover figs with water to which a pinch of baking soda has been added to take away dust and fuzz. Add the sugar, and bring to a boil slowly, and let stand overnight. Repeat the boiling and standing three times, adding spices or a lemon slice to the last boil. On the third day, pack in jars.

Fig pudding: two cups cooked rice; two cups milk; one whole egg beaten; ¼ stick butter or margarine; one cup chopped figs; ½ cup chopped nut meats; ½ cup brown sugar; ¼ teaspoon ginger; ¼ teaspoon nutmeg; ½ teaspoon vanilla. Add the sugar to the beaten egg, and fold in rice, milk, figs, nuts, and spices. Add vanilla and melted butter. Pour into greased baking dish and bake in a 350° oven until mixture is set and slightly browned on top. Serve with cream, ice cream, or vanilla sauce.

Honey figs: peel figs and cut in half. Arrange in serving dish and pour a mixture of equal parts honey and hot water over them. Chill well and serve with cream.

Figs with ham: peel figs and arrange with finely sliced ham on a platter.

Ripe fig preserves: Place figs in the sun for a short while to harden their outer skin, then prick each fig with a darning needle. Prepare syrup (use one pound sugar in ½ cup water for each pound figs) by stirring water until all sugar has dissolved, and bring to a boil. Add fruit and boil one minute. Add three to four tablespoons lemon juice and boil until fruit is clear and transparent. Bottle and seal while hot.

Fig preserves: six quarts firm, ripe, unbroken figs; six cups sugar; four cups water. Wash figs and pat dry. Bring sugar and water to a boil, add figs, and cook until tender. Pack in jars and process thirty minutes in a hot-water bath.

Mayapple (*Podophyllum peltatum*) (family *Berberidaceae*)
   (maypop, mandrake, hog apple, wild lemon)

Colonial in habit, mayapples appear in large colonies on rich bottom lands and open hillsides. The large, umbrella-like leaves hide the pretty white

PLATES 258–259   Florence Brooks with mayapple.

flowers and later the oval fruits. The lemon-yellow fruits are edible, with a strawberry-like flavor. Green mayapples can give you a terrific stomach ache. CAUTION: ALL THE REST OF THE PLANT IS POISONOUS IF EATEN.

Jake Waldroop described the mayapple to us. "It'll have one stem come up to a bunch and have a broad leaf. Sometimes it'll fork. It has a great big white bloom that sheds off and it'll bear an apple. They're pretty good to eat. Black draft medicine is almost all pure mayapple. The plants die in the fall and come back every year." Mayapples are delicious candied, preserved as jam, and in pies.

Mayapple drink: squeeze out the juice from the fruit, and add sugar and lemon; or add to white wine.

Mayapple marmalade: gather ripe fruits, and simmer until soft. Strain through a colander, and boil the pulp with sugar to taste.

Pawpaw (*Asimina triloba*) (family *Annonaceae*)
  (custard tree, custard apple, frost banana)

The pawpaw is a small slender tree, found in rich woods and along streams. It is always easily identified by its obovate green leaves, and its very ill-smelling twigs. Three-petaled dark red flowers appear before the leaves in early spring. The fruits are green, then yellow, and finally brown, and look like stubby bananas with a thick, sweet pulp. They are ripe in late autumn, and are about an inch in diameter. One has to develop a taste for pawpaws. Someone said they "feel like sweet potatoes in your mouth, and taste somewheres between a banana and a persimmon." Gordon Underwood said you "eat them just like a pear. They're yellow on the inside."

Baked pawpaws: bake in skins; serve with cream.

Pawpaw pie: one cup sugar; one cup milk; one egg; ¼ teaspoon salt; 1½ cups pawpaws, peeled and seeded. Place in a stew pan and stir together. Cook until thickened. Pour in an unbaked pie shell and bake until done.

Pawpaw flump or float: beat up pulp with egg white and sugar like an apple float.

Pawpaw bread: add pawpaw pulp to nut bread. It gives bread a lovely rose-red color.

River plum (*Prunus americana*) (family *Rosaceae*)

The river plum is a small tree which grows to twenty feet. It has thorny branches and can be found along rivers and streams in the mountains and piedmont. Leaves are ovate and toothed. The sweet, white, five-petaled flowers appear before the leaves in early spring (April–May). The very tart fruits are red or yellow and can be dried for winter use.

Sloe plum (*Prunus umbellata*)
   (hog plum)

The sloe plum is a small tree found in pine woods and along roadsides, mostly in the piedmont. Its bark is scaly and the leaves are oval and shiny. Its pure white flowers appear several weeks later than those of the chicka-saws or river plums. The dark-colored fruit ripens from July to September. Fruits are small and tart, sometimes rather bitter.

Chickasaw plum (*Prunus angustifolius*)

Chickasaw plums were once native to areas west of the Mississippi River. The Creeks and Cherokees planted them near their villages and they have naturalized in old fields, roadsides, and open woodlands all over the moun-tain areas. The chickasaw is a small tree, with narrow leaves, which usually grows in clumps. The white flowers appear before the leaves. Chickasaws have the best-tasting plums—large red-yellow fruits that are very sweet when ripe and make superlative plum jelly, plum butter, preserves, and spiced plums.

In the old days, it was the fashion to have plum-gathering picnics, going by horse and buggy or wagon to the plum thickets to gather bushels of fruit and dry them for winter use.

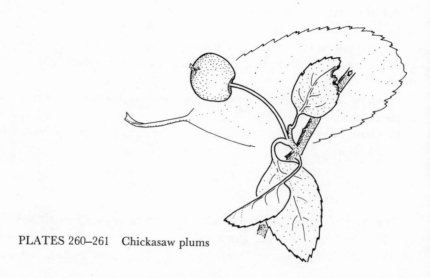

PLATES 260–261   Chickasaw plums

LATE 261

Wild plum catsup: five quarts wild plums; four pounds sugar; one pint vinegar; one pint water; 1½ teaspoons cinnamon; one tablespoon allspice; one tablespoon cloves. Boil plums with one teaspoon soda. Bring to a rolling boil, then strain through a colander. Simmer with sugar, vinegar, and spices until thick as catsup.

Plum cobbler: cook and pit one quart plums. Roll biscuit dough thin and cut in strips. Grease a pan well and add a layer of plums and strips of dough, topping with sugar and dabs of butter. Repeat until pan is almost full. Bake in medium oven.

Plum pudding: put pitted, cooked, sweetened plums two inches deep in bottom of a baking dish. Beat one cup sugar, four tablespoons butter, and one egg to a cream. Add one scant cup of milk, two cups all-purpose flour, and two teaspoons baking powder. Mix well, and pour over plums. Bake one hour at 350°.

Wild plum conserve: seven pounds wild plums; five pounds sugar; two pounds of seeded raisins; three oranges. Wash and pick over plums. Cover with boiling water, and add ½ teaspoon soda. Bring to rolling boil. Pour off the soda water, rinse plums, and strain through a colander. Slice oranges in thin slices, rind and all, removing seeds, and grind the raisins. Combine fruit and sugar, adding enough water to keep them from sticking. Simmer until thick and clear.

Wild plum jam: Three-fourths pound sugar for each pound plums. Place in alternate layers in kettle and let stand until juice flows freely. Boil 15 minutes. Press through a sieve, return to fire, and boil until thick, stirring constantly.

Wild plum preserves: take half-ripe plums, and boil for three minutes. Pour off the water and add one pound of sugar to one pound of fruit. Boil for thirty minutes, or until the syrup is thick.

Plum preserves: pour boiling water over large plums, then remove the skins. Make a syrup of a pound sugar and a cup of water for each pound fruit. Boil, and pour over the plums. Let it stand overnight, then drain saving the syrup. Boil syrup again, skim, and pour over plums. Let them stand in this another day, then cook in the syrup until clear. Remove the plums with a skimmer and pack them carefully in cans; boil the syrup until thick and pour into the cans and seal.

Plum jelly: cover ½ gallon half-ripe plums with water in a porcelain kettle, and boil ten minutes. Pour off the juice and strain through flannel. Add one pound sugar to each pint juice and boil until it will harden when cold (about twenty to thirty minutes).

Plum sauce: gather plums, wash, and lift gently from water. Add one cup sugar for each cup fruit. Do not add extra water as that clinging to fruit is enough. Cook slowly at low heat. When mixture has thickened, strain through colander to remove seeds and skins.

OR: take ½ gallon almost green plums, wash and cover with water, and boil fifteen minutes. Pour off the water; add to the plums two pounds sugar and one cup good apple vinegar. Boil for thirty minutes. Take from the fire and flavor with one teaspoonful each of extract of cloves and ginger.

OR: boil three quarts of half-ripe plums fifteen minutes. Rub through a colander and add one pound sugar, one cup apple vinegar, and ½ teaspoon each of ground cloves, mace, and cinnamon. Place again on the fire and boil for half an hour.

Plum sweet pickle: take ½ gallon almost green plums and scald until the skins are tender. Drain them well and place in jars. Have ready a syrup made of two pounds sugar, one pint apple vinegar, and a teaspoon each whole cloves and mace. Pour over the plums while hot, and seal.

Salt wild plum pickle: take ½ gallon large green plums, wash and put in self-sealing jars. Make a pickle of one quart water, one teaspoon vinegar, and one teaspoon salt. Boil a few minutes, pour over the plums, and seal while hot. Keep until the cool weather and they will be ready for use.

Sour wild plum pickle: take ½ gallon green plums, and pierce them each two or three times with a needle. Put in jars. Boil one quart vinegar, two cups sugar, one teaspoon cloves, and one stick cinnamon. Pour over the plums and seal while hot.

Green wild plum pickle (imitation olives): pick plums that are grown, but not at all ripe. Boil a mixture of one tablespoon white mustard seed, one tablespoon salt, and one pint vinegar. Pour this over the plums. Repeat this three mornings in succession and seal in jars.

Spiced wild plums: boil ½ gallon plums five minutes, pour off the water and add three pounds sugar, one teaspoon each ground cloves, allspice, and cinnamon, and one pint vinegar. Boil a half hour, stirring constantly. Seal while hot.

Peach (*Prunus persica*) (*P. amygdalus*)
    (Indian peach)

Indian peaches are small trees, spreading with scraggly branches, said to be descendants of those trees planted by the Cherokees around their villages. Other, more modern varieties are planted by the birds, or persist around old homesites. Leaves are very narrow and shining, and beautiful pink blossoms appear before the leaves in very early spring. The fruit of the Indian peach is white with a rosy cheek, white-meated with a red heart. Other old peach trees have small, yellowish or pinkish fruits. All have a most delicious flavor, raw or cooked. Peaches are rich in iron, and peach leaf tea was a medicine for bladder troubles or used as a sedative.

Peach and apple butters were made with molasses before the early settlers had sugar.

PLATE 262 Terry and Teresa Tyler with Indian peach.

Pickled peaches: peel fruit, quarter, and put in a pot. Make enough brine of two parts vinegar, one part water, and two parts sugar to cover fruit. Add ground cinnamon, nutmeg, and allspice to taste. Cook until tender. When done, lift the fruit out and pack in jars. Keep brine simmering and pour into jars over fruit leaving a half inch at the top. Seal at once. (Apples can be used instead of peaches.)

Peach tarts: for the tart pastry use two cups flour; one teaspoon salt; two teaspoons sugar; two egg yolks; ½ cup sweetened soft butter; a few drops of water. Sift dry ingredients together. Place in bowl and make a hollow in center. Put egg yolks and butter in hollow and work in with the fingers, gradually blending in dry ingredients. Add a few drops of water to hold the mixture together. Wrap in wax paper and chill thoroughly. Roll out ¼-inch thick and fit loosely into an eight-inch pan. Bake, cool, and brush with glaze. Peel and slice the peaches, roll in lemon juice, drain, arrange in shell, and spoon on glaze, covering all pieces well. Chill. For glaze use ¾ cup orange juice; two tablespoons sugar; one tablespoon cornstarch. Mix in saucepan and cook, stirring until thick and clear. (Blackberries or grapes may be used instead of peaches.)

Pincherry (*Prunus pensylvanica*) (family *Rosaceae*)
   (red bird cherry)

The pincherry is a small tree found in the high mountains with a shining, lenticeled bark, and slender, almost drooping branches. The leaves are very narrow, thin, and a shining green. Solitary five-petaled white flowers appear before the leaves in the spring. Cherries are small, sour, and a bright red in color. They make a particularly pretty, bright red jelly.

Wild cherry (*Prunus serotina*)
    (black cherry, rum cherry)

    The black cherry can be a tall tree (100 feet high in the mountain coves), or it can be smaller and almost shrubby on rock outcrops, along fencerows, or in old pastures. It grows in all habitats, and is a common tree in the mountains. The bark is satiny, the leaves are oval and shiny green. Flowers appear in a white raceme with the new leaves and the cherries are black on red stems.

    The wild cherry has always been a "medicine" tree. Its bark was used in cough medicines and known as "lung balm" bark. To prepare wild cherry bark for tea, boil the cherry bark and make a cough syrup out of it. Take the bark and a little whiskey. They claim it's the best medicine there is for the stomach.

    Jake Waldroop says, "The wild cherries are ripe about the last of September and the first of October. They're ripe when they drop off the trees. They're mostly a hull and a great big round seed. They've got a pretty good flavor, not too bitter. They're pretty plentiful."

PLATE 263   Wild cherry

Cherry wine: crush the cherries, put them in a large crock and cover with boiling water. Cover the crock and let it sit until the juice stops working. Then strain through a cloth squeezing out all the juice. Put the juice back in the crock, add three cups sugar to each gallon, cover, and let sit nine to ten days, or until it stops working. Put in bottles, but don't seal too tightly until it has stopped fermenting completely. The wine is supposed to be very potent.

Wild cherry jelly: wash three quarts cherries, and place in a vessel with two cups water. Boil until very tender. Pour off the juice, measure and add one measure sugar to each measure juice. Boil until jellied. Put in molds and cover when cold with writing paper dipped in brandy.

Wild brandy cherries: fill a large jar with cherries. Make a syrup of a half pound of sugar for each pound of fruit. Scald the fruit in this syrup, but do not boil. Remove the fruit, boil the syrup until it is reduced by one third, and add one third as much brandy. Pour over the cherries, and seal while hot.

Southern negus: take a quart red cherries, three pounds black wild cherries, and four pounds currants. Mash and mix all together, and store in a cool place for three or four days. Strain, and boil the juice. To every pint of juice, add ½ pound sugar. Let cool and bottle. Add two or three tablespoonfuls to one glass ice water.

One-flowered haw (*Crataegus uniflora*) (family *Rosaceae*)
    (haws, thornapples)

This is a small shrub found in open oak-pine woods and on rock out-crops. Its leaves are leathery and toothed. White blossoms appear in the spring with the new leaves. The haws are brownish-red, globose, and very seedy.

October haw (*Crataegus flava*)

This is the most common haw in this area, a shrub or small tree with rounded, serrate-edged leaves. The white flowers appear rather late in the spring, followed by reddish-yellow haws late in August–September. This haw is common in open, dry, or rocky woodlands.

River haw (*Crataegus punctata*)

River haw forms a very thorny shrub or small tree, found along stream banks and rich, rocky woods. The leaves are almost obovate, and its white flowers, purple-centered, are followed by bright red fruits.

PLATE 264 October haw

PLATE 265 River haw

Mrs. Norton described the haws as "haw berries. They're very seedy, and they are usually eaten plain. We used to call them rabbit apples; they grow on thorny bushes, and are just little, round, red things. I've eaten some of them. I prefer them to groundcherries any time."

Thornapple relish: pick over and wash one gallon thornapples. Remove blossom ends and cut the apples in half. Put in a kettle with barely enough water to cover the fruit, and simmer until soft. Drain, and strain through a colander. Add one cup brown sugar, two teaspoons pepper, two teaspoons salt, two teaspoons cinnamon, and three finely chopped onions. Mix together. Add one pint vinegar, and boil until onions are tender. Bottle.

Hawthorn jelly: ½ pint water, one pound fruit. Simmer haws, mash, and add one pound sugar to one pint liquid plus a dash of lemon juice. The result will be a brown jelly that tastes like guava.

Red haw (hawthorn): crush three pounds fruit (not too ripe). Add four cups water and bring to a boil. Simmer ten minutes and strain the juice through a jelly bag. Bring four cups of juice to a boil and add seven cups sugar. This shows a jelly test soon after it begins to boil (for test, jelly flakes rather than pours off a spoon). Pour in jars and seal.

Haw marmalade: cook haws in very little water, and press through a sieve. Use 1½ cups strained pulp and juice. The juice of a lemon or orange improves the flavor. Add five cups sugar, boil hard for one minute, and seal in jars.

Pear (*Pyrus communis*)

Old pear trees are found at homesites, and sometimes naturalize at the edges of open woods. They are tall trees, often with scraggly branches. They have fragrant white flowers very early in the spring. The pears are of varying size and flavor, often very hard, and need cooking to be edible. Pears can be substituted in any recipes using apples or dried for winter use.

Baked pears: put halves in baking dish, cover with honey and a dash of cinnamon. Or, scoop out the cores (but leave the peeling) and fill the center with honey and chopped nuts. Bake half hour at low heat.

Pear conserve: one cup pears and one cup apples. Grind fruit, add two cups sugar, and mix thoroughly. Boil for twenty minutes and seal.

Apple (*Pyrus malus*) (family *Rosaceae*)

Old apples persist where orchards once covered the mountains, and around old homesites. Apples also come up along fencerows and woods' edges where apple cores have been thrown. These old apple trees may be gnarled and crooked, but often have small apples with a very good taste. The sweet white apple blossoms appear with the leaves in early spring.

Dried apples: apples are either sliced into thin slivers, or cored and sliced into rings. The rings were strung on a pole; slices were spread out on boards. They were then set out in the sun or in front of the fireplace, depending on the weather, until the slices were brown and rubbery. This usually took two or three days, and they were turned over frequently so they would dry evenly. When dry, the apples were stored in sacks for use during the winter. Mrs. Grover Bradley says, "Those make the best fried pies I ever ate." (Peaches were dried just like apples. Small berries such as blackberries were simply spread out on boards and were not sliced.)

Apple beer: peel apples and dry peelings as above. Put peelings in a crock, and add enough boiling water to cover. Cover crock and let sit for about two days until the flavor comes out in the peelings. Strain and drink. Add some sugar, if desired.

Scalloped apples: use six tart cooking apples, one cup graham cracker crumbs, ¾ cup sugar, ⅛ teaspoon cinnamon, butter or margarine, water. Pare, core, and slice apples. Roll out crackers and add sugar and cinnamon mixture. Place in baking dish in layers, covering each layer with crumbs dotted with butter. Add hot water to moisten. Bake in a medium oven three quarters of an hour until apples are well cooked and crumbs browned.

Dried apple cake: mix your favorite white or yellow cake, and bake in four thin layers. Mix one pint dried apples with one pint water and cook until thick and the apples are mashed up. Sweeten apples to taste and add spices. Let cool and spread between layers and on top of the cake.

Fruit vinegar: Mrs. Tom MacDowell said that she used to make fruit vinegar. "We had a cider mill and we ground the apples up and made it out of the cider. Before the cider mill ever come, they mashed up the apples and put them in a barrel and let'em rot, and then drained the vinegar off."

Apple vinegar: mash up two or three bushels of apples. Put them in a barrel or crock and fill with water, using one quart syrup to 2½ gallons water. Cover with a coarse cloth and keep in a warm place. The vinegar will make in a few months, but will not be good for pickles until it is eighteen months to two years old. Vinegar may also be made from one gallon cider using one cup syrup and "mother" from other vinegar.

Baked apples: wash, core, and fill with honey and chopped nuts. Bake at low heat.

Apples on a stick: alternate chunks of apples and pears on a stick. Broil over an open fire.

Cider apples: peel and cut apples in small pieces. Cook slowly on low heat in enough cider to cover the apples.

Apple sauce: cook peeled, cored apple slices with butter and brown sugar.

Apple grunter: use little, sour wild apples. Grease a baking dish with butter, put in two inches sliced apples, and shake on cinnamon, nutmeg, and salt. Tuck six ¼-inch cubes fat salt pork into the apples. Pour ½ cup molasses over the whole thing. Put on a biscuit dough crust. Make holes in the crust with fork tines so the juice can bubble up. Bake.

Crabapple (*Pyrus coronaria*) (family *Rosaceae*)
    (northern wild crab)

The northern wild crabapple is a wide-spreading tree of the mountains, found in thickets, rich coves, and often along streams. It has oval leaves and rather spiky twigs. The beautiful pink flowers appear in early May and spread a spicy fragrance over the woods. The fruits are round, yellow-green, and very hard. They are considered the best of all apples for apple butter.

Crabapple (*Pyrus angustifolius*)

The southern crabapple is a small, spreading tree, usually growing in thickets, with prickly branches and very narrow, toothed leaves. The flowers are deep pink and very fragrant. The little apples are hard, shiny, and green, and will hang on the tree until January. Jake Waldroop says, "We used them mixed with other apples for jelly. The crabapples are ready now (in September). They never do get sweet. Nothing affects them—they're always sour."

PLATE 266   Crabapple

Crabapple jelly: one gallon crabapples and one gallon golden delicious apples. Peel apples and quarter. Cook together for thirty minutes. Strain the juice. Put into a cooker with two cups sugar for each cup juice. Boil for one hour.

Crabapple jelly: simmer crabapples twenty minutes. Mash in a pan. Strain, and for each pint juice add one pound sugar; boil ten minutes. Add mint leaves if desired. Put in jars, and set in a dark place to thicken.

Virginia jelly: four quarts crabapples, two quarts grapes. Wash and clean fruit, cook and strain juice. Add sugar and boil until it reaches the jelly stage.

Crabapple preserves: small hard crabapples are picked from the ground in December or January. Cook with sugar and a few red cinnamon candies. Juice thickens into jell overnight.

Sweet pickled crabapples: two quarts crabapples, $2\frac{1}{2}$ cups sugar, two sticks cinnamon, two teaspoons whole allspice, one teaspoon whole cloves, two cups vinegar, $1\frac{1}{2}$ cups water. Wash crabapples. Cut out blossom ends, but leave stems intact. Tie spices in cheesecloth. Combine in large pot with spices, sugar, vinegar, and water. Boil five minutes. Add enough fruit to cover the surface without crowding. Cook slowly until just tender. Fill jars, and seal at once.

Crabapple butter: four quarts crabapples, three cups sugar, four cups water, two teaspoons cinnamon, one teaspoon cloves, one teaspoon salt. Cook crabapples with peelings and run through a food mill. Boil slowly over low flame until thick. Seal boiling hot.

Crabapple preserves: peel the crabapples and drop them in water. When all are ready, place them in a porcelain kettle and let them just come to a boil. Remove from the fire, pour them with the water into an earthen bowl and let them stand twenty-four hours. Then take them out of the water and remove the cores. Drain them and then pack in sugar, using one pound sugar for each pound fruit. Let them stand twelve hours; pour off the syrup and boil it twenty minutes; then put the apples in and let them boil until clear, when they will be ready to seal.

Crabapple jelly: remove the stems, wash the apples and rub them well with a coarse cloth. Put them in a porcelain kettle, cover with water and let them boil until very tender. Strain out the juice and return it to the fire and boil ten or fifteen minutes longer. Then add one pound of sugar to each pint of juice, and boil until it jellies. This will take only a few minutes.

Crabapple pickle: peel and core the apples. Put them in a jar and over them pour hot vinegar, sweetened and spiced, as for peach pickles. Let this remain twenty-four hours; then drain off the vinegar, heat it, and pour over the apples and seal.

Crabapple pickle: peel and core the apples. Put them in a jar and over them pour hot vinegar, sweetened and spiced with choice spices. Always use good apple vinegar not less than two years old. Always seal the jars with three layers of brown paper put on with a flour paste when it is not convenient to use jars that are self-sealing.

Pasture rose (*Rosa caroliniana*) (family *Rosaceae*)

The pasture rose is a familiar low bush which grows to six feet high, found in old fields, on rock outcrops, and on roadsides. It has variable divided leaves and prickly stems. The roses are single, pink, and very fragrant. The red hips are extremely rich in vitamin C.

Swamp rose (*Rosa palustris*)

The taller swamp rose is found in marshes, bogs, and along rivers and

PLATES 267–268   Rose hips

streams. The flowers are small but fragrant, and the red hips are equally edible. The hips of various cultivated roses such as the dog rose (*Rosa canina*), the sweet brier (*Rosa eglanteria*), and the multiflora rose (*Rosa multiflora*) can all be eaten.

Rose hip tea: cook the hips and strain off the juice. Then reheat juice with honey or sugar. It has the taste of apple. The darker the hips, the better the tea.

Rose hip juice: wash and remove ends from hips. Use 1½ cups water to one cup rose hips. Cover, and let stand twenty-four hours. Strain, and bring to a rolling boil. Add two tablespoons of vinegar or lemon juice and bottle.

Rose hip jelly: put in a boiler with water according to how many rose hips you have. Just let them simmer. Strain. Let juice start simmering and add a cup sugar for each cup juice.

Rose hip soup: four ounces dried rose hips, three cloves, cinnamon stick, lemon rind, one tablespoon white wine, one ounce flour, one ounce fat. Soak rose hips, and boil in one pint water with the lemon rind, cinnamon, and cloves until they are soft. Rub through a fine sieve. Brown flour in fat and gradually add the soup. Sweeten to taste. Add the wine and serve hot.

Haggenbutten: simmer rose hips gently. Strain the juice, and add honey. (Haws can be substituted.)

Rose hip jam: cook one pound of fresh rose hips with two cups boiling water. Press. Add pectin and sugar to juice and boil.

Rose hip jelly: boil equal parts of sugar and rose hips in enough water to keep from scorching. As soon as hips are soft enough, mash them in this brew, and boil five minutes longer. Strain, add pectin to juice and boil again.

Rose hip juice: four cups rose hips, two cups boiling water. Wash hips, chop coarsely, add boiling water. Cook five minutes. Strain. Add sugar to taste. Drink hot or cold, use on puddings, or add to cold milk to make a pudding by thickening rose juice with ground rice or tapioca. Makes a good drink with a dash of cinnamon or ginger.

Rose soup: cook hips. Strain, add ½ cup sugar and one tablespoon cornstarch. Cook until slightly thickened. Serve hot or cold.

Rose petal jam: one pound rose petals; two cups sugar; ½ cup water. Pinch white part from petals, wash, and dry. Dissolve sugar, stir in the petals, and place in a shallow pan. Cover with glass and place in the sun for eight hours. Then put in a kettle and simmer for twenty minutes.

Rose sugar: bury a fragrant rose in a glass jar full of powdered sugar. Put the top on tightly and place in the sun for several days. Use sugar in tea or on fruit.

Fried rose petals: dip in whiskey, then in batter. Fry in deep fat, dip in sugar, and serve.

Rose dew: gather roses in early morning. Pull petals into small pieces and to each cupful add two cups sugar. Mix well and pack in jars. After two months, drain off the liquid that has formed and bottle it for use in flavored drinks, whipped cream, or puddings.

Rose syrup: four cups rose hips, two cups boiling water. Cook five minutes, and strain through a cloth. Add sugar and boil until it begins to thicken slightly.

Rose petal tea: four cups boiling water over three teaspoons dried rose petals. Steep three to five minutes, and sweeten with honey. Add mint or basswood blooms for dyspepsia.

Maypop (*Passiflora incarnata*) (family *Passifloraceae*)
(wild passion flower, apricot vine, granadilla)

The maypop climbs ten to twelve feet by means of tendrils, but usually is found looped over other foliage. Leaves are three-lobed and indented. The showy lavender and green flowers are followed by the pulpy yellow-green fruit, juicy and edible when fully ripe.

Rev. Rufus Morgan told us, "The passion flower is supposed to have in the flower the various symbols of the crucified Christ—the nails and such, I've forgotten just what the symbols are. It is a fruit children like."

Fanny Lamb said, "Just after frost, they go to turning yellow. Wild apricots are very different from the tame ones. They are about the size of an egg and are very seedy inside."

PLATES 269–270   Maypops in flower

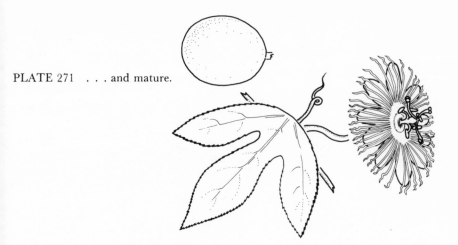

PLATE 271 . . . and mature.

Yellow passion flower (*Passiflora lutea*)

This small flowered relative to the maypop is a higher climber. It has small, deep green, blunt, three-lobed leaves that may be variegated, or streaked with white or yellow. The flowers are small and pale yellow. The purple fruits are about one inch long.

Maypop drink: pour hot water over maypops, squash out the pulp, strain, drink hot.

Maypops (wild apricots): gather maypops when they are very green. Take off the peeling, cut in halves, and take out the seed. Drop them in lime water, made in the proportion of one cup lime to one gallon water. Let them stand twelve hours. Boil fifteen minutes in weak alum water; then boil in clear water until they are clear. Drain well. Pack in granulated sugar using ¾ pound sugar to each pound fruit. Let stand twelve hours, then boil twenty minutes. Flavor strongly with ginger root. Either seal in jars or dry as crystallized apricots.

Maypop jelly: Use the seed and pulp of ripe maypops. Boil them fifteen minutes and strain. Add one pint sugar to each pint of juice and boil twenty-five to thirty minutes, or until it jells. To make maypop syrup, boil only until a thin syrup tests. It's good with biscuits or pancakes.

Fox grape (*Vitis labrusca*) (family *Vitaceae*)

The fox grape is a high-climbing vine, with very large, rather smooth leaves. It is found in low woods and along streams in the mountains and upper piedmont. Flowers are intensely sweet scented and grapes are small and rather sweet.

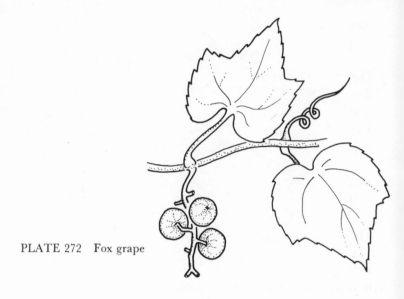

PLATE 272   Fox grape

Chicken grape (*Vitis vulpina*)
(possum grape, river grape, winter grape, frost grape, bull grape)

This grape is high climbing by means of dark red tendrils. Its bark shreds with age. The young leaves are pinkish in the spring, and toothed and three-lobed when mature. The flowers have the odor of mignonette. Grapes are small, black, or very dark blue, with a musky odor. They ripen after frost. The high-climbing possum grape (*V. baileyana*) of the mountains is a variety of the *Vitis vulpina*.

PLATE 273   Possum grape

Summer grape (*Vitis aestivalis*)
    (pigeon grape, bunch grape)

The summer grape is found along streams, usually loosely draped over bushes and small trails. It has large dentate leaves, white on the underside. Its leaves may be cobwebby when mature. The grapes ripen in September, and are blue-purple with a bloom. They may remain on the tree until they become wrinkled and raisin-like.

Muscadine (*Vitis rotundifolia*) (family *Vitaceae*)
    (scuppernong, bullace)

The muscadine is our most common grapevine, climbing everywhere. It can go to one hundred feet in the trees, in all habitats. Its bark is white-speckled, and the leaves are small and glossy on both sides. Small green flowers are followed by large, thick-skinned, richly flavored grapes. Grapes on individual vines may vary greatly in texture, color, or flavor. Grapes are rich in vitamins B and C, and iron. They are said to stimulate the appetite. The wild muscadine is the ancestor of many cultivated varieties.

There is a tremendous variety of wild grapes in the mountains: possum, river, summer, fall, muscadine, scuppernong, and fox. They are usually eaten plain, or made into jelly, juice, or wine. The leaves can be used in making cucumber pickles. Place them between the layers of cucumbers in a crock, but do not eat them. They add a nice flavor and help pickle the cucumbers.

Jake Waldroop told us about fox grapes. "The Japanese beetles just killed ours out. There were a big grape. They looked like a concord, only bigger. When they go to getting ripe, they have the best smell. You can make wine, jelly, preserves. The fox grapes were something wonderful—plenty of them. They ripen in the later part of August on into September. There is also a fall grape. One vine will be in several trees, and have just bushels of grapes from this one vine. They are sweet. They can be eaten skin and all."

Cora Ledbetter told us, "If you cooked grapes down and used no sugar at all, what you'd get would be juice but it'd be so sour you couldn't drink it. Wild grapes made better jellies than domestic. Cook down, strain (to get seeds out) and use about two cups sugar to one cup juice. Cook till it jellies. It doesn't take long. There's plenty of pectin in the grapes. Seal with paraffin or put in glass jars. Not too much jelly was made back then. It depended on molasses and honey for sweetening."

Dried grapes: grapes can be sun-dried for future use.

Possum grapes preserved: wash, put in jars, cover with syrup.

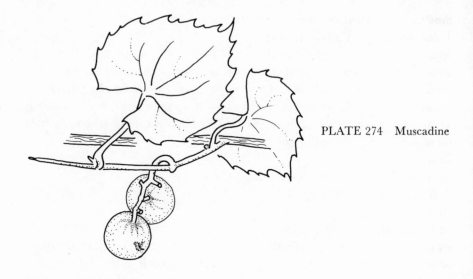

PLATE 274   Muscadine

Grape jelly: pick about a gallon of wild grapes, and wash, removing the stems. Crush in a large pan, add a pint of apple vinegar, and some cinnamon if you wish. Cook for about fifteen minutes slowly, strain through a cheesecloth, and boil for about twenty minutes. Add three pounds of sugar and cook until it starts to jell. Put into jars.

Fox grape jelly: Wash and stem one peck grapes, drain and mash. Cook, strain. Measure five cups juice and cook twenty minutes. Remove from fire and add five cups sugar, stir until all is dissolved. Pour in glasses and let stand. It will gradually thicken and will have a good grape flavor.

Grape leaves: grape leaves can be put up in June for future use. Alternate a layer of leaves with a layer of salt until you fill a jar. Soak overnight before using.

Stuffed grape leaves: wash leaves, roll, stuff with rice and chopped chicken or ham, salt, and pepper. Broil lightly.

Rolled grape leaves: gather large leaves in June, snap off petioles. For filling, use one pound minced lamb or beef with a little suet, one cup rice, salt and pepper to taste. Place tablespoon of filling in each leaf, roll, fold, stack in pot. Add cold water to 2/3 depth. Boil gently one hour. It is wise to put a pie plate under the leaves to prevent burning.

Grape juice: Sterilize quart jars. Place two cups washed grapes, fully ripe, in each jar. Add 1/2 cup sugar. Fill to top with boiling water and seal. Let stand three to four weeks before straining for use. This makes a good-smelling, pale juice.

OR: pick and wash grapes, put in a kettle, barely cover with water, and cook. Strain, add 1/2 cup sugar to each quart of juice, boil five minutes. Pour into jars and seal at once.

Possum grape juice: Gather, shell from stems, and wash. Stew the grapes and mash them. Strain. Add a little cornmeal for thickening, and boil again.

Spiced grapes: for this relish (used with meat, bread, etc.) use seven pounds fox or possum grapes, one cup fruit vinegar, two teaspoons cinnamon, five pounds sugar, one teaspoon cloves, one teaspoon allspice. Wash, stem, and pulp grapes. Put pulp with seeds over fire and cook until seeds come free. Add skins and pulp together with sugar, vinegar, and spices. Cook until thick, and can.

Crock grapes: collect dry, sound fox grapes, and pack them in a churn. Pour boiling hot fresh molasses or syrup over them. Take two clean cloths and dip the first in hot beeswax and the second in hot tallow and tie each cloth separately around the top of the churn. Make this in the fall when the grapes are fresh and ripe, and set the churn in a cool place until winter. They can be eaten during the winter after they have mildly fermented.

Scuppernong preserves: cook grapes until seeds are free, and strain. Add ½ cup sugar to one cup juice, and cook until it jells. Pack in hot jars and seal. For spiced preserves, add cinnamon, mace, and one cup vinegar.

Scuppernong juice: wash grapes, crush, and barely cover with water. Heat until pulp is soft. Remove from heat, and let sit five minutes to deepen color. Pour in a jelly bag and squeeze. Add one cup sugar to each cup strained juice, and stir until sugar is dissolved. Heat to 180°, stirring constantly. Bottle, leaving ¼-inch head space.

Scuppernong pie: one cup scuppernongs, seeded; one cup sugar; one tablespoon flour; one tablespoon butter; one egg, beaten; few grains salt. Heat grapes, add salt. Cream butter, sugar, flour and egg. Pour over grapes, and then pour all that into uncooked pie shell. Lattice top with pastry. Bake one hour at 300°.

Grape wine: use five gallons crushed grapes and five pounds sugar. Mix grapes and sugar together, and let work nine days. Strain, and let work nine more days. Then strain again and seal loosely in jars. The wine might work a little more, and if the tops are too tight, they may blow up. When it has quit working completely, seal jars tightly and store in a dark place.

Muscadine marmalade: Aunt Lola Cannon told us that this is "the finest thing in the way of preserved fruits. You cook the muscadines until all the pulp looks like a mass of mush. Then you put it through a colander. The product is real thick. Put sugar in and cook it down like a preserve. You have to cook the marmalade a long time, unless you add pectin or Sure-jel."

Muscadine jelly: take the pulp and juice of half-ripe muscadines. Nearly cover them with water. Boil a few minutes and strain through a jelly bag. Measure the juice, and add one pound white sugar to each pint juice. Boil until it will congeal when dropped on a cold, dry surface. This usually takes from twenty to thirty minutes.

To preserve muscadine pulps: take half-ripe muscadines between the thumb and forefinger and press the pulp into an earthen vessel; continue until the desired amount of pulp is ready. Then press the seeds from the pulp in the same way. When the seeds have all been removed, put the pulp in a kettle with just enough water to cover, and boil two or three minutes. Add 1½ pounds sugar to each pint pulp and boil twenty minutes, or until the syrup is thick.

To make a firm jelly that is nice to serve with whipped cream, put the pulps in their strained juice and add a pound sugar for each pint juice and boil for fifteen or twenty minutes.

Preserved hulls of muscadine: take the hulls, after using the pulp, and boil them in enough water to cover, until they are tender. Pour off half the water and add 1½ pounds sugar to each pint hulls. Boil until the syrup is quite thick, and put in jars.

OR: use the hulls in the same way, with one pound sugar to each pint hulls and leave all the water in which they are boiled. Seal while hot. Some people prefer these to those having more sugar.

Persimmon (*Diospyros virginiana*) (family *Ebenaceae*)

The persimmon is a common southern tree, found at the edges of woods, in old fields, and along roadsides. It grows to fifty feet, with a very rough trunk, and oval, leathery-looking leaves. Small leathery, greenish bell flowers attract honeybees. The fruits are one to 1½ inches in diameter, orange or peach colored, with several flat seeds. They are very sour and astringent

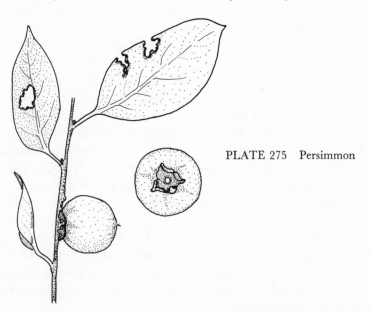

PLATE 275   Persimmon

until they are fully ripe, when they become sweet and edible. They do not need frost to ripen, but many people prefer not to pick them until after the frost. Individual persimmon trees may vary greatly as to the size and flavor of their fruits. Tree-ripened persimmons are best. To be good, a raw persimmon must be soft and squishy to the touch. Persimmons are very high in food energy. The leaves, rich in vitamin C, can be used for tea. Persimmons can be eaten plain, put into bread, or made into jam or beer.

Persimmon bread: use one cup cornmeal, one cup flour, one cup crushed persimmons with seeds removed, one spoonful of baking soda, a dash salt, and ½ cup buttermilk. Mix everything together. Add water if mixture is not thin enough. Bake like cornbread.

Persimmon beer: gather persimmons and a good number of honey locust seed pods. Wash them both well and place them in a large crock in layers until the crock is full. Pour enough boiling water in to cover them, cover the churn, and let it sit at least a week. Pour off or dip out the beer as desired. When drained, the churn may be filled with boiling water again to make a second batch.

OR: gather and wash persimmons and place them in a churn. Pour enough boiling water in to cover them and let them work. Skim off the foam, add sugar to taste, and let them work some more. The beer is supposed to be very potent.

Locust and persimmon beer: break honey locust pods into small pieces. Place in bottom of barrel or churn. Add layer of crushed persimmons, then another layer of locusts, and another of persimmons. Cover with water and let stand until fermentation stops. Drain off and bottle or use from churn. (Sometimes a layer of syrup cane pumice was added in the bottom and on top of the persimmons and locust to add more sweetening and a mellow taste to the beer.)

Persimmon pudding: 1½ cups persimmon pulp; 1½ cups sugar; ½ teaspoon salt; 1½ cups buttermilk; 1¼ cups flour. Strain persimmons through a colander. Stir all ingredients and put in greased pan. Bake one hour at low heat.

OR: two cups ripe persimmon pulp; one cup brown sugar; ½ cup white sugar; ½ teaspoon cloves; one teaspoon cinnamon; dash of nutmeg; ½ teaspoon salt; two cups flour; ½ teaspoon soda; four tablespoons melted butter; two egg yolks; two egg whites, stiffly beaten; three cups sweet milk. Remove stems, cover with warm water. Leave persimmons in water until they are soft, then drain water and discard. Put persimmons through a colander to separate pulp from the seeds. Add sugar and spices to the pulp. Mix thoroughly. Add the two beaten egg yolks. Blend dry ingredients and milk alternately. If lumpy, beat with rotary egg beater, as batter should be very thin and smooth. Add butter and fold in egg whites. Pour in buttered baking dish until ¾ full. Bake at 325° until firm (about one hour). Serve plain or with whipped cream and broken pecan nuts.

Persimmon frosting: cut and mash one cup persimmons. Add ⅓ cup butter, and cream together. Then add three cups powdered sugar and ¼ teaspoon vanilla. Beat until creamy.

Persimmon pie: one cup persimmon pulp; two cups sugar; one cup milk; one tablespoon flour (or cornstarch); three eggs; one teaspoon nutmeg; ½ teaspoon salt. Peel and crush persimmons until smooth. Add sugar and beat. Add three egg yolks and one egg white. Add milk, nutmeg, and salt. Beat until smooth. Pour into nine-inch pie shell and bake until done. Make meringue by beating whites of eggs until stiff. Add four tablespoons sugar. Put on top of pie and brown in moderate oven.

Candied persimmons: pack persimmons in jars, alternating with layers of sugar. Put on lids and store in a cool place until they become candied.

Stuffed persimmons: wash and stone firm persimmons. Stuff with nut meats. Roll in granulated sugar. Serve at once.

Persimmon pulp (to top pudding or ice cream): peel, strain, and mash, removing seeds. Stir in one tablespoon lemon juice. Spoon over pudding, fruit cocktail, or ice cream.

Persimmon marmalade: cook ripe persimmons in a double boiler; strain through sieve. To two quarts pulp, add ½ pint orange juice. Cook down, add sugar to taste. Bottle and seal.

Persimmon butter: cook and strain persimmons. Add ½ teaspoon soda to each cup pulp. Sweeten and flavor with spices or orange rind. Cook thoroughly and bottle.

Persimmon-nut bread: ⅓ cup shortening; ½ cup sugar; two eggs; 1¾ cups flour; two teaspoons baking powder; ½ teaspoon salt; ¼ teaspoon soda; one cup mashed persimmons; ½ cup chopped hickory-nut or black-walnut meats. Cream shortening, add sugar and eggs; beat well. Sift dry ingredients, add to creamed mixture alternately with persimmons and nuts. Pour in greased loaf pan and bake at 350° for one hour.

Persimmons can be used instead of prunes or pineapple for upside-down cake, or used as a topping with nuts and sugar on coffee cake.

Groundcherry (*Physalis virginiana, Physalis heterophylla, Physalis pubescens*) (family *Solanaceae*)
  (cape gooseberry, husk tomato, bladder cherry)

The groundcherries are low, spreading plants, the various species differing mostly in the amount of hairiness on the leaves. These natives of Peru and Mexico often appear in cultivated gardens or in waste places. Leaves are variable in shape or form. Flowers are an inverted bell, pale yellow with

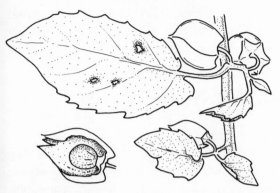

PLATE 276   Groundcherry

a brownish center. The edible cherries, yellow when ripe, are enclosed in a papery husk. The husk also turns yellow when the cherry is ripe. The cherries are used in preserves or pies. DO NOT EAT THE LEAVES, for they have the poisonous properties of most members of the nightshade family.

Physalis viscosa is a closely related species distinguished by very sticky stems and leaves. *Physalis edulis* (*oxocarpa*) the cultivated garden ground-cherry, or strawberry tomato, will also escape and naturalize or reseed itself in old gardens. This plant has slightly larger fruits with a bright yellow or purplish-red cherry.

Many people are very fond of groundcherries, others have to develop a taste for them. Mrs. Norton said, "I had a daughter who was always picking groundcherries and eating them, but I never did like them. I'd have to be real hungry to eat them."

Jake Waldroop says, "They are a sweetish, good-flavored thing. They are small, something like the end of your little finger. They come up in the summertime and die down in the fall. You don't use them much until after the frost falls on them. That's when they're really good. They're white-looking with little stripes and have a husk on them. You take the husk off and the cherry is inside."

Groundcherries are often dried and used for sweetening. When preserved, they need very little sugar.

Groundcherry pie: one pint hulled cherries; $\frac{1}{2}$ cup white sugar; $\frac{1}{2}$ cup brown sugar; one tablespoon butter; one tablespoon quick-cooking tapioca; juice and grated rind of $\frac{1}{2}$ lemon. Combine and bake between two pie crusts.

Baked groundcherries: mix groundcherries with eggs, milk, and a little flour. Bake at low heat until firm. Serve with milk or cream.

Groundcherry sauce: one quart washed groundcherries; two cups honey; one cup water; $\frac{1}{2}$ teaspoon cinnamon; one tablespoon lemon juice. Boil.

Tops, bottoms, and in-betweens—this is a designation for a variety of wild plant foods that do not fit any specific category. We might bring them under miscellaneous but that seems a dull way of treating a most interesting assortment of plants. They are given here in botanical order.

Cattail (*Typha latifolia*) (family *Typhaceae*)
(reed-mace)

This is the familiar cattail of marshes and stream banks, with tall stalks, broad grassy leaves, and a brown flower spike. Early in the season, the flower spike is double and the top, or staminate part, rich with yellow pollen. All parts of the plant are edible, from the rhizome roots to the young green spikes. Young shoots can be a substitute for asparagus. The bulb-like sprouts can be peeled and boiled as a vegetable, or pickled for salads. The young shoots are a good substitute for poke salad. Roots can also be ground into meal or flour said to be the equal of corn or rice. Rich in pollen, this yellow substance can be gathered and used in baking.

Cattail shoots may be boiled or creamed. Cut the whole sprout up and roll in meal. Add salt and pepper and fry them. Or, boil young cattails one inch long for fifteen to twenty minutes and cover with cream sauce.

PLATE 277   Cattail

Cattail flapjacks: two cups pollen; two cups flour; four teaspoons baking powder; one teaspoon salt; two eggs; one cup milk; 1½ cups water; one tablespoon sugar or syrup; bacon drippings. Mix and fry in a greased pan.

Cattail pancakes: boil roots into gruel, then dry. Mix with an egg, milk, ½ teaspoon salt, and margarine. Drop by tablespoons into a well-greased cast-iron skillet. Serve with cooked blueberries or stewed apples.

Cattail soup: cook in water until tender and drain. Add water, milk, salt, and pepper; top with cubes of toasted bread before serving.

Nut grass (*Cyperus rotundus*) (family *Cyperaceae*)
(coco-grass, earth almond, rush nut, ground nut)

A small weedy sedge, native of Europe, but naturalized everywhere in waste places. It has long, running rootstocks bearing small, hard tubers at intervals. These are usually too hard to eat raw, but can be cooked and used as you would use any nuts. Nuts can be ground into meal that makes a good cooked cereal.

Nut sedge (*Cyperus esculentus*)
(coco-sedge, yellow galingale, chufa, ground nut)

This larger sedge grows in damp, weedy places. It has rather stout stems up to eighteen inches high, with yellowish divided flower heads. Sweet nutty tubers with a tough, dry rind occur on the roots. These can be ground into flour.

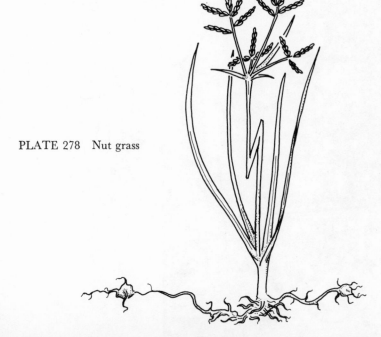

PLATE 278   Nut grass

Chufa drink: soak tubers eight hours. Mash, add one quart water and ½ pound sugar to each ½ pound of tubers. Strain through a sieve and serve as a drink.

Chufa (ground nut) bread: 2½ cups warm water; two packages active dry yeast; one tablespoon salt; one tablespoon melted margarine or butter; seven cups unsifted flour; one cup peanut butter; ¼ cup softened margarine or butter; one egg white; one tablespoon cold water; ¼ cup chopped ground nuts. Measure warm water into a warm mixing bowl. Sprinkle in yeast and stir. Add salt and melted margarine. Add flour and stir until dough is sticky. Place in a greased bowl; let rise one hour. Turn dough on a floured board. Roll half into an oblong pan, cover with peanut butter, softened margarine, and ground nuts. Cover with rest of dough. Roll up and seal. Brush top with egg white. Bake in 450° oven for 25 minutes.

Chiney-brier (*Smilax pseudochina, Smilax bona-nox, Smilax glauca, Smilax rotundifolia*), (family *Liliaceae*)

> (greenbrier, ground nut, sarsaparilla, saw brier, prickly bamboo, China brier, cat brier, biscuit leaves)

The chiney-briers are weedy vines found everywhere, with tough prickly stems, oval to arrow-shaped leaves, and fuzzy, very sweet-scented green flowers followed by blue or black berries. The tips of the arching new shoots

PLATES   279–280 Greenbriers: *Smilax glauca* (left) and *Smilax rotundifolia* (right).

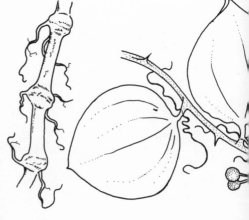

are very good to eat. Before the days of commercial gelatin desserts, the knobby roots of all four species of Smilax were dug and used for food. The berries have been used for seasoning.

Gather greenbrier shoots when tender enough to snap, and use them raw in salad, or cook into a cream soup. They can be combined with lettuce or other greens, or used as a substitute in any recipe that calls for asparagus.

Chop up or grind roots, and cover with water; strain, leaving powdery residue. This will be an edible powder of a reddish color. Mix with warm water and honey for a delicious jelly; cook into gruel for invalids; fry in hot grease for hotcakes; or use as a cornmeal substitute for fritters or bread.

Wild bean vine (*Phaseolus polystachios*) (family *Leguminosae*)
(wild kidney bean)

A slender, twining vine, found in rich, damp woodlands and along streams. It is a perennial with tri-divided bright green leaves, and small bunches of white or pale purple flowers. The beans occur in small pods, are edible, and can be used as one uses dried garden beans, but they are difficult to obtain, as the pods coil up and expel the seeds as soon as they ripen. The round, white tubers on the roots are called ground nuts.

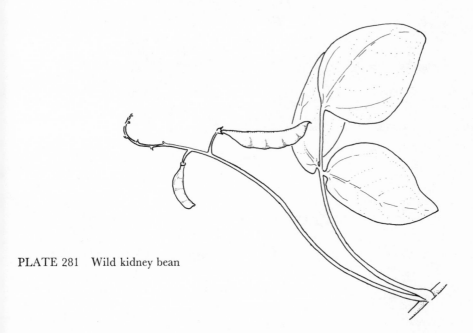

PLATE 281   Wild kidney bean

Hog peanut (*Amphicarpa bracteata*)
   (wild peanut, hog vine)

This slender vine twines to seven feet over other shrubbery. It has tri-divided light green leaves followed by two kinds of pods: those at the upper part of the vine have slender pods with small mottled beans; those near the base of the plant bend and go underground (like peanuts) where they form fleshy underground pods. Both are edible after boiling, but have a rather poor taste.

PLATE 282   Hog peanut

Ground nut (*Apios americana*)
   (sprig nut, Indian potato, bear potato)

A four- to five-foot vine found in very wet places, usually growing in great patches. Leaves have five to seven leaflets. There are clusters of maroon, sweet-smelling flowers in midsummer. The roots have a string of small rhizomes, or thickened tubers, that have a delicious, nutlike flavor. They can be roasted, boiled, or sliced and fried. Cooked in syrup, they are superior to yams. THEY ARE NOT CONSIDERED EDIBLE UNTIL COOKED.

PLATES 283–284   Ground nut: flowers (left) and tubers (right).

In the mountains, the names wild sweet potatoes, or pig potatoes, seem to be given to the tubers of the wild bean (*Phaseolus*) or the ground nut (*Apios*). The hog peanut (*Amphicarpa*) is not as common as the other two leguminous vines, but was probably used for food where it was available.

Roast the wild sweet potatoes in ashes; or peel and slice, boil in salted water so they won't turn dark, and fry in grease, adding brown sugar, salt, and pepper.

You can make a delicious pudding out of ground nuts by steaming them. Tie them in a cloth with a mixture of flour, sugar, and an egg and hang over your boiler to steam.

Honey locust (*Gleditsia triacanthos*) (family *Leguminosae*)

The honey locust is a small, very thorny tree found in hedge rows and waste places, woods' edges, and rocky outcrops. It has compound leaves, and small, honey-sweet, greenish-yellow flowers in April and May. The long pods contain many small seeds, and a small amount of sweet edible pulp. These have been used to make a drink, ground into meal, or used with persimmons in persimmon beer.

The honey locust tree produces long, flat seed pods which are dark brown or black when ripe. They may be eaten raw, as there's a honey flavor in the pod.

Honey locust beans: shell beans from pods, soak overnight, and boil.

Locust bread: dry pods and grind into meal for bread.

Jerusalem artichoke (*Helianthus tuberosus*) (family *Compositae*)
   (bread root)

   This tall sunflower grows to twelve feet in rich bottom lands where it has naturalized. It is also found in waste places and persists in old garden sites. The leaves are opposite, ovate, and rough-hairy. Large yellow flowers with greenish centers appear in autumn. The root tubers are high in calories and are a very desirable food. They can be used raw or cooked, and should be harvested in late fall or early spring. Attached to the roots of a tall, straight plant, they look similar to a knobby potato, and can be cooked and eaten like regular potatoes. They are good sliced raw and salted. They're also good sliced and fried in grease. Some use them diced in relish along with peppers and onions or just boil them until they're tender and serve with a plain white sauce.

   Boiled artichokes: one pound unpeeled, shredded, or diced artichokes. Simmer in hot milk, add a pinch of salt and parsley or onion before serving.

   Baked artichokes: slice thin in a baking dish, cover with white sauce and bake. Or combine with wild onions and grated cheese in a baking dish and bake.

   Artichoke relish: five quarts Jerusalem artichokes; three pounds white cabbage; six green peppers; one quart onions, coarsely ground; three pounds

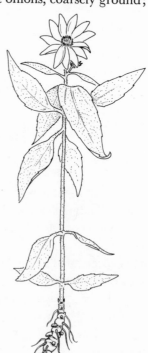

PLATE 285   Jerusalem artichoke

sugar; one small box mustard; one gallon vinegar; two tablespoons turmeric; one tablespoon black pepper; three tablespoons white mustard seed; 3/4 cup flour. Scrub artichokes, cut fine, and soak in one gallon of water with two cups salt for twenty-four hours. Coarsely grind the peppers, cabbage, and onion, and mix with sugar, black pepper, mustard seed, dry mustard, and vinegar. Bring mixture to boil, and cook until vegetables are clear. Add artichokes, return to a boil, and stir in turmeric. Pour immediately into hot sterilized jars and seal.

Pickled artichoke: 1/2 peck artichoke root; two quarts vinegar; 1 1/2 pounds brown sugar; 1/4 pound mustard; one ounce white mustard seed; one ounce pepper; one ounce turmeric; 1/2 teaspoon cloves; three teaspoons allspice; two sticks cinnamon. Peel artichokes and sprinkle well with salt. Slice and salt a few white onions. Let stand twenty-four hours, then wash off well. Cook apple vinegar, sugar, and spices together a few minutes. Drop in artichokes and onion to heat through. Seal while hot. [NOTE: Spices may be omitted and horseradish used instead.]

Jerusalem artichoke pickle: two quarts artichokes, scraped and peeled; one pint vinegar; two onions or several white multiplying onions; 1 1/2 cups brown sugar; two tablespoons salt; one teaspoon allspice; one teaspoon turmeric. Boil vinegar, sugar, and spices ten minutes. Add onions and artichokes, and boil ten minutes. Seal in jars.

Thistle (*Cirsium altissimum*) (family *Compositae*)

The thistle is found in damp fields, marshes, and along streams. It has a tall, straight stem from a perennial root. Leaves are sparingly spiny-edged, and a gray-green color. The showy lavender flower heads attract many bees and butterflies. Seeds are winged. The young thistle stems, when peeled, are edible and pickles can be made from them. Make them as you would a sweet cucumber pickle.

Fried thistle rings: peel young thistle stems, cut into rings. Fry in butter and serve hot.

Stuffing: boil peeled thistle stems in salt water. Use to stuff fish.

WILD TEAS

A variety of plants can be gathered and used to make pleasant-tasting teas. Some of these (sassafras, sweet birch, and spicewood) were included in the section of spring plant foods in *Foxfire 2* (pp. 49–53). The plants given here, gathered in midsummer, seem to have a special quality, as if all the goodness of summer sun and showers was embodied in their leaves and flowers.

Sometimes various plants are combined in special mixtures. For example, "fatigue tea" combines nettles, dandelions, and yarrow. Garden tea is a mixture of strawberry leaves, grape leaves, and rose petals.

The mountain people used teas as beverages and as tonics. They would usually gather the plants in the proper season, remove the leaves or roots, and dry them. The dried material would be stored in jars or in a dry place and used as needed. They would keep all year if dried properly. Honey or syrup was used for sweetening, if desired.

Agrimony (*Agrimonia parviflora, Agrimonia rostellata*), (family *Rosaceae*) (tormentil, church steeples, cathedral plant)

The small agrimony (*A. parviflora*) and the large agrimony (*A. rostellata*) are very similar, except for size. Both are found along roadsides, in wet ditches, and around old homesites. They are perennials, with hairy stems and compound leaves. The leaves are very spicy when crushed. The small yellow flowers appear in midsummer and are followed by sticky seeds that adhere to clothing.

Though not as well known as some of the tea plants, both the flowers and the leaves make a fragrant tea. A lady near Blairsville called it "spice-tea," and said it tasted like "apples with cinnamon." Gather the leaves and flowers and boil, strain, and serve with lemon or sugar.

Red clover (*Trifolium pratense*) (family *Leguminosae*)

Red clover is common along roadsides and in old fields and pastures. It grows to two feet, with tri-divided leaves, each leaflet often marked with white. Occasionally leaves produce the lucky "four-leaf clovers." The deep rose-red flowers appear in May, but blossom late in autumn. The flowers are very sweet-scented and favorites of bumblebees.

The flowers are edible and can be used in spring salads or brewed into

PLATE 286   Red clover

tea. It is known as a "spring bracer" and when combined with honey made a good-tasting tea that was also a spring tonic. Clover blossoms are often combined with mints in midsummer or used in "old field tea"—made of sage, mullein, clover blossoms, and basswood blooms. Most of these teas were used to relax the drinker, and they did.

It is said that red clover blooms can be combined with apples to make a pleasant-tasting jelly.

Basswood (*Tilia americana*) (family *Tiliaceae*)
   (linden, bee tree, bast, daddywort)

The basswood is a tall tree of the rich mountain coves, with large, heart-shaped leaves and smooth bark. The very fragrant, creamy-white flowers appear in early summer. Bees seek out basswood after sourwood, and basswood honey is a clear white, flavorsome honey produced in some areas of the mountains. The nectar within the flowers is about 50 per cent pure sugar. The blossoms are gathered for tea or used in fruit desserts and candy.

Basswood blossom tea: a teaspoonful of flowers for each pint of water. Strain and add sugar or honey, or drop a couple of cloves into the pot.

Basswood bark tea: peel the bark and boil it. Strain and add sugar to taste. It was sometimes used for colds and flu.

MINTS

Our most flavorsome midsummer teas come from the many species of aromatic mints. Used alone, or in combination with other plants, they are considered very healthful as well as good-tasting.

Ground ivy (*Glechoma hederacea, Nepeta glechoma*) (family *Labiatae*)
   (jill-over-the-ground, lizzie-run-around-the-hedge, hedge maids, tun-hoof, maymaids, catsfoot, field-balm, heart's ease, run-away-robin)

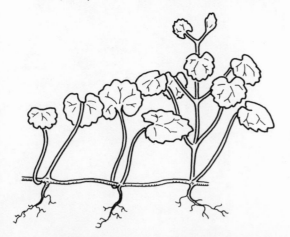

PLATE 287   Ground ivy

Ground ivy is a small, creeping ground cover which roots at the joints, with oval, scalloped leaves and small blue mint flowers. It forms large patches in waste places or in damp meadows. It is naturalized from Europe.

Ground ivy tea: gather the vine in summer and fall. Make the tea by boiling six or seven leaves in a pint of water. Strain and sweeten to taste. Ethel Corn said, "Ground ivy does make a pleasant tea for anybody t'drink, and old people was bad t'give it to babies for colic." Jake Waldroop says it was given to babies with hives to break the hives up. Another recipe for tea is to use ¼ cup fresh-picked, chopped leaves with one cup water. Boil and strain, sweeten with syrup or honey. Use hot or cold to reduce fever.

Catnip (*Nepeta cataria*) (family *Labiatae*)
  (owl eyes)

Catnip grows from one to three feet high in waste places. It has pale green, woolly, very odorous leaves, and a dense whorl of velvety, lavender-white flowers. It is a native of Europe which was brought over to this country by the first settlers, and became a naturalized weed.

Catnip has a very strange effect upon most cats—they find it exhilarating. When catnip is brewed into tea it has just the opposite effect upon humans, for it acts as a sedative, calming nerves and inducing sleep. Catnip tea

PLATES 288–289   Catnip

would prevent nightmares and lighten nervous disorders. The leaves were often chewed to relieve the pain of toothache. Catnip was given for colds with boneset or mint. The leaves have a high content of vitamins A and C. It is best to gather catnip when it is flowering. Jake Waldroop says catnip was also called rabbit tobacco. "Lots of people would smoke it."

Catnip tea: pour a pint of boiling water over a half cup of broken stems and leaves. Let stand several minutes, then strain. Combine catnip leaves with peppermint and chamomile for a good-tasting tea.

Oswego tea (*Monarda didyma*) (family *Labiatae*)
(red bee balm, red horsemint)

Bee balm grows in rich, wet places in the mountains. It has ribbed stems to three feet high, with dark green, opposite leaves that are very aromatic. The flower heads are bright scarlet and attract hummingbirds. The flowers are sometimes floated in lemonade or iced teas for flavor or color. Leaves are gathered and used fresh or dried for an invigorating tea. Oswego tea is supposed to stimulate the appetite and induce sleep.

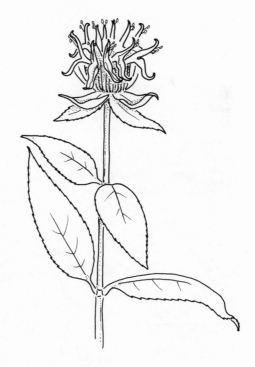

PLATE 290   Oswego tea

Bergamot (*Monarda fistulosa*)
  (purple bee balm)

The lavender bee balm has opposite green leaves, often purple-tinged, and purplish stems. It grows in colonies in open woodlands and along roadsides. The leaves are aromatic. Flowers vary from pale lavender to a deep magenta or purple. Leaves have been used as flavoring in sausage, and it is a favorite for mint tea.

Pale bergamot (*Monarda clinopodia*)

Pale bergamot grows in mountain woods. It has flowers of a pale greenish-white, less showy than those of the other species. The narrow green leaves have a mint-camphor odor.

Mountain mint (*Pycnanthemum incanun*) (family *Labiatae*)
  (calamint, little fish flower, white mint, white horsemint)

Mountain mint is common on hillsides, in open woods, and along trails and roadsides. It is a tall plant, and its leaves have a frosted appearance. The flowers are white and very aromatic.

The leaves make a very pleasing tea, and are especially good combined with lemons or oranges in a cool drink. They may also be used for candied

PLATE 291   Mountain mint

mint leaves or as flavorings in candies or frostings. Gather mint leaves in the summer when the plant is young, just before or after it blooms. Boil the leaves in water, strain, and sweeten with honey.

Mrs. Hershel Keener said that she used to make it all the time. "Make a good strong tea out of it. It's good for colds and it might keep you from having pneumonia if you took it in time."

Pennyroyal (*Hedeoma pulegioides*)
(penny-rile, squaw-mint)

American pennyroyal is a small annual plant, with very odorous leaves and small lavender flowers. It grows in waste places, often appearing as a weedy garden plant. It has been called the best-tasting of the wild mints, making tea that was both potent and healthful, supposedly helpful in curing coughs and colds.

Mrs. Mann Norton described it as "a kind of springy little bush. Gather it when it's green and tie it up in the house and keep it for tea. You can use it after it's dried just the same as when it's green."

Rev. Morgan told us that "they would sell pennyroyal in the apothecaries. People would boil the pennyroyal plant, the whole plant, and then catch the fumes from it and condense the fumes through a wormlike still. Then they bottled the fumes. I don't know what it was used for, but the druggists used it in medicines."

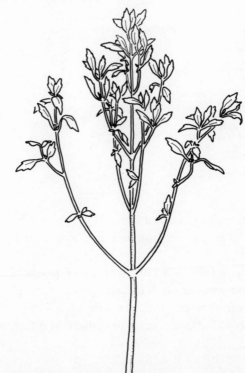

PLATE 292   Pennyroyal

Cora Ledbetter said that her family used to boil it and "just pour a person who was snake-bitten full of that to make him vomit."

Pennyroyal tea: use fresh or dried leaves. Do not boil. Merely pour hot water over it and let stand for a few minutes. Flavor with syrup or honey.

Pennyroyal shoots can also be added to fruit salad. A few sprigs of pennyroyal rubbed on your face or hands will keep gnats and other insects away.

Curled mint (*Mentha crispa*) (family *Labiatae*)

Curled mint persists around old homesites and is sparingly naturalized along streams. It has very woolly, gray-green leaves, and a pleasing mint odor. It is good to use in iced tea, or to make mint tea.

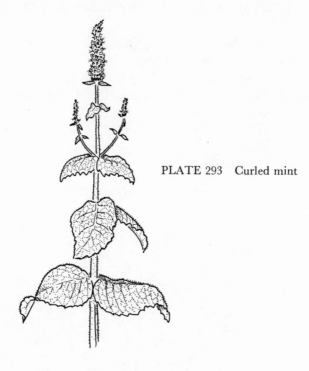

PLATE 293   Curled mint

Spearmint (*Mentha viridis*)
(green mint, roman mint, lamb mint)

Spearmint is a one to two foot perennial growing in old garden sites or along streams. It has dark green, very pleasant-smelling leaves, and pale purple flowers. It can be dried for winter use as flavoring or for tea. It is favored for lamb sauce, or cooked with English peas.

Spearmint tea: steep mint in water to desired strength. Sweeten with honey.

PLATE 294   Spearmint

Peppermint (*Mentha piperata*)

Peppermint grows in wet places, and is naturalized around springs and streams. It has very strong-smelling dark green foliage and pale purple flowers. Peppermint tea is a remedy for colic, and is considered a sleep-inducing sedative.

PLATE 295   Kenny Runion with peppermint.

Ethel Corn told us that people used to drink it for a sick stomach. The leaves and stems are gathered, boiling water is poured over them, and the tea is allowed to steep for a few minutes, then strained and sweetened. Either spearmint or peppermint can be used in the following mint recipes.

Mint with new peas: tear young mint leaves in pieces and cook with very young peas.

Mint syrup: two cups sugar; one cup water; one tablespoon fresh or dried mint leaves chopped fine. Stir together and simmer until sugar is completely dissolved. Cover and let stand one hour. Strain and use over fresh fruit or puddings.

Mint-carrot salad: add chopped mint leaves to carrot slaw or to fruit salad.

Mint jelly: do not boil leaves, but pour boiling water over them and let steep. Strain, add sugar and pectin, and cook until it jells.

Mint vinegar: two cups tender mint leaves; one cup sugar; one quart cider vinegar. Let mint stand covered by sugar for five minutes. Bring vinegar to a boil. Add mint and sugar to vinegar and boil three minutes. Strain through cheesecloth and bottle. Let stand several weeks to ripen.

Mint sauce: one bunch mint; ¾ tablespoon sugar; ¾ cup vinegar. Chop mint very fine. Dissolve sugar in vinegar. Add mint and let stand one hour. Then strain.

Mint frosting: chop young mint leaves fine, mix with powdered sugar, soft butter, and drops of cream.

Blue-mountain tea (*Solidago odora*) (family *Compositae*)

Blue-mountain tea, so-called because it grows in the Blue Ridge Mountains, is really a goldenrod, but the only one that has fragrant, anise-scented

PLATE 296   Blue-mountain tea

foliage. It is a slender plant with narrow, shining whole leaves, and a curving head of pale yellow-green flowers. The odor of the foliage is distinctive and it is impossible to mistake the licorice taste and odor for any other plant. It is common in open oak-pine woods, and along trails and roads.

The leaves make a delicious tea, either hot or cold. Steep green or dry leaves in hot water until the tea is a pale golden color. Add sugar, honey, or lemon.

Yarrow (*Achillea millefolium*) (family *Compositae*)
  (woundwort, nosebleed weed, bloodwort)

Yarrow is a colonial plant, with finely cut gray-green foliage and heads of small white flowers. Both leaves and flowers are strong-smelling. Yarrow grows along roadsides and in old fields. It is a native of Europe naturalized and common in this country.

Originally a "woundwort," the bitter-tasting and aromatic yarrow was said to cure almost any internal or external human ill. Leaves placed on the brow would relieve headache, placed in one's shoe they would help ease sore or blistered feet, and they were often used to bind up wounds.

Leaves are brewed into a bracing, not unpleasant tea, good and warming in cold weather. Yarrow is also used as a flavoring or as a potherb.

PLATE 297   Yarrow

Yarrow tea: place dry or green leaves in a cup, pour hot water over them, steep only until color shows. Drink without sweetening.

Fried yarrow: fry in butter until brown and serve hot, sprinkled with sugar and the juice of an orange.

Yarrow salad: use very young leaves; mix sparingly with cress, sorrel, or violet leaves. Add oil and vinegar, salt and pepper.

Chamomile (*Anthemis nobilis*) (family *Compositae*)

Chamomile is a low-growing annual, with finely cut, very pleasantly scented foliage, and topped by small white, daisylike flowers with bright gold centers. It is a native of Europe that persists around old gardens. Flower heads are gathered and make very pleasant-tasting tea. They should be gathered at noon, when the sun is shining, for then the dried blooms will have the most flavor.

Chamomile tea: gently steep a teaspoon of leaves in hot water until it is a pale golden color. Add sugar, honey, syrup, or a dash of ginger.

FLAVORINGS

Some wild plants are used mainly as accents, or seasoning, in salads or with other potherbs.

Wood sorrel (*Oxalis filipes, Oxalis corniculata*)
(sour grass, shamrock)

Wood sorrels are delicate small plants, with clover-like tri-divided leaves. They have small, bright yellow flowers. They are found in open woodlands,

PLATE 298   Sour grass or wood sorrel

on damp trails, and as a weed in gardens or cropland. The leaves have a deliciously tart taste, but must be used sparingly, for they contain oxalic acid. Sometimes they are called "sweet and sour" for the leaf stems are sweet and the leaves themselves are sour.

Wood sorrel lemonade: boil leaves 15 minutes, cool, strain, add honey and lemons.

Fish sauce: one cup of chopped leaves mixed with a spoonful of flour, melted margarine, and a tablespoon of vinegar. Spoon over fried fish. OR: chop leaves into melted butter or margarine, add salt and pepper, and use over fish.

Wood sorrel cream sauce: two cups of finely chopped sorrel, water, sugar, salt, pepper, and one cup of sour cream. Cook and drain sorrel, add sour cream and seasonings. Mix well and use over other greens.

Dill (*Anethum graveolens*) (family *Umbelliferae*)
   (dilly weed)

Dill is an annual which grows to four feet, with striped, hollow stems, and finely cut, very odorous leaves. Flowers appear in rather good-looking, large, flat, yellow-green umbels. Dill will naturalize as a garden weed, and grow in waste places.

The leaves are the main flavoring ingredient in dill pickles. Dill water was used for stomach troubles. It is also used to flavor vinegar, beans, and salads. The seeds are also edible and used as flavoring in salads and cooked vegetables.

PLATE 299   Dill weed

Fish sauce: chop dill fine, blend with melted butter, pour over fish. OR: mix together ¼ cup butter or margarine, half teaspoon salt, dash pepper, half teaspoon dill weed (or seeds), one teaspoon parsley. Spread over fish and broil.

Tansy (*Tanacetum vulgare*) (family *Compositae*)
     (bitter buttons)

Tansy is a tall herb, with dark green stems, and very strong-smelling, deeply cut leaves. The stalks are topped by a cluster of yellow button flowers. This European plant has naturalized along roadsides and is found around old gardens. It was planted in orchards in the belief it would keep pests away from the fruit. Leaves were rubbed on new beehives to make the bees feel at home. People used to gather tansy to flavor puddings, omelets, salads and cheeses, and special cakes called "tansies."

PLATE 300   Tansy

NUTS

There is a tremendous variety of nuts which grow on trees in the mountains. White and black walnuts, hickory nuts, and hazelnuts are usually eaten plain or used in baking. Chinquapins, beechnuts and wild chestnuts are sometimes eaten plain, but more often they are roasted or boiled in water for twenty to thirty minutes. Chestnuts are sometimes used in stuffing for turkey. Any kind of nut can be stored for the winter. Take the hull off the nuts, except beechnuts, before storing.

Black walnut (*Juglans nigra*) (family *Juglandaceae*)

Black walnuts are large trees up to 150 feet high, in rich mountain coves or along streams. They have frequently been planted and mark old homesites long after the dwellings are gone. Walnut wood has been prized for gunstocks and fine furniture, and as a result walnut trees have been almost completely eliminated in some areas. The bark is dark, often moss-covered. The black walnut has twigs with a light pith and very large leaves with many leaflets. Twigs and foliage have a characteristic odor. The flowers are green catkins that appear with the new leaves.

Walnuts are round and dark with a hard four-celled kernel, covered by a thick, greenish husk. The hulls yield a brown dye. Nut meats are prized for candies, cakes, and cookies.

PLATE 301   Black walnut

Black walnut pudding: ½ cup finely chopped walnuts; one tablespoon butter; four teaspoons cornstarch; ½ cup milk; two egg yolks; three egg whites; ¼ teaspoon salt; tiny bit of cream of tartar; ¼ cup granulated sugar; one teaspoon maple flavoring. Butter a baking dish. Mix all ingredients except egg whites. Place in greased baking dish. Top with well-beaten egg whites. Bake at 350° about forty-five minutes.

Walnut pickle: Gather the nuts when they can be easily pierced with a needle. Soak in brine one week. Remove and sun for a few hours. Soak in cold water for twelve hours. Put in jars and pour over them boiling-hot vinegar to which has been added one teaspoonful each of ginger, cloves, mace, and pepper; two onions; a small quantity of horseradish; and two pods red pepper for each quart vinegar. Cover well. The pickles will be ready for use in a month or more.

Butternut (*Juglans cinerea*) (family *Juglandaceae*)
  (white walnut, oil nut)

The butternut is a rather uncommon tree, found in rich river bottoms and valleys in the mountain regions at lower altitudes. It is a medium-sized tree with smooth gray branches and dark bark. Green flowers appear with the leaves, which have eleven to seventeen leaflets with sticky petioles. Nuts are oval in a very thick, sticky hull and can be ground into flour or oil, or can be pickled when green. They can be substituted for black walnuts in any recipes calling for such nuts.

Jake Waldroop says that butternuts "are mostly just to eat. They're sweet. You let them dry and crack them up and they're good."

PLATE 302   Butternut hickory

Pecan (*Carya illinoensis*)
    (king nut)

The pecan is not native to the mountain area, but often is found growing around old homesites, and sometimes in woods' edges where the nuts have been planted by squirrels or bluejays. It is a large tree, fifty to one hundred feet high, with brown bark. Leaves have seven to nine slightly downy leaflets. Flowers occur with the young leaves. The oval nuts have very thin husks and shells and very sweet kernels.

Shagbark hickory (*Carya ovata*)

The shagbark is a tremendous tree found on mountain slopes and in rich coves. The shaggy bark separates in layers and is a distinctive feature of this hickory. Leaves are very large with eleven to seventeen leaflets. Nuts have thin shells and are very sweet and edible.

Shellbark hickory (*Carya laciniosa*)

The shellbark is more commonly found in the Mississippi River Valley or in the central heartlands. It is occasionally found in the mountains along streams. It has a flaky bark and one- to two-foot leaves, with seven leaflets. Nuts are in a thick, bony shell.

Mockernut (*Carya tomentosa*)
    (white heart hickory)

Mockernut is a common tree found in oak-pine woods and on chestnut-oak ridges. It is a large tree with ridged gray bark, and leaves with seven large, rather smooth leaflets. The nuts are large, with thick shells and on individual trees vary in size and thickness of hulls and in edibility.

Pignut hickory (*Carya glabra*)
    (sweet pignut)

The pignut hickory is a small or medium-sized tree found in oak-pine woods in dry, light soil. It has ridged bark and smooth leaves with three to seven (usually five) leaflets. Nuts are small and slightly flattened in a thin hull. Nuts on individual trees vary greatly—some are acrid and bitter, others sweet and edible.

Hickory nuts have always been good eating worth the effort of getting them out of their shells. If a girl really liked a young man she would go

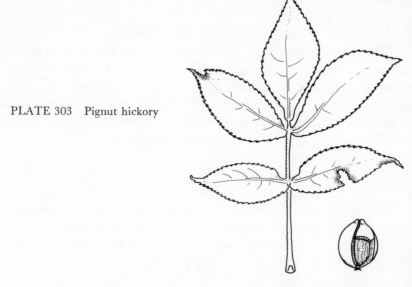

PLATE 303   Pignut hickory

to the considerable trouble of making him a hickory nut cake. Nuts were also used in candy and cookies. Hickory bark was broken off and chewed by many as chewing gum, as with the bark of the sweet birch.

Jake Waldroop told us, "That was the wild hog's feed for all winter. The nuts fall off and the leaves fall on them, and they'll lay there all winter. You take the scaly bark nut—now you can crack them if you've got good sound, strong teeth. Why, I've cracked many of'em with my teeth. They have the biggest kernel of any hickory nut. I've gotten bushels on the ridge right up there."

Hickory nut cake: ½ cup butter; one cup sugar; three egg whites, beaten stiff; half cup milk; 1½ cups flour; ¾ cup chopped hickory nut meats; one teaspoon cream of tartar; ½ teaspoon soda. Preheat oven to 350°. Cream butter and sugar, add milk and flour alternately. Add eggs and nuts, and beat until smooth. Then sprinkle in cream of tartar and the soda dissolved in one teaspoon milk. Beat and place in a greased and floured pan and bake forty-five minutes.

Nut brittle: spread hickory nut meats in a shallow pan. Melt white or brown sugar in a saucepan; pour over nuts quickly, shaking it all the time. Let set. Break into small pieces.

Hickory nut pie: Use one cup syrup; three eggs; ¾ cup chopped hickory nuts; ½ cup sugar; ¼ pound butter; one teaspoon vanilla. Place hickory nuts in unbaked pie shell. Mix syrup, sugar, and eggs together well. Add melted butter and vanilla. Pour mixture over nuts. Place in 400° oven. Bake ten minutes (IMPORTANT!) and then reduce heat to 300° and bake thirty minutes. (Pecans or walnuts may be used, instead.)

Hazelnut (*Corylus cornuta, Corylus americana*) (family *Corylaceae*)
 (beaked hazelnut, filberts)

The American hazelnuts are shrubs found in thickets on hillsides and along streams. Both shrubs have soft brown bark. Male flowers appear as long catkins, called lamb's tails, which form in late autumn, and lengthen into masses of yellow pollen in early spring. Both species have similar round-toothed leaves, but the American hazelnut has its nut in a ruffled husk, while the beaked hazelnut has a long, beaked nut covering.

PLATE 304   Hazelnut

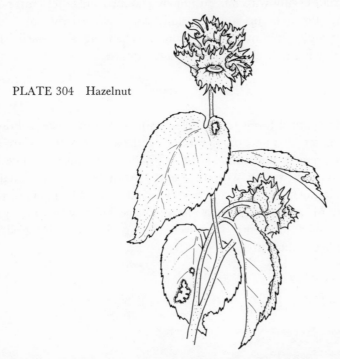

Besides being good to eat, especially roasted, the nuts would be used to tell fortunes on Halloween. If you named the nuts for your sweethearts and placed them on an open fire, the nut that jumped or cracked first represented the lover who would come calling first.

Nuts could be ground into meal to make filbert bread, or grated hazelnuts added to cake frostings.

Toasted hazelnuts: heat ½ cup butter or margarine. Add one pound shelled nuts. Cook until the nuts are a deep brown, stirring often. Drain on a paper towel. Sprinkle with salt.

Hazelnut cookies: one egg white; one tablespoon sugar; ½ cup flour; one teaspoon baking powder; one cup grated nuts. Mix, drop in small spoonfuls on a greased tin. Bake in moderate oven.

Sugared nut meats: ¼ cup vegetable oil; two cups powdered sugar; two teaspoons rum flavor; dash of cinnamon; dash of nutmeg; dash of ginger; 1½ cups shelled nuts. Cream oil, sugar, flavoring and spices. Spread nuts on cookie sheet, heat in moderate oven ten minutes. Turn hot nuts into the cream mixture and stir. Separate and spread on a cookie sheet to cool.

Many recipes using nuts can be adapted for whatever species is available, or various kinds of nuts can be used in combinations. The recipe given below can be used for walnuts, hickory nuts, or hazelnuts.

Nut brittle squares: butter the outside bottom of an eight-inch-square pan, and spread evenly with one cup finely chopped nuts. Set pan, nut side up, on a tray. Put one cup sugar in skillet and heat, stirring until golden brown and syrupy, pour over nuts at once. When slightly cooled, remove in one piece to a board and cut into two-inch squares.

Beech (*Fagus grandifolia*) (family *Fagaceae*)

Beech is a beautiful forest tree with smooth bark and graceful branches. It grows along streams and on rich bluffs and banks. Its leaves are shiny, very regularly veined, and turn bright yellow in early autumn. The beech flowers in the early spring with the newly green leaves. The small, triangular, edible nuts are encased in a very prickly bur. The nuts are rich in protein, calcium, and phosphorous. Roasted beechnuts were once ground and used as a coffee substitute. They were also ground for cooking oil, meal, or made into beechnut butter.

PLATE 305   Beechnuts

Chestnut (*Castanea dentata*) (family *Fagaceae*)

The American chestnut was once a dominant tree of the mountains before the chestnut blight spread across the hills and devastated the chestnut forests. Jake Waldroop said, "I've seen the time when you could go out on this hill and pick up about three bushels a day. They was laying there by the thousands of bushels—hundreds of acres covered by chestnuts. Now we don't have any chestnuts. A blight hit up here and killed'em all. Some people think that they'll come back again, but as for me, I don't know. I don't think they will. I'll find some (the trees) every once in a while as big as my leg and then there'll come a big brown spot on it and it'll die."

Sprout growths of chestnuts still struggle for existence on the hills. Occasionally a tree reaches a size large enough to bloom with showy white flower spikes, and bears a crop of rough husked nuts. The chestnut is enclosed in a hard brown outer shell and a bitter inner skin that is usually peeled off before using. The nut is made up almost entirely of carbohydrates and water. They can be ground into flour or added to bread.

Chestnut croquettes: mix one cup mashed, boiled chestnuts with ¼ teaspoon vanilla, two beaten egg yolks, two tablespoons cream, one teaspoon sugar. Shape in balls, roll in crumbs, and fry in deep fat.

PLATES 306–307   Chestnuts

Chinquapin (*Castanea pumila*) (family *Fagaceae*)

The chinquapin is a spreading shrub, or small tree, found on mountain-sides and in the piedmont oak-pine woods. It is more resistant to blight than the American chestnuts, and is still abundant in some areas, bearing a crop of small, but very sweet and edible nuts. Leaves are slender, toothed slightly, and dark green in color. Racemes of white flowers appear in the early summer. The nuts are enclosed in very prickly burrs.

Rev. Morgan told us about a chinquapin tree they used to play in as children. "We would climb and make a treehouse in it. We didn't use chinquapins in cooking. We would boil them and the girls would string them on threads and wear them as necklaces. Then, if they could get by with it, they'd eat them during school. We'd play games with chinquapins, one was jack-in-the-bush."

Chinquapin stuffing: use finely chopped or ground nuts instead of bread crumbs in your favorite stuffing recipe. The small, sweet chinquapins can also be used in any chestnut recipe.

PLATE 308   Chinquapins

White oak (*Quercus alba*) (family *Fagaceae*)

The white oak is a common forest tree, growing to gigantic size, with flaky white bark and scalloped, thin, green leaves. Catkins appear with the new leaves in early spring. The large acorns mature in one year, and can be made into flour, or boiled or roasted for food. Today few people will bother with the slow process necessary to make acorn flour, but it was once a staple of pioneer diet. Acorns were used to make flour when, as Laurabelle York said, "Times were rough." It was usually mixed half and half with regular flour. To make it, peel and roast acorns until they are

PLATE 309   White oak leaves and acorns

thoroughly dry, but not burned. Pound them into a powder and use this powder as flour.

The large acorns of the chestnut oak (*Quercus prinus*) and the yellow chestnut oak (*Quercus muehlenbergia*) can also be prepared for food but aren't as sweet as those of the white oak.

Coffee: parch acorns, and grind. It makes a red coffee—"real good, just as good as bought coffee."

Baked acorns: make slit in the acorn shell. Bake until shells crack off.

Acorn Indian pudding: one cup acorn meal; four cups water; sorghum syrup. Put three cups water on to boil. Mix meal with remaining cup, stir until smooth. Add to boiling water, stir until thickened. Add syrup. Cover and cook fifteen minutes at low heat.

Acorn meal: grind acorns, spread meal ½-inch thick on a porous cloth and pour hot water over the meal. Repeat several times. Meal can be used instead of cornmeal. OR: boil acorns two hours, pour off black water; soak in cold water three to four days, then grind into a paste. This makes bread dough. OR: pulverize acorns. Allow water to trickle through meal for twenty hours. Dry and grind again. Use one cup acorn meal to one cup regular flour in muffins.

WOODROW SHOPE
BUILDS A SMOKEHOUSE

Most old-timers would laugh at us if we told them that one of the biggest things to happen on Middle Skeener this year was that Woodrow Shope built a smokehouse—but it's true. And everyone in the community turned out for it.

When we stopped at the little country store near his home to find out exactly where he lived, the men there all commented on how well the building was progressing. A bread man stocking shelves in the back called out that he had just been by there and lots of neighbors were out watching. When we got there, one of the neighbors was splitting boards to cover the roof. He hadn't done it in so long he just wanted to see if he still knew how. School was almost out for the day, and some of the parents had left to get their children and bring them by just so they could see it going up.

Woodrow, a recently retired Forest Service employee who now does things like this to help fill up his days, laughed when we commented on the attention his log building was getting. "People even stop on the road and look as they go by," he said. "Everyone's talking about it. I saw one neighbor in the doctor's office this morning. He said, 'That thing sure is looking good. We was all in hopes you'd cover it with boards, and sure enough, you *are*.' "

Woodrow has spent all his life working—mostly in the woods—and even though he's retired now, he's not about to stop. He believes in staying active; staying tough: "When the Lord made a man, He made him good. He made him tough. And this old body is really put together, buddy. It takes something to pull it apart. You just can't hardly tear it apart it's so well put together."

And he believes in observing the world closely and in learning by experience. Through years of close observation he learned how to do most of what he does best. "On splitting boards, [see *The Foxfire Book,* page 45] you have to learn how to take advantage of your timber. There is a skill to anything you do. I don't care what it is. You might think anybody can dig with a mattock or shovel with a shovel. They cannot do it. They can *pretend* to, but there's a skill to using them tools. There's a right way and a wrong way to anything you do. I've seen people work theirselves to *death* with a mattock or a shovel and *still* never shovel no dirt! They'll stomp down more than they dig up.

"Those old people used their experience that they'd had, and they'd watched stuff till they *knew* what the story was; and that's the best idea that you've ever had of anything. You can read in books—you can't get by anymore without that—but still you've got to have a little bit of mother wit and common sense about anything. And they ain't no book knowledge that beats experience. I don't care what you say. No book knowledge can take the place of experience because you know that stuff like you know your name. You know exactly what's going to happen. The

PLATE 310   A smokehouse below, a storage loft above, and a covered space out front for firewood and yard equipment.

PLATE 311 *Foxfire* editors watch as Woodrow splits the white oak boards for covering the roof.

PLATE 312 A group of *Foxfire* editors watch as Woodrow nails on row after row of 24″-long hand-split white oak boards. He is placing them on board fashion (see *Plate 315*).

only difference between a professional and a non-professional is a piece of paper. That's all they is to it."

Though people might disagree with some of his beliefs, he can back them all up through personal encounters and experiences. When we asked him about clearcutting, for example, knowing that he had seen lots of it with the Forest Service, he took a stand formulated on the basis of what he'd seen—not what he'd heard: "It's fine if it's applied where it *needs* to be applied. Now if you've got a southeast exposure back in these mountains —and the most of them you've got a lot of it—and if you go there and look at the timber before it's clearcut, it'll be pretty scrubby stuff. And it's been there—if you get down and count the rings of it—no telling how long it's been there. Now I say, and I've said it all the time, that that needs clearcutting and completely doing away with whatever's there and setting it in pine or something—something that will grow in that site. They've tried for years to grow hardwood there and it hasn't grown. It just ain't there. It's pretended to grow, but it's just got up maybe pulpwood. Only occasionally will you find a saw log.

"And then you spoke of the game business. Now it's *exactly true* that the best game pasture you've ever seen for deer browse is those sprouts coming back [after clearcutting]. It really works. It's good for that. I've seen it happen. Them clearcut areas makes a deer pasture *right* for about three years.

"But I don't believe in going out here in a place where there's good, rich land and the timber is growing [and clearcutting]. The thing you want to do in them places is to thin and give the rest of it room to grow. But you needn't expect to go up here on a southeast exposure and be able to grow big tall red oak timber, or black oak. It just don't grow there. That just isn't the site for it."

This concentration on personal observation has made him a man who is leery of beliefs that smack of superstition. When we asked him about mad-stones, he chuckled and told us a story: "They supposedly come out of a white deer's paunch. I've never seen one, but they claim they can cure a snake bite or anything. No matter what it was, it was good for everything. That's what the old people said. I know one time there was a fellow told me, said a fellow hollered at him, 'Run down here right quick with that madstone. A snake's bit me!'

"And he said he went down with this madstone, washed it, and they applied it to the place and it wouldn't stick. He said if it was the poisonous kind, the madstone would stick and draw the poison out. It'd have a tendency to hold to it. And he said he washed it three times, put it on, and it wouldn't stick. Said he come to find out a darn *lizard* bit him. It wasn't even a snake.

"But I've never seen one, and frankly I don't think there *is* such a thing, between you and me and the gatepost."

But the real thing we had come to find out about was smokehouses. There was little doubt that he knew, again, what he was talking about. He had a beauty standing behind him to prove it. Here's what we learned.

There is no specific size for a smokehouse. They were tailor-made to a family's needs. Sometimes they stood alone among a complex of outbuildings. Sometimes they were part of another building that had several uses. He has seen one in the top floor of an apple and potato cellar, for example. His own building is a smokehouse below, a storage loft above, and a covered space in front for firewood and yard equipment. It is based on the design for the old-style corn cribs: the wagon would pull up in front under the overhang, the corn would be tossed through the door into the lower storage area, and the top could be used for storage, a hay loft, or a smokehouse. With the logs chinked to prevent freezing temperatures inside, the bottom could have been used for a potato cellar and storage for canned goods.

The only real recommendation Woodrow would insist on for a smokehouse is that it be animal- and insect-proof. To keep out flies, he tacked aluminum screen wire to the inside of the logs (since he isn't going to chink them) and to the underside of the ceiling between the rafters. The salt will eventually eat holes in the wire, but it's easy enough to replace when that happens. To keep out rats, he dug a trench six inches into the ground under the bottom logs, and cemented this all in to make a solid barrier that rats can't get through and won't tunnel under. A door and the walls themselves will keep out animals such as dogs. And the 24-inch overhang that the eaves provide will keep out most rain and sunlight. The floor will be left as dirt to help keep it cool inside. He used a board roof to keep the building from accumulating heat, or sweating on the underside. The comb of the roof is turned so that it will shed all blowing rain from the southeast, the direction from which most of the rains in the valley come.

The logs Woodrow used are pine. They came from a beetle kill nearby and were snaked in with a horse, peeled, trimmed up and treated with a half-and-half mixture of creosote and diesel oil brushed on to preserve the wood and keep powder beetles away. He used treated telephone poles for the sills, and set them slightly off the ground on stone pillars. Traditionally, the sills would have been locust and the sides poplar or chestnut. He

PLATE 313   Two rows on and six more to go. The 1×6 at Woodrow's foot is tacked on to help him keep the boards' bottom edges straight and true.

PLATE 314   The smokehouse from the side.

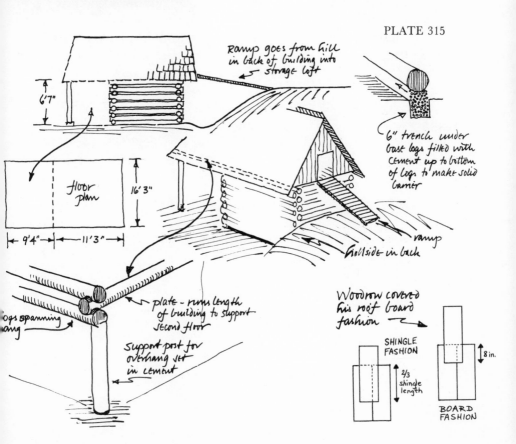

PLATE 315

Ramp goes from hill in back of building into storage loft

6'7"

floor plan

16'3"

9'4"   11'3"

6" trench under base logs filled with cement up to bottom of logs to make solid barrier

ramp

hillside in back

plate - runs length of building to support second floor

logs spanning

support post for overhang set in cement

Woodrow covered his roof board fashion

SHINGLE FASHION

2/3 shingle length

8 in.

BOARD FASHION

chose pine, however, since the wood had to be used in some way or destroyed.

Inside the smokehouse room, wooden, waist-high meat benches will be built out of two-inch-thick lumber to set the curing pork on.

His method for curing is to kill the hog in November as the weather turns cold, coat it completely (top, sides and bottom) while still warm with a heavy coat of plain white salt, and then let it absorb the salt for about three days. He then slides one-inch-thick, narrow slats under the meat to raise it off the counter—otherwise the moisture the salt draws out of the meat will keep it damp and make it soggy.

When the weather begins to turn warm again in the spring, he removes the meat from the racks, washes it well, dips the joints into a tub of boiling water and then coats it with 20 Mule Team Borax. Then he hangs the meat in cloth sacks, tying them to the rafters with white oak splits or rope.

He doesn't smoke the meat himself, but if he did, it would be done in the spring, and the smokehouse would have to be closed (he'd have to chink his logs) to keep the fire smothered and smoking. A fire of hickory wood chips would be built in an iron wash pot, and then smothered so it would just smoulder.

He intends to use it. The only thing that worries him is that our winters seem to be getting warmer, and pork requires a good cold winter to keep the meat from spoiling during the four-month curing process. But he's got high hopes.

And even if he can never use it successfully as a smokehouse, he at least has caused some excitement in the community.

As we left, he asked, laughing, "Well, you boys think you could build a smokehouse if you had to? It's not complicated. You just got to get in there and pitch."

WILLIAM HORNE, STEVE HELMERS AND RICKY WARE

Photographs by Kenny Taylor and Russell Arthur.

BUILDING A LUMBER KILN

Today there are many kilns used for drying green lumber quickly, but thirty years ago they were hard to find. To fill that need at one farm in our county, Claude Darnell constructed one for the Jay Hambidge Art Foundation. Mrs. Jay Hambidge asked Claude, a master mason who built all of her chimneys and rock walls, to build one so that they could dry and produce their own lumber for Foundation studios.

When we talked to Claude about it, he told us that he obtained the pattern from Lex Darnell and built the kiln in 1942. Between the twenty-foot foundation walls, a "V"-shaped trough was dug into the ground extending from the front of the building to the back (see diagram, *Plate 316*), its walls and top made of "blue rock" (flat, granite slabs) strong enough to withstand the intense heat. This trough doubled as both the dual firebox and as a flue connected to the chimney in the back wall. Wood was put into the fireboxes through the two ground-level openings in the front foundation wall. The system was totally enclosed to prevent the flames from igniting the drying lumber.

Above the foundation was the floor on which the green lumber was stacked (leaving plenty of air spaces between the boards). Two small holes in the front foundation (see diagram, *Plate 317*) and a larger hole in the center of the kiln's roof acted as an air circulation system to draw off the steam while the kiln was being fired.

Shortly after Claude completed it, he stacked it full of fresh lumber and fired it up. For thirty-six hours he kept the fire burning steadily, using green wood for fuel. Neighbors gathered to watch the process, turning it into a community event. Mrs. Hambidge was there. But to everyone's disappointment, when the door was opened at the end of the thirty-six hours, it was found that the wood was still wet. It hadn't worked.

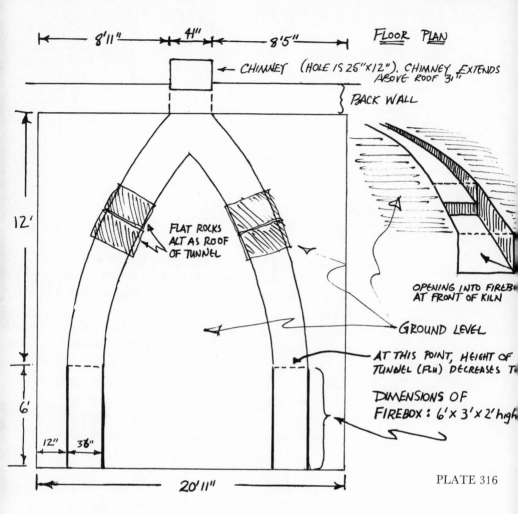

FLOOR PLAN

8'11"   4"   8'5"

CHIMNEY (HOLE IS 25"x12"). CHIMNEY EXTENDS ABOVE ROOF 31"

BACK WALL

12'

FLAT ROCKS ACT AS ROOF OF TUNNEL

OPENING INTO FIREB AT FRONT OF KILN

GROUND LEVEL

AT THIS POINT, HEIGHT OF TUNNEL (FLU) DECREASES T

DIMENSIONS OF FIREBOX: 6' x 3' x 2' high

6'

12"   36"

20'11"

PLATE 316

To this day, Claude is not sure why. He knows the heat was intense enough. It was so hot, in fact, that the pressure split a portion of the front wall leaving a crack to the left of the door that can still be seen today. The closest he can come to a remedy for anyone that might want to try to build one today is to suggest that they increase the size of the three air circulation holes so that the steam will be drawn off faster instead of being allowed to build up on the inside. He said that if he were to build another one, he might even put two vent holes instead of one in the roof.

He also suggests that the roof be made peaked instead of flat to give more working room inside the building for stacking the lumber, and that steel reinforcing beams be added to the kiln walls.

PLATE 317   Claude Darnell, the builder of the kiln, with David Dillard.

PLATE 318   The lumber kiln from the front.

PLATE 319 Note the rock work above the door frame, a good example of the kind of work for which Claude is noted.

PLATE 320 Detail of the vent below the front door.

PLATE 321 Claude explains the construction of the kiln to Terry York (left) and David Dillard.

PLATE 322   Looking down on the kiln from the bank that runs behind it. Note the
chimney, and, barely visible at the extreme left, the vent hole in the roof.

PLATE 323   The opening into one of the fireboxes.

PLATE 324   Three-quarter view of kiln from
the front.

FRONT OF BUILDING:

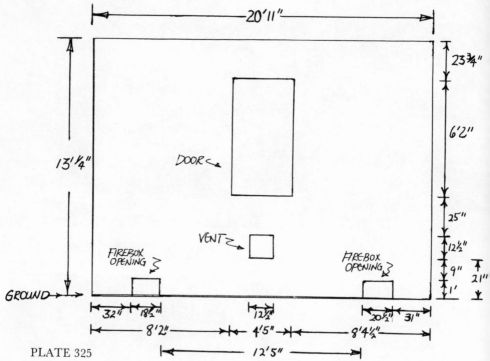

PLATE 325

But he'll never build another one. This first one was abandoned after its first trial and never used again. Another was not built to take its place, and it still stands, slowly wearing away.

Written and photographed by Roy Dickerson, David Dillard and Terry York.

Dick Harrison also remembers building lumber kilns, but they were much simpler than the one built by Claude Darnell. The ones he remembers were made of wood and sometimes some tin was used for the roof.

When asked for possible reasons for the failure of the kiln Claude built for the Hambidge Foundation, Mr. Harrison gave two possibilities: 1) They did not burn it long enough (Mr. Harrison's kiln's required an eight- to ten-day burn); 2) they didn't leave enough ventilation for the steam-laden air to escape quickly.

Kilns like the one that follows were makeshift things. They were usually used once and then might be torn down after they served their purpose. Generally wood was not kilned unless it was to be used as flooring or weather boarding. Framing lumber was generally air-dried.

The length of the lumber to be dried determined the size of the kiln. The dimensions used in the following instructions are for a kiln to dry twenty-foot lumber.

Step 1: Get thirteen 6″ to 8″ (dia.) poles. You can use whatever kind of wood you want. You'll need six 16′ long, one 14′ long, and six 12′ long; or you may use the same length (app. 12′) for all (see *Step 5*).

Step 2: Either set the poles in the ground or brace them up well enough so they can stand alone when you start nailing slabs to the outside. Set the poles as shown in *Plate 326*.

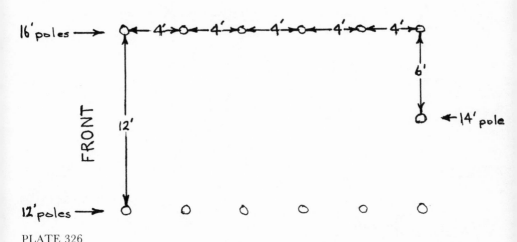

PLATE 326

Step 3: Run stringers across the width. Notch them into the poles as in *Plate 327*, starting with the second pole from the front and going back. It is a good idea to use about a 2″×8″. Don't just nail these, as they have to support too much weight. Make sure the stringers are set evenly about 8′ above the ground so the lumber you lay across them rests equally on all.

PLATE 327

Step 4: Nail rough boarding around the outside within 4″ to 6″ of the top of the poles, leaving the front of the building open.

Step 5: The roof can be of any type you want. Mr. Harrison recommends the shed-type roof (slanting in one direction) as the best and easiest to build. If you want to build an "A"-type roof, however, cut all the poles in *Step 1* the same length.

Step 6: Dig a pit 6″ to 8″ deep starting about 4′ back from the front and going to about 4′ from each of the walls. Throw the dirt up against the walls. Don't make the pit any deeper than about 8″ or the fire won't burn well.

Step 7: Stack the lumber as shown in *Plate 328,* continuing the pattern to as near the roof and walls as you want.

PLATE 328

Step 8: Start a fire in the pit. Build it up to a good low flame (Mr. Harrison remembers getting the fire too high and burning one up one time)—a good barbecue fire—and keep it at about this level. It will take eight to ten days to dry a load of green lumber. Someone will have to stay with it all the time.

There are gauges to determine when the lumber is dried thoroughly, but if you don't have one the best idea is cut into one of the boards and feel it to see if it is dried out.

Step 9: When you remove the lumber from the kiln it will be black with smoke and soot and "the nastiest stuff to handle you ever saw" but it will dress down beautifully.

BUTTER CHURNS

Many years ago men who worked skillfully with wood were indispensable to those around them. Everything from houses to banjos required wood, and men who knew how to work with wood were needed in every community. One essential trade was that of a cooper—someone who made kegs, barrels, buckets, and other related vessels. These wooden containers were used to hold cornmeal, water, salted meat, nails—anything that could be stored or carried in them.

We at *Foxfire* had been interested for a long time in finding a master of this trade, but could not locate anyone who was still actively working at it. Finally, Mr. Bill Henry, a member of the Southern Highlands Handicraft Guild and one of our subscribers, told us of a friend of his in Sneedville, Tennessee who was still making churns, buckets and large wooden tubs. He offered to direct us there and introduce us, and we gratefully accepted. Four of our staff members went to Sneedville and ended up spending an entire day with Alex Stewart—watching, listening, and recording as he made a churn. We found him to be one of the most interesting men we have ever met.

Born and reared on Newman Ridge within sight of his present home, Mr. Stewart grew up watching and learning from his father and grandfather, both of whom had worked with wood all their lives. From them he learned to cut and season his own wood and make all his own tools by hand. The outbuildings on his farm include a small sawmill and a blacksmith shop where he forges the tools he works with. He has power tools as well, but he prefers his own handmade manual and foot-powered tools, feeling that he has better control with them and gets the job done just as quickly.

In the course of the day we spent with Mr. Stewart, we were not only

PLATE 329   Alex Stewart

PLATE 330

impressed with his work, but with the things he said. He readily answered all our questions and often made interesting comments of his own.

"I've made all my tools, matter a'fact, ever'thing I got. Well, this [shaving horse] I guess is about fifty years old. I used t'have another'un. It got old, an' I made this'un. If I've got it right, this is th'second one there is in the United States made like this. They's one more like it, and I made it. My grandfather, I learnt this from him. He made ever'thing—wheels, anything could be thought about, he made it, an' I got th'pattern off'a his'n. An' m'daddy—he worked at it as long as he lived. I've been doin' it since I'uz old enough t'do it . . . about sixty-five or seventy years. When I'uz young, ever'time I'd get a chance, I'uz a'foolin' with it. Yeah, I just delighted in it. Anything that you delight in, it ain't any trouble for you t'do it, but somethin' you don't delight in, it's pretty hard.

"Yeah, I made these tools. I used t'make about anything I wanted to. It's a lot better than stuff you buy. It makes me feel good. I've made many of a churn an' sold it for two dollars. No, not a regret, not in this line [of work]."

Mr. Stewart also displayed a ready humor and often had us smiling or laughing as he worked and talked. One of the most pleasant and touching surprises we had that day occurred at noon when we discovered Mr. Stewart's daughter had prepared a wonderful dinner for all of us. The large table fairly groaned under the weight of all the good food. We ate an incredible amount and then trooped back out to continue our work, well satisfied.

A description of Alex Stewart would not be complete without telling about the workshop where he spends so much time. It is located in the barn which stands behind and to the left of his house. Probably the first thing one notices in walking into the barn is the sight and smell of cedar, stacked in the corner to dry, and lying all over the floor in the form of chips and shavings. Mr. Stewart uses cedar to make his churns, buckets, and other containers because cedar doesn't shrink when drying out after it has been wet. Some people use poplar as it is also easy to work with, but it is apt to shrink after it has been wet if water is not left in it.

On the right-hand wall hang the handmade tools. In their respective places stand the handmade shaving horse, foot-powered lathe, and jointer. Also scattered about are various things he has made—churns, barrels, buckets, piggins, and a big, wooden washtub. It was here that we discovered that he also makes rolling pins, bread boards, brooms, ingenious little wooden puzzles, and many other things. His son, Milum, showed us many of these things and told us about them.

Alex Stewart did indeed become a person for whom we developed a vast amount of respect and admiration as we watched and listened to him, and at the end of the day, when we were forced to say good-by and head back, we all agreed that we came away with much more than the directions for this chapter.

LAURIE BRUNSON

[Ed. note—Since this was written, Alex Stewart has retired and donated all his tools to a museum in Tennessee.]

Photographs by Stan Echols and Gary Warfield.

PLATE 332   **Step 1:** Cut the cedar in the fall
when the sap is down. Stack it up to dry
for about six months. When you're ready to
make a churn, split the cedar into staves with
a stave froe.

PLATE 331   Alex poses with examples of his work: a churn, piggin (foreground),
tub, and bucket. The dimensions of the churn follow.
Capacity: approximately five gallons; height: 20¾ inches; diameter of top: 7¾
inches; diameter of bottom (head): 10 inches; circumference at top: 24⅞ inches;
circumference at bottom (head): 34 inches; average width of staves at top: 1½
inches; average width of staves at bottom: 2⅟₁₆ inches; width of hoops: 1¼ inches;
length of dasher: 32 inches; dasher crosspieces: 2 inches wide by 6¼ inches long;
diameter of dasher: 1 inch.

PLATE 333 **Step 2:** Measure fifteen to twenty staves and saw them off to the same length. The length is decided by the size of the churn needed. (The churn featured in this chapter has staves $20\frac{3}{4}$ inches long. Sixteen staves were used.) Smooth the staves on a shaving horse and start tapering slightly "by guess." All the staves should be tapered so that they are narrower at the top than at the bottom.

Front View of Stave

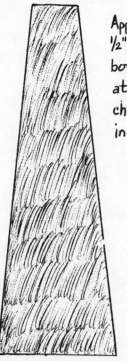

Approximately $\frac{1}{2}$" wider at bottom than at top for churn pictured in this article

PLATE 334 This churn's sixteen staves had an average width of $1\frac{1}{2}$ inches at the top (no stave was less than $1\frac{1}{4}$ inches, nor more than $1\frac{3}{4}$ inches wide) and $2\frac{1}{16}$ inches at the bottom (no stave less than $1\frac{11}{16}$ inch, nor more than $2\frac{3}{8}$ inches wide). Fitting in the last stave (**Step 5,** *Plate 347*) compensates for the inconsistency in stave width.

PLATE 335 **Step 3:** Shave off the sides of the staves at the top end so the staves will be about $\frac{1}{4}$ inch thicker at the bottom end than at the top end. This helps to keep the hoops from sliding down when they are added later.

Side View

$\frac{1}{4}$" thicker at bottom

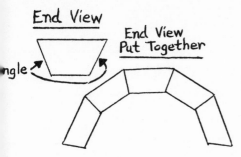

PLATE 336 Decide what the diameter of the head will be (8 inches, 10 inches, 12 inches, etc.). The diameter of the head (which is the bottom of the churn) determines what angle the stave edges must have to fit together correctly.

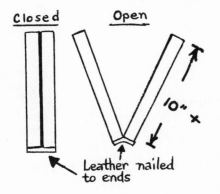

PLATE 337 Mr. Stewart made a gauge to use as an easy guide for angling his stave edges. The gauge is simply two small boards, $10'' \times \frac{3}{4}'' \times \frac{3}{4}''$, joined on one end with a leather hinge.

PLATE 338 These two diagrams illustrate how the gauge is marked for various diameters. The placement for the marks on the gauge are determined by measuring off the radius of each desired diameter (using a compass) from the hinged end of the gauge. The hinged end is treated as the center of the proposed circle (head), with the marks on the gauge representing a part of the circumference of that circle.

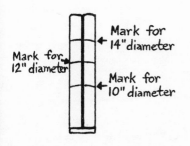

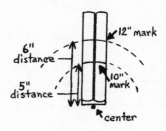

PLATE 339 Alex uses a compass to mark his gauge for different-sized churn heads.

PLATE 340 Using a long-jointer, wood is planed from the edges of each stave until the angled edges fit the gauge.

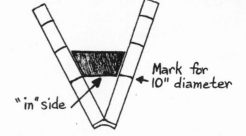

Checking edge angle of stave used for churn with 10" head diameter:

"in" side

Mark for 10" diameter

PLATE 341 The angled edges must fit the gauge as illustrated. The "in" side of the stave is the side placed on the mark.

PLATE 342 Alex checks his stave angle on the gauge. The correct angle should be maintained as closely as possible for the full length of the stave. However, the angle does not have to be perfect. The wood, being pliable, seats itself. The last stave to be fitted (**Step 5,** *Plate 347*) has to be driven into place. This closes most of the cracks which may result from slight errors in the angles of the other staves.

PLATE 343 **Step 4:** After staves are tapered and sides angled, Alex prepares to fit them into two temporary hoops.

PLATE 344 The large hoop goes around the bottom (head) and the small one around the top. (Alex used a metal hoop for the top end and an old wooden hoop with a double knot fastening it at the bottom end.)

PLATE 345 Alex pushes a straw-filled bag between the hoops to hold the shape as the staves are added.

PLATE 346   The staves are added carefully.

PLATE 347   **Step 5:** Use a hammer to fit in
the last stave. If it won't fit, adjust the other
staves with the jointer. A tight fit is absolutely
necessary.

PLATE 348 A chisel can be used as shown to help fit the last stave.

PLATE 349 **Step 6:** Pull out the bag and hammer the staves until they are even.

PLATE 350 Trim off uneven edges on the bottom with a pocketknife. Use a hammer to adjust the bands to higher or lower positions (for a better fit).

PLATE 351 **Step 7:** Using a round-shave, smooth (or dress) the inside of the churn. It is especially important to smooth the inside near the bottom end, where the head will be fitted.

PLATE 352 **Step 8:** Use a rasp to smooth the outer edges of the top and bottom. The churn must sit straight and flat.

PLATE 353 **Step 9:** Use a croze (*Plate 354*) to cut a groove for the head to fit in.

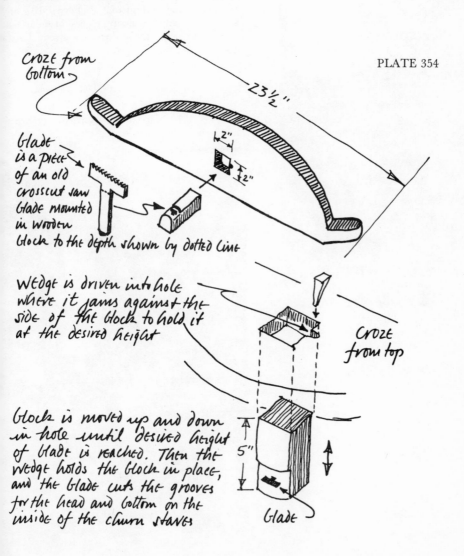

PLATE 354

Croze from bottom

23½"

Blade is a piece of an old crosscut saw blade mounted in wooden block to the depth shown by dotted line

2"

2"

Wedge is driven into hole where it jams against the side of the block to hold it at the desired height

Croze from top

Block is moved up and down in hole until desired height of blade is reached. Then the wedge holds the block in place, and the blade cuts the grooves for the head and bottom on the inside of the churn staves

5"

Blade

PLATE 355   This groove was cut one inch from the bottom edge of the staves.

PLATE 356   **Step 10:** Use cedar board(s) for the head (the bottom of the churn). Use any size board and as many pieces of board as needed to make the proper size circle. Use a compass to mark the proper size.

PLATE 357   Cut off the board piece with a handsaw.

PLATE 358   For this churn, Alex used two
pieces of board to make two half-circles.

PLATE 359   **Step 11:** Use a shaving horse
and drawing knife to smooth both pieces.

PLATE 360 Remark a half-circle on each
piece with a compass.

PLATE 361 Begin to cut the half-circles out
with a handsaw. Saw as close to the edge of the
half-circle as possible.

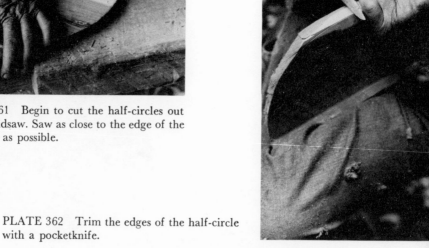

PLATE 362 Trim the edges of the half-circle
with a pocketknife.

PLATE 363 After trimming, hold the half-circles together and check the smoothness of the circumference.

PLATE 364 **Step 12:** Begin to bevel the edges of the half-circles with a drawing knife.

PLATE 365 Finish beveling the edges, and smooth off with a pocketknife.

PLATE 366 **Step 13:** Take the bottom (head) hoop off. Fit the two halves of the head into the groove made by the croze. Put another temporary hoop on that fits in the middle of the churn. (Alex replaced the bottom wooden hoop with a metal middle hoop.)

PLATE 367   With a chisel and hammer, force the middle hoop down as tightly as possible.

PLATE 368   Tap the staves with a hammer to make sure the head is in the groove tightly. Keep tightening the hoop with a chisel and hammer.

PLATE 369   When the middle hoop is tight, the staves and head should be secure if the churn is lifted.

PLATE 370 **Step 14:** With the temporary bands still on, smooth outside of the churn with a wood rasp.

PLATE 371 **Step 15:** To measure for a permanent bottom hoop, take a string and measure the very bottom of the churn.

PLATE 372 **Step 16:** For the hoops, use green white oak. If the oak is dry, soak it overnight. Split the oak into strips using a froe and mallet. Measure the length with string, allowing six extra inches for the notch and lock.

PLATE 373 **Step 17:** With a drawing knife and shaving horse, smooth the oak pieces to ⅛ to ¼ inch thick and 1 to 1¼ inches wide.

PLATE 374 Mark the length of the circumference of the churn on an oak piece, allowing three extra inches on each end for the lock. The top edge (edge toward the small end of the churn) should be made thicker than the bottom edge for a tighter fit. Use a pocketknife to smooth, if necessary.

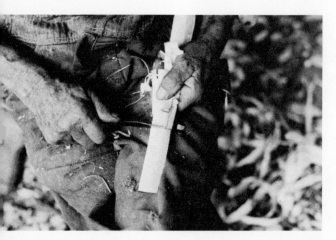

PLATE 375 **Step 18:** Begin to shape one hoop end with a pocketknife; the hoop end is shaved as it is shaped. Each hoop will eventually fit around the churn and the ends will fasten together.

PLATE 376 To create the notch, place the chisel down on the hoop and hammer it through the hoop to make the first hole.

PLATE 377 Make a second hole with the chisel.

PLATE 378 Using a pocketknife, begin to cut out and shape the notch. Continue to shape the notch as shown.

PLATES 379–381 On the opposite end of the hoop, cut with a knife as shown, until the inner side (*Plate 380*) and the outer side (*Plate 381*) are finished.

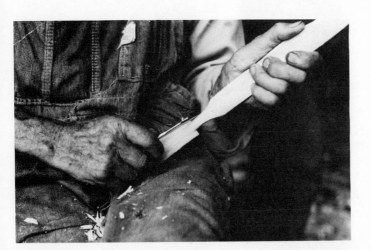

PLATE 380

PLATE 381

PLATES 382–383 **Step 19:** Bend the hoop
around your knee to make it curve, and hook
the ends of the hoop together (*Plate 383*).

PLATE 383

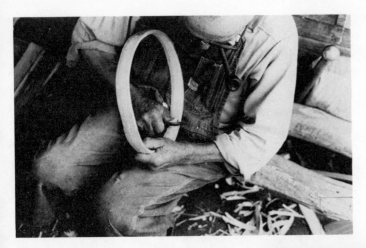

PLATES 384–385 Trim the edges with a pocketknife (*Plate 384*), and shave the inside of the joint (where the ends come together) with a pocketknife to fit flush with hoop. Finished hoop should appear as shown (*Plate 385*).

PLATE 385

PLATE 386 **Step 20:** Put the hoop around the churn and force it down to the bottom (head) of the churn with a hammer and stick of wood—keep the thick edge of the hoop up, toward the narrow (top) part of the churn.

PLATE 387 **Step 21:** With a pocketknife, trim off some of the thickness of t**h**e top side of the hoop. Smooth the outside of the churn with a rasp again.

PLATE 388   **Step 22:** Add three more hoops, using the same procedure. With a handsaw, cut off the staves at top to even them. Use a rasp to smooth the top and bevel the edge.

PLATE 389   **Step 23:** For the lid, obtain the circumference using the same procedure as for the head (*Plates 356–365*). For groove on the underside of the lid, use a handsaw and trim with a pocketknife and rasp. Drill a hole slightly larger than the diameter of the dasher handle in the center.

PLATE 390   The top should fit right on top
of the churn, with a hole in the middle that
the dasher handle can easily slide through.

PLATE 391   **Step 24:** For the dasher handle,
use oak or maple and turn on a foot-powered
lathe (*see Foxfire 2,* p. 164), leaving an extra
chunk of thickness toward the bottom to prevent the crosspieces from being forced up the
handle.

PLATE 392   Use two pieces of cedar for
the crosspieces, shaped as shown. Drill a hole
in the middle of the crosspieces to fit the stick
in. Smooth with a pocketknife and force the
crosspieces onto the handle. Small nails or pegs
can be driven in the bottom to hold the crosspieces securely to the handle.

PLATE 393

PLATE 396

PLATES 393–396 This 145-year-old churn, passed on to one of our contacts by his grandmother, shows how accurately Alex Stewart has maintained the traditional pattern for his own churns. The difference is that the churn (and the equally old wooden bowl) pictured here are made of yellow poplar—a wood more frequently used than cedar, as it would not affect the taste of the butter in the way cedar might.

PLATE 394

PLATE 395

BEULAH PERRY

Beulah is one of the most beautiful people we have ever met. No matter how she feels, she always gives us a warm smile and makes us feel at home. She is eighty years old, but acts and looks much younger. Her belief in God and the Bible are the main forces in her life. She was brought up in a very religious atmosphere and these qualities shine through.

Born before the turn of the century, Beulah has been through many changes during her life, many of which she'll tell you about. She lived on a farm when she was young and gardening became one of her main interests. She still loves to work in her small vegetable garden behind her house, and in her yard where she has planted lots of flowers and shrubs, many of which she hiked into the mountains to get.

Although she grew up in the South Carolina Piedmont region, and moved around to many different places, she loves this area best. "This is the best and most beautiful part of the country to me, here in the mountains. I love Clayton."

BEVERLY JUSTUS AND VIVIAN BURRELL

This material about Beulah Perry was collected over a period of three years by Jan Brown, Mary Garth, Beverly Justus, and Vivian Burrell.

My grandfather came here from Africa as a slave when he was young. Of course, this was before the Civil War. I don't know what part of Africa [he was from], but he was with a bunch of slaves that came from Africa. They came to Augusta—where the ocean is, where the big ships come in. Down there in some part of South Carolina, the slaves were all brought there and sold in a slave market. He was first a slave in [eastern] South Carolina, somewhere close to where they were brought in.

He couldn't have been too old, because the people that owned him educated him—he was well-educated. I just don't remember [how old he was], because back in those days, people grew old much quicker than they do now. Back when I was a girl, a person fifty years old was considered a very old person and now people seventy and seventy-five years old still work.

It must've been quite a place because he said that he would have to go over all the plantation, that was his biggest job. They would send him and he would have to bring back a report, what every bunch of slaves [was doing], or wherever they were, he would have to bring back a report of what had happened and what they were doing and all.

PLATE 397

PLATE 398

My grandfather said that when they educated him, they called the lady "Miss," and she would take him and give him his lessons every day and she would dare him to tell any of the other slaves anything that he was taught. He wasn't supposed to tell anything. He must have been a very unusual black. Back in those days, she would take him in a room and give him his lessons and she educated him well enough so that he could teach school after he was freed. He could teach school and that was a little unusual. In those days, there weren't many colored people that knew anything about education.

He said he did everything—all of their business and everything. He was the overseer of everything. He had a big horse he would ride, and he went all over the big plantation, from place to place.

I don't think that my grandfather's slave people were very cruel to him. He didn't say anything [about that]. Mostly he said what the slaves would do and that the [slave owners] didn't allow them to have church, or pray and sing—nothing like that. No, [the white people] were bitterly against that. They would punish them for that as quick as they would anything. He just said praying and singing—that was a crime. My grandfather said sometime in the big slave plantations, a bunch of them would get together and they would pray and sing, but they had to be real low.

Seemed like they were more religious than people are now—but I don't know if it was their African religion, or a Christian religion. Did you know back in Africa, they had a religion—I don't know where, don't know what it was, but they had a religion over there.

Some of the slaves were treated awful bad, because my grandfather would talk—I don't know, maybe it was just one of God's plans for somebody to tell a little of both sides. You know, most of the people just tell the bad side of it and the distressing side, but my grandfather had good slavemasters and he wasn't treated what you'd call bad, like others, because they trusted him and he was educated.

His name was Wartlaw—my mother's father. I don't know too much about my father's parents because my father's slave people didn't educate him—his father nor him. He didn't read and write, and none of them ever taught me any African words.

My grandfather must have been getting on up in age when they freed him, because they gave him seventy-five acres, and I know where the spot of land is. I go by that place most every time I go to Anderson [South Carolina]. I used to hear my mother talk and she said from time to time the different white people around would take a little of Grandpapa's land and maybe another one would come in and would take a little bit, so eventually they just took all of it. [I didn't grow up on that land.] When we learned anything about the property, we were just little kids. Sitting around on the floor, my grandfather would tell us things just like people'll tell a fairy tale to children. We were all very small, but I can remember lots of things.

I don't know how long [after he was free] that he lived on that land, but I don't think he lived on that place very long, because I remember when I was just a little toddling thing, he had a little store on his little tract of land. His store was a very small place—it wasn't much bigger than this room. I guess I was maybe four or five years old, and my mother would send us to Grandpapa's store to get soap or anything like that. She would give us a tin cup, just like we have now—a tin cup, and she said, "Take this cup and Grandpapa will give you some molasses."

We would take that cup and when we'd get ready to go, Grandpapa would give us that cup about half full of molasses, old black molasses, and we were just little things—we thought we had a fortune.

Some of the things he would tell us—why the poor white people didn't like the colored, black people. Said the white people would do something wrong, and the old master'd make the colored slaves go get this white person and bring him to the old master and they would punish'em for it. That was the biggest way they would have catching the white people that would do anything wrong. It don't seem to me that there was any law or anything. They said that was one of the biggest reasons that white people didn't like colored people. It just kind of grew up as a hatred. The colored people *knew* to go get [the white people who'd displease the master]. They *knew* not to come back without them. Sometimes they'd run'em all day, just like dogs. But they *knew* they better not come back without them.

"Back in those days . . ."

I grew up in the country in Anderson County [South Carolina] about ten to twelve miles from Anderson. I married in 1915.

I guess I must have been about thirteen or fourteen [when we started dating]. We'd sit around home, read the Bible, talk about things done at church, things like that. We didn't run around and make loud noises on Sunday. That was the law. It had to be a real quiet date. There wasn't much to be done—just sit talking and playing. You know, we played like other children do, but not too loud and rough. They were strict about who we dated. Most of the time when we were old enough to date, it would be on Sunday, not any other day. I think we called it courting.

I guess it was pretty rough [when I first got married]. People now might think it was bad, but we were used to living on a farm, and eating things we raised on the farm. We were taught to raise chickens, hogs and cows, and that's just the way we started out.

The white people that raised my husband gave him a little spot of land. It had one little house on it and they gave that to him and we lived in it. You could lay down at night and look through the loft and see the stars. I remember once, one night it snowed and the snow had come through those cracks and the bed and the floor were covered with snow. I waked up my husband and said, "It's rained in here." He made a light and looked, and everywhere in that room—even our bed—had just a little white coat of snow. It had come in the cracks overhead. It was fun to us. We got up and put some sheets up by the side of the walls to keep the snow from coming in. Well, it didn't keep it out but it didn't go all over the house. We did things like that and it was fun to us. I married just before my eighteenth birthday. I married the fifteenth of January, and the twenty-eighth was my birthday.

You know, back in those days when you married, you went to your own home. You didn't stay with your parents. We moved out on that plantation where the white people had raised my husband.

We stayed there for about eight or nine years. Then moved to another plantation—about six or seven miles from that place. We stayed there until we went to Atlanta. I was the mother of four little boys; they all died babies, but one. He lived to be fifteen.

In Atlanta, I did domestic work and housekeeping, and from there came to Clayton. I went to Washington, D.C., after I came to Clayton. I came to Clayton in '25 and I was here about ten to twelve years. My health got bad and Dr. Green advised me to go to Florida or some place other than Clayton, because the climate would be better. I stayed down in Florida seven or eight years and after I got tired of going down there, I went to Washington and stayed up there six or seven years.

I came back to Clayton for good twenty-one years ago. This is the best and most beautiful part of the country to me, here in the mountains. I love Clayton. I think the country people are more friendly than the city people. They're more lovely and they seem like they love each other better; and I always feel like they're more Christian-like in the country than the city people. City people have to work all the time if they have a job. In the country, on a farm, you have rest periods. In the summertime, you get through working your crop and you have a little rest time. From the time you lay your crop by and from the time you have to go back to picking cotton, back on the farm, you have a little rest between that. So I guess that makes it a little better than living in the city.

"That's how crazy we were."

I never will forget. My father and mother were big churchgoers. One day while they were gone, we decided we wanted to go horse-riding. We caught the mules we could catch the easiest (the horses and mules belonged to another person). My brothers got mules, and I got the big black horse. I never will forget that! We got up on blocks and I got up on that horse—and the horse just reared right straight up. I just slid off his back, and I led him back up to a block and got back on him—that's how crazy we were. He commenced prancing around and my brother got that big buggy whip and got behind me and hit the horse as hard as he could—and off we went. They got on their mules right behind me and up the road we went. We couldn't go too far, because we were afraid Papa would come back and see us! Some of those horses and mules were wild—I don't know why some of us didn't get killed. But the Lord was with us.

Papa would go to the woods and catch a possum. He'd catch them at night. He had possum dogs and he'd go and catch'em and sometimes bring in two or three. In the morning Papa would kill them and put on a big pot of hot water, dip'em down in that hot water and scrape the hairs off them. It'd come off nicely. Then you take the insides out and parboil them a little bit. I know you've heard about possum and sweet potatoes. When the possum gets about done you take and put some sweet potatoes around it. They're better than squirrel or rabbit—they're very good.

When I was a kid, the possum head was my favorite. Mother would always pay me to do things, and she says, "Now, Beulah, if you do so and so, I'll leave the possum head on." When it got done, she'd cut that head off and give it to me.

"We helped my father with the farming."

We stored our own vegetables. Like leather britches—dry your green beans in the summer—string them, hang them up to dry. We also dried pumpkin, apples; but we always had fresh vegetables in the winter (in western South Carolina)—turnip greens, collards, mustard, and things like that. They grow in the winter here.

Now peas we'd dry—my father'd put about a couple of acres in peas, and we'd go through there with big sacks and pick those peas when they got ripe. We'd pick them maybe every other week, and maybe we'd have this room about half full of peas. Now we didn't have a thrasher, and we'd

put them out on a big sheet, and take sticks, and beat those peas out of the
hull. A windy day would take all the little trash out of them. We'd just take
'em out in the yard on a sheet and hold'em up, and the wind blew through
and got'em clean.

We canned some blackberries and apples, and peaches. We didn't make
too much jelly, but we made applesauce. We dried most of the fruit. We
had a smokehouse in which we kept all the peas and canned food, and
dried food and meat.

My father always made our own syrup. People in the neighborhood
would have a mill, maybe the whole neighborhood would have only one,
and people from far and near would go to the place and make their syrup.
Carry all those loads of cane to the mill!

[We helped my father with the farming.] We didn't have any machinery,
just used hoes and mattocks and shovels and plows. We'd get in the garden
and clean it off with our hoes and rake up the trash. There was a lot of
trash on the ground and we'd pile it up and burn it. That would make beds
with a lot of ashes to start tomatoes, cabbages. They called them hot-beds
then.

We took the manure out of the barn and put it in a pen as big as this
room. [My father'd] clean out the stalls of the mules, cows, hogs, and
chickens. Then he'd go to the woods and get a load of leaves to throw
in there. From time to time, he'd mix it up and keep adding to it till it was
time to use it. We had big sacks we made into big aprons, and we'd go to
the pile and fill up our aprons and go scatter it around the garden. We'd
have to carry at least a half a bushel. We had big paling fences around the
garden so chickens couldn't fly over them. My daddy made the palings
out of a certain kind of pine.

We grew one kind of corn for us and the animals; we didn't have any
sweet corn. To harvest the corn we were going to keep over the winter,
we waited way late, till after several frosts. That was so the corn would
get good and dry. If it didn't, when you gathered it, it would rot. We'd go
in and pick the corn and heap it up, and then somebody would come
through with a wagon, loading up that corn and carrying it to the barn.
Sometimes we'd pile it out in the yard and have a corn shucking with 25–
30 men, and have a great big dinner. We took the corn to the mill any time
after we picked it. My father used to take a half a bushel of corn and have
it made into grits—didn't buy no little packages of grits—not with so many
kids. For seed, we'd pick out good ears to put back.

Now crows would eat up your corn crop if you didn't keep them scared
out. We'd make scarecrows and put around the edge of the field—
that'd scare'em out. Sometimes they'd get so bad, people would get out in
the edge of the woods and shoot at'em.

Back when I was a kid, we had big cotton patches to sell. You'd clear off your fields, plow them up, lay off your rows, and put your fertilizer [composted manure] in, and go along with a great big cotton planter. I'd say we'd plant along the middle of April. You'd have a mule pulling your planter, and you could do sometimes four to five acres a day. To get it in, you'd put five or six big baskets, like the one I made for *Foxfire* (see *The Foxfire Book,* pp. 119–27), out in the field, get you a sack and put that on your back and go along and pick cotton. It was ready to pick when those big green cotton bolls would pop open—all that white cotton ready to pick out. We didn't have boll-weevils then. Nothing really bothered the cotton, but some years we'd have a very good crop, some years it wouldn't be very good. When we got it in, we'd put it on a wagon, take it to a gin house and have it ginned, made it into bales, carried it to the market— that was a big time. That was the only way poor people had to make a living.

We grew our wheat and oats—at harvest time you cut your wheat and have a thrasher thrash that wheat out, sack it up, take it to the mill and get your flour. The oats were for the animals.

My grandfather grew tobacco for his own use, a patch about as big as this room. When those leaves began to turn—now that was his job, we couldn't do that—he'd go through the field when those bottom leaves began to turn, he was very careful, and he picked one off at a time and put them in a basket, and he'd go over his little patch two to three times a week. He'd take those big tobacco leaves, tie a bunch together, take them and hang'em up in the barn so they'd get good and dry. He'd put'em where we couldn't get to them. It was hard to grow—seems like every three to four days checking those leaves looking for worms. I always wanted to work with him in his tobacco, but no, that was apart. When he got ready to twist his tobacco, he would make a sweetened water with homemade syrup, and he'd put a big wagon sheet down, put his nice leaves down on that sheet, and take that sweetened water and sprinkle it on the tobacco. When it got pretty damp, why he'd twist it. He'd keep on until he got it done. Some parts he'd have for chewing, and some for smoking. I'm pretty sure he saved his seed. Some people had big old tobacco patches—they didn't sell it— they made their tobacco, and they divided it with people who didn't have any.

We raised great big turnips. People don't raise turnips like they did then—old people had great large turnips back then—and they had'em all the winter. Lot of times, they'd have t'plow those old turnips up and push them aside to plant again in the spring. And my father went to the field with a big basket [to gather the cast-aside turnips] and we'd put on pots of them to cook for the hogs.

Seems to me like the vegetables were better then. I don't know whether it was because we cooked them with so much meat. You know people don't season things much any more now.

You take people that use stable manure for their garden—I think that makes a difference in the flavor of the food; it grows off better. Now I garden with store-bought fertilizer, and I don't like it either. I can't get a good garden—a pretty garden like I want to. I think about back when I was a kid and my father used t'have those pretty gardens. Stable manure is really good for a garden.

[On the farm, the mules were very important] because that's what my daddy used to make his crop with—they would have been our most valuable thing. He used them for hauling wood, getting back and forth to the market. That was the biggest way people had of getting around—a mule and wagon.

About the house—my mother's garden, her milking and her churning, and fixing her butter and milk took most of her time. She took care of the garden most of the time. Of course, Papa would do the plowing, but the rest was her job.

I don't think my father ever did anything but just farming and he also learned to make baskets and to bottom chairs; he made fish baskets and things like that. [A lot of people use those fish baskets], particularly people that liked to fish and had ways to get out to the rivers and big creeks. So many people didn't have convenience to get out to places like that; my father had his one-horse wagon. He could go a long distance. I remember once we were on the big creek, on the plantation that we worked, and a creek then was about like a river now, and my father would take small baskets like that and put in those deep places in that creek. Sometimes we'd be in the bottom land working, sometimes we'd go with my father, and see him take that basket out and get the fish out.

I never will forget once we went with him and Papa took out one or two eels. They were long and I thought that was something terrible. They looked just like snakes. My father just took them out like they were fish. Of course you have to use a little more pain and patience; I don't know whether they'd bite or not.

Back when I was a child, we didn't know too much about buying things. Everybody had about the same things—some people weren't as lucky as others. The biggest thing we had t'buy were clothes, and my mother mostly made those. She taught us to sew. I'd sew for most of the other little girls around in the community. As I grew older, I was the dressmaker. I really enjoyed that, and I like to sew yet . . . when I have the time.

Once in a while we would buy flour—we never had enough wheat to do from one wheat season to the next. Maybe a little meal—sometimes we

PLATE 399

wouldn't have enough corn to last till the next crop-gathering. We had
to buy salt, and once in a while sugar—not too much because we made
syrup, and that syrup in the winter would go to sugar stored in a big
barrel. We raised our own spices and teas—sage, catnip, boneset, and
some other things.

Most of the time, Papa would swap things he had—eggs and chickens—
sometimes he'd go to town in the wagon and load up different things
we had, cabbage or corn or tomatoes, or whatever and go to town on
Saturdays and sell those things. Sometimes we'd have milk and butter to
send, just anything we could spare.

My father was a busy man—he had to be!

Back when I came up, people didn't sell things; they gave to each other.
Now my father always had two-three milk cows, and Mother would churn,
and she'd give some of us kids a bucket of milk and some butter, and she'd
send us across the field, or up the road to take Mrs. So-and-So some butter
and milk. We churned every day.

We lived out in the country, close to a spring, and my father would put
a big box in the spring. He would make holes in that box for the water

t'run through. And we would take the buttermilk and sweetmilk down and put it in that box and [the cold water] kept it fresh. It was churned every day and put to keep in that spring.

You know, [giving away farm products] was the way most poor people paid their doctor bills. When the doctor would come, my father would catch him three or four chickens, or give him a bag of corn; just put it on his buggy.

In my young days, people didn't have money to hire anything done. If we wanted to do something for one of our neighbors, we just had to go and do it; we didn't have money to hire things done. Say if some of our people in the community got sick and got behind with their crops, why the people in the neighborhood, sometimes maybe as far as from here to Mountain City, would just come in with their wagons and tools and work that crop out maybe in a day. That's the way they done things. Women would come in, wash and clean up the house and things like that, and maybe one bunch would come in a day or two and do things, and for the next two or three days, another bunch would come in. There wasn't no money, nobody paying, because people didn't have anything to pay with, only the little things they made out of their crops and gardens. They would divide.

We lived in one settlement where we had two families of German people. I was very small. I can just remember that. They didn't have things like lots of people. I can't understand it. It might have been because they hadn't been in this country long. I don't remember very many German people from back when I was a child. Those two families were our very close neighbors and he could mend shoes, and he taught me how to mend shoes. I'd go carry milk and things, and he would be mending shoes and he would show me how. I can mend shoes today.

"We were all raised out in the country."

It's so different now from what it was then. Well, we had our house chores to do; we had just about everything to do—a little bit of everything. When my mother passed away, why we just had to take over. There were nine of us children, and I was the second girl. We just had to be a mother and do everything around the house that had to be done, and take care of those small children. My father—he worked every day. When we got to be ten or twelve years old, we would go to the fields. After I got big enough, I worked right along with the boys. We usually had to do about everything we could do; I don't think we had any choice.

I didn't like picking cotton; I don't know what it was about it. It was different. I had it to do and a lot of it, but I never did like to do it. My father had a great big, three horse farm—something like that. We had between twelve and fifteen bales of cotton a year.

We picked it in the field and my father would put it on the wagon, carry it to the gin house and it'd be made up in large bales.

Once in a while on Sunday evenings, some of the neighbors' children would come in and play. People didn't let the children go just any place and play in those days. They picked places they thought where nice people were for their children to go. We would go to homes like that and play a while with the children on Sunday evenings after church and Sunday School. Once in a while the children would come and visit us on Sunday. That was about all the visiting we did. We walked and we'd go to church. Our churches were usually a long way off and Papa would put us in the wagon—two horse wagon—and have straw in the wagon and all of us kids would sit down in that straw to go to church.

We were all raised out in the country—I think the happiest days I had in my life were along then because I imagine we didn't know anything else. We didn't have any movies or anything to go to. We didn't know anything about buying clothes. We were raised in a good, old-time Christian home. What our parents said was right—there wasn't anything else said about it.

Now my parents would sit and spend the evening, the night, and read the Bible to us. And my father would have a prayer every night, and most of the time in the mornings—'round the table. Sometimes my father would have to get up early and leave before we were up, and my mother taught me and my older sister t'pray. She would say, "Now you all got to pray this morning. Your papa had to leave early." And we didn't know anything about praying, and Mama said, "Well, you'll have to learn. Don't you know how it's done? You know how to ask me and your father for things."

We said, "Yes, ma'am."

And she said, "Well, that's just the way you talk to the Lord."

You know a lot of people are blaming the young folks for a lot of things, like losing interest in the Bible and church life. Well, I don't. I'll be different. I believe we older people, people who have children, are responsible for part of it. They just haven't taken the time, and you know, it takes time. People have got to have a lot of patience with children. We didn't go to bed without having that prayer. We'd go to the table in the morning—we had a great big country dining room, with a big bench. It would seat about six of us on one bench, and we would have the morning prayer. Then we would eat. Rainy days, maybe, we'd have a little leisure and Mother would get the Bible down and read it to us. Nowadays people don't have time. Or they don't make time. Back when I was a girl, people's mothers and fathers worked at home—they didn't go out and work. It was on the farm, around the house.

My parents were very good to their children, very strict, so much different from now. You would say the children now are bad, if you compared them to the way children were when I came along. Once in a while we would get good spankings.

Maybe they would tell us to do something and we wouldn't do it right. They would tell us, "Now you go back and do that again and do it right." My mother particularly would say, "Now if you have to do this over, you are going to get a switching." And sometime, we would be careless and think we were going to get by—things like children do now, and we didn't do it just like she wanted it done. We'd get a spanking; she'd make us do it over again and then we'd do it right the next time.

I would advise the young people to just be sweet children, honor their mother and dad, go to church and Sunday School and by all means go by that blessed Bible. Then you won't make a mistake. Just try to do right. You know if you want to do right and try to do right, you've got lots of help, our heavenly Father standing there waiting with a mending, helping hand—He's right there to help. [Young people today are different from the way we were] and my heart goes out for the youths. I just live with them in my mind; I love young people and so many people now don't give the young people credit for lots of their goodness.

I take up for the young folks. Of course, I know some of them are very naughty, but I can't help but feel that the parents have to take some of the blame. And we live in a different age now and we can't expect it now to be like it was back when I was a girl. That's a great big space. My time is passed, and it's the young people's time, and all we can do—anything we can do—we ought to help them and do it with them. The Bible says Christian people have to become as little children. I feel that way, and we have a lot of fun here when I have the little children in the neighborhood come over. We have a lot of fun here.

My people went more on the Bible times, you know. We'd go to church and hear the preacher and read our Bibles. Now we don't keep up with it like they did; they read it and went by that Bible.

One of the greatest things I remember and it stays with me today was when we were small children, our father used to gather up things and go to Anderson to sell at the market—he'd carry chickens and watermelons and eggs, just whatever he had. He'd get a nice little load and in blackberry time, he would say, "Now you children, you go pick some blackberries. I'm going to town tomorrow and you can make you a little money." We'd get out and pick our blackberries. When we had the buckets just barely full, we

PLATE 400

thought we had enough. When he'd get through shaking the berries down
in the buckets, they'd lack that much being full, and we'd say, "Papa, we
had the bucket full."

And Papa would say, "No, you didn't."

Papa said, "The Bible says, 'Give full measure, shake down and run
over.' You haven't done that. Now you've got to put more in there until
that bucket runs over."

So that's just how strict they were. We might get out playing or something, and cheat each other, but that wasn't the way they wanted it done.

It's so different from now—back when I was a girl. I wouldn't hardly
know how to start telling you, it's just that much different. We read the
Bible and we tried to go by that. My mother would say (when we were out
playing and something didn't go right), "That wasn't your Sunday School

lesson. You know the preacher said this or that yesterday (or Sunday). That's what you go to church for—to learn."

That was the way they chastised us.

I think the parents are partly the blame for the problems so many young people have. The reason I say that is that I don't ever think I would have been as good a girl as I tried to be when I was grown, if I hadn't been taught that when I was a girl. Parents took a lot of time with their children. It wasn't just once in a while—on rainy days or at night-time or in the morning, my parents would read a little Bible scripture, or they'd tell us about something that was said in Sunday School. That's just part of young people's lives and that's the reason I love the young people. I can look back and see where parents have failed; they haven't taken the time that maybe my parents or some other parents did. Most of these people now just say, "Well, go ahead, I don't want to be bothered." They didn't say that when I came along; they had time.

I do know people were happier then than they are now. Back in those days, maybe people didn't have so many different things to go to. Back when I was a child we went to school, and church and Sunday School. Didn't do too much visiting; children didn't do much visiting, just once in a while. But we were happy. I look at the children now; they don't seem to have any happy days like we had. I don't know why, but I think sometimes maybe they have too much.

We didn't have the privilege of getting everything we wanted like children do now. A dime's worth of candy would be that big around. And my father'd come home, and sometimes he'd give us half a stick of candy. There were nine of us children. He hardly ever had enough to give us a whole stick, but he'd divide that. We were much more pleased with that than the children are now with fifteen cents' worth. He'd go to town in the winter and buy apples, and take a whole apple and quarter it. That's about all we would get. That would kind of pay us off for something!

We didn't have entertainment as people think of it today. We went to church, Sunday School, and we were just satisfied around the house. And we would have our little handmade dolls—our mother'd make'em, or maybe one of the neighbors would say, "Now if you'll be a good girl, I'll make you a doll," and make us a big rag doll, stuff it with cotton. And that would be our doll.

We'd get out in the yard and take sticks and make doll houses and things like that, and we made mud pies. That was the way we passed the time.

We didn't know anything but eating what we raised, and once in a while, Papa would go to town and get something. Mother would go to town and get material to make our clothes. We didn't know too much about buying things.

"Me and money, we're so far apart."

The world has changed so from my young child days and from the Bible days, you don't know hardly how to say what's the cause of this and what's the cause of that, but we do know all wrong things.

You know, to my little judgment, when you see all those great people [in the government] that's so far ahead of me and know so much more than I do, and have had so much experience, and making *such* great mistakes as they're making now, you wonder. You can't help but think it's sin—the cause of it. Sin is the cause of a lot of bad things today and there are some people that don't know and don't understand. What we don't know, the Lord don't require that of us, because He's so wise and all of His creations, He knows in our hearts, He knows what we think and what we know right, we're to do right.

Seems like our country now is more for money, regardless of how it comes or how it goes, or who suffers, who lives or who dies. Seems like money, the big people are just for the money, regardless of how they have to get it, because most of our trouble now is with the big people and the money-making people. All the money being taken from each other is the big talks taking money from each other. Well, the Bible says, "Money is the root of all evil."

Me and money, we're so far apart. I like to make it and I like to have it, but just following after money like I see some people do, that's the least thing I think about.

I know I never will forget, I have worked with people and when pay-day would come, seem like I would forget and they would say to me, "Beulah sure don't care nothing about money. You just walked right out and left your check or money. You sure don't care nothing about it."

And it's the truth. I like it and I need it. I just don't know if I knew I was going to get it or what, you know; some people just money, money, but I never did think of it that way.

It's a strange thing to say. I've got an old Bible here. When we went from the country to Atlanta and the second job I got in Atlanta, I worked for Ku-Klux-Klansmen who ran a dairy farm about four or five miles out of Atlanta. They were the nicest people. My little boy was a baby about six or seven months old and I could get in a street car every morning to that job and I got a Bible—that old Bible—and I love it better than anything. When I hear people talking about Ku-Kluxes, the first thing I think about is, "Well, they must not have been as bad as people said, because my first Christmas gift that I got in Atlanta was this Bible and they gave it to me." They were the nicest young people and they had two little children. They were the nicest, sweetest people to me. I wish I knew where some of them were now. There must have been some good somewhere because they treated me and my baby just the same as one of the family.

"We have so much to be thankful for."

There's one thing I want to do. I want to go to Africa and go on a foreign mission field. I've been wanting to do that ever since I was thirteen. My father had an uncle and he sold his plantation and took his family, and they all went to Africa. Back in those days, I reckon you had to go by ship. There weren't any planes.

When Uncle Joe and his family went, I wanted to go. I asked one of his daughters who was much older than I. Uncle Joe said, no, that it would break my father's heart if I was to do that. He told me to keep studying my Bible and maybe someday the mission or the church might send me. He said, "We're going to pray that you might come see us some time."

I've been wanting to go ever since. At my age now, sometimes it comes to me that I'm going to see some part of the foreign mission. I've seen and studied so much about it.

You know, we didn't know too much about the people coming from Africa—the colored people. It was the mission work they were doing and it seemed like the people there needed mission studies so much more than we here needed them. That was my thing that I wanted to do—to go there. I used to tell people that I've always been a missionary. I don't know why I want to go to Africa or another foreign country, because I've been a missionary all of my life [right where I'm living].

The religion's the only part of my life that stays with me today. My Bible, teaching and training from back as far as I can remember—that's the sweetest part of my life. The Bible is our guide. We wouldn't know how to serve the Lord if we didn't know a little about the Bible. It's through God we have all of our enjoyments, all of our good things. It's through Him that we get it—we know that's for sure. We see some of His handwork every time we look out and see something because He made everything on the earth and He is the Creator of all the beauties everywhere.

The first thing when I get up of a morning that I want to do is get to a door or window and look out and I stand there and look, and thank the Lord for being able to see that beauty one more time. It's a wonderful thing to try to live a Christian life and to love the Lord. We have so much to be thankful for.

APPLE BUTTER

I've eaten apple butter all my life. Both my grandmother and mother have made it, but I had never seen it made in a brass kettle until I went to Rogersville, Tennessee. We were very lucky to find Mr. and Mrs. Pat Brooks, their family and grandchildren, who still make it the old-time way.

"Back years ago, you either made it or you didn't eat it. This day and time everybody has got enough money. They don't have to work like us poor folks. Nobody wants to take the time to make it, but they've all got their hand out for a jar."

Pat was humorous and fun to be with. "Well, Honey, I'm going to tell you something. My daddy was this way [humorous] and I ain't never seen a stranger in my life. Just enjoy your life, for when you're dead, you can't."

Obviously he lives by his word. "I have fun everywhere I go. That's what we're here for."

I remember when I was left in charge of the tape recorder, Pat asked me, "You got your tape recorder on? You want to give me some sugar!" Pat just naturally does things like that.

As we were pouring the apple sauce into the brass kettle to cook, he told us about a trick he pulled on his wife. "Now I've got to tell you about my wife when she put on her first pair of shorts. She came outside and when she did, I just wheeled my chair around in front of the door. Here come these people down the road in a car. She was just a'jerking me trying to get in the house, so in order for them to see her [wearing shorts], I just screamed and hollered like I was dying, so they would look. And she said, 'I'll never put the dern things on again, I bet you.'"

We were taking turns at stirring the apple butter when he brought out

PLATE 401   The apples must first be washed and peeled.

a rolling pin that belonged to his grandmother. "I'd like to sell this rolling pin. We're going to have a little auction. What do you bid?"

Bids started at five cents and ended with $4.75.

. . . going once, going twice, gone—sold to Laurie.

Later he told his wife, "We had a sale here a while ago—a rolling pin. I got three neck hugs, four squeezes and nine kisses with it."

After the first stir came off the fire, everyone was sampling the product with hot, homemade biscuits. Meanwhile, Pat had gone in the house and brought out his banjo and was making a deal with Barbara and Mary to buck dance. We had our own little outdoor concert. He sang a couple of songs, gave us each some apple butter, and we were on our way back home.

VIVIAN BURRELL

The making of apple butter was once a quite common event. We talked to a number of people about it, and we found that, in addition to the Brooks method (illustrated in this chapter), there were many variations.

Pauline Henson and Mrs. Charlie Ross Hartley of Vilas, North Carolina, for example, used molasses instead of sugar. Here's their recipe:

Wash, slice, core and peel the required number of apples. Put a little water in the brass kettle first and heat, and then add the slices of apple filling the kettle nearly full. Cook them down, and stir them

PLATE 402 The apples are cooked on a stove for fifteen to twenty minutes, then run through a colander.

to prevent sticking. After they are cooked down, add molasses to thicken. The molasses is added after the apples are cooked down to keep the butter from being lumpy.

Just before it's done, add sticks of cinnamon to taste. Then, when it's so thick you can almost cut it with a knife, put it up in half gallon or gallon crocks; place a cloth over the top, and seal the crocks with paraffin.

They can also remember apple butter being made in the molasses boiler during the last runs to get rid of the extra apples and keep them from going to waste.

Aunt Arie made hers in an iron washpot instead of a brass kettle, as she never had one of the latter. She told us:

"We always had so many good apples. See, we had an apple orchard there at home. We had hundreds of bushels of apples, till it come that storm and blowed the trees all up and Ulysses never did set'em back out. The few trees that were left made up more than we could use and he got old and crippled on both sides, couldn't dig much. And you can't hire people to do what you want done. You just have to do what you can do. Of course, we had plenty of apples. We've done away with three hundred bushels in one year. I tell you, I got so tired of picking up apples and carrying them to the house and giving them to everybody in Georgia and everywhere else, till I was glad when they were gone! Now that's the truth. Of course, I was stout then and could do it, but you done so much of it,

PLATE 403   The applesauce is poured into a twenty-gallon brass kettle heated by an open fire. (The kettle must be cleaned with a solution of vinegar and baking soda prior to use.) Mrs. Brooks said, "Brass is the only kind [of kettle] I would have. It just makes better butter somehow. I don't like a copper kettle because it makes the butter taste, I think."

Pat told us, "You can use any kind of wood for the fire except pine. [Pine would make the butter taste.] Don't let the wood touch the bottom of the kettle or the butter will burn."

PLATE 404   Pat made the butter-stirring stick himself out of cypress. Wood with acid in it can't be used because it will impart a taste. He likes yellow poplar the best.

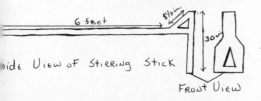

PLATE 405   Pat's stirring stick.

PLATE 406   The applesauce is constantly stirred until it's hot enough to melt sugar. Then, using one five-pound bag at a time at regular intervals, fifty pounds of sugar are poured in. The mixture must cook for about two hours, stirring it constantly.

"When you stir, you go once on one side, once on the other side, and once in the middle. You see, the bottom is narrow, and that way it won't stick."

PLATE 407 As the apple butter cooks, Pat brings out his banjo to liven up the proceedings.

PLATE 408 After two hours' cooking, the mixture is taken off the fire, and 4¼ fluid ounces of imitation oil of cinnamon (used by the Brooks) or other desired flavor is added.

you got tired of it. What I mean, you got give out of it—I'll put it that way. Your strength give out.

"Use good ripe, soft apples. Peel the apples and cut them up—not too fine. Add just enough water to prevent the apples from sticking while they cook. When the apples begin cooking good, mash them with a potato masher as fine as possible. Make the apple butter thick. Then add lots of sorghum to it for sweetening (if you don't, it'll sour). If you don't get the apple butter good and thick, and boil it down good, a five-gallon jarful will sour. Add ground cinnamon for flavoring. If you can't get cinnamon, use lemon.

"To store it, use five six-gallon crocks; tie the tops with cloth, then cover with paper and tie with string. When we wanted apple butter, we opened a crock and got out a bowlful, ate it, and went back for more.

"Lord, they loved apple butter at my house, mercy alive. See, there was so many boys and you know what boys will do. And Papa loved it! I can eat apple butter, but I never did love it like they did."

The Brooks family has been making apple butter every year for over forty years.

It takes three bushels of apples to make a stir. You can keep the apples for three or four days before using them in the apple butter. Mrs. Brooks explains, "I wouldn't have nothing but the Winesaps. That's the only kind that makes good butter. The other kind won't cook up good. Sour apples do. An apple that has a sweet taste to it [won't] make good butter."

Mrs. Brooks says, "Sometimes [we sell it], but most of the time we keep it. The family likes it. They must; every time I turn around they're asking for some."

I understand!

Aunt Arie also told us of other recipes that were brought to mind when we asked her about apple butter. "Now another thing that really I like a little better in one way is apple preserves. You make preserves out of the kind of apples that don't cook all to pieces—that stay whole.

"You peel the apples and cut them up into little pieces—they don't cook up. Put cinnamon or whatever you want to flavor them with. We put them in big old jars and tied them up. People don't can stuff now like they did then. Of course, if I was to make apple butter now, I'd want to put it in smaller jars and seal them up. And then eat it. You'd have it good all the time. Apple preserves are good!

"I've helped make gallons of apple cider. You have to have a cider mill to grind up your apples most of the time. Squeeze that all out and put it up. It's hard to make. I don't like apple cider much. Boys, they loved it at

PLATE 409 The apple butter is now done
and ready to be poured into jars. Each stir
(three bushels of apples) yields about seventy-
five jars.

PLATE 410 "It's s'good that if you put some on your forehead, your tongue would
slap your brains out trying t'get to it!" PAT BROOKS.

home, though. We'd make it by the gallons. We'd fix the apples and put them in a big old wooden trough. We'd take a maul and beat up them apples and make cider out of them. They'd strain the cider out and put it in jugs or whatever they wanted to keep it in. How they did love it! Especially when it's sharp, as they called it. They left it till some of it commenced to sour just a little [and then they really enjoyed it.]

"You make pumpkin butter like you do apple butter. Cut the pumpkin up and peel it and cook that good. Then just mash it up and put sugar and flavoring in. That's all you have to do. We always made ours with cinnamon, and how good it was! Really pumpkin butter is easier to make than apple butter. We grew as high as a hundred big pumpkins in one year. We'd make it up to last a year and eat it every bit up before spring. We'd have to make a'many a gallon to have enough to do us a year, 'cause we loved it. Then there was so many of us. You take a houseful of boys—they eat something!"

SORGHUM

At one time, syrup made from juice crushed out of sorghum cane was highly prized as a sugar substitute and sweetener. In some communities, aside from honey, it was the only sweet substance available, as sugar cost money, and money was the rarest commodity of all.

Some families in the mountains still produce sorghum (or molasses) for their own use, but the method of production, in most cases, has undergone some refinements. Nowadays, the mills that are used to crush the juice out of the cane are, more often than not, run by a gasoline engine or a belt connected to the power take-off of a tractor. Years ago, the rollers of the mill were turned by a horse or mule. The animal was hitched to the end of a long rein pole or "sweep." A rod mounted horizontally in, and at right angles to, the butt end of the sweep was tied to a line that went to the horse's halter so that as the horse pulled the lead end of the sweep forward, the line connected to the butt end would keep him pulling himself around in a never-ending circle (see *Plates 411* and *412*). The sweep turned a crusher roller in the mill, which in turn engaged a second (and sometimes a third) roller, forcing it to turn also. The cane was fed in between the rollers and crushed dry of its juice.

Since few people could afford these mills, it was common that men who owned one would move them from settlement to settlement, grinding and making the syrup for everyone in the area. In return, they were given a "toll"—usually every fourth gallon—in payment. Those who had helped the farmer harvest his cane were also paid in syrup. Making it was a long, slow process, however. Many mills could only turn out about sixteen gallons a day.

Today, those who grow sorghum grow it in much the same way as their families did before the turn of the century. In early April, the ground is

PLATE 411 A horse-operated sorghum mill in the reconstructed pioneer settlement at the Cherokee, North Carolina, entrance to the Smokies.

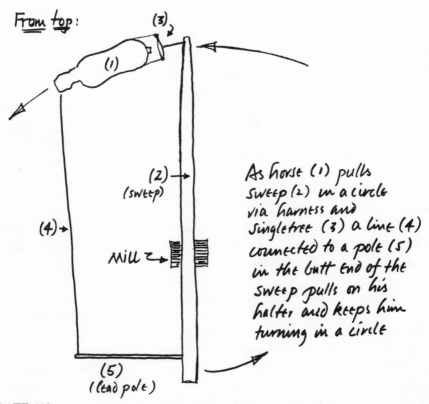

From top:

(3)

(1)

(2)
(sweep)

(4)

Mill

(5)
(lead pole)

As horse (1) pulls sweep (2) in a circle via harness and singletree (3) a line (4) connected to a pole (5) in the butt end of the sweep pulls on his halter and keeps him turning in a circle

PLATE 412

plowed and readied for planting the patch. Noel Moore claims that the soil the cane is planted in makes a big difference in the final product: gray soil for light, thin syrup; and red clay for thick, clear syrup. The seeds, which were saved from the crop the year before, are planted sometime between the middle of May and the first of July (often when the moon is in its growing phase, according to Noel Moore) so that it will be ready for harvest in mid-September—after the corn and before the first frost. It is planted in hills approximately a foot apart and with seven to twelve seeds per hill.

When the stalks are up, the farmer cultivates the rows and thins the number of stalks per hill to five to prevent the cane from growing too tall and thin, thus making the juice watery for lack of enough sun.

All through the summer months, the cane grows. It is ready to be harvested when the seeds turn red and hard. Hopefully, this will be before the first frost, for even though the frost won't necessarily destroy the crop, cold weather makes the plant turn tough and the leaves become harder to strip off. If wind, rain, or other bad weather knocks the stalks down before harvesting, some farmers just give the crop up and plow it under. Others, like Burnett Brooks, try to use it anyway.

At harvest time, the family goes through the field stripping off the stalks' leaves and cutting off the heads (the large red seed pods at the tops of the stalks). The leaves can be mixed with the cornstalks and used as silage. Some of the heads are saved for next year's seed, and the rest are fed to the chickens or put out for the birds.

This job done, the farmer cuts the stripped cane stalks off at the base, using a sharp hoe or mowing blade, and stacks them in piles to be picked up immediately by horse and wagon, or tractor and wagon. The stalks are rarely left for long after they've been cut, as they will dry out in a matter of a very few days. Also, the cut ends can start to rot, souring the juice and ruining it. The stalks are taken to the mill as quickly as possible for crushing.

This fall, we were lucky enough to find one family producing sorghum for themselves in the most traditional way of all. Tim DeBord and Shanon Jackson drove up with Margie to cover it.

After a short winding drive up a narrow, black-top road, we found the Brooks family hard at work making sorghum syrup. As we stepped out of the Blazer, we were greeted by a bunch of people—mostly kids.

They had saved a dozen or so stalks of cane and left Roxy, the nine year old horse, hitched up just to show us how the process of grinding the sorghum cane is done. The grinding had started at five that morning when one of their relatives, Lowell Buchanan, got up, hitched up the

PLATE 413 The cane is stripped and the tops removed. It is now ready to be ground by the mill.

PLATE 414 Some of the sorghum seed tops are saved to start for the following year's crop.

horse, and sat down in the dark to grind cane. Some people would think that's a lot to ask but this man was not asked; he volunteered.

When we asked about another type of furnace, this same man loaded two of us in his jeep and took us several miles up the road just to show us one. On the way, he told us some good hunting stories.

Mr. Burnett Brooks was the owner of the furnace and boiler-box he built in 1969. When people stopped by to see how it was going, Mr. Brooks was always there to say hello, and found time to talk about ground-hog hunting or bear season. People were just dropping in constantly. One man came by and skimmed the boiling juice for an hour and then left. He was "just a friend." Another friend, Robert Sutton, came by and stayed all day—just helping out.

Mr. Brooks made small paddle-spoons to scrape down the sorghum from the bottom of the boiler. These were about eight inches long and made of wood. They were given to the children when the sorghum was finished, and were good for getting a sample of sorghum. We found the kids getting ahead of the rest of us—they would slip their spoons into the sorghum while it was still boiling hot. They thought it was good—hot or not. And Mr. Brooks had just as much fun as the kids did.

As the morning passed, the amount of boiling juice in the box diminished. We were invited to lunch at a table loaded with food—green beans, chicken, corn relish, creamed corn, pickles, potatoes, fresh garden tomatoes, light bread, and sweet milk. We were given plates and filed by the table filling them with a taste of everything—then headed for the back porch shade. We all sat on the cracked edge of the cool, moist back porch. As one of us was about to take a big bite of crisp chicken, Mr. Brooks said, "Yeah, I pinched the head off that ol' rooster this morning."

We changed the subject and got him to talk about sorghum. He explained the whole process to us.

When the cane is harvested, the mill is oiled and the wood gathered to make ready for the cane-grinding. The Brooks have two wooden barrels, one thirty-gallon and one fifty-five-gallon, to be used for collection of the cane juice. A few days before the grinding, the barrels are filled with water so that the staves will swell making the barrels water-tight. Poplar and oak wood are used for the fire under the boiler. By the time the juice is prepared and added to the boiler, the fire has burned down to a bed of coals. Then more wood is added to bring the temperature of the boiler up, or the fire is doused with water to cool the boiler when the juice is boiling too vigorously.

Mr. Brooks has a three-roller mill. One of the rollers is stationary, the second is set at one-eighth inch, and the third at one-sixteenth inch from the stationary roller (*Plate 415*). As the horse turns the mill, the sorghum

PLATE 415   Mr. Brooks's mill has three rollers (one is concealed in this photo).

is fed into one side of the mill. The bright green juice drops into a trough
and down to a burlap-covered barrel. It is then taken to the boiler where
it is poured through several layers of cheesecloth into the boiler. The
boiler is filled to within two inches of the top for each batch. No more
juice is added after that until that batch is completely cooked down and
poured into containers for storage.

When the juice begins to boil, a dark foam forms on the top. A handmade tool called a skimmer is then used. The skimmer is an eight-and-
one-half-inch-square piece of metal attached to a broom handle. It is per-
forated so that the juice will run out and leave the foam on the skimmer.
The skimmings are discarded into a hole nearby and later the hole covered
with dirt. Usually the dogs get to the skimmings before they are covered
and really enjoy this treat. We have been told that the skimmings were
used at one time to help sweeten moonshine.

The juice has to boil for three to four hours. It is kept at a rolling boil
by controlling the heat of the fire as mentioned. The boiler-box holds
about eighty gallons. From this eighty gallons of juice come eight to ten
gallons of syrup. The juice turns from bright green to a rich caramel color
as it is cooked and thickens. When the syrup has cooked long enough, the
boiler is lifted from the firebox and placed onto two logs, so that one end
of the boiler can be tilted up and the syrup scraped to the other end with
a long wooden paddle, about two feet long and flat on one end, made by
Mr. Brooks. It is then dipped out of the trough with a small boiler (or
saucepan) and poured through several layers of cheesecloth into five-gallon
lard cans. After it cools, it is stored in smaller containers—quart jars or
gallon cans.

After all the sorghum is finished, and all the syrup cooked and poured into containers, the boiler-box is washed thoroughly and mutton tallow is spread on it to keep it from rusting. After the tallow hardens, the boiler is stored upside down in a shed or barn. The barrels are washed and dried and stored away. The boom pole, which is attached to the mill, and the lead pole, which is attached to the boom pole, are taken down and stored until next year. The mill is covered with a tarpaulin and left for the kids to play on.

PLATES 416–418   As the horse turns the mill (*Plate 416*), cane is fed through it, several stalks at a time (*Plate 417*). The mill pulverizes the cane, leaving it dry and flaky on the inside (*Plate 418*). The pulpy ground cane will be spread on fields as mulch. The extracted juice runs into a burlap-covered barrel.

PLATE 418

PLATE 419 The burlap bag spread over the barrel serves as a strainer. This is the first of three strainings during the entire sorghum-making process.

PLATE 420 The furnace is prepared for lighting.

PLATE 421 More wood is added to the furnace.

PLATES 422–423 The juice is poured through a cloth (strainer) into the trough, or boiler-box (*Plate 422*), until it is filled to within two inches of the top (*Plate 423*).

PLATE 423

PLATE 424 The juice is brought to a boi
Some evaporators are slightly different than
the Brooks's. Another example is shown as a
diagram (*Plate 425*); numbers 1 through 6
indicate the sequence of the flow of the juice,
number 7 refers to the boiler.

PLATE 425

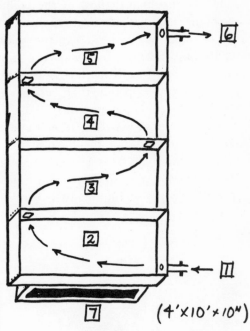

PLATE 426 Robert Sutton skims the foam
off the boiling juice.

Some evaporators are slightly different from the Brooks's. One variety is shown in *Plate 425*. The syrup enters from the storage barrel at (1) through a valve that allows the operator to admit it at a controlled rate. The evaporator is tilted slightly (the exit end is about ⅜ of an inch higher than the entrance end) and gates in the bars which divide it into sections allow the syrup to pass from one compartment into another. The arrows show the direction of flow of the boiling syrup which is slowly forced to the higher end by the pressure of the incoming syrup and the heat.

The cane juice is heated to the boiling point in the first two compartments (2) and (3). In the third compartment, the impurities left in the juice are forced to the surface where they are skimmed off by a man with a wooden strainer-paddle that has a long wooden handle.

In the fourth compartment (5) the juice is brought to the proper thickness for syrup. A cut-off gate at the entrance to this compartment allows the operator to admit the juice at a controlled rate. The syrup is ready to be drawn off (6) when the bubbles that rise from the bottom are about two inches in diameter and burst in the middle. If the bubbles are tiny, the syrup is still not ready to be released.

PLATE 427   Mrs. Brooks holds the skimmer. Note the holes in its bottom—juice runs through them but foam doesn't.

PLATES 428–430   The boiler-box is removed from the furnace (*Plate 428*), and the sorghum is scraped down to one end of the boiler-box (*Plate 429*). The sorghum is then dipped out of the boiler-box with a small saucepan (*Plate 430*).

PLATE 430

PLATE 429

Ready syrup is drained off at (6). It proceeds down a trough, through another strainer, and then into the clay jugs that were used to store it for use during the winter.

Often the skimmings would be saved, boiled separately, and then worked into candy at a "candy pulling" which was one of the social events most looked forward to in the fall. "The candy," said Bill Lamb, "tasted *pretty well*, but mostly people came for the fun of it."

PLATE 431   Finally, the sorghum is poured through several layers of cheesecloth into five-gallon cans (the Brooks use empty lard cans), where it cools before being stored in smaller containers.

BROOMS AND BRUSHES

THE MONROE LEDFORD VARIETY

Through Maco Crafts in Franklin, North Carolina, we were introduced to Monroe Ledford, a delightful person who has raised broomcorn and made brooms for several years as a hobby. He uses the same technique as his parents and grandparents used. He will be retiring soon from road construction and plans to make brooms to supplement his retirement income.

As we drove up in the Ledfords' yard, we noticed bunches of sticks in neat piles, lumber near a workshop, and a shock of corn nearby. Off to the side of the house were woods, where Mr. Ledford showed us sourwood saplings that he prefers to use for broom handles.

Beyond the house, down the hill a short way, was his broomcorn field—about two acres. As we were visiting him in February, the field was bare, but we're hoping to go back in August and see the broomcorn in full growth.

Mr. Ledford makes his brooms in the garage adjoining his house. There on the rafters, he has all kinds of sticks to choose from for broom handles and walking sticks. He has his broom straw spread out on timbers in one corner to keep it dry and flat, and convenient to choose from as he makes each broom.

Interview and photographs by Ken Kistner,
Phil Hamilton, and Lanier Watt.

PLATE 432   Monroe Ledford and his brooms.

PLATE 433   Broomcorn

PLATE 434   The harvested straw drying.

PLATE 435 First the seeds are combed out of the tassel or head. Seeds that are not saved for planting the next year are simply plowed under in a nearby pasture.

PLATES 436–439 Set two small nails in the handle to prevent the stalks from slipping off after they have been tied in place (*Plate 436*). Surround the end of the handle completely with one layer of stalks (*Plate 437*) and tie them down in two places with strips of cloth or string. With a knife, shave off or taper the ends of this first layer of stalks to reduce bulk (*Plate 438*). Then add a second layer of stalks and tie them in place temporarily (*Plate 439*).

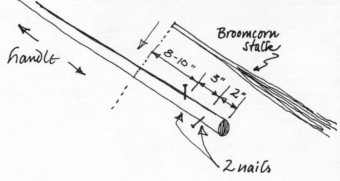

PLATE 437

PLATE 438

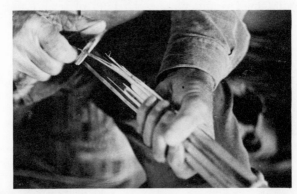

PLATE 439

I started to make brooms just for a hobby, that's all. Just thought I'd make a few brooms, and if somebody wanted them, I would have them to give. And that's what I did, till I gave away two or three hundred dollars' worth. The most expensive part of the broom is your time. This little ball of twine that I'm weaving with costs 75¢. It'll make five or six brooms, maybe more.

They make a nylon cord that won't break, but it's not good to use for weaving brooms because it won't hold—it's too slippery. You can't keep nylon cord tight. The cord I use is made of cotton; it doesn't stretch.

I use a type of carpet needle—bowed a bit so that it goes in and out of the stalks easy enough when you're weaving the string through. It probably costs about 35¢ at the dime store in Franklin.

About the first of June, I prepare my soil and plant the broomcorn; it's just like planting corn or sorghum. Only I plant it a lot thicker. Broomcorn [can be planted] about every five inches apart. I guess if your ground is good enough, you probably wouldn't have to use much fertilizer. It's not too hard to grow. An acre of broomcorn will make lots of brooms.

I save most of my seed for the next year. I don't imagine any stores around here would handle the kind of seed I use. Now that's something I've never done—gone to a store for seed. I guess you could order them from a seed book somewhere.

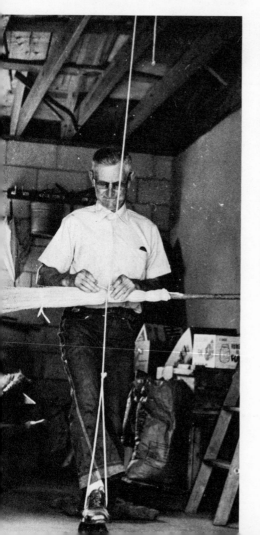

PLATE 440   Lay the broom on a cement floor or in a long trough of some type. Cover it with a burlap sack and pour scalding water over the broom to soften the stalks so that they will be pliable enough to stitch through them. Leave them under the wet sack about ten to fifteen minutes. String will now be tied tightly around the broom to hold the stalks in place permanently. To do this, Mr. Ledford uses an apparatus of the same type used by his parents' generation (*Plate 440*). Hang a rope from a rafter; it must be long enough to allow a loop at the bottom for the broom maker's foot, four to six inches above the floor. Wrap the rope once around the broom near the point where it will be tied. Push down on the rope with your foot to tighten the loop around the broom. Twisting the broom upward will tighten the loop more.

PLATE 441   When it seems quite tight, take a five- or six-foot piece of heavy-duty cotton string threaded through a carpet needle. Run this through the center of the brush right below the point at which the stalks stop and the brush begins (*Plate 441*). The needle will have to be pulled through with pliers. Then bring the needle out and twist string all the way around the broom and tie very tightly. As the broom straw dries, it will expand around the string, tightening it further. Twist the loose end of the string so that it goes into the center of the broom and will not be seen.

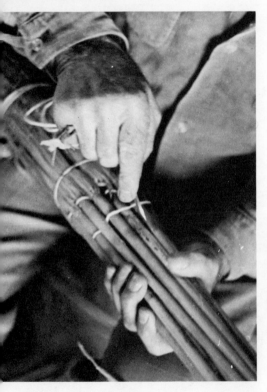

PLATE 443

PLATES 442–443   If you want to weave the stalks instead of simply ringing them in four places, start weaving the string from the brush and weave toward the bare handle in a standard over one, under one pattern. If you end up needing to weave two stalks at one time to keep the pattern, go ahead (*Plate 443*). Mr. Ledford says he has tried to put an odd number of stalks around, but it rarely works out that way, so he doesn't worry about it any more. He just catches up two stalks if he needs to.

PLATE 444 To finish up, put the broom back in the loop of the rope apparatus near the top of the stalks and tighten. Tie the string very tightly at the top to finish off the weaving (*Plate 444*). The excess string may be used to make a loop there to hang the broom by the fireplace. Trim off the excess stalk at the top of the string. Leave a string or rag wrapped around the lower part of the broom to keep the brush from spreading until the broom is hung by the fireplace or wherever it will be kept.

PLATE 445 Several handle designs are common. The style chosen depended on personal preference.

About eight years ago, a neighbor gave me a handful of broomcorn seed. I never thought to ask them where they got the seed. I planted them and that's how I got started in the broom business. About ten or fifteen years ago, my stepmother gave me some seed—I don't know where she got them, South Carolina, maybe—and I grew the corn to make that broom there [standing in the corner of the garage]. I had enough corn for several brooms, but I was busy, and just made that one and left the rest to lie around and ruin.

September is when I start cutting it—before frost—when the head begins to be pretty well filled out, while the seeds are still green. This happens before you know it. Then I go and break the stalk about three feet below the top, and let that hang down. This helps the brush to stay straight. If the stalk is not broken over like this, the straw becomes too heavy with seeds and begins to fall down and turn the wrong way.

So that's the first thing I do. After a few days I cut it. Broomcorn should be cut while still green. It makes tougher brooms this way.

You want to leave it out to cure, but you must be careful not to let it get rained on too much; it mildews and deteriorates pretty quickly while it's green. I don't like to leave it out in the field after it's cut; I'd rather not have it rained on. I like to keep it dry and just put it out in the sun each day—it's got to have sunshine to cure.

Some people like a red-colored broom. If the broomcorn is not harvested, or cut, until after it is completely ripe, the straw will be red. The straw is more brittle, and the broom not quite so durable, as one made with broomcorn cut before it is fully ripe, but for some people this is suitable because the broom will be used for ornamentation more than utility.

After I cure it, I cut the stalks in the shape I want them. I cut them at an angle or split off part of the stalk to reduce bulk around the handle of the broom.

I comb the seeds of the straw with a child's saw that one of my grandsons had left around here. Any kind of sharp-toothed tool could be used, just to rake out the seeds and fluff up the straw.

My brooms are generally three and a half to four feet long from the top of the stick down to the end of the brush. I have to pick out stalks that match, that are pretty much the same length. Sometimes I put the best corn inside just to get the right length to match around the outside. Sometimes I put the big, long brushes inside; the bigger and longer the brush, the tougher and better broom you've got, you know.

Then they're ready to place on the broomstick. Now what they call a hearth broom, if I understand it right, is just stalks—no broomstick. Although some people do put a small stick in them, long stalks of broom-corn can be used and just bunched together and the stalks woven as for a regular broom. Just use long stalks, and use the stalk handle to hold it. It's the same length as those longer stalks that aren't split. Well, to make a hearth broom, I do split part of them that won't show, and then leave the ones on the outside unsplit.

THE AUNT CELIA WOOD VARIETY

"How does it feel to be one hundred years old?" was one of the first questions we asked Aunt Celia Wood. "Well, not much different from ninety-nine," was all the answer we got.

Aunt Celia is our oldest contact, and even at one hundred she still keeps her house spotless. She also makes her own brooms out of broom sage and twine. As she showed us how, she talked of various things. She has definite opinions on many current subjects, and we were fascinated by her spirited comments on such things as politics and religion.

PLATE 446

On Going to the Moon: I don't believe there is no such business. When God made this world, he gave man authority t'subdue [animals]. Gave control over fowls, beasts, fish. Well, God left space for himself. He's got th'sun, moon, stars. Man ain't got no business a'foolin' with'em.

On Politics: They's a lot of things goin' on that oughtn't. Hit's th'leaders of th'country. Congress, and th'President said America was sick. Doctor it! Congress is treatin' America like a doctor who don't know what he's a'doin'.

[When women got the right to vote] I registered. I voted several years. I didn't care whether I did or not, but my husband wanted me t'register and vote. Said th'other women was all a'doin' that, and most of'em did. I wish they hadn't, 'cause they gave'em that privilege and now they're a'tryin' t'take over. I don't like that—even if I am a woman. I think that's men's work. 'Course they're makin' a right smart mess out of it. Maybe if th'women had it all they *might* do better.

On Religion: Well, I couldn't live without it. When I'uz thirteen years old, I joined th'Baptist church. I've been a Baptist ever since. I don't fall out with th'other denominations because hit's not th'church that saves'y'. Don't do you any good t'join th'church if you ain't saved.

I'm a'lookin' forward to a better time than I've got. I've enjoyed life. I've had a lot a'sorrow. I'd a'never went through it all if it hadn't a'been for th'Lord.

My parents treated us strict. There were parties. We never went to 'em. My daddy said dances would lead you wrong. They trained me that they was a Lord over us all. And they'd read th'Bible to us every night. Had a big fireplace. I can see m'old daddy. After supper he'd throw in a piece a'pine wood, lean his chair back, and read th'Bible to us. I wuz th'oldest. Then he'd get his songbook and they'd set there and sing. We enjoyed it. We knowed t'behave. I think that has a lot t'do with our young people. Young people get into mischief, but you'll think about what daddy and mommy said.

I was married eighty-six years. I didn't have no children, but I've always had children around me. I always tried t'give th'boys good advice. I got after a boy one day. I'uz a'settin' here, and he cussed. I says, "I'm not a'gonna' have anybody around me that cusses." I told all of'em that. They never did cuss any more around me. And I had that boy tell me after he married that if it hadn't'a'been for my advice, he didn't know what he'd'a'made.

I'uz just a'studyin' about that—advice to a person just startin' out. Now one of th'boys married a girl who had never been saved. I talked

t'her. I advised her. I asked her what church she belonged to just t'start
it off, y'know. I said t'her, "Ain't y'never been saved?"

She said, "No."

I told her, "You're married now, and most ever'body is apt t'have
some children," and I says, "Y'can't raise up your children right without
th'Lord. When y'go in yer new house, y'ought t'take th'Lord with you."
I told her that.

All my boys was church members. But one day I found a deck a'cards
in a drawer. But I never said a word. So one night after supper, he said,
"Let's have a game."

I said, "Lamar, I don't know how."

He said, "Oh! I'll show y'."

I said, "No, I won't play cards."

He said, "Why? Hit won't be a bit a'harm fer you and me t'sit here
and play a game a'cards."

I said, "I don't believe it'll stop there. Playin' cards is like drinkin'
liquor. Hit will grow on y'."

He said, "Oh!" He wouldn't let it.

I says, "Y'can't help it if y'play awhile with me'r'anybody." I says,
"You'll get t'where you can play pretty good, and you'll want t'bet some."

"Oh," he said, "I wouldn't."

I said, "If I was t'play cards with y', and later you was t' get into a
rarr [argument], then you'd think back and say, 'Well, Aunt Celia learnt
me.' I'd be t'blame. I'd be th'cause of it."

He still thought he'd get me t'play, so he kept on. He said, "Well, if
y'don't play with me here, I'll go t'somebody's that will. And I'll bet my
farm!"

I said, "See there? Already you're a'thinkin' about bettin'." He never
did ask me, ner I never did see that deck of cards n'more. They got
missin'. He got t'thinkin' about what I'd said t'him.

If I could go back, I would want t'live closer and do more for th'Lord.
Go t'church and all. I've tried t'live a pretty good life.

I've never harmed anybody.

Done my part.

The brooms Aunt Celia makes are of bundles of broom sage trimmed
to about twenty-four inches long and bound at the base by twine or a
narrow strip of cloth wrapped around the straw eight to ten times (*Plate
446*). "This used to be all th'kind of broom we had. They last me about
three months. 'Course I don't do much sweepin'. I have t'hold to a chair.
I sweep out th'corners twice a week. I don't do no moppin' though. I got

a woman t'get me a bundle of straw and I made six of'em. You can have this'n now. You sweep with it!"

It was my hope that we would be able to interview Aunt Celia often, but she grew ill, and died in October.

This was a personal loss for me. She was a friend, but more than that I was attached to her like close kinfolk.

Aunt Celia will not be forgotten, and what she told us will be preserved, and cherished by our staff for years to come.

She has set an example and hopefully, many will follow it. I won't think of Aunt Celia as dead—just gone home.

KATHY LONG BLALOCK

SCRUB BRUSHES

A durable brush or mop was needed to clean the rough-hewn wooden floors of log houses. Here's a description of one type we've found used in earlier mountain homes.

This scrub brush was made from a small white oak sapling trunk about two inches in diameter and four feet long. From the bottom, the trunk is shaved into thin, narrow splits (as for white oak splits) about twelve inches long. Be sure not to cut the splits away from the main part of the trunk (see *Plate 447*).

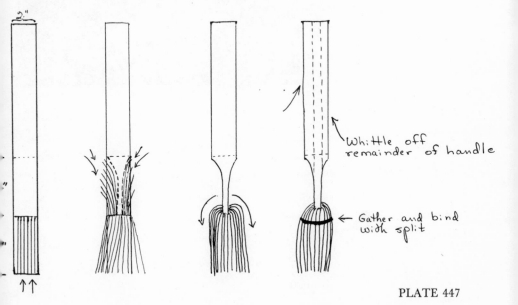

PLATE 447

Then split the wood down about twelve to fourteen inches and bend these splits over to form the outer "bristles" of the brush. Use a narrow leather strap or another split to hold the bristles together (*Plate 448*).

To scrub, throw sand and water on the floor and scrub with the brush. Sweep the sand off and the floor will be white.

PLATE 448

CORNSHUCK MOPS, DOLLS AND HATS

We heard from a number of people that Mrs. Kate Hopper, who works in the Rabun Gap Craft Shop, knew how to make scrub mops from cornshucks. As we were interested in this subject, we went to investigate. Luckily, she agreed to make one for us, and as she made it, we took a set of photographs so you could see how it is done.

Photographs and interview done by Jan Brown and Mary Garth.

PLATE 449   L. D. Hopper (Kate's husband) works on the board for the mop. The board should be 5½″ wide, 13¾″ long, and 1½″ thick. Eighteen holes (one inch in diameter) should be placed in three rows of six holes each, as pictured.

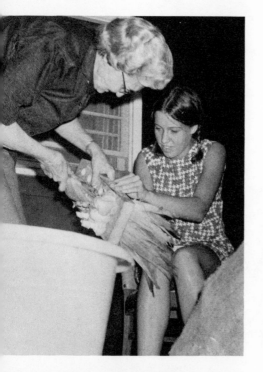

PLATES 450–452   Kate soaks the cornshucks in a tub for several minutes to make them pliable. Then she and Jan Brown (right) fit the dampened cornshucks through the holes (*Plate 450*). The loose ends of the shucks are put through first. Note that the whole shuck is used; the shank is not cut off until after the mop is completed. When all the loose ends are through, they should be pulled firmly until they are tight (*Plate 451*). Then Kate trims the shanks and ends to make them even (*Plate 452*).

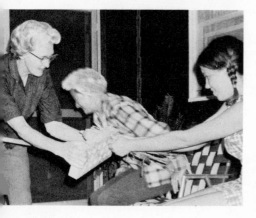

PLATE 453 Mary Garth demonstrates the effectiveness of the new mop on Kate's porch.

DOLLS

The cornshuck dolls we have photographed were made by Daisy Justice and Lassie Bradshaw. Not many of our contacts remember making or playing with cornshuck dolls as children. They remember more about home-made rag dolls, although they did make little horses and dogs from shucks. The cornshuck dolls now are usually made for doll collectors more than for toys.

The materials needed are a ball of twine or crocheting thread (not nylon as it stretches); scissors; a bowl of water to dampen the shucks; clean shucks—white, or any available colors (mildewed or dark shucks may be used for the bottom layers of the skirt and the inside parts of dolls); and corn silks—blonde, red, and brown—for hair.

Different people have told us varied lengths of time to wet the shucks before using. It seems the best formula to follow for dolls is to trim a few shucks, dip them in water for three to five minutes, then drain and use.

PLATE 454   Daisy Justice works on a cornshuck doll.

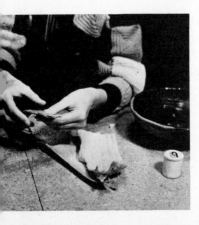

PLATES 455–459 To make the head, cut a cornshuck two inches wide and six inches long. Fold it over lengthwise, making it one inch wide (*Plate 455*). Begin folding shuck down several times to make the filling for the head (*Plate 456*). When finished, the filling for the head should appear as shown (*Plate 457*). Cover the filling with another shuck as illustrated (*Plate 458*). This shuck will extend below the neck to form the upper body of the doll. Tie the shuck at the neck (*Plate 459*) to secure it tightly.

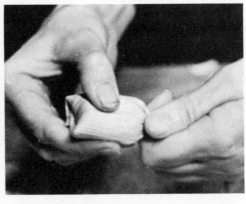

PLATE 456

PLATE 457

PLATE 458

PLATE 459

The shucks seem easier to use when dampened a short time rather than soaked. As the shucks dry on the newlymade doll, they will fluff out. The sashes will tighten so that they don't come untied when dry.

There are many variations of the cornshuck dolls ranging in sizes from three to twelve inches high. Some wear dyed dresses (the shucks are dyed just like fabric before making the dolls); some are boy dolls with pants on.

We believe that the pattern shown is a basic style, and once you get the gist of making a cornshuck doll, you will develop your own techniques and try out various ideas.

Interviews by Shanon Jackson, Julia Justice, and Annette Reems. Photographs by Phil Hamilton. Text by Annette Reems.

PLATES 460–462 For the arms, pick two shucks about the same size (one will be used for each arm). Twist each shuck as pictured (*Plate 460*). Bend each twisted shuck in half (*Plate 461*) and tie one on either side of the body of the neck with string. Attached arms should appear as shown (*Plate 462*).

PLATE 461

PLATE 462

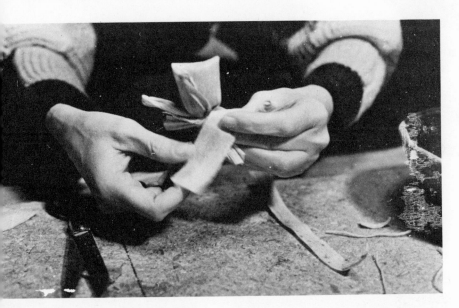

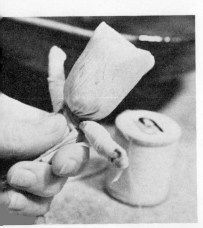

PLATES 463–465 Take another shuck and wrap it around one arm—forming a sleeve beginning about ¼ inch from the folded end (hand) of the arm, and wrap back toward the head (*Plate 463*). Bring the end of the wrapped shuck across the back of the doll diagonally to the waist. Go through the same process with the other arm. Sleeved arms should appear as pictured (*Plate 464*). The sleeve strips crisscross in back. Tie them at the waist with a piece of string (*Plate 465*).

PLATE 464

PLATE 465

PLATES 466–467 Now cover the body with two shucks. One goes diagonally across each shoulder (*Plate 466*). These shucks crisscross in back and front. Tie them at waist with string (*Plate 467*).

PLATE 467

PLATES 468–470 Place several shucks lengthwise (one at a time) around the waist. The shucks will overlap to form a full, long skirt (*Plate 468*). Use as many shucks as needed for desired fullness, and tie at waist with string (*Plate 469*). Trim the skirt to make it even, so the doll will stand straight (*Plate 470*).

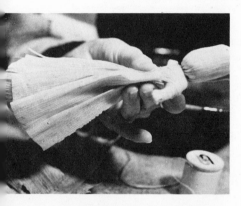

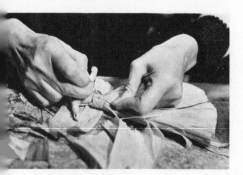

PLATE 469

PLATE 470

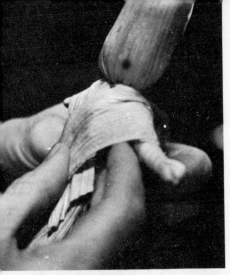

PLATE 472

PLATES 471–472   Next crisscross two shucks over the shoulders (*Plate 471*) and bring them down below the waist in front and back. Fold another shuck into a long, narrow strip. Put it around the waist and tie as a sash in back to hold the bodice secure (*Plate 472*). (An apron may be added before the sash is tied by cutting a shuck into a heart shape and placing it around the waist.)

PLATES 473–474   Dampen corn silks and put them over the doll's face. Tie the silks around the forehead with string (*Plate 473*). Flip the silks to the back, exposing the face (*Plate 474*). The string will be completely covered by the "hair."

ATES 475–476   Take a 1½-inch-wide p of shuck about six inches long and place ver the head, leaving the hair exposed just ve the face (*Plate 475*). Fold the hat down r the back of the head. Then fold in the e to the middle, bunching in back (*Plate*). Tie with string and cover with a nar- shuck for the hat tie. Finish the doll by wing a face with pen and ink.

PLATE 476

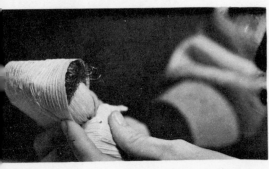

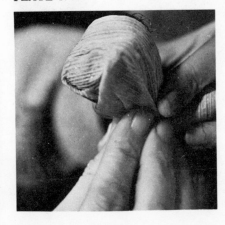

PLATES 477–479 Other accessories may be added, such as a bucket (*Plate 477*). Use any small, deep container, such as a plastic bottle cap. Punch holes in each side of the "bucket" and run a twisted shuck through the doll's hand (loop formed by folded arm shuck), and then through the holes of the bucket to form a handle. Small dried flowers stuck through the doll's hand are another option (*Plate 478*). Touch a little glue to the stems and hand to secure the flowers. For a broom (*Plate 479*), take several shucks about three inches long and tie with a string about a third of the way down. Take a straight pin and shred the lower two thirds. Stick a toothpick, or other small stick, in the top for handle. Put glue on the end of the stick to make it stay on the shucks. Then slide the "broom" handle through the doll's hand.

HATS

Many people have inquired about the cornshuck hats that were sometimes worn to church. We heard that Mrs. Ada Kelly made these cornshuck hats. We went to see her and she was willing to make one for us. As she made it, we took a set of photographs and have made a list of instructions to show how one can be made. The hat Mrs. Kelly made for us was a miniature, but there is a drawing of the pattern including the dimensions for an average-sized head.

Shuck several ears of corn; discard the outer shucks and any shucks with blemishes. Put the shucks in water until they are wet and pliable (about fifteen minutes). To make a pattern for the hat, you need to cut the pattern out of a newspaper or piece of brown paper. Materials needed are stiff buckram, muslin for the lining, cornshucks dried in the fall, thread, a needle, and a pan of water to keep the cornshucks wet.

ANNETTE REEMS

Photographs by Barbara Taylor and Stan Echols.

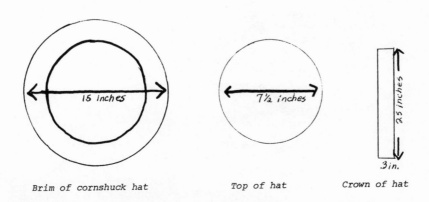

Brim of cornshuck hat   Top of hat   Crown of hat

PLATE 480   This diagram is a pattern for an average-sized cornshuck hat.

PLATES 481–482   Mrs. Ada Kelly cuts the shucks into 1½" squares (*Plate 481*).
Take each square and fold it in half and then in half again, causing the folded shuck
to have a point like the one Mrs. Kelly is holding (*Plate 482*).

PLATE 483 Sew the shucks on buckram, starting at the outer edge and going toward the center.

PLATE 484 Sew the shucks on the crown with the points of the shucks downward; then sew the ends of the crown together.

PLATE 485 When the crown is finished, place it down on the brim and sew the crown onto the brim.

PLATES 486–488   Sew the cornshucks on the top, starting at the outer edge and moving toward the center (*Plate 486*). The shank of a cornshuck can be used at the center of the top, making it look like a flower (*Plate 487*). Place the top of the hat on the crown and sew it on (*Plate 488*). Take muslin or other soft material and sew it onto the underside of the buckram for a pretty lining.

AUNT NORA GARLAND

It seems like each time we visit Aunt Nora, she's in the kitchen cooking something that really smells good. She always has a basket of homemade biscuits sitting on the table. "I cook twelve biscuits every day and if Raleigh doesn't eat them, the kids will, so they're all gone by the end of the day."

Aunt Nora lives in a stone house north of Clayton, Georgia. She doesn't live on a dirt road way back in the hills, but right on the highway next to a block building which she and her husband, Raleigh, owned and in which they operated a grocery store for many years. They sold out last year, but she still has many things to remind her of the store—cartons of Coke bottles stacked against a wall; the building itself; and an old cash register which they bought secondhand twenty-five years ago. The time-worn register is perched on an ancient cabinet, both cracked and peeled, showing the effects of age and use. There is also an old meat-chopping block and a big black pot sits in the back yard.

It's difficult to characterize Aunt Nora because so many "little things" make her unique. She has made quite an impression on me; I hope I am able to convey this to you. Aunt Nora has that loving kindness toward humanity that everyone should have. She's not afraid to tell a person how much she cares about him, or to help a neighbor when he's in need. Her faith in God is so amazing that she spreads His love to everyone without even realizing it. She's worked with God for a long time through faith healing as you can read on pages 352–55 in *The Foxfire Book*.

ANNETTE SUTHERLAND AND ANNETTE REEMS

"Back then . . . "

I was lying on the bed the other night just thinking about how I love country life. We lived in a great big log house. The living room was fixed pretty on the inside. I can almost see it in my dreams. There was a door going through there and a big stairway. You'd go upstairs a piece, turn back and go upstairs again, and there was a big room. Back then people didn't have a living room—just one big room, with two beds in the back of the house, but how nice we kept them. Just white as snow, and we had a pink bedspread on one with a big peafowl and a blue one on the other. I can see them sitting up against the head of the bed. People used to have pillow-shams, they called them. They'd tack them up over the headboard of the bed and they came down over the pillows. Oh, we thought they were pretty. [We had a] great big kitchen with a fireplace and [another] fireplace in the living room.

We used to live up near Sylvan Lake. You don't go right by Sylvan Lake, you keep on that road along by that big mill. I went to that mill there a'many a time. I used to go and watch them grind the meal we had to eat. There's been a mill [there since] before I was born, I guess. It works now. They probably don't grind it, I reckon, but they could if they wanted to. That's where we ground it. I carried many a pail. My uncle owned it, you know.

My parents treated me real good. Daddy was seventy-five year old when he died and Mother was eighty-four. That's been a long time and I don't have any family [anymore] of my own but a sister and she's in a rest home. Oh, we had a happy home. We all had thanks at the table and they was real good to us.

We'd go out and play ball. That's about all we had to do. It was awful fun. We played town ball. If you was caught three times you came out of the ring. Generally I was caught out.

On Christmas we would go a'serenading—a whole crowd of young people. We'd all gather up and put on old things and go a'serenading. Then after we got to the last place, we'd play till about one or two o'clock.

Really we never did play much because we worked. Very little did we play, but on Sunday all we had to do was to go off. If it was springtime with all the leaves, then we'd make leaf dresses and hats and things. We'd come back with dresses and hats made of leaves and sit all day and swing on grapevines. It's a wonder we hadn't been killed going from one hill to another on a grapevine. Never thought about getting hurt.

We lived close to the graveyard and it was right down the hill to Taylor's Chapel. The pine needles was just as thick as can be over there. We'd make

PLATE 489

us a sled and get right up there at the graveyard and slide from it to the road. That's about all the recreation we had when I was little.

We all got along like babies. I had two sisters and five brothers. I'm the baby of the flock though.

We'd have a cornshucking and after that we'd have a candy drawing. You had a lot of corn. People gathered the corn then and they'd go around the evening before and invite them to the cornshucking the next day. Two or three women would come help get dinner and we'd kill the hogs and have plenty of backbones and ribs, a big pot full. Mother had a big pot and she cooked that mess of backbones and ribs, and she cooked chicken, you know, and made dumplings, a sweet potato pie, a grape pie and all these things. Yes, we had plenty. We had lots of good things to eat. I guess things that people wouldn't notice now. That would go on for about six to eight weeks but switching to other people's houses. If we didn't get done, and sometimes we didn't, then we'd have two cornshuckings, but you know, it didn't cost a thing. We'd just have to fix dinner and if it was late when we got through, we'd fix supper. We never thought about charging for anything like that.

If anyone was sick, you'd chop up their wood and carry it in the house for them, and wash their clothes, clean their house for them, and do everything you could for them. "Love your neighbor as yourself" and you know we believed that.

We had candy-pullings too. We'd make up the syrup. We always had a big cane patch and we'd make the syrup and begin to pick it up and get it through. A crowd would gather around and we'd have a circle candy-pull. This was sort of dating, too. The boy would choose the girl that he wanted to pull candy with and he'd pull candy with her.

We went to church twice [on Sunday], and the one that lived farthest away, why all the other young people would go visiting to get to be together. Then when the chinquapins came in (Ral's family had a big orchard then, just little trees that had just been set out) we'd all gang up there and hunt chinquapins and things like that. That was a great thing for us to do. They're like a chestnut, only smaller. We used to string them up on great big long strings. My sister came one time and my mother had strung up about four big strings and hung them up, you know. We had a big dinner and she thought Momma would give them to her and she asked, "Momma, what are you going to do with those chinquapins?"

Momma said, "Nothing. I just hung them up there for children to beg for." We thought that was real funny.

My daddy wouldn't let me go nowhere unless my brothers went. They generally went and we had to be in at a certain time—not later than eleven. Some Christmases we went a'serenading and that made it later because we'd gather at somebody's house after we serenaded. We had to walk; didn't have no other way to go. We all walked together and coupled off. We wasn't in a hurry walking so we got to talk more.

We worked in the field—us children would hoe corn. Mother did the cooking. I believe she had a harder job than we did. I didn't think so then but I can almost see her now. She'd scrape her potatoes; she didn't peel them, she scraped them. Now we don't take time to scrape them; we peel them—Irish potatoes. Land! you'd put them in a pan of water and all that would come off with a knife. I can almost see her a'sitting on the porch. She'd hunker down a'scraping those potatoes and cook a big black pot of beans and potatoes. We'd all eat hearty. We knew it wouldn't be long when we saw her go to the springhouse after the milk and butter till she'd call us for dinner. We had the cows and we made our own butter. She'd churn and she'd take the milk and butter every morning and set it in the springhouse, and before she'd call us to dinner she'd go and get some. She'd cook that big pot of beans and put them long potatoes right beside those on top of the beans. They'd just burst open and be so good with onions and things. She'd put a big piece of streaked meat in it. We'd eat and then she'd hunker down scraping more potatoes to fix another pot for supper.

We made cottage cheese. We grew everything we had nearly. Dad would kill four or five big hogs—big, fat hogs—and we'd salt them down. You can't keep them that way now. But he'd salt them down and we'd have plenty of meat to do us. Oh, I dreaded that fried sausage. We just fried sausage and canned it, you know; we had it the rest of the winter. We dried sweet potatoes and dried apples, and boiled them too. We cooked them and made pies. We dried [the potatoes and apples] on a scaffold. We used an old door laying across two pieces of wood. You boil those potatoes till they get to where you can stick a fork in them, and then peel and slice them and lay them on a cloth on that big table and dry them. We'd have them all winter. Everybody did that—not only us, but everybody.

We had four big cherry trees and they were always just as red. I looked like a flower pod and I was little. Well, I was so slim, you know. I've always been little. Up to here lately I weighed a hundred pounds. So I was the one that could get up in the cherry tree and pick cherries. I never saw the like. And we always canned and picked fifty to seventy-five cans of wild strawberries. Daddy's field was just red with them. And we'd also put up apples. Apple sauce it's called now. We put that up in churns. We made apple butter out of syrup. We had just as many good things to eat back then, or we thought it was just as good. It would be a treat for people now to have what we had back then. Mother would bake

PLATE 490

five or six fruit cakes, real thick, of sweet bread, which she made out of syrup. You know, people never heard of a [layer] cake. We didn't know how to make [layer] cakes. All we could make was great big cakes out of syrup and sweet bread because [we didn't have] stoves.

You know, the first stove I ever saw was a Wilson Patent Stove. I'll tell you about the first [cook] stove I ever saw in my life. My mother had been to her Aunt Jane's, right here in town. She found out that her aunt had a stove. Well, she came back home and wanted Daddy to know about it. It had two little eyes at the top and we wanted it. He told us to go back to Aunt Jane's [and find out where she ordered it]. It finally came and they put it up, built a fire in it, and we just got the wood, thinking that it was the awfullest thing in this world—people [still] cooking in a fireplace. We hadn't had a stove and that was the first one that came out. The neighbors came in to see it and it began to smoke. Well, Momma watered the fire out of it and she walked to Aunt Jane's to see what the matter was with it. Aunt Jane said, "Honey, the newness is burning off it. The polish will soon burn off and it will be all right." Well, we were so happy with that stove. We baked bread on it, just a batch, you know. We had had to bake bread in that fireplace but we didn't have to after that. The stove had an oven in it and little eyes. The people came in to see what was a'happening and from then on nearly everybody just tried to get three dollars to get them a stove.

This must have been about nineteen and five and I was born in about nineteen-one. Now I'm seventy-one but I must have been about five or six. It might have been nineteen and six. I remember that stove so well and we even made a poem about it:

So well do I remember
The Wilson Patent stove
That Father bought and paid for
With cloth the girls had wove.

All the neighbors wondered
When we got the thing to go.
They said it would burst and kill us all
Some twenty year ago.

But twenty year ago, ago
Just twenty year ago
They said it would burst and kill us all
Just twenty year ago.

It never did burst. It was a stove like any other stove, but you know, we hadn't never saw one before.

On Christmas we had a big stack of apple pies, maybe a dozen of them, made out of dried apples. Well, Momma would make a big stack like that and pumpkin custards and make some sweet bread. We baked it on the fireplace. We wouldn't of known how to bake regular cakes. Daddy would always put a big barrel of apples away and they'd keep so good and he'd have a pretty good size barrel full of chestnuts. We'd roast them in the fire and we'd hear the serenaders coming and Daddy would go and get a basket of apples and bring them out when he heard them coming down the hill. He would always reach up to get his gun and shoot straight up in the air. That meant the treat was on them; 'course we always treated them. Oh, I can almost see him reach up and get that gun, then shoot it straight up. That would be on Christmas eve night. We just set around the big old fire. We had a great big fireplace. We'd always get hickory wood for the fire and we'd have it all in and we'd roast chestnuts in the ashes.

We had a Christmas tree but we didn't have anything on it . . . only a string of popcorn, that's all. We'd string up popcorn and have it real pretty and white. Santa Claus came and he'd bring us a piece of candy and maybe an apple or an orange, and a piece of sweet bread that Mother had baked. We'd hang our stockings, great big long stockings, and that's what would be in it, but now we never let on that we knew Mother had done that. We just took that as the best treat. We couldn't wait to get up every [Christmas] morning to see what was in our stockings. We didn't exchange nothing though. Nobody bought nobody nothing. [We] didn't get a thing but a big dinner on Christmas Day. We got up at four o'clock everyday, but if we thought there was something in our stockings, my brother and I would get up before then [on Christmas morning] just to see what was there. We'd act like it was so good and us knowing Mother made it.

She did a lot for us. She'd weave our material and spin it too. All of us could spin. It was wool, and Mother had to have it to weave with. We'd spin the thread. Everyone, even my brother, could knit. He could knit a pair of socks as fast as Mother could and there wasn't any shame in it: no, not a bit in the world. Everybody was just alike.

We even made our own soap. Daddy would always fix Mother an ash hopper and burn hickory wood and she'd put the ashes out in the hopper and burn her lye slow, and she made the soap. We washed the dishes with homemade soap and you know, now it would eat our hands up. It didn't then. We used grease and lard for our hands. We didn't have any kind of lotion.

I ordered the first lipstick I had. I sent off to where you get something to paint your face with. It was in a little box and there wasn't a thing but grease in it. We'd use a little of that on our face—just red grease. They used that to paint their cheeks with. We painted our faces a right smart. It wasn't paid much attention back then, but when my lipstick come, I let all my girlfriends use some of that old greasy stuff on their faces.

It wasn't like this generation. We all wore long dresses. We wore our dresses 'way down to our feet. 'Course that's coming back in style. I've got my girls' pictures with their dresses way down below their knees and their hair done up in a ball. [We] never seen no short hair. [There] wasn't no such thing.

Now I had so much pretty brown hair that I put it up in three big balls behind me. We thought that was pretty and it was. When the style changed, we wore a big bow in our hair back there.

We'd watch other people and if somebody else made something new, we made it too. We didn't have no fashion books or nothing to sew by.

My sister was a dressmaker and she could make a dress in a little while. She sewed for people. She'd look at a picture and cut it out, and then sew it. [She] didn't have a pattern or nothing. She cut it out of the newspaper sometimes—the pattern to fit you—and you'd just tell her how you wanted the dress made and she'd make it. She'd sew after dark and a lot of times put the sleeves in backward, and I'm the one that would have to take them out. Oh, I dreaded that job worse than anything.

We wore a lot of underclothes but they were made out of sheeting. Yes, we had nice underclothes. They was as white as they could be, with lace on them. They were made out of what you make sheets out of today.

Back when I was young, we wore middy blouses and skirts and gingham dresses. Of course they were nice clothes and made real nice, but it was nothing special from what they have now. I never wore a store-bought dress. You could get a very nice dress for a quarter back then.

I know one time my sister went to town. She wanted something to sew; she got material for a dress for me and some for her. It hurt my feelings awfully bad because she gave a quarter for my material and gave fifty cents for hers. Every chance I got, I wore that dress. I was kind of jealous. That hurt my feelings awfully bad, though.

You could even get a hat for a quarter. They wore lots of hats then, just covered up with flowers or "blossoms" as my sister said.

We didn't have no slippers back in my days. We wore button shoes and then after button shoes went out of style, we wore laced-up shoes—way up to here. Couldn't hardly get to church on time! You'd have to lace up shoes or button them up. There was a thing you'd button them with, a shoe buttoner. It took all you could do to get them on and get them fastened up in time to go to church.

I don't believe in the real short mini dresses. I don't. Now the pants look all right [and] my grandchildren wear them. Pants look a lot better than the mini dresses. I still don't approve of it but that's what they're doing. I don't think the Lord is pleased with it; I just don't. You ought not judge people by the way they dress. No, that's up to them—what they want to do about that—but I think they'll have to do something about it. I'm not saying that I'm the most religious person and I'm not exactly old-fashioned, but I like to see a decent dress come below your knees, just barely below your knees. I'll be glad when styles like that come back. You don't see nothing hardly but pant suits now and old people, as old as I am, I guess, that wears pant suits. I never did have one on; I just approve of dresses and them at decent lengths.

No, pants [were never worn by women and girls] when I was young. And they wouldn't come out in front of a man barefooted for nothing in the world. Now they go to school barefooted and any way they want to. When you see a picture of our Lord or Mary Magdaline, they've got on robes, long ones, and they don't have them in mini.

I hear folks say that they don't know what kids are coming to. I hear that. I wouldn't say that . . . I never did say that. They might be good Christian people before they die—wear decent clothes. You know, this is just the world a'changing. It's like the seasons you see changing.

Used to, a woman, if she had eight or ten children, would come into church and she'd bring all those children. Calico cloth then was all the kind of cloth they had. That's the cheapest and it was the next thing to cheese cloth. But you'd see that woman with a dress on with ruffles all over it and a ruffle around the tail and it nearly dragging the ground, and high top shoes you could hear squeaking from the time she started into the door—just a'squeaking all over the house. Everybody could tell when she had on a new pair of shoes. I don't know what made them shoes squeak like that. Every child she had could have on a dress just like hers, you know—plumb down to their feet—and a bonnet made of the same calico material. Well, the least child would have on a dress with sleeves of a different kind of material and a collar of another kind to piece it out, because there wouldn't be enough of that material to make a full dress. Everytime I hear the cost of new clothes, I think of that.

People had to be saving [with] their shoes back then. I've known people to carry their shoes over their shoulders till they got to the foot of the hill just below the church and then put them on and wear them into the church. When they started back down the hill after church, why

PLATE 491   Excavating for the lake at Taylor's Chapel.

they'd pull them off again. Babies wore homemade shoes or those button shoes.

We had a lot of nice things like sleds and ox-drawn wagons. They plowed with oxen, you know. We didn't, but there was a lot of people that did. We had cows at home and a big saddle horse. The saddle horse's name was Henry. We just named our animals anything. That was my treat on Christmas to go and ride on Henry. We also had a big pair of mules that were just as fat as could be, and there wasn't a soul who could get them out of the stable but my sister. She just trained them, I reckon. I'll never forget their names—Pete and Kit. Daddy would have to holler for my sister, because if he was going to plow or anything, she would have to go get those mules out. They'd turn their backs in the door, but she could just walk to the door and say, "Come here." They'd turn around and she'd put the bridle on them.

Oh, I can see that little homeplace. They're building a lake there now. They call it Taylor's Chapel, because so many Taylors lived up there. They've even got a new church up there. That's where I was raised. Right there where they're building that lake. It'll be under water soon. That's my Daddy's old homeplace where I lived till I was married.

A couple would generally court about five years. People didn't get married so early back then, you know. They used to say if you married in blue, you'll always be true; if you married in red, you'll wish you were dead. I imagine people married in just anything they had. Most people married at home. You didn't kiss your bride back then. The usual marrying age was about eighteen to twenty. Usually a man had some sort of living he could offer his bride.

Ral and I went to school together. You know the first time I ever did see [Ral], he was just big enough to think about going with the girl he loved; I just fell in love with him then right from the beginning. Seemed like I was marrying my folks. He always called my folks Uncle and Aunt, and we called his folks Uncle and Aunt. I love him very much, better and better every day. By the time we were through courting, we knew each other pretty good.

Ral and I went to Anderson, South Carolina on our honeymoon and spent a week. That was a big trip back then. There's my ring. My other ring was white gold. It got too little and my daughter wears it around her neck on a chain.

Now we've been married fifty-two years and raised seven children. I thank the Lord for it. You know, my family will never leave me. I just turned my kids over to God and they all go to church. They've all accepted Christ and I'm proud of them. We're an awful close family. One never

PLATE 492   Aunt Nora with her grandson, Stephen Brown.

comes in this house without giving me a big hug and kiss. I raised a sweet
family. You know, every Wednesday we have a coffee break at one of our
houses and we get together and talk and just enjoy being together. My
children all come and we drink a cup of coffee and have a piece of cake.

I believe the Sabbath ought to be a day of rest. The Savior rested that
day. He made everything wonderful and everything good, and on that day
he rested—the seventh day—and I think we ought to. The old Bible said
not to kindle a fire on Sunday. I cook breakfast every morning. I cook
breakfast on Sunday morning, but we usually eat out for Sunday dinner.

"We had all kinds of hard times."

Doctors in them times was sometimes hard to find. I was with Dr. Dover
one time and he told me, "The first place I ever went was back up the road
here. There was a baby being born—her first child." They called him in
there and he stopped. He said he was scared so bad that he left her just in
that shape and got on his horse and went home. He said he got to studying
and said, "I took an oath. I took an oath to do my duty and I got to go

back up there." He said that the baby was there when he got back there and he was never so happy in his life. That was the first baby he delivered. Every child I've got was delivered in the home, but one.

If it was an emergency you just had to wait. We used Dr. Neville most of the time. He'd ride a horse until in the late years when they got T-model Fords. But people'd ride a horse plumb to Dillard to get Dr. Neville. We'd just have to go and see if the doctor was there. If he wasn't, you'd just have to do it by yourself. [There wasn't] a thing in the world to kill pain. I always had a doctor every time but a baby was generally born [before] the doctor came. He did what he had to do. A neighbor would fix the baby. We got along just as good as you do today.

Ralph Taylor was our dentist. We had Dr. Taylor as far back as I can remember. He's been dead now for several years. A man pulled teeth and he never bothered to deaden your gums or nothing—just pull them. He had "tooth-pullers" as he called them. It might have been wire pliers as far as I know.

If you worked a little, you had a little money. If you didn't work, you didn't have any. Back then young girls could work; I did. You could help can for the government and make some money like that. I'd hoe corn for people and make money. Of course I've never worked out a day since I've been married. My husband has always provided for me and our family.

You couldn't trade things much. You'd pay three hundred dollars now for a milk cow, and back then you did good to get twenty-five dollars for a milk cow. The money is the root of all evil. People worship money and money is what they're looking for. It's the least thing from my mind. I'd like to have some. I like to have spending money, but as far as having just loads of it, I don't care a bit for that unless I had some to help some poor person.

We had all kinds of hard times. About twenty or thirty years ago, a tornado struck through here. We lived at Clayton then. It took furniture in the houses and blew it up on the mountain. My aunt got killed. Why, it was awful. She was blown way down in the meadow and they almost never did find her husband, but he was alive and he lived several years after that. Well, anyway, my mother got up that night and she said, "I want you to get up." My daddy said it was the awfullest roaring. He'd never heard the like in his life. He said, "You'd better get back into the bed before you take a cold."

She said, "No, I'm not going to bed. There's something happening."

At midnight somebody come and knocked on the door and said his sister was blown away—the only sister he had. They found her under a big pile of lumber. She was asleep in the house and everything blew away.

There was a family that lived up there at Rabun Gap and it took

PLATE 493

the upstairs off [their house]. The lady said there was some firewood on
the back porch and a piece landed right in between her and her husband,
right in the bed—never touched one of them. It took the whole top of the
house and sat the children down *on their bed* over there near the York
House—all the way from Rabun Gap. It didn't hurt a one of them.

I can also remember back when there was [the old] jail in Clayton.
There wasn't much to hinder a jailbreak if a body didn't turn it down.
The jail had a chimney and if [someone] took a notion to break out, they'd
go out the chimney. It happened pretty often.

The streets were plank—cases on the sides with planks nailed across them.
And sometimes the boards were loose and sticking up, and you had to be
careful to keep from stumping your toe and falling. That happened to lots
of people.

There were only two stores. One was Henry Cannon's and the other Bill Long's general stores. That's about all there was. Well, Bud Richey had a market, no showcases or anything like that. You bought your meat out in the open.

A long time ago, we had panthers. They used to be as thick here as rabbits. My mother said that there used to be a house right down this side of Black Rock where her brother lived. His wife was afraid to stay by herself, so she'd start from Germany [a nearby community] about four o'clock every evening through a path across Black Rock and she said you could hear them on every side, just a'hollering. She said they sounded like they were coming right at her. She'd get on down to the house and build a big fire. It'd be late when my mother's brother got in at night and they said there'd be panthers on top of the house just a'scratching at the boards, trying to get in the house. On account of that fire, they couldn't come down the chimney. My mother told us that story many times. Now that was in my mother's time, not in mine. I imagine [panthers] were something like a big dog. I've seen pictures of them, but never a live one. There's still wild cats around here. Back then there was a little bit of everything.

I used to have a greenhouse awhile back, but I've sold it now. I worked with flowers but [I couldn't] get help. My husband had to stay in the store and that left me right by myself. I had all kinds of flowers. I sold a lot of them. I made good in the flower house. I worked that for about five years.

But religion holds all in my life. I'm Baptist, you know, and I work on the mission field. I've traveled and been in every house in this county, and I've had prayer with them. On Christmas, I [used to] deliver Christmas boxes. The last time I went around, I delivered fifty-two boxes to the poor. They'd have cakes and jellies and different kinds of food—oranges, apples, candy, bananas. I know I went to a place that the lady herself had built her house. It was a little shack. That was the worst I'd ever been hurt. The little girl was over here that morning and I said, "Honey, did you get anything for Christmas?" And she said they only got fifty cents a week for food. Well, I went around and delivered the boxes and I came back by there. I never had been in there; it's just a little shack and the cracks were wide. There was a big old wood stove sitting there just barely a little heat in it. I delivered a toy there. I came on back out to the car and told my brother that they had to have some help. I was crying. I delivered their box for Christmas, and came home and baked them two cakes.

My sister can cure the thrash. There's a lot of people come here that think I can, but I can't. My brother wanted to teach me how, but I didn't want to know.

PLATE 494

[When someone comes for help and you can help them] they just com-
mence to getting better. I've seen it happen. A faith healer just says a little
verse from the Bible. You say one to take off warts and to stop blood, too.
I'm called every week for something like that, but I can't tell you how.
That's between God and me.

There was a man here a while back standing against a truck. I'd been
to town and when I came back, the kids called to me. I went down and
that boy's nose was a'gushing. I said, "Son, do you believe I can stop that?"

He said, "Yes, I do." It stopped. A person has to have some faith in
what you're doing.

I can draw out fire and that's the most wonderful thing there is nearly.
You have to be present to draw out fire. I know this lady. She has bleeding
ulcers and comes to me nearly every week saying her ulcers are bleeding.
I can draw that fire out, but she's got to be here and believe that I can do
it. I believe God is working in me to help people. That's another part of
my mission.

I was a young woman when the flu epidemic hit our community. There
wasn't anybody in the community that didn't take it but me. My folks all
had it and it killed more people than the war did. I was the only one up.
Every morning I'd see that my folks were cared for and all in the bed. Then

I'd go down the road and fix people some soup or something to eat. Then I'd come back and walk to Germany and fix those people something to eat, and try to care for them. There was a family that lived right down below us (the man died here a while back). I went to their house one morning and they were laying all over the house on quilts and things with nothing but a big old fireplace. I made them some soup and fed them. The next morning his wife and two children were dead and there was nobody to dig graves. I reckon this man dug the graves himself. The next day I saw him carrying his wife and two children to the graveyard.

The doctors just couldn't get around to every place. Dr. Green, Dr. Neville, and Dr. Dover and I just traveled all the time trying to fix people something, and trying to do something for them. I felt like I was doing what the Lord wanted me to do and that he spared me to take care of the rest. A lot of young people today would hardly go see them, much less do anything for them, but I've done everything I could. That's what I mean by the mission field.

All this was going on during the war. Me and my husband were married during war times. Sugar was thirty cents a pound. Imagine that! You were allowed a sack of flour once a month and five pounds of sugar, I believe it was. That was World War I. But I'm not going hungry, because God will take care of His children.

INDEX OF PEOPLE

THE KIDS:

Ken Kistner
Suzanne Krieger
Don MacNeil
Curtis Malan
Billy Maney
Dennis Maxwell
Ray McBride
Gena McHugh
Scott McKay
Joyce Moore
Ernie Payne
Mike Pignato
Gary Ramey

Annette Reems
Claude Rickman
Joe Sabin
Steve Smith
Kevin Speigle
Randy Starnes
Greg Strickland
Annette Sutherland
Barbara Taylor
Kenny Taylor
Mary Thomas
Gary Turner
Teresa Turpin

Sheila Vinson
Ricky Ware
Gary Warfield
Linda Warfield
Steve Waters
Lanier Watt
Mac Westbrook
Craig Williams
Dana Williams
Jeff Williams
Randall Williams
Terry York
Carlton Young
David Young

THE CONTACTS:

Uncle Alex
C. M. Arrowood
Joe Arrowood
Mr. and Mrs. Grover Bradley
Lassie Bradshaw
Burnette Brooks
Florence & Lawton Brooks
Mr. and Mrs. Pat Brooks
Mrs. Varn Brooks
Mrs. E. H. Brown
Harry and Marinda Brown
Raleigh Bryans
Louin Cabe
Mary Cabe
Mrs. Cecil Cannon
Lillie Cannon
Lola Cannon
Rose Cannon
Guy Carawan
Aunt Arie Carpenter
Bertha Carpenter
Carl Carpenter
Harley Carpenter

Mary Carpenter
Mr. and Mrs. Buster ("Buck") Carver
Doc Chastain
Mrs. Norman Coleman
Minyard Conner
Ethel Corn
Imogene Dailey
Claude Darnell
Fred Darnell
Lester Davis
Mack Dickerson
Mimmie Dickerson
R. M. Dickerson
Barnard Dillard
Bobbie Dills
Bertha Dockins
Glen Dockins
Lon Dover
Happy Dowdle
Harriet Echols
Turner Enloe
Ernest Franklin
Simmie Free

RELATED GROUPS:

This list of related groups was supplied by IDEAS, Inc. (1785 Massachusetts Ave., N.W., Washington, D.C. 20036) which is in part responsible for their development. Subscription rates not quoted below are available upon request from the respective publications.

ADOBE
Centennial High School
San Luis, Colorado 81152

ALL-AH-WEE $6.00 per year
Nazareth High School
St. Thomas
U.S. Virgin Islands 08001

BITTERSWEET $6.00 per year
Lebanon High School
416 North Adam Street
Lebanon, Missouri 65536

CITYSCAPE $2.00 per issue
Western High School
Washington, D.C. 20007

CLINGSTONE
Greer High School
Greer, South Carolina 29651

DOVETAIL $2.00 per issue
Ronan High School
Ronan, Montana 59864

FOXFIRE $6.00 per year
The Rabun Gap–
    Nacoochee School
Rabun Gap, Georgia 30568

FURROWS
Mount View High School
Thorndike, Maine 04986

GUARIQUEN $4.25 per year
Associacion Dominicana de Boy Scouts
Santiago
Dominican Republic

KIL-KAAS-GIT $6.00 per year
Prince of Wales High School
Craig, Alaska 99921

KO KAKOU $6.00 per year
Kailua High School
Kailua, Hawaii 96740

LAULIMA $7.50 per year
Ka'u High School
Pahala, Hawaii 96777

LOBLOLLY $5.00 per year
Gary High School
Box 88
Gary, Texas 75643

NANIH WAIYA $8.00 per year
Choctaw Central High Sschool
Route 7, Box 72
Philadelphia, Mississippi 39350

PIG'S EYE
New City School
St. Paul, Minnesota 55101

SALT $5.00 per year
Kennebunk High School
P.O. Box 302A
Kennebunkport, Maine 04046

SEA CHEST $6.00 per year
Cape Hatteras High School
Box 278
Buxton, North Carolina 27920

SHENANGO
College for Senior Americans
Edinboro State College
Farrell, Pennsylvania 16121

SKIPJACK
South Dorchester High School
Church Creek, Maryland 21622

THISTLEDOWN
Watkins Memorial High School
Pataskala, Ohio 43062

TSA'ASZI $8.00 per year
Ramah Navajo High School
Box 35
Ramah, New Mexico 87321

WINDFALLS
North Buncombe High School
Weaverville, North Carolina 28787

Italic numerals *1, 2,* and *3* refer to *The Foxfire Book, Foxfire 2,* and *Foxfire 3* respectively.